Textbook on Constitutional Law

The daring publisher, Universal Law Publishing Company, among the foremost in the law publishing field and progressive in venturing to bring out rare legal literature of avant garde *character has rightly enriched the* corpus juris *of India*

Justice V R Krishna Iyer
Random Reflections, page 14

Textbook on
Constitutional Law

Dr. Veena Madhav Tonapi

B.Sc. (Hons.); LL.M.; Ph.D. (Law)
Principal, J.S.S. Sakri Law College,
Hubli, Karnataka

Universal
Law Publishing Co.
NEW DELHI - INDIA

2013 Edition

ISBN: 978-93-5035-254-0

Published by
UNIVERSAL LAW PUBLISHING CO. PVT. LTD.
C-FF-1A, Dilkhush Industrial Estate,
(Near Azadpur Metro Station) G.T. Karnal Road,
Delhi-110 033
Tel.: 011-47082254, 27438103, 27215334
Fax : 011-27458529
E-mail *(For sales inquiries)* : unilaw@vsnl.com
E-mail *(For editorial inquiries)* : edit@unilawbooks.com
Website : www.unilawbooks.com

Recommended citation: Dr. Veena Madhav Tonapi, *Textbook on Constitutional law* (New Delhi: Universal Law Publishing Co. Pvt. Ltd., 2013).

Computer Typeset at Aesthetic and *Printed* at Mudrak, Delhi.

This book is dedicated to the memory of my father late Prof. Mohan Venkatrao Kowjalgi who was an incessant driving force in all my academic ventures.

PREFACE

As in my earlier text book on Jurisprudence – in this book also I have made a conscious attempt to keep the language simple and explain the meanings of difficult words/phrases/concepts as and when required - but this time in foot notes itself rather than in an Independent Glossary, to facilitate simultaneous reference.

Every chapter begins with a detailed synopsis of contents and important case-laws which nearly sums up the salient aspects of the chapter for easy remembrance.

As the Constitution provides for more or less parallel provisions in respect of the Legislature, Executive, Judiciary at State and Union Level – I have clubbed the provisions pertaining to State and Union Legislature; State and Union Executive; State and Union Judiciary in respective chapters. Given my own teaching experience of more than two decades I feel this will avoid turning pages back and forth to get at the differences between the State and Union provisions.

I hope that the Tabulations which gives an immediate grasp of the differences will make the Constitution of India – the "Law of all Laws" more comprehensible specially for the students.

DR. VEENA MADHAV TONAPI

WORD OF THANKS

I owe a word of thanks to all the persons directly and indirectly instrumental in the writing of this book. I specially thank my husband- Madhav- the man behind all my academic endeavours, my sons- Kedar, Pramod, my daughters-in-law –Medha and Gayatri and the little-baby grand-kids- Adithya, Pranav and Tejaswini and my mother Pramila- who have willingly given up their claim over my time –so that this book could come up.

Above all- all my thanks to Dr. Manish Arora for his ever encouraging attitude and useful suggestions and the whole Universal Team.

DR. VEENA MADHAV TONAPI

CONTENTS

INTRODUCTION

CHAPTER 1
SALIENT FEATURES OF THE INDIAN CONSTITUTION

CHAPTER 2
NATURE OF THE INDIAN CONSTITUTION (FEDERAL OR UNITARY)

CHAPTER 3
UNION AND ITS TERRITORIES

CHAPTER 4
CITIZENSHIP

CHAPTER 5
FUNDAMENTAL RIGHTS

CHAPTER 6
RIGHT TO EQUALITY

CHAPTER 7
RIGHT TO EQUALITY (PROHIBITION OF DISCRIMINATION ON RELIGION, ETC.)

CHAPTER 8
EQUALITY OF OPPORTUNITY IN PUBLIC EMPLOYMENT

CHAPTER 9
ABOLITION OF UNTOUCHABILITY, TITLES

CHAPTER 10
PROTECTION OF FREEDOM OF SPEECH ETC.

CHAPTER 11

PROTECTION IN RESPECT OF CONVICTION FOR OFFENCES

CHAPTER 12

RIGHT TO LIFE AND PERSONAL LIBERTY

CHAPTER 13
PROTECTION AGAINST ARREST AND DETENTION IN CERTAIN CASES

CHAPTER 14
RIGHT AGAINST EXPLOITATION

CHAPTER 15
RIGHT TO FREEDOM OF RELIGION

CHAPTER 16
CULTURAL AND EDUCATIONAL RIGHTS

CHAPTER 17

RIGHT TO CONSTITUTIONAL REMEDIES

CHAPTER 18

DIRECTIVE PRINCIPLES OF STATE POLICY

CHAPTER 19
FUNDAMENTAL DUTIES

CHAPTER 20
UNION AND STATE EXECUTIVE

CHAPTER 21

UNION AND THE STATE LEGISLATURE

CHAPTER 22

UNION AND STATE JUDICIARY

CHAPTER 23
PARLIAMENTARY PRIVILEGES

CHAPTER 24
PANCHAYATS AND MUNICIPALITIES

CHAPTER 25
RELATIONS BETWEEN THE UNION AND THE STATES

CHAPTER 26

PROPERTY, CONTRACTS, RIGHTS, LIABILITIES, OBLIGATIONS AND SUITS

CHAPTER 27

CONSTITUTIONAL RIGHT TO PROPERTY

CHAPTER 28

FREEDOM OF TRADE, COMMERCE AND INTERCOURSE

CHAPTER 29

SERVICES UNDER THE UNION AND THE STATE

CHAPTER 30
TRIBUNALS

CHAPTER 31
ELECTIONS

CHAPTER 32
SPECIAL PROVISIONS RELATING TO CERTAIN CLASSES

CHAPTER 33
EMERGENCY PROVISIONS

CHAPTER 34
AMENDMENT PROVISIONS

TABLE OF CASES

A

B

E

F

I

J

L

M

N

R

S

T

INTRODUCTION

SYNOPSIS

Introduction

A. The need to study Constitutional Law

Constitutional law is the law of all laws and is therefore all encompassing. It is an umbrella in whose shelter every activity of the Nation and its people must survive. This means that every law and every statute and every Order or a bye-law or an Ordinance in our country; every appointment to a public post; every policy of the Government and every judgment given by the court must be in accordance with the Constitution. If not they would be quashed as being unconstitutional "because the Constitution is in hourly use as a benchmark and measuring stick for citizens and officials touching the lives in ways great and small, learning of its working truly opens a window into India."[1] The Constitution of India is such a sacrosanct that some call it *Dharmashastra*.

Constitution has an influence on our lives, on our day-to-day living; it speaks of our rights, our duties, our powers, immunities, about our Legislature, Executive, Judiciary, the Municipalities, the reservation policy, the mode of election, the mode of amending the Constitution. It lays down how you can enter into a contract with the Government, when can you file a legal proceeding against the Government etc., thus, the Constitution has a say on the quality of our lives. Hence the need to study Constitutional Law.

It should be remembered that before the Constitution came into force the country's major units were called 'Provinces' and the leaders of their ministries were called 'Premiers'.

B. Constituent Assembly

It is noteworthy that our Constitution is not the result of a revolution but it is the result of studied discussions by persons who were true to the issues. The discussions about what provisions must be incorporated in the Constitution were discussed in the Constituent Assembly at length. The Assembly took 2 years 11 months and seventeen days to finish the task *i.e.*, from 9th December 1946 to 26th November 1949. 7635 Amendments were received out of which 2473 were moved and considered by the Assembly. Adopting a Constitution by any country marks a fresh start in the life of a nation where the country and its people intend to have their own indigenous system of governance.

It was a tough task. More than 300 million people belonging to different religions, culture, customs and languages had to be united through a common Constitution. In addition, the dalits, the backward classes, the tribals, the minorities had to be accommodated.

C. Journey from the entry of the East India Company to Indian Independence to Adoption of the present Constitution—From 1600 to 1947 to 1949[2]

(1) Establishment of East India Company

The East India Company formed in England in 1600 established its trading centres at several places in the country and the factories at Bombay, Madras, and Calcutta became the chief presidencies. During this period the English settled in India with the license of the Indian Government. But the sovereignty of Bombay had been ceded to the British Crown. The island of Bombay was gifted as dowry by the King of Portugal to Charles II who in turn transferred it to the East India Company. Yet the English people were not governed by the *lex loci* (law of the locality) because the personal laws in India and its peculiar way of thinking was impossible of being applied to the English people. Hence they were allowed to retain their own English laws and the English Government in their own settlement. So the Crown granted certain legislative and judicial powers to be exercised by it over the English servants of the company and the Indian settlers who sought their protection.

---

1. *Granville Austin:* Working of Democracy in India, p. 1.
2. V.N. Shukla: Constitution of India: Eastern Book Company, Lucknow pp. Ai-A23.

(2) Queen Elizabeth's Charter of 1601

Queen Elizabeth's Charter of 1601 permitted the Governor and the Company to make and revoke the laws and to impose penalties. But the laws were not to be contrary to the laws of England. Similar powers were given in 1609 and 1661.

(3) Charter of 1726

The Charter of 1726 issued by George I, the Governors in Council were given power to make laws etc., but they had to be approved and confirmed by an order in writing of the Court of Directors. The Charter also introduced the Mayor's Courts in all the three Presidencies of Bombay, Madras and Calcutta.

(4) Administration of Diwani

Until the 18th century the British remained mainly as merchants. But after the victory of Plassey (1757) and Buxar (1764) they became the virtual masters of Bengal. The Company obtained the grant of Diwani from Shah Alam whom it accepted as the rightful claimant to the throne of the Moghul Emperors. The Company began administration of Diwani – *i.e.,* revenue and civil justice from 1772 and promulgated a body of laws commonly known as the plan of Warren Hastings. It consisted of 37 rules dealing with civil and criminal justice.

(5) 1773 Regulating Act—The first Act for better management of Company's affairs

Even before 1773 the Company had acquired a *de facto*[1] sovereignty over a vast territory in the northeast of India. The 1773 Regulating Act was the first Parliamentary Act which provided for establishing certain regulations for the better management of the affairs of the Company. The Act set up a Government of Bengal in whom the civil and the military government of the Presidency of Bengal would vest. The Crown was empowered to establish a Supreme Court in Bengal with civil and criminal jurisdiction over the British subjects and their servants. The Governor General and the Council were empowered to make laws for good governance and impose penalties subject to condition that it should not be opposed to laws in England. The laws had to be registered with the Supreme Court and the Supreme Court could veto it. An appeal from the registered law lay before the King in Council in England.

(6) Act of 1781—Personal and proprietary rights of the Indian subjects

By the Act of 1781 the Governor General and Council were empowered to frame regulations extended to the territorial acquisitions of Bengal, Bihar and Orissa *i.e.,* the Diwani Kingdoms. Literally interpreted the power was to be exercised only for prescribing procedure and practice of the provincial courts. But in fact it was extended to making a regular code to affect the personal and proprietary rights of the Indian subjects and others amenable to the company's courts. The same provisions were extended to the local Governments of Madras and Bombay.

---

1. '*De facto*' *i.e.,* 'in fact' as distinguished from 'de jure' *i.e.,* 'in law'.

(7) 1813 Charter Act—Duties and taxes

By the 1813 Charter Act the powers were enlarged and subjected to greater control by the Parliament. They were empowered to make articles of war, and impose custom duties and other taxes. They had to be annually laid before the British Parliament.

(8) The Charter Act of 1833—Legislative power in India

The Charter Act of 1833 (1833 - 1856) introduced important changes in the system of legislation of India. The sole legislative power in India was vested in the Governor General-in-Council. It could make laws for all persons, places, things and courts in every part of the Company's possession in India. The powers of the Councils in Madras and Bombay were superseded. But it was the Parliament which had the right to make laws for India.

(9) Act of 1853 – Legislative and the Executive machinery

The Act of 1853 differentiated the legislative and the executive machinery. For the first time legislative business of India came to be transacted in public. Lord Dalhousie started the new Legislative Council with considerable formality on the lines of the English House of Lords.

(10) First War of Indian Independence in 1857 (1857-1918)

The First War of Indian Independence in 1857 brought an end to the career of the East India Company. In 1858 the Government of India was placed directly under the Crown through the Secretary of State for India. The legislative power of the Governor–in–Council was extended over all persons – whether British or Indian – within the Indian dominions of her Majesty and over all courts of justice. By the Minto–Morley Reforms of 1909 the membership of the Councils was increased and functions widened. Until 1919, legislation was primarily the prerogative of the Executive.

(11) Important policy statement—Towards realization of responsible Government

On August 20, 1917 an important policy statement was made by the Secretary of State for India in the House of Commons. Namely, that there would be increasing association of Indian in every branch of the administration and the gradual development of self governing institutions with a view to the progressive realization of responsible Government in India as an integral part of the British Empire and that the Government in India is in complete accord with the policy.

(12) Government of India Act, 1919

The main provisions of the Government of India Act, 1919 were—

(a) Diarchy

Introduction of the system of diarchy in the Provinces, that is subjects were classified as Central and provincial.

(b) Indian Government responsible only to UK Parliament

The Government of India remained with the Governor General-in-Council. It was responsible only to the United Kingdom's Parliament through the Secretary of State for India.

(c) Simon Commission – Federation of Indian States and Provinces – The ultimate goal

The system of Provincial diarchy embodied in the reforms of 1919 failed to fulfill the hopes built upon it. The Commission was appointed in 1927 to report on the condition of India under the new Constitution. It reported that diarchy had outlived its usefulness and recommended a large extension of responsible Government in the Provinces. It recommended that establishment of a Federation of Indian States and Provinces should be the ultimate goal. Until then problems affecting British India and the States should be discussed between the parties in a consultative consisting of representatives drawn from the States and the British and not legislative council of Greater India. But in 1930, unexpectedly, the Indian Princes agreed to accede to a federal system. So a Round Table Conference of the representatives of the British Government, the Princes, and British India was scheduled. Government White Paper was prepared based on its results. The Paper was submitted to a Joint Select Committee of the Parliament, which was assisted by an Indian Delegation. Based on the Report, Government of India Bill was introduced and passed with extensive amendments as Government of India Act, 1935.

(13) *Government of India Act, 1935 (GI Act)—Model for the present Constitution*

Our present Constitution is largely based on the model of the Government of India Act, 1935. Following are the main provisions of the Government of India Act, 1935:

(a) Division of legislative powers

Powers were divided between the Centre and the Provinces. Legislative powers were divided into three categories—

1. Federal list: Those that were exclusively assigned to the Central/ Federal Legislature;
2. Provincial list: Those that were exclusively assigned to the Provincial Legislatures; and
3. Concurrent list. Those assigned to both the Centre and the Provinces.

(b) Federal system substituted

The Act substituted a federal system of Government for the unitary one. The Federation was to consist of the Governor's Provinces and the Indian States. The Indian States had the option to join or refuse to join the Federation. If it agreed to join, the Indian Ruler had to sign the Instrument of Accession. In fact the Rulers never gave their consent and therefore the Federation never came into existence.

(c) Federal Executive based on diarchy

The Federal Executive was composed of the Governor-General and a Council of Ministers who were chosen and appointed by the Governor-General. Thus, the Federal Executive was to be based on the principle of diarchy. Federal subjects were divided into two categories - reserved and transferred. Matters like defense and external affairs were reserved for the Governor-General who was to be assisted by three Councillors who were *ex-officio* members of both the Houses without the right to vote. In respect of the transferred subjects, the Governor General was normally to act on ministerial advice yet he could act independently in respect of matters specially entrusted to him.

(d) Federal Legislature

The Federal Legislature was to consist of King represented by the Governor General and two Houses the Legislative Assembly and the Council of States.

(e) Provincial Government

Executive Government of the Provinces vested in the Governor and a Council of Ministers to advise him. The Act provided for responsible Government in the Provinces subject to two limitations: special responsibilities were given to the Governor akin to those of the Governor-General except as regards finance and secondly, certain matters were within the absolute discretion of the Governor like power to make temporary Ordinances or Acts.

(f) Federal Court

Federal Court consisted of a Chief Justice and not more than 6 judges. It had 3 kinds of jurisdiction. It had exclusive original jurisdiction in any dispute between the Federation and the Units.

(g) Appellate jurisdiction

Appeals lay to the Federal Court from the High Court if the High Court certified that the case involved a substantial question of law as regards the interpretation of the Government of India Act, 1935 or of an order-in-Council made under the said Act. An appeal lay to the Privy Council from the original jurisdiction of the Federal Court in constitutional matters and by its leave or that of the Privy Council in all other matters.

(h) Advisory jurisdiction

The Governor could refer any question of law to the Federal Court and obtain its opinion. Law declared by the Federal Court and the Privy Council was binding on all the Courts in British India.

(i) Drawbacks in Government of India Act, 1935

There were vehement drawbacks in the Act: Indians were not given control over the Government of their own country; diarchy at the Centre was thought to be a mistake; choice given to the States whether to join or not to join the Federation was thought to be a mistake; indirect elections to the Federal Assembly was against the spirit of true democracy; territorial constituencies elected their representatives by separate communal electorates.

1935 Act came into effect in 1937. At the Provincial elections the Congress formed ministries in 7 out of 11 provinces.

(j) Second World War—India unilaterally declared a belligerent country

In 1939 when Second World War broke out the British Government unilaterally declared India as a belligerent country at war with Germany without consulting the Indian Legislatures and the Indian leaders. This was protested by the Congress. The Congress ministries resigned as they were not satisfied with the aims of war declared by the British Government and the Indian participation in the war. The Governors of the 7 Provinces took over the administration in their hands.

In October, 1940 the Viceroy announced that the coming into operation of the federal part of the Constitution would be indefinitely postponed.

(k) Muslims demand a separate nation

After the Congress formed ministries, communal tension between Hindus and Muslims increased and the Muslims demanded a separate nation by grouping together areas where the Muslims were in numerical majority. The Muslim League's objective was realized with the passing of the Indian Independence Act, 1947:

(l) The Cripps Mission 1942 – Elect a body for framing a Constitution for India

Sir Stafford Cripps – member of the War Cabinet came to India to discuss about the Indian problems and to secure their co-operation for the Second World War. The proposals suggested were that immediately after the war steps would be taken to elect a body for framing a Constitution for India; that Indian States would participate in the framing of the Constitution; that the British Government would implement the Constitution so framed, but it recognized the liberty of the provinces to reject the Constitution so framed; or to have an independent Constitution of its own.; until the Constitution was framed the British Government would retain the control and direction of the defense of India as part of their world war efforts. The Mission failed because the Congress insisted on full Cabinet and the Muslim League rejected the offer and demanded for a partition.

(m) Wavell Plan 1945 – Failed

It proposed for a reconstitution of the Executive Council so as to consist entirely of Indians in addition to the Viceroy and the Commander-in-Chief. The proposal failed as no agreement could be arrived at regarding the composition of the Executive Council.

(n) Cabinet Mission 1946

Acceptance of India's claim to freedom: After the Labour Party came to power with Mr. Attlee as the Labour Prime Minister there was a definite change in attitude of the British Government. There was an unequivocal acceptance of India's claim to freedom.

Three Ministers arrived[1] and a Conference was held in Shimla with the representatives of the Congress and the Muslim League, but no settlement could be arrived at. So the Mission recommended proposals which were acceptable to all parties and elections to the Constituent Assembly took place in July 1946.

Following were the proposals:

- There should be a Union of India consisting of both British India and the States.
- All subjects other than the Union subjects and all residuary powers should vest in the provinces.
- The paramountcy of the Crown was to lapse.

1. *Lord Pethick Lawrence – Secretary of State for India; Sir Stafford Cripps – President of the Board of Trade; and Alexander – the First Lord of Admiralty.*

The procedure for election to Constituent Assembly: It was to be as follows:

(i) The members of each Provincial Group were to be divided into two groups – General and Muslim (except in Punjab where they were divided into 3 groups – General, Muslims and Sikhs).

(ii) Each group was to elect its own representatives to the Constituent Assembly.

(iii) The method of election would be by the method of proportional representation with single transferable vote.

(iv) The number of representatives allotted to each Province and community were to be proportional to its population in the ratio of one to a million.

(v) The total number of representatives from the Governor's Provinces was to be 292 plus 4 members to represent the Chief Commissioner's Provinces and not more than 93 members from Indian States. Method of electing the members from the Indian States was left to be decided by the Consultation.

(vi) The States in the preliminary stage were to be represented by a Negotiating Committee.

(vii) The Constituent Assembly thus elected was to meet in a plenary session to elect its Chairman and other officers; settle general order of business and set up an Advisory Committee on the rights of the citizens, minorities and tribal and excluded areas. The Provincial representatives were to divide up into three sections A, B, C. These sections were to settle the Provincial Constitution for the respective provinces and were to decide whether any Group Constitution was to be set up for those Provinces. After the Provincial Constitution had been formed the representatives of the sections and the Indian States were to reassemble for the purpose of resettling the Union Constitution.

(viii) An interim Government was to be set up having the support of the major political parties.

Elections to the Constituent Assembly took place in July 1946. An interim Government of 14 members was formed- 5 representing the Congress; 5 the Muslim League and one each representing the Sikhs, Anglo Indians, Parsis and the Indian Christians.

The first session of the Constituent Assembly began on December 6th, 1946, the Muslim League members did not attend despite the statement of December 6 which had accepted the Leagues' interpretation of the Cabinet Mission provisions relating to voting in sections of the Constituent Assembly. It demanded 2 separate Constituent Assemblies – one for Pakistan and one for Hindustan and declared that it would never participate in any single Constitution making body.

(14) Mountbatten Plan – Partition – The only solution

Mountbatten succeeded L. Wavell. On June 3rd, 1947 he issued a statement declaring that the partition of India and partition of the Provinces of Bengal, Assam and Punjab was the only solution for solving the political tangle.

(15) *Indian Independence Act, 1947*

L. Attlee declared while moving the Bill that it was an enabling Bill which enabled the representatives of India and Pakistan to draft their own Constitutions and to provide for the difficult period of transition. Following are the main provisions:

(a) *Two independent Dominions:* Two independent Dominions were set up in India known as India and Pakistan headed by the Governor-General for each Dominion appointed by the King.

(b) *Its Legislatures Supreme:* Legislatures of the Dominions were to be supreme. British Acts passed after 15th August, 1947 were not to be applicable to them.

(c) *British paramountcy lapse:* The British Government would not have any responsibility after 15th August, 1947 in respect of India or Pakistan as its paramountcy was to lapse.

(d) *Constituent Assembly – Supreme*: Powers of the Legislature of the Dominion were to be exercised by the Constituent Assembly. The constituent powers of the Assembly were without any limitations. That is the Constituent Assembly was to be supreme.

(e) *Government of India Act, 1935* to remain until new Constitution framed:

(i) Until the new Constitution was framed, the Government of India Act, 1935 was to remain the Constitutional law of India.

(ii) Act received royal assent on July 18th 1947 and the British rule ended on 15th August, 1947.

(Thus, note that we have received the authority and the power to frame the present Constitution from the Indian Independence Act passed by the British).

(f) *Framing of the present Constitution*:

(i) Constituent Assembly first laid down the objectives by moving the Objectives Resolution. It was moved by Pandit Jawaharlal Nehru.

(ii) It said that India was to be proclaimed as an Independent Sovereign Republic and that provisions for further governance would be drawn up.

(iii) That India shall be a union of all territories comprised in British India the Indian States, the parts of India as are outside British India and such other territories as are willing to be constituted into the independent sovereign India.

(iv) The said territories shall retain the status of autonomous units together with residuary powers and exercise all Governmental and administrative functions except those which are vested with the Union.

(v) That independent India derives its powers from its people.

(vi) That justice, social, economic and political; equality of status, or opportunity and freedom of thought expression, belief, faith, worship, vocation, association and action shall be secured to all people subject to law and public morality.

(vii) That adequate safeguards shall be provided for minorities, backward and tribal areas and depressed and other backward classes.

(viii) Integrity of the territory of India and its sovereign rights on land, sea and air shall be maintained in accordance with justice and the law of civilized nations.

(ix) That it would make full and willing contribution to world peace.

(x) Different committees were formed to deal with different topics: the Union Powers Committee, the Union Constitution Committee, the Provincial Constitution Committee, the Advisory Committee on Minorities and Fundamental Rights, Committees on Chief Commissioners and financial relations between Union and the States and the Advisory Committee on Tribal Areas.

(xi) The Reports were considered by the Constituent Assembly and their recommendations were considered and adopted as basis for preparing the Draft Constitution.

(xii) The Draft Constitution contained 315 articles and 8 schedules. It was considered at great length at the second reading stage. The Constituent Assembly finalized the Constitution on November 26th 1949. It came into force on January 26th 1950.

(g) What is Constitutional law?

Basic law

Constitutional law of any country- whether a written or an unwritten Constitution is its basic law. All laws/rules/laws/bye-laws/ordinances etc., have to ultimately conform to the Constitutional law of the country.

For governing a country several rules of different nature are needed. Each country has a set of rules/laws/etc., which serve different purposes. What is it that holds these set of rules together and converts them into a legal system? It is the basic law of the land which holds the set of rules together and converts it into a legal system.[1]

Basic law in unwritten Constitution

Where there is an unwritten Constitution as in England –the basic law is to be seen in common law principles, judicial decisions, in conventions and practices and different statutes. It is not something that has been evolved the way in which our Constitution was evolved where the representatives sat together with an intention to make a Constitution for India; deliberated over the structure of the different organs that the Constitution would provide for; debated over the rights; duties, powers, immunities, privileges etc., of the different stake holders in the country etc. In short where they sat together and prepared a holistic picture of the way in which the country should be governed. In Britain, they do not have a single document called the 'Constitution of Britain'. So for them the Basic law is the common law principles, judicial decisions etc., which are

1. Keelson calls it grundnorm.

not found in one single document but are spread over in various documents and practices. The central doctrine of the unwritten British Constitution is the sovereignty of the Parliament *i.e.,* the Parliament can make and unmake the laws. There is no distinction between the Constitutional law and an ordinary law. In India it is the Constitution which is supreme and not the Parliament as in England.

Basic law in written Constitution

Where there is a written Constitution the Basic law is the Constitution of a country. Thus in India it is the Constitution of India which is the basic law which holds all the laws/rules/bye-laws/regulations/ordinances etc., together and weaves them all into a sound and an integrated legal system. It can be said that the Constitutional law is a common strand that runs through all these rules etc. Hence all other laws etc., have to be in tune with the Constitution.

Legal system of a country

A legal system of a country is broadly divisible into Public laws and Private Laws. Public laws are laws governing the State, like the Constitutional law and the Administrative law. Private laws are laws which regulate the conduct of its members in their day-to-day dealings like contract laws, Tort laws, Consumer laws etc.

Constitutional law establishes the different organs of the Government, describes how they shall be constituted (*i.e.,* their structure and composition); their powers and functions; their responsibilities. It deals with the inter-relationship between different organs and its political relationship with the people at large.

Structure of a State

The three Organs of a State are: (1) Legislature to make laws (2) Executive to execute and implement laws (3) Judiciary to interpret laws. The Constitution deals with the mutual relationship between these 3 organs; how far one is independent or dependent on the other; and the role each plays in the set up of a Nation with reference to the people of the country. In addition the Constitution may create any other orgân which it thinks fit as *for example,* the Finance Commission, the Election Commission in our Constitution.

Federal or a unitary Constitution

Constitution of a country may be federal or unitary. In a Federal Constitution the Central Government exercises powers over the entire country. But there are State Governments which exercise powers over their regions and they are supreme within their realm. There is a definite relationship between the State and the Centre which is described in the Constitution. India has a Federal Constitution.

Unitary Constitution is one where all powers are concentrated with the Central Government and it can delegate powers to different agencies.

Constitutional conventions: The Constitutional law of a country also consists of conventions which are not mentioned in the Constitution but are the result of practices followed again and again over a passage of time. According to Jennings "within the framework of the law there is room for the development of the rules of practice, rules which may be followed as consistently as the rules of law which determines the procedure which the men concerned with the Government follow"[1] *For example,* under our Constitution the convention has been to transfer the judges only after obtaining their consent. Hence when the unwritten convention was not followed during the internal emergency it was challenged in *Sankalchand Singh* v. *Union of India.*[2] According to C.J. Ahmadi- conventions grow in areas where law is silent. Adoption of such conventions do not breach (violate) the law but fill up the gap.[3] Likewise in India Constitutional conventions are significant in the relationship between the Legislature and the Executive.

Constitution and Constitutional law

Note that the term 'Constitutional law' is broader than the term 'Constitution'. Constitutional law comprises the Constitution, the relevant statutes, judicial decisions and conventions.

(h) Constitutionalism

There is a difference between Constitution and Constitutionalism. A country may have a Constitution but not Constitutionalism. *For example,* a country with dictatorship – where dictator's word is law there is a Constitution but no Constitutionalism.

Where the Constitution confers not only powers but also restrains those powers because power corrupts and absolute power corrupts absolutely there is Constitutionalism. Where the Constitution embodies checks and balances so that power must not be misused; where Constitution provides for in-built restrictions to keep a sane Government in place, there is Constitutionalism. Constitutionalism is the antithesis (direct opposite) of arbitrary powers/despotism, tyranny, authoritarianism.

Aquinas, Paine, Locke, Grotius and Rousseau have promoted the thought of Constitutionalism.

A written Constitution, independent judiciary with powers of judicial review over Legislative and Executive actions, and power to decide on the disputes of the people of the country – whether an individual dispute or a dispute with the State; free and fair elections to the Legislature; transparent democratic Government, fundamental rights, directions to the State in the form of directive principles; decentralization of powers; amendments to the Constitution through majority promote Constitutionalism. Right to seek information strengthens Constitutionalism.

---

1. W.I. Jennings, Law and the Constitution.
2. AIR 1977 SC 2362.
3. *S.P. Anand* v. *H.D. Deve Gowda,* AIR 1997 SC 272: 1997 AIR SCW 18: (1996) 6 SCC 734.

CHAPTER 1

SALIENT FEATURES OF THE INDIAN CONSTITUTION

SYNOPSIS

- A. Preamble
  - (1) Elaborate
  - (2) Does not grant powers
  - (3) Enacting clause
  - (4) Aims and the objects
  - (5) Nature of Indian Polity
  - (6) Preamble is a part of the Constitution
  - (7) Preamble can be amended under Article 368
- B. Lengthiest written Constitution
  - (1) Drawn from the experience of other Constitutions
  - (2) Administrative details
  - (3) Fundamental rights
  - (4) Union-State relations
  - (5) Division of powers
  - (6) Directive principles
  - (7) Fundamental duties
  - (8) Independent judiciary
  - (9) Constitution of the Union and the States
  - (10) Administrative details
  - (11) Diverse interests protected
  - (12) Inculcating democratic values
- C. Establishment of a Sovereign, Socialist, Secular, Democratic Republic
- D. Single citizenship
- E. Special provisions
- F. Elections
- G. Independent Judiciary
- H. Federation with strong centralizing tendencies
- I. Blend of rigidity and flexibility
- J. Fundamental law
- K. Parliamentary and Presidential System of Government

Salient features of the Indian Constitution

Let us briefly go through the salient features of the Constitution so that we get a bird's eye view of the entire Constitution in order to get a holistic picture of the provisions that we will be studying in detail.

A. Preamble

(1) Elaborate

We have an elaborate Preamble covering such important aspects that in *Keshvanand Bharati's*[1] case the Supreme Court has held that Preamble is a part of the Constitution. This has rendered it all the more a salient feature of the Constitution.

(2) Does not grant powers

It does not grant powers but it lays down the objectives of the Constitution. It shows the directions towards which the country must move in order to do full justice to all its citizens.

---

1. His *Holiness Keshvananda Bharati Sripadgalvaru* v. *State of Kerala*, AIR 1973 SC 1461: (1973) 4 SCC 225: 1973 Supp SCR 1.Thus it has reversed the ruling in *Berubari* case where it was held that Preamble is not a part of the Constitution.

(3) Enacting clause

It contains the enacting clause which brings the Constitution into force. It says "We the People of India ... do hereby adopt, enact, and give to ourselves this Constitution" on twenty-sixth day of November, 1949. This shows that sovereignty (power, independence, no control by others) vests with the people. In other words it conveys that we have a "Government of the people, for the people, by the people"; that the interests of the people are at the centre-stage of every State activity; It thus vests political power in the people of the Republic of India. It also indicates that the Constitution is not imposed on us but we have deliberated over the provisions and given it to ourselves.

(4) Aims and the objects

It lays down the aims and the objects of the Constitution *viz.* to secure justice, liberty, equality and fraternity to all the citizens. The Preamble is the key to open the mind of the makers of the Constitution.

(5) Nature of Indian Polity

It declares the nature of Indian Polity- *viz.*, that India is to be a 'Sovereign, Socialist, Secular Democratic Republic'. Fraternity brings about brotherhood amongst all the people which is relevant in the Indian context having regard to social backwardness and the untouchability practice prevailing in the country. The Constitution thus aims at attaining an egalitarian society (classless society). Preamble must be read with the Directive Principles as the latter lay down the goals to be attained by the Government.

(6) Preamble is a part of the Constitution

Preamble is the key to open the mind of the makers of the Constitution. Whether Preamble is a part of the Constitution arose for the first time as early as in 1960 in *In ref. Berubari's* case[1]. It was held that it is not a part of the Constitution and hence it cannot be regarded as a source of any substantive powers or prohibitions. It can be resorted to where there is an ambiguity in the words used in the Constitution. If it has two meanings – then to decide which of the two is applicable – Preamble can be relied upon. *Berubari* case was reversed by the Supreme Court in *Keshwanand Bharati* v. *State of Kerala*[2] and it was held that Preamble is a part of the Constitution.

(7) Preamble can be amended under Article 368

Preamble is a part of the Constitution. Hence it can be amended like any other provision in the Constitution but the basic features cannot be amended. If the basic features are amended it will not remain the same Constitution. What are the basic features were not laid down. They are determined as and when the cases have come up before the courts. Thus, secularism, socialism, judicial review have been held to be the basic features of the Constitution

42nd amendment has inserted 3 new words in the Preamble – Secularism, Socialism and Integrity. These concepts were there already in the Constitution. They have now been expressly mentioned.

---

1. AIR 1960 SC 845: 1961 (1) SCA 22: (1960) 3 SCR 250.
2. AIR 1973 SC 1461: (1973) 4 SCC 225: 1973 Supp SCR 1.

B. Lengthiest written Constitution

When originally enacted it had 395 articles and 8 Schedules. Today it has 441 articles and 12 Schedules. Following are the reasons for the lengthy Constitution:

(1) Drawn from the experience of other Constitutions

It has drawn from the rich experience of the working of the Constitutions of the other countries in the world in order to avoid committing the same mistakes. Thus the Parliamentary form of Government is based on the British modes; Fundamental rights are drawn from the American Bill of Rights; Directive Principles of State Policy – on the Irish model; Emergency provisions – on the German model and the Government of India Act, 1935; Constitutional amendments is a modified version of the American provisions; Centre – State financial relationship is based on Australian experience;

(2) Administrative details

Administrative details are reproduced from the Government of India Act, 1935.

(3) Fundamental rights

It contains elaborate provisions regarding fundamental rights which are basic human rights and freedoms like the freedom to life and personal liberty; to speech and expression etc., right to enforce the fundamental rights by the Supreme Court is itself a fundamental right under article 32. In addition under article 226, the High Court also can enforce the fundamental rights. The Supreme Court has held that the attempt of the court must be to expand the reach and ambit of the Fundamental Rights rather than to attenuate their meaning and content in the course of judicial interpretation.[1]

(4) Union-State relations

It contains elaborate provisions about relations between the Union and the States

(5) Division of powers

Division of powers between the Union and the States are extensively dealt with as the Constitution is federal in nature. It has created a substantially strong Centre.

(6) Directive Principles

Detailed provisions regarding the Directive Principles of State Policy are provided so as to provide guidelines to the Government in framing laws and policies and in general in order to attain efficient governance in the country and to attain social welfare and equality.

(7) Fundamental duties

Fundamental duties have been inserted in 1976 by 42nd Constitution Amendment.

---

1. *Maneka Gandhi* v. *Union of India*, AIR 1978 SC 597: (1978) 1 SCC 248: (1978) 2 SCR 621.

(8) Independent judiciary

It has provided for an independent judiciary and laid down detailed provisions regarding the appointment of the judges of the High Court and the Supreme Court.

(9) Constitution of the Union and the States

It has included the Constitution of the Union and also of the States though they are substantially parallel provisions.

(10) Administrative details

It contains detailed provisions regarding administrative details such as citizenship, official language, Government services, electoral machinery, State liability, property rights etc.

(11) Diverse interests protected

India is a land of varying cultures, different religions and various communities, castes and Tribes. The Constitution contains elaborate provisions to protect their interests. *For example,* problems of Anglo-Indians, the Scheduled Castes and the Scheduled Tribes and other backward classes etc., have been addressed.

(12) Inculcating democratic values

Being under a long spell of foreign rule – the country was more exposed to dictatorial culture than democratic culture while being aware of the inherent strengths of the democratic system. Hence detailed provisions have been included so as to inculcate democratic values by laying down detailed norms of administration and Government services.

But this does not mean that all problems of governance are one hundred percent settled by the Constitution. There is scope for the growth and development of conventions.[1] *For example* – relationship between the President or the State Governor and his Council of Ministers; the concept of ministerial responsibility for the acts of the officials, the relationship between the Prime Minister or the Chief Minister in a State and his Council of Ministers or the appointment of a State Governor; relations between the President and the Governor are left to be evolved by conventions.[2]

It should be noted that British conventions are not *suo motu* (of its own force) operative in India. Some conventions have been questioned and either upheld or modified by the courts according to the demands of the situations.

C. Establishment of a Sovereign, Socialist, Secular, Democratic Republic

Sovereign means that India is not subject to any external authority and that the State has power to legislate on any subject in conformity with Constitutional limitations.[3]

'Socialist and secular' have been added by the 42nd Amendment Act, 1976 (*i.e.,* during the internal emergency). Term socialist is not defined in the Constitution. Socialism in its strict and doctrinaire sense would mean State ownership of material

---

1. W.I. Jennings, Law and the Constitution.
2. M.P. Jain: Indian Constitutional Law (Nagpur: Butterworths Wadhwa), 5th Ed, 2009 at p. 11.
3. *Synthetics and Chemicals Ltd.* v. *State of Uttar Pradesh,* AIR 1990 SC 1927: JT (1989) 4 SC 267.

resources of the Nation. But this is not what is meant under our Constitution. It does not totally exclude private enterprise. Socialism was always implicit in our Constitution. It has now been expressly provided. Hence it enables the courts to lean more and more in favour of nationalization and State ownership of industry.[1] Democratic socialism aims to end poverty, disease, and inequality of opportunity. Socialist concept of society should be implemented in the true spirit of the Constitution.[2] Social justice is people's justice where the tyranny of power is transformed into the democracy of social good.[3] Establishment of the egalitarian social order through rule of law is the basic structure of the Constitution.[4] J. Bhagwati has observed[5] that "the Constitution makers have given us one of the most remarkable documents in history for ushering in a new socio-economic order and the Constitution which they have forged for us has a social purpose and an economic mission and therefore every word or phrase in the Constitution must be interpreted in a manner which would advance the socio-economic objective of the Constitution." Socialism aims at distributive justice wherein there has to be an equitable distribution of the material resources and no concentration of wealth in the hands of the few. Indian economy is based on the concept of mixed economy – wherein both the public and the private sector have a role to play. It may also be noted that after India has signed GATT and thrown its economy open to the world at large, there has been a considerable increase in private ownership of the material resources of the country.

Secularism: It is not defined under the Constitution. Though India has a number of religious groups and the people belonging to the Hindu religion are in the majority – there is no State religion. All religions are treated equally. The State is not concerned with the relationship between man and God. It only regulates the relationship between man and man. It guarantees the freedom of religion and worship and prohibits discrimination only on the ground of religion. Freedom of religion is subject to the powers of the State to make laws in the interest of social reform. No one is disabled from holding any public office on the ground of his religion. There is only one electoral roll containing the names of all the qualified voters. There is no communal based electorate (persons entitled to vote). Secularism has been held to be the basic feature of the Constitution[6] and hence cannot be amended.

'Democratic' means that India has a responsible and Parliamentary form of Government which is accountable to an elected Legislature. Supreme Court has declared democracy to the basic feature of the Constitution.[7] It means that we have a Government of the people, by the people and for the People. It means that the Government derives its authority from the 'will of the people'. The

1. *Excel Wear* v. *Union of India,* AIR 1979 SC 25: (1978) 4 SCC 224: (1979) 1 SCR 1009.
2. *G.B. Pant University of Agriculture and Technology, Pantnagar, Nainital* v. *State of U.P.,* AIR 2000 SC 2695: 2000 AIR SCW 2870: (2000) 7 SCC 109.
3. Iyer, K.I.: Social Justice: Sunset of Dawn p.17-18 (Lucknow: Eastern Book Company, 1987).
4. *Samatha* v. *State of Andhra Pradesh,* AIR 1997 SC 3297 (3330): 1997 AIR SCW 3361: (1997) 8 SCC 191.
5. *Sanjit Roy* v. *State of Rajasthan,* AIR 1983 SC 328 (332): (1983) 1 SCC 525: 1983 (I) LLJ 220.
6. Supra note 1.
7. *S.R. Bommai* v. *Union of India,* AIR 1994 SC 1918: 1994 AIR SCW 2946: (1994) 3 SCC 1.

rulers are elected by the people and are responsible to them. But this does not mean that the people are above Constitution. People's will is respected if it is within the limits of the Constitution[1]. Thus, the rule is 'Be you ever so high the law is above you.'

Republic: It signifies that there shall be an elected head of the Government unlike a hereditary monarch (person inherits the office of the king- the King dies and his son succeeds) as in England.

Responsible Government through Parliamentary form of Government: To make the people supreme – Parliamentary form of Government is established under which the executive is responsible to an elected Legislature.

America also has a democracy but the system differs as they have a Presidential system of democracy based on the separation of powers between the Executive and the Legislative organs. The Indian system is based on the principle of co-ordination and co-operation of the two organs. It is based on 'co-operative Federalism'.

In India people elect the Lok Sabha members (Lower House- referred to as House of the People under the Constitution) at the Centre and the Legislative Assembly members at the State by direct election. In the Rajya Sabha (Upper House- referred to as the Council of States under the Constitution) representatives of the States are elected by the Legislative Assembly members. The President is elected by an electoral college consisting of the elected members of both the Houses of the Parliament and the Legislative Assembly. This ensures that the President is the choice of the people and he represents both the Centre and the States. The Executive power formally vests with the President but is actually exercised by the Council of Ministers headed by the Prime Minister and responsible to the Lok Sabha. Members of the Lower House at the Centre and the Legislative Assembly at the State level – are directly elected by the people on the basis of adult franchise normally for 5 years. Hence the Government is known as Responsible Government.

D. Single citizenship

It has provided for a single citizenship of the Union. There is no dual citizenship as in America. There a person has the American citizenship and also that of the State *e.g.*, Virginnia citizenship.

E. Special provisions

It has provided for special provisions in favour of Scheduled Castes and Scheduled Tribes and the Backward Classes and the minorities to promote a sense of security amongst them and in order to bring them into the mainstream fold.

F. Elections

Elections are based on the principle of one man one vote. Every citizen who has attained 18 years is entitled to vote. The Constitution has established an autonomous Election Commission to supervise and conduct elections to the Parliament and State Legislatures.

1. *B.R. Kapoor* v. *State of Tamil Nadu,* AIR 2001 SC 3435: 2001 AIR SCW 3720: (2001) 7 SCC 231.

G. Independent Judiciary

A well structured and well-regulated judicial machinery has been provided for with the Supreme Court at its apex (head). It is the general court of appeal from both civil and criminal and revenue and other matters. It can issue writs for the enforcement of Fundamental Rights. It has an advisory jurisdiction under which it gives its opinion over legal questions referred by the President. It is the custodian of the rights of the citizens. It is the ultimate arbiter (judge, authority) in all constitutional matters. Likewise there exists a High Court in each State. They also decide disputes between a private party and the Government and between the Governments *inter-se*. Constitution contains provisions to safeguard their tenure, their salaries and they can be removed only by a special procedure. India has a unified judicial system of courts. The Supreme Court, the High Court and the Lower Courts constitute a single unified judiciary having jurisdiction over all cases arising under any law enacted by the Parliament or the State Legislature. In U.S.A. there is a dual system of courts- a Federal Judiciary with Supreme Court at the top and a parallel judicial system at the State level.

H. Federation with strong centralizing tendencies

Indian Federal System differs from that of USA, Canada and Australia. We have a two-tier Government system with the Central Government at one level and the State Government at other. Thus two sets of Governments function simultaneously. Seventh Schedule of the Constitution lays down 3 lists – the Union, State and the Concurrent Lists. The Central Government legislates on subjects mentioned in the Union list; the State Government legislates on subjects mentioned in the State List and both can legislate on subjects mentioned in the Concurrent List subject to certain provisions which give primacy to the laws enacted by the Centre. There is an elaborate distribution of Legislative, Administrative and financial powers between the State and the Centre. Each is supreme in its own area. But during emergency situations it tends towards unitary system.

The Indian Federal scheme has developed novel techniques so that it incorporates the advantages of the Federal system and also attempts to mitigate (lessen) the weaknesses of rigidity and legalism. During the Proclamation of an emergency the Union Parliament is empowered to legislate on any subject mentioned in the State List. Central Government can give directions to the State Government as to the manner in which it should exercise its Executive powers.

Thus, we have a dual polity but with a single citizenship – *viz.*, the Indian citizenship. Hence an Indian enjoys practically the same political and civil rights of citizenship throughout the country no matter in which State he resides. Our Constitution has been described in different ways- *quasi* federal (partly federal); unitary with federal features; federal with unitary features, centralized federation etc.[1] However note that the States are not the agents of the Centre. They exist under the Constitution; they derive their power from the Constitution and not

1. *Supra note* 6 at p. 19.

from Central laws; federal provisions can be amended not unilaterally by the Central Government but with the co-operation of the Centre and the States.

In USA, the States are free to draft their own Constitutions unlike in India.

What is to be noted is that Centre and the States are not rivals. They are intended to work harmoniously (amicably). Justice Sarkaria Commission was appointed by the Centre to examine and review the working of the existing arrangements between the Union and the State regarding powers, functions and responsibilities in all spheres. The report has emphasized on greater decentralization in the decision making process and its execution up to the village level. The Constitution has been amended in 1992 in order to ensure participation at the municipal and village level to attain a responsive and democratic local self-Government.[1] This has created a third tier of local Governments – Panchayats and the Municipalities. In order to maintain the Federal character the Supreme Court in *S.R. Bommai's* case has laid down several procedural safeguards before the Centre can take over the administration of a State during an emergency under article 356.[2]

I. Blend of rigidity and flexibility

Even with a written Constitution it is sufficiently flexible. It is only a few provisions of the Constitution which require the consent of half of the State Legislatures for amendment. The rest of the provisions can be amended by a special majority of the Parliament. Our Constitution has been amended 95 times up to 2009.

J. Fundamental law

In a legal system we have the Constitution laws and the other laws. Constitution law is the basic or a fundamental law. This means the following:

(a) All other laws, Legislative actions, Executive actions must derive their validity from the Constitution.

(b) No Legislature can make a law so as to contravene the Constitution.

(c) No act – whether that of the Legislature, Executive, or Judicial or *quasi*-judicial or any administrative agency can stand if contrary to the Constitution.

(d) It is for the judiciary to see that the Constitutional organs do not violate the Constitution.

K. Parliamentary and Presidential System of Government

Presidential form in USA	Parliamentary form in India
Based on the strict doctrine of separation of powers.	Doctrine not that strict. Thus *e.g.*, Executive has Legislative powers.
President is the real head of the Executive. All Executive powers are vested in him.	President is the nominal head of the Executive. Real powers vest with the Council of Ministers headed by the Prime Minister. Thus the functions

1. Constitution 73rd & 74th Amendments 1992.
2. Under article 356 the Centre takes over the affairs of the State Government if the State is not being carried on in accordance with the provisions of the Constitution.

	of the head of the State are by and large separated from that of the Head of the Government.
Members of his Cabinet are not members of the Legislature. They are appointed by the President out of the best talent available in the country. He is free to dismiss them.	Council of Ministers are members of the Legislature. People directly elect the members of the Lower House for 5 years.
Cabinet members are responsible to the President alone and not to the Legislature.	Council of Ministers are collectively responsible to the Lower House.
President exercises his own discretion. President is not responsible to the Council of Ministers *i.e.,* the Congress.	President has to act in accordance with the aid and advice of the Council of Ministers headed by the Prime Minister.
Legislature does not dictate to him the political and administrative policy to be followed by him.	When the President addresses the Parliament – he reads out the policy statement prepared by the Government.
President is elected directly by the people for 4 years.	President is elected by an electoral college consisting of the elected MLA's and MP's- thus indirectly elected by the people.

(a) Advantages of Presidential System

(a) Relatively free from sectional and party disputes, President can hence devote time for developmental activities.

(b) He chooses his team of ministers from the best available talent.

(c) President being the real Executive Head is powerful.

(d) Discourages defections and horse trading.

(b) Advantages of the Parliamentary System

(a) It is a responsible Government. Ministers are accountable to the Legislature whose members are elected by the people. Assessment of the responsibility of the Executive is both daily and periodic. Question hour and Zero hour[1] puts the Government on trial during the sessions.

(b) Executive is accountable to the Legislature for its policy formulations. Survival of the Executive depends upon the mercy of the Legislature which may at any time pass a vote of no-confidence. The Legislature also is not hampered in any way as long as it adheres to the policies and the programmes of the party which was elected to power.[2]

(c) Ensures harmony between the Executive and the Legislature.

(d) The Prime Minister also can select the best talent from outside the Cabinet and get them elected or nominated to either house of the Parliament.

(e) Prime Minister who enjoys the majority in the House is more powerful than the President in USA.

Defections and horse trading are the greatest defects. During Emergency (1975-77), there appeared to be a serious move to replace the Parliamentary

---

1. Coined by the Press because the time slot allotted is at 12 noon. No such term is there in the Constitution.
2. Shukla, V.N. Constitution of India (Lucknow: Eastern Book Co.) 10th Ed at p.A-41.

system with the Presidential system, but then it was not carried any further. Since then the form of Government has not been seriously debated.[1]

(c) Disadvantages of Parliamentary Form of Government

(a) Multiplicity of political parties.

(b) Evil of defection.

(c) Lack of leadership in national parties.

(d) Illiteracy of the voters.

(e) Growth of regional parties.

(f) Criminalization of politics.

(g) Our ministers and legislators are subjected to the pulls and pressures of the elected representatives. It affects efficiency.

(h) Executive can become all powerful and conduct itself by an authoritarian rule if the opposition does not play its role properly.

Parliamentary democracy becomes unworkable if the candidates contesting the elections are not committed to the ideology, policy and programme of their political party. Hence the political parties have to be very careful in admitting persons as members of their party only for the sake of numbers.

---

1. *Supra note* 20 at p. A-42.

CHAPTER 2

NATURE OF THE INDIAN CONSTITUTION (FEDERAL OR UNITARY)

SYNOPSIS

Introduction

Constitutions are either unitary or federal. In a unitary Government powers of the Government are centralized in the Central Government. The States are subordinate to the Centre. In a Federal Constitution there is a division of power between the States and the Central Government and both are independent in their own spheres.

There is a difference of opinion amongst different Constitutional experts regarding the nature of the Indian Constitution. One view is that it is:

- o Federal with unitary features;
- o Unitary with federal features;
- o *Quasi* federal;
- o Dr. Ambedkar termed it 'Federal' in spite of provisions where the Centre has powers to override the States in case of emergencies.

A. Essential characteristics of a Federal Constitution

(1) Distribution of powers

Distribution of powers between the Centre and the State is in such a way that matters of national interest are looked after by the Centre and matters of local interest fall within the purview of the States.

(2) Supreme law

Constitution in a Federal State is the supreme law of the land.

(3) Written Constitution

A Federal Constitution is almost necessarily a written Constitution.

(4) Rigidity

Written Constitution are necessarily rigid. The amendment procedure is very complicated. This does not mean that the Constitution should never be amended. But amendment should not remain exclusively with the Central or the State Government. Constitution is considered a permanent document to remain in operation for generations to come. Its supremacy can be maintained only if its method of amendment is rigid.

(5) Judiciary – Final authority

The *judiciary is the final authority* to interpret the Constitution and is the guardian of the Constitution.

B. Nature of the Indian Constitution

Federation with strong centralizing tendencies

Indian Federal System differs from that of USA, Canada and Australia. We have a two-tier Government system – with the Central Government at one level and the State Government at other. Thus, two sets of Governments function simultaneously. Seventh Schedule of the Constitution lays down 3 lists – the Union, State and the Concurrent Lists. The Central Government legislates on subjects mentioned in the Union list; the State Government legislates on subjects mentioned in the State List and both can legislate on subjects mentioned in the Concurrent List subject to certain provisions which give primacy to the laws enacted by the Centre. There is an elaborate distribution of legislative, administrative and financial powers between the State and the Centre. Each is supreme in its own area. But during emergency situations it tends towards unitary system.

The Indian Federal scheme has developed novel techniques so that it incorporates the advantages of the Federal system and also attempts to mitigate (lessen) the weaknesses of rigidity and legalism. During the Proclamation of an emergency – the Union Parliament is empowered to legislate on any subject mentioned in the State List. Central Government can give directions to the State Government as to the manner in which it should exercise its executive powers.

Thus, we have a dual polity but with a single citizenship- *viz.*, the Indian citizenship. Hence an Indian enjoys practically the same political and civil rights of citizenship throughout the country no matter in which State he resides. Our Constitution has been described in different ways – *quasi*-federal (partly federal); unitary with federal features; federal with unitary features, centralized federation etc. However note that the States are not the agents of the Centre. They exist under the Constitution; they derive their power from the Constitution and not from Central laws; federal provisions can be amended not unilaterally by the Central Government but with the co-operation of the Centre and the States.

In USA, the States are free to draft their own Constitutions unlike in India.

C. Factors modifying the strict application of the Federal principles in India

(1) Appointment of Governors

They are appointed by the President and are answerable to him. Governor is required to send certain State laws to the President for his assent. *e.g.*, articles 200, 288(2). President can veto (rejection) those laws. The only example of such a veto is where the Kerala Education Bill was sent back after obtaining the Supreme Court's opinion.

(2) Legislating on State list matters

Parliament can legislate in the national interest on matters enumerated in the State list of the 7th Schedule.

(3) Forming new States

Parliament has power to form new States and alter boundaries of the States.

(4) Emergency provisions

Three kinds of emergencies are contemplated: (1) caused by war, external aggression or armed rebellion[1] (2) caused by failure of Constitutional machinery in States (3) financial emergency.

Important affairs of the State – like making laws on matters in the State List; modifications of the provisions for distribution of revenue; directing the State as to the manner in which the Executive powers are going to be exercised —are taken over by the Centre when there is a Proclamation of Emergency. Dr. V.N. Shukla opines that these provisions are a plus point to the Federal System and not a negative point. This is because it takes into consideration the contingencies which would destroy the basic assumptions of the Constitution and provides a remedy to face the crisis.

(5) Emergency provisions in aid of Federalism

It should also be noted that in case of USA, Canada, Australia which are strictly federal the courts enlarged the defence powers of the Federal Government in order to tackle the emergent situations arising out of the two World Wars. During this period the countries behaved more like unitary than federal.

(6) Partly federal – Partly unitary

The Indian Constitution is neither purely federal nor purely unitary. It has a harmonious mix of both. It has contemplated the problems that the country may face if the Constitution were to be purely federal and therefore has made provisions converting it into a unitary mode on a temporary basis until the crisis is overcome. Whichever may be the form of Government – ultimately what is needed is competent, sincere and honest persons, true to the interests of the Nation and the welfare of its people.

---

1. Before the 44th Amendment it was: 'Internal disturbance'. But going by the unfortunate experience of the country during the internal emergency in 1975 where without anything alarming on the law and order front or financial front, Smt Indira Gandhi –the then Prime Minister had got an Emergency Proclaimed. Hence 'internal disturbance' was replaced by 'armed rebellion'.

CHAPTER 3

UNION AND ITS TERRITORIES

(Articles 1-4)

SYNOPSIS

Introduction

Constitution lays down that India *i.e.*, Bharat- shall be a Union of States.[1] Dr. Ambedkar has observed that there are 2 advantages in using the term 'Union' rather than that of 'federation'- *viz.*,—

- it shows that the Union of India is not the result of an agreement between the units like in USA and
- that the States have no right to secede (break away) from the federation.

'Bharat'- comprises of the States, the Union territories[2] specified in the First Schedule and such other territories as may be acquired.[3] They are mentioned in the First Schedule. Today we have 29 States and 7 Union territories.[4]

Parliament may **by law** admit new States on such conditions as it deems fit.[3] It means no amendment is needed to admit a new State into the Union.

A. Formation of a new State—Alteration and its Procedure

The Parliament may by law—

(a) Form a new State – by separating a territory from the existing State (*e.g.*, Jharkhand out of Bihar and Uttaranchal carved out of Uttar Pradesh) or by uniting 2 or more States; or parts of the States; or by uniting any territory to a part of any State. It can also[5] unite a part of a State or a part of a Union Territory to any other State or Union Territory and thus form a new State or a new Union Territory.

---

1. Article 1.
2. Union Territories are administrative units which do not form a part of any State but are kept separate due to several historical, cultural and political reasons. A Union Territory is administered by the President. Governor of an adjoining State may be appointed as an Administrator for the Union Territory. In that capacity the Governor acts independently of his Council of Ministers.
3. Article 2.
4. Andhra Pradesh, Arunachal Pradesh, Assam, Bihar, Goa, Gujarat, Haryana, Himachal Pradesh.
5. Explanation II, article 3.

(b) It can increase or decrease the area of any State.

(c) It can alter the boundaries.

(d) It can alter the name of any State.[1]

Note that under this Article only States can be admitted by a law of the Parliament. But to admit or establish a Union territory, Constitutional amendment under article 368 is needed. *For example* Portuguese and French territories were admitted as Union Territories of Goa, Daman, Diu, Dadra and Nagar Haveli and Pondicherry by an amendment to the Constitution.

Procedure: However such a Bill for the formation of a new State can be moved either in the Lower House or Rajya Sabha

(1) Recommendation from the President

Only after obtaining the recommendation from the President.

(2) Views of the State Legislatures ascertained

If the Bill affects the area, boundaries or name of any of the States then the President must refer the Bill to that State in order to ascertain the views of the Legislatures of that State. If it does not so affect there is no question of referring the Bill to any State. But, the Parliament is not bound by the views. If the State fails to express its views within the specified time- Parliament may proceed with the matter. For amending the Bill after receiving the views, no fresh reference is needed to ascertain the views on the amendment[2]. However in case of Union Territories- no such reference to the concerned Union Territory is needed.[3]

(3) 1st and 4th Schedules to be amended

The First and the Fourth Schedules to the Constitution are related to the topic under discussion. The First Schedule deals with the list of the States and the Union Territories in India and the Fourth Schedule deals with the number of seats reserved for different States in the Council of States. When a new State etc., is formed under articles 2 and 3 the Parliament shall also make such amendments to the First and the Fourth Schedule as may be necessary to give effect to the law and may contain such consequential and incidental provisions as may be necessary when a new State is to be formed like- representation of new units in Parliament, setting up of Legislative, Executive and Judicial organs necessary for effective administration.

Note that any such law is not regarded as an amendment to the Constitution under article 368 and hence it can be passed by a simple majority and it does not require 2/3rd majority as laid down for Constitutional amendments. But this does not authorize the Parliament to override the Constitutional scheme. Thus a State cannot be set up without effective Legislative, Executive and Judicial organs.[4] When Haryana State was established in 1966 the strength of the interim Legislature was 54 whereas the minimum prescribed was 60 under article 170. Supreme Court upheld it as it could not be treated as an amendment to the Constitution under article 4(2).

1. Article 3.
2. *Babulal Parate* v. *State of Bombay*, AIR 1960 SC 51: (1960) 1 SCR 605: 1960 SCJ 107.
3. Article 3.
4. *Mangal Singh* v. *Union of India*, AIR 1967 SC 944: (1967) 2 SCR 109: 1968 (1) SCJ 240.

Thus, the boundaries can be altered only by a law made by the Parliament and not by any State Legislature. It speaks of the unitary character of our Constitution.

In *R.C. Poudyal* v. *Union of India*[1] Sikkim was conferred a full-fledged Statehood. A seat was reserved for the representative of the group of religious institutions to be elected by them; and seats were reserved in favour of a tribe far in excess of its population. The Supreme Court held that the provisions were not inconsistent with the principles of secularism and equality laid down in our Constitution. They were upheld on the ground of historical, cultural political background of Sikkim.

Parliament has passed 23 Acts under articles 2 and 3 to bring about a change in the area, boundaries and names of the States. States were divided on linguistic lines by the States Reorganization Act, 1956.

B. Cessation of the territory

Supreme Court has held[2] that power to reorganize the States under article 3 cannot be used to cede Indian territory to a foreign country. Article 3 deals with internal adjustments of the States in such a manner that ultimately the newly formed or altered States remain within the jurisdiction of India. If a portion of the Indian territory is to be ceded to the foreign country it has to be done only by a Constitutional amendment.

C. Settlement of boundary dispute

But settlement of a boundary dispute is different from cessation of territory. Hostilities broke out between India and Pakistan on a boundary dispute in Kutch. It was referred to a Tribunal for arbitration. The question in *Maganbhai* v. *Union of India*[3] was: can the award be executed by an executive act of the Parliament or does it require a Constitutional amendment. It was held that an executive action is sufficient because it does not involve cessation of territory, but only drawing a boundary line on the surface of the earth.

---

1. AIR 1993 SC 1804: 1993 AIR SCW 1620: (1993) 1 SCR 891.
2. *In Ref. on Berubari,* AIR 1960 SC 845: 1961 (1) SCA 22: (1960) 3 SCR 250.
3. AIR 1969 SC 783: (1969) 3 SCR 254: (1970) 3 SCC 400.

CHAPTER 4
CITIZENSHIP

(Articles 5-11)

SYNOPSIS

Introduction

Population of a country is divided into citizens and non-citizens (aliens).

India is a Federation with Union Government at the Centre and State Government at the State level. Yet, the citizens have only a single citizenship *viz.*, the Indian citizenship.[1]

A. Advantages of citizenship

Citizenship carries with it the following advantages:

(1) Fundamental right

Most of the fundamental rights are available to the citizens and are not available to the non-citizens. *For example* – right against discrimination only on the grounds of religion, race, caste, sex or place of birth;[2] right to equality in public employment[3]; right to fundamental freedoms under article 19 - that of Speech and expression, association, assembly, residence, movement, profession are available only to the citizens.

(2) Cultural and educational rights

Cultural and educational rights *viz.*, protection of the interests of the minorities[4]; and rights of the minorities to establish and administer educational institutions[5] – is available only to the citizens.

---

1. In *Dipali Katia Chadha* v. *Union of India*, (1996) 7 SCC 432, the court entertained a possibility of dual citizenship, but did not decide the point but referred it to the Central Government.
2. Article 15.
3. Article 16.
4. Article 29.
5. Article 30.

(3) Holding offices

To hold the office of high Constitutional authorities like that of the President, Vice President, Governor, judges of the High Court, Supreme Court; Advocate General of the State, Attorney- General, one has to be a citizen of India.

(4) Voting and contesting elections

Right to vote at elections to the House of People and the Legislative Assembly of States; and to contest for such elections is available only to the citizens.

B. Ways of acquiring citizenship

Articles 5-11 in the Constitution lays down the persons who shall be citizens of India at the commencement of the Constitution. They are:

(a) By domicile – Article 5.
(b) Those who have migrated to India from Pakistan - Article 6.
(c) By registration – Article 7.
(d) Citizenship of Indians abroad- Article 8.

(1) Citizenship by domicile

Fact of *actual* residence *plus intention* to reside there permanently constitutes domicile. Every person who has his domicile in the territory of India at the commencement of the Constitution *i.e.,* 26th January, 1950 and

- Was born in India; or
- Either of his parents (father or his mother) were born in India or
- Who has been ordinarily resident in India for not less than five years immediately preceding the commencement of the Constitution (*i.e.,* for a minimum period from 26th January, 1945 to 26th January, 1950).

Note that what is required to acquire Indian citizenship under this category is – domicile in India and one of the 3 requirements mentioned above and not all the requirements. Thus, if a person was born in India *and* has his domicile in India, he becomes a citizen of India – it does not matter if his parents were not born in India; likewise it is sufficient if either his father or his mother was born in India coupled with the fact of his Indian domicile.

Note that in all the three cases mentioned above nationality of the person or of his parents is immaterial.

Domicile – what is

Domicile is a complex legal concept (idea). It is not defined under the Constitution. But it is essential for the purposes of Citizenship. It means the fact of residence and his intention[1] to make it his permanent home. It is the fact of residence coupled with a certain state of mind – *viz.,* to reside there permanently. Supreme Court has held in *Central Bank of India* v. *Ram Narain*[2] *that* mere residence is not enough. Intention to reside permanently is equally necessary. The court further observed that "a person may not have a home, but he cannot be without a domicile, and the law may attribute to him a domicile in a country where in reality he has not. A person may be a vagrant, as where

1. *Animus manendi.*
2. AIR 1955 SC 36: 1955 Cr LJ 152: 1955 SCR 777.

he lives in a yatch, or a wanderer from one Hotel to another yet the law will ascribe to him a domicile on one particular territory." Thus, all persons must at all times have a domicile

(2) Classes of domicile—Of origin and by choice

Domicile of origin – which attaches to a person by birth and domicile by choice which he acquires by residence in a territory subject to a distinct legal system coupled with an intention to reside permanently. Whether there is an intention to reside there permanently is a question of fact and circumstances of the case. *For example,* say a person goes to England to pursue his medical studies and after completion of his studies takes up a job there for say 10 years. Meanwhile he is constructing a hospital and a residential building in India – circumstances indicate that he has an intention to come and reside in India permanently and therefore he has an Indian domicile.

A person – Louis was staying in India on the basis of a foreign passport with the permission of the Indian authorities. The Supreme Court held that there was nothing to even remotely suggest that he had formed an intention to reside in India permanently.

Minor's domicile follows that of his father; a married woman's domicile follows that of her husband. In India the domicile of a posthumous child is that which his father had at the time of his father's death. Widow retains the domicile of her late husband until she changes it by her own act.

In *Pradeep Jain* v. *Union of India*[1] the Supreme Court has held that the Constitution speaks of only one domicile *viz.,* 'the domicile in the territory of India'. Domicile and nationality are different.

In *Mhd. Raza* v. *State of Bombay*[2] – the appellant came to Bombay in 1938, went on a pilgrimage to Iraq in 1945. On return he was registered as a foreigner and his stay was extended several times in India. In 1957 his application for extending stay period was refused. He contended that he must be regarded as a citizen under article 5. His appeal was dismissed. It was held that though he was originally in India he did not acquire Indian citizenship; that he took up a job as a cashier was insufficient to establish that there was a change of mind of the kind necessary to acquire a new domicile in India. His application for extending his stay showed that he had no intention to stay permanently.

(3) Citizenship of migrants to India from Pakistan (Article 6)

Such migrants from Pakistan are classified into two groups:

- Those who came to India before July 19th 1948[3]

---

1. AIR 1984 SC 1420: (1984) 3 SCC 654: (1984) 3 SCR 942 it has thus overruled the view in *Joshi* v. *Madhya Bharat,* AIR 1955 SC 334 that theoretically it was possible to have a State domicile because domicile has reference to the system of law by which a person is governed in respect of succession, minority and marriage. Hence when in one country there are different rules of succession prevailing in different areas- then each area having a distinct set of laws can be considered as a country for the purpose of domicile. – *see* Jain, M.P.: Indian Constitutional Law (Nagpur: Lexisnexis Butterworths: Wadhwa) 5th Ed. 2009 at p. 793.
2. AIR 1956 SC 1436.
3. This is the date on which the Influx from Pakistan (Control) Ordinance introduced a permit system to control the admission into India of persons from West Pakistan.

- Those who came to India after July 19th 1948

A person who has migrated to India from Pakistan is deemed to be Indian citizen at the commencement of the Constitution if

(1) He or either of his parents or either of his grandparents were born in India as defined in Government of India Act, 1935. In addition one of the following two conditions must be satisfied:

- If he has migrated before July 19th 1948 – he must be ordinarily resident in India since the date of his migration;
- If he has migrated after July 19th 1948 – he must be registered as a citizen of India with the officer appointed by the Government for the purpose. But no such person can be registered unless he is residing in India for at least 6 months immediately before the date of registration.

(4) Citizenship by Registration (Article 8)

A person who was born in India or either of his parents or grand-parents were born in India before independence – but is ordinarily resident outside India may register himself as Indian citizen with the Diplomatic Representative of India in the country of his residence.

(5) Termination of Citizenship (Article 8)

A citizen of India by domicile or by migration ceases to be Indian citizen if he has migrated to Pakistan after March 1st 1947 (Article 7) but if he returns to India under a permit of resettlement or permanent return he can register himself as Indian citizen in the same manner as a person migrating from Pakistan after July 19th 1948.

This article speaks of termination of the citizenship of only those persons who migrated to Pakistan between March 1st 1947 and January 26th 1950.[1] In respect of persons migrating after January 26, 1950 it has to be decided under the provisions of the Indian Citizenship Act.

'Migration' means people going from one territory to another – whether or not with intention of permanent residence. In *Kulathil Mamma* v. *State of Kerala* migration is used in the broad sense as meaning- 'going from one State to another State' without bringing the meaning of domicile. The movement should be voluntary and should not be for a specific purpose and for a short and limited period.[2]

(6) No dual citizenship

No person can be a citizen of India if he has voluntarily acquired the citizenship of a foreign country.

C. Citizenship under the Citizenship Act, 1955

The Act[3] provides for acquiring and terminating citizenship after commencement of the Constitution.

---

1. *State of Madhya Pradesh* v. *Peer Mohd.*, AIR 1963 SC 645: (1963) 1 Cr LJ 617: 1963 (1) SCA 649.
2. AIR 1955 SC 1614.
3. Citizenship, naturalization and aliens' fall in entry 17 List I. Hence the Parliament has the power to make laws with respect to citizenship.

Citizenship can be acquired in Five ways: Birth, descent, registration, naturalization, incorporation of some territory in India.

(1) Birth: Born on or after 1-1-1950

Every person born in India on or after January 1st 1950 is an Indian citizen by birth. But he shall not be an Indian citizen if at the time of his birth:

(a) His father possesses diplomatic immunity and is not an Indian citizen.

(b) His father is an alien enemy and his birth occurs at a place under enemy occupation. Alien enemy is a person who belongs to a country which is at war with our country.

(2) Citizenship by descent – may occur in 2 ways – Born outside India between 26-1-1950 and 10-12-1992 or born after 10-12-1992

- A person is an Indian citizen by descent if was born outside India on or after 26th January 1950 but **before** the commencement of the citizenship (Amendment Act) 1992, *i.e.,* 10-12-1992 (*i.e.,* between these 2 dates).

and at the time of his birth his father is a citizen of India.

- A person who was born outside India **after** the commencement of the Citizenship (Amendment Act), 1992 is an Indian citizen if either of his parents is a citizen of India at the time of his birth—

  provided that if either of his parent also was a citizen of India by descent only—

  —then such person shall not be an Indian citizen under this provision unless his birth is registered at an Indian consulate or either of his parents is at the time of his birth in service under Government in India.

(3) Citizenship by Registration (section 5)

The following categories of persons, if not already citizens of India can be registered as Indian citizens after taking an oath of allegiance:

(a) persons of Indian origin ordinarily resident in India and residing there for 6 months immediately preceding the application for registration.

(b) Persons of Indian origin who are ordinarily resident outside undivided India.

(c) Women married to the Indian citizens.

(d) Minor children of Indian citizens.

(e) Persons of full age and capacity who are citizens of a Commonwealth country. The Central Government has to keep due regard to the conditions on which an Indian citizen can become a citizen of that country by registration.

Citizenship Act does not have any provision for cancellation of the certificate of registration issued under section 5 as held in *Hari Shanker Jain* v. *Sonia Gandhi*[1]

1. AIR 2001 SC 3689: 2001 AIR SCW 3557: (2001) 8 SCC 233.

(4) Citizenship by naturalization

A person of full age and capacity who is a citizen of a non-Commonwealth country may become a citizen by naturalization if the Central Government is satisfied that he fulfils the conditions laid down in the Act. These conditions are:

(1) He is not a subject or a citizen of a country where Indian citizen are prevented from becoming citizens by naturalization.

(2) He renounces the citizenship of that other country.

(3) He has resided and/or been in Government service for 12 months immediately preceding the date of application.

(4) During 7 years prior to these 12 months he has resided and/or has been in Government service for not less than 4 years.

(5) He is of good character.

(6) He has an adequate knowledge of a language recognized by the Constitution.

(7) After naturalization he intends to reside in India or enter into Government service or serve an international organization of which India is a member or under a society, company or body of persons established in India.

If the Central Government is satisfied that the applicant has rendered distinguished service to the cause of science, philosophy, art, literature, world peace, or human progress generally – these conditions may be waived.

(5) Citizenship by incorporation of territory (section 7)

If a new territory becomes a part of India the Central Government may notify the persons who shall be citizens of India by reason of their connection with that territory.

D. Commonwealth citizen

A citizen of a Commonwealth country has the status of a Commonwealth citizen in India. The Central Government may make provisions on the basis of reciprocity for the conferment of all or any of the rights of an Indian citizen of a Commonwealth country.

E. Corporation is not a citizen

Whether a Corporation is a citizen has engaged the attention of the courts. Note that fundamental rights are available only to the citizens and persons. An interesting question that arose was whether juristic persons like a company registered under the Companies Act of a statutory corporation can be treated as a citizen and given the benefits of the fundamental rights under the Constitution.

In the earlier cases it was held not to be a citizen and that only natural persons can be citizens but in the later cases – the strategy adopted was of joining a natural person alongwith the company in writ petitions in order to avail the benefit of fundamental rights.

In *State Trading Corporation* v. *Commercial Tax Officer*[1] – the Corporation was a Government company registered under the Indian Companies Act consisting of the President of India and the Secretary of the Ministry of Commerce as its shareholders. The Corporation filed a writ petition to quash sales tax on the ground that it was illegal and hence infringed its fundamental right under article 19(1)(g) of the Constitution. Supreme Court held that the Corporation can have a nationality but it cannot have a citizenship. Nationality is an international law concept but citizenship is a municipal law concept. Nationality is determined by the place of incorporation of the company.

In *Tata Engineering* v. *State of Bihar*[2] – it was a public Limited Company with a large number of Indian citizens as its shareholders. But the court held that it could not have a citizenship. It refused to pierce the corporate veil of the Tata Company and held that the company has a separate entity and therefore though its shareholders are citizens of the country the company cannot be regarded as a citizen.

The trend changed from 1963 onwards. In *Sakal Newspaper* v. *Union of India*[3] the company and a reader of the *Sakal* filed writ petition challenging the Daily Newspaper (Price and Page) Order, 1960 under article 19(1)(a). In *Bank Nationalisation* case[4] bank nationalization was challenged by the banking companies, a shareholder and a current account holder in the bank. The Supreme Court held that petition was maintainable as the rights of the companies as well as the shareholders- who were the citizens, were involved.

In *Bennett Colman* case[5] the Newsprint Control Order was challenged under articles 19(1)(a) and 14 in writ petitions filed by several newspaper companies and several readers, newspaper editors and shareholders. The petitions were held maintainable as the fundamental freedom of speech of the individuals also was involved.

In *D.C. & G.M.* v. *Union of India*[6] the Supreme Court has held that the rights of the shareholders and that of the company which the shareholders have formed are co-extensive with each other. If the rights of the company for enforcement of fundamental rights are denied – that of the shareholders also will be denied. Thus the trend seems to be that the courts are willing to recognize the rights of the company as a citizen.

Unlike a corporation which has a legal entity of its own and which is separate from that of its shareholder – a partnership firm stands for all the partners collectively and therefore a petition is deemed to have been filed by all the partners who are the citizens of India.

However in the case of a Limited Liability Partnership registered under the LLP Act, 2008 – the LLP is a separate legal entity and is separate from that of

---

1. AIR 1963 SC 1811: 1964 (2) SCA 201: (1964) 4 SCR 99.
2. AIR 1965 SC 40: 1965 (1) SCA 365: (1964) 6 SCR 885.
3. AIR 1962 SC 305: 1962 (2) SCJ 400: (1962) 3 SCR 842.
4. AIR 1970 SC 564: (1970) 1 SCC 248: (1970) 3 SCR 530.
5. AIR 1973 SC 106: (1972) 2 SCC 788: 1973 (1) SCJ 177.
6. AIR 1983 SC 937: (1983) 4 SCC 166: (1983) 54 Com Cas 674.

its partners.[1] – hence it would attract the same comments as in the case of an incorporated company.

F. Citizenship (Amendment) Act, 2003 – Double citizenship

It has been enacted mainly to provide for double citizenship to 'overseas citizens of India'. An overseas citizen means[2] a person who:

(i) is of Indian origin being a citizen of the country specified in the Fourth schedule; or

(ii) was a citizen of India immediately before becoming a citizen of the country specified in the Fourth Schedule[3] and is registered as an overseas citizen of India by the Central Government under section 7A(1) of the Act.

Sections 7A, 7B and 7C have been added to the Citizenship Act and provision has been made for registration of overseas citizenship if

a. he is a person of Indian origin, full age and capacity who is a citizen of a specified country; or

b. or he is of full age and capacity and has obtained the citizenship of the specified country on or after the commencement of the Citizenship (Amendment) Act, 2003 and who was a citizen of India immediately before such commencement or

c. that person is a minor of a person mentioned in clauses (a) or (b).

Under the Act citizenship is terminated in three ways:

(i) renunciation of citizenship – being a citizen of another country – the person renounces his Indian citizenship by making a declaration to that effect and by registering it.

(ii) termination of citizenship: if an Indian citizen voluntarily acquires the citizenship of another country he ceases to be the Indian citizen.

(iii) Deprivation of citizenship.

Deprivation of Citizenship

It is a compulsory termination of the citizenship of India.

(a) If registration or naturalization was obtained by fraud, false representation or concealment of material fact,

(b) Or he has shown himself to be disloyal to our Constitution,

(c) Or he has unlawfully traded or communicated with the enemy country or

(d) Within 5 years of his registration or naturalization he has been sentenced to imprisonment for not less than 2 years, or

(e) He has been ordinarily residing out of India for 7 years continuously.

---

1. Section 3(1). Limited Liability Partnership is a sort of a hybrid between a Company and a Firm.
2. Section 2(ee).
3. Australia, Canada, Finland, France, Greece, Ireland, Israel, Italy, Netherlands, New Zealand, Portugal, Republic of Cyprus, Sweden, Switzerland, United Kingdom, and USA.

CHAPTER 5

FUNDAMENTAL RIGHTS

(Articles 12-13)

SYNOPSIS

Introduction

Part III of the Constitution deals with fundamental rights. Man has certain basic, inalienable rights and it is the function of the State to protect, preserve and nourish them. This thinking which is there since the 17th century is reflected in Part III of our Constitution. They are rights or freedoms which are necessary for all round development of a person.

A. Reasons for Fundamental rights to be incorporated into our Constitution

Following are some of the reasons for fundamental rights to be incorporated into our Constitution:

1. The then Congress was demanding these rights against the British rule as a part of human rights.
2. Indian Society is divided into religious, cultural, linguistic groups. Hence fundamental rights had to be specifically laid down to give a

sense of security and confidence and to lay down the rights and the limitations of the authorities.

3. *In the Constituent Assembly–* Debates centered round not whether fundamental rights are required but whether any restrictions must be imposed on fundamental rights.
4. *J.P.N. Bhagwati–* has observed that "fundamental rights represent the basic values cherished by the people of this country since the Vedic times and they are calculated to protect the dignity of the individual and create conditions in which every human being can develop his personality to the fullest extent. They weave a pattern of guarantee on the basic structure of human right and impose negative obligations on the State not to encroach on individual liberty in its various dimension."[1] The whole purpose is to establish a rule of law and not of men.

Fundamental rights are grouped under the following seven heads:

1. Right to equality.
2. Right to freedoms.
3. Right against exploitation.
4. Right to freedom of religion.
5. Cultural and educational right.
6. Right to property.
7. Right to Constitutional remedies.

B. Fundamental rights are not absolute

These fundamental rights are not absolute. It means that there are limitations and restrictions in the exercise of these rights. *For example* right to Speech and Expression is a fundamental right. This does not mean that one can go on talking, writing anything even if it means endangering the security of country or the minds of the people with obscene publication. Hence these fundamental rights can be curtailed with reasonable restrictions in the interest of sovereignty, security etc. Each individual has to exercise the right with due regard to the rights of his fellow beings, because X has a freedom of speech- he cannot use it to defame B; he cannot use it to create a disharmony amongst the various groups and communities in the society. Hence no civilized legal system provides for absolute and unrestricted individual rights. Absolute freedom leads to chaos in the society and it ruins it.

At the same time if State has absolute power to determine the extent of personal liberty without any rules to govern its powers the result will be anarchy, exploitation and favouritism. Hence there is a need to balance the individual right on one hand and that of the State and the Society as a whole on the other.

On the whole, in non-economic matters like freedom of speech and expression, right to life; right of movement etc., the emphasis is towards individual freedom. In case of economic rights emphasis is shifting towards

1. *Maneka Gandhi* v. *Union of India,* AIR 1978 SC 597 (619): (1978) 1 SCC 248: (1978) 2 SCR 621.

State control. This has been attained through judicial interpretation and through Constitutional amendments. However note that in the post Globalization era – emphasis is on Liberalization Privatization Globalization (LPG). Hence State control over economic rights of the people is diminishing; privatization and private ownership is getting more emphasis.

There was complete freedom of contract *i.e.,– laissez faire* doctrine in the 17th century. In India until we opened up our economy under Globalization principle in 1994 we had a mixed economy with both private and State players. But the recent trend is towards more and more economic freedom to private entrepreneurs not only from India but from across the world and less and less State control.

J. Mathews says that "the major problem of human society is to combine that degree of liberty without which law is tyranny with that degree of law without which liberty becomes license and the difficulty has been to discover the practical means of achieving this grand objective.[1]

Our Constitution seeks to attain a balance between conflicting interest of the individual and of the society by enumerating fundamental rights and laying down reasonable restrictions in the interest of the society and provisions for suspension of the fundamental rights.

C. Suspension of Fundamental Rights

Fundamental rights can be suspended in the following emergency situations:

(1) Automatic suspension of article 19

The President can proclaim an emergency under article 352 on grounds of armed rebellion, war or external aggression. When emergency is proclaimed freedoms granted under article 19 are automatically suspended as provided in article 358. Thus, freedoms of speech and expression; of assembly, of association; of movement; of profession; of residence are all automatically suspended. This means that the restrictions on the State are removed and therefore they can make laws taking away these rights. Hence any law or executive order which is inconsistent with these rights cannot be challenged on the ground that they take away these fundamental rights. But as soon as the Proclamation of emergency ceases to operate – article 19 freedoms automatically revive. But things done or omitted to be done during emergency cannot be challenged even after the emergency is over.

(2) Suspension by Presidents' order under article 359

During the Proclamation of emergency under article 352 the President is empowered to suspend the right to move any court for the enforcement of right conferred by Part III of the Constitution (except articles 20 and 21) *i.e.,* the fundamental rights during the continuance of emergency. Such suspension is not automatic as in the case of article 19. The President has to specifically order the suspension of such of the fundamental rights as may be necessary under the circumstances under article 359.

1. *Indira Nehru Gandhi* v. *Shri Raj Narain,* AIR 1975 SC 2299 (2380): (1976) 2 SCR 347: 1975 Supp SCC 1.

D. Are Fundamental rights available against the private citizens

Fundamental rights are available against State action and not against private actions. In *P.D. Shamdasani* v. *Central Bank of India*[1] the Supreme Court held that fundamental right to property under article 19 and article 31 were not available against the private person *i.e.,* the Central Bank of India in this case.

However there are some fundamental rights which are available against the private citizens also like article 23 (trafficking in human beings), 17 (untouchability).

E. Definition of State under article 12

It is important to study the definition of State because if the fundamental rights provided under Part III are taken away by a law made by the State it is void to that extent. If fundamental rights are taken away by State action a citizen can file a writ petition.

Article 12 defines State. Most of the fundamental rights are available against the State only and not against private persons. In Part III unless the context otherwise requires State includes:

1. Government of the Parliament of India,
2. Government and the Legislature of each State and,
3. All local or other authorities within the territory of India or under the control of Government of India.

This means that if the 'context requires otherwise'- 'State' may not mean what is mentioned in article 12.

If the actions of the bodies mentioned in article 12 takes away the fundamental rights it can be challenged before the courts as violating article 13(2) because it lays down that the State shall not pass any law which takes away or abridges the fundamental rights. If it does so- it is void to that extent. State includes executive and legislative organs of the Union and the States.

(1) 'Other authority' under article 12

The term 'other authority is not defined under the Constitution. Hence most of the court decisions centres round the term 'other authority'. To put it in a gist- in the earlier cases up to 1966- this expression was held to be *'ejusdem generis'* with Government or the Legislature *i.e.,* of the 'similar category as the Government.' Hence it included only authorities exercising Governmental functions. Later, Supreme Court rejected this restricted interpretation because there was no common genus running through the bodies already mentioned in article 12. It was held in *Electricity Board, Rajasthan* v. *Mohan Lal*[2] that 'other authorities' would include all authorities created by the Constitution or statute on whom powers are conferred by law though not engaged in performing sovereign functions.

(2) Important rulings on 'other authority' under article 12

Following are some important rulings on the interpretation of 'other authorities' under article 12:

1. AIR 1952 SC 59: 1952 SCR 391: 1952 SCA 36.
2. AIR 1967 SC 1857: 1968 (1) SCJ 461: (1967) 3 SCR 377.

1. Test to determine whether Company, Corporation etc., are 'State' under article 12?

   International Airport Authority is a State: *R.D. Shetty* v. *International Airport*: International Airport Authority – being a statutory body- it was held to be an authority. Under our Constitution the Government performs a large number of welfare functions. Hence it has to act through natural persons and also through juridical persons. A Corporation may be a statutory body set-up under a statute or a body registered under general laws like the Companies Act, Societies Registration Act etc. Supreme Court has held in *R.D. Shetty* v. *International Airport*[1] that the manner in which the Corporation comes into existence is immaterial but the purpose of its being brought into existence is relevant. Any body which can be regarded as an instrument of State falls under article 12. If Government acting through its officers is 'State' then it follows that Government acting through its instrumentality or agency of Corporation should be subject to same limitation.

   Corporation may or may not amount to 'State' under article 12 depending on following factors:

   (a) It would be a 'State' if the Corporation is wholly controlled by Government in its policy-making and in discharge of its functions.
   (b) It would be a 'State' if the entire share capital is held by Government though the Corporation is autonomous in its working.
   (c) It may or may not be a 'State' if the Corporation established by statute has no shares or shareholders but if administration is in hands of a Board of Directors appointed by the Government, but the Directors have complete freedom in discharge of the function.
   (d) If the Corporation discharges functions of public importance it is an instrumentality of Government.

   However the Supreme Court wondered whether the distinction between Governmental and non Governmental functions is valid in a social welfare State where *laissez faire* is an outdated concept. Hence it is necessary to consider the above factors in their totality to determine whether a Corporation is a 'State' or not.

2. In *Electricity Board, Rajasthan* v. *Mohan Lal*[2] the test is to find out whether authority is invested with statutory power to issue binding directions to the third parties and its disobedience would result in penal consequences.
3. In *Ajay Hasia* v. *Khalid Mujib*[3] Supreme Court held that where a Corporation is an instrumentality or agency of the Government it must be held to be an authority under article 12 and hence bound by the obligation to obey the fundamental rights. If it were held not 'other authorities' it would be the easiest thing for the Government to assign almost every Government function to different Corporations and deprive the people of India of the fundamental rights guaranteed to them.

---

1. AIR 1979 SC 1628: (1979) 3 SCR 1014: (1979) 3 SCC 489.
2. AIR 1967 SC 1857: 1968 (1) SCJ 461: (1967) 3 SCR 377.
3. AIR 1981 SC 487: (1981) 1 SCC 722: (1981) 3 SCR 79.

4. In *M.C. Mehta* v. *Union of India*[1] - There was oleum gas leak from Shriram Fertilizers Ltd – a private corporation. J. Bhagwati left the question open as to whether it was a 'State' under article 12. It was held that the measure of damages must be co-related to the magnitude and capacity of the enterprise so that compensation has a deterrent effect.
5. In *Som Prakash* v. *Union of India*[2] J. Krishna Iyer has held that if the Corporation is an agency of the Government it is 'other authority' under article 12. He observed that article 12 is a special definition with a broader goal. It enlarges the scope to embrace all authorities under the control of Government. In a welfare State the 'State' takes up a large number of welfare activities. This role cannot be played by curtailing the cherished right of the people in Part III of the Constitution. Bharat Petroleum Corporation – a Government company registered under the Companies Act was held to be a 'State' under article 12. These judgments have widened the net of article 12.
6. *Indian Statistical Society*- A society registered under the Societies Registration Act was held to be an instrumentality of the Central Government being under the complete control of the Government of India.
7. *Indian Council of Agricultural Research* – Registered as a society, it was wholly funded by the Government – it was held to be an 'authority.'[3]
8. An aided school which received Government grant of 90% , a Children's Aid Society registered under the Societies Registration Act were held to be a 'State' as being an instrumentality of the State.
9. In a case decided in 1969 in *Prag Tools Corporation* v. *C.A. Immanual,* (1969) 3 SCR 773 even with 88% share capital held by the Central Government and the AP Government together – it was held not to be a State because it was a non-statutory body incorporated under the Companies Act. Thus, the concept of 'instrumentality of the State' developed in later decisions have widened the ambit of article 12.
10. Food Corporation of India has been held to be 'other authority'.[4]
11. Housing Board is a 'State'[5].
12. State Bank of India and Bank of India are 'State' under article 12.[6]
13. In *Zee Telefilms Ltd* v. *Union of India*[7] the Board of Control for Cricket in India is not 'State' because it is not financially functional or administratively dominated by the Government nor is it under the control of the Government
14. *Central Inland Water Transport Corporation*- A corporation registered under the Companies Act was held to be an authority. It is to be seen whether

1. AIR 1987 SC 1086: (1987) 1 SCC 395: 1987 (1) Supreme 65.
2. AIR 1981 SC 212.
3. *P.K. Ramchandra Iyer* v. *Union of India,* AIR 1984 SC 541: 1984 Lab IC 301: (1984) 2 SCC 141.
4. *Workmen of the Food Corporation of India* v. *Food Corporation of India,* AIR 1985 SC 670: (1985) 2 SCC 136: 1985 (II) LLJ 4.
5. *Bhagat Singh Negi* v. *H.P. Housing Board,* AIR 1994 HP 60.
6. *Bank of India* v. *O.P. Swarnanakar,* AIR 2003 SC 858.
7. AIR 2005 SC 2677: 2005 AIR SCW 2985: (2005) 4 SCC 649.

behind the corporate veil there is the face of the agency of the State. If there is such a face- it is the instrumentality of the State.

(3) Bodies held not to be authorities

1. Cochin Refineries Ltd., incorporated under the Companies Act; Central Government holding 53% shares, private foreign company holding 23% shares, Government not exercising much control- it was held not to be an 'authority'.[1]

2. Institute of Constitutional and Parliamentary Studies- registered as a society, receiving Central Government grants, - with the President of India, Vice-President and the Prime Minister as its honorary members[2]

3. NCERT – a registered society, autonomous body, activities not wholly related to Governmental functions, Government control restricted to seeing that the funds are properly utilized, funding is not entirely from Government sources- held it was not an authority.[3]

4. Private educational institution though recognized and affiliated to a university is not an instrumentality of the Government under article 12. Recognition is for conforming to the standards laid down by the State.[4]

5. In *Sabhajit Tewari* v. *Union of India* Supreme Court held the Council of Scientific and Industrial Research (CSIR) as not an authority under article 12. This case is overruled in *Pradeep Kumar Biswas* v. *Indian Institute of Chemical Biology*[5] and has held that CSIR is an authority.

(4) Incidents of being an authority under article 12

Once a body is held to be an authority under article 12 following are the incidents that follow:

(a) The actions and decisions of the body can be challenged with reference to the fundamental rights under the writ jurisdiction of the High Courts under article 226 and of the Supreme Court under article 32.

(b) The body becomes subject to principles of Administrative law.

(5) 'Local authority' under Article 12

It refers to the unit of local self-Government like a municipal committee or a village panchayat. *For example* – Delhi Development Authority is a local authority. Calcutta State Transport Corporation was held not to be a local authority. It is meant only for providing road transport services and has no element of popular representation in its constitution. It is more in the nature of a trading service.[6]

(6) Is Judiciary "State" under Article 12?

The question was raised in *Naresh* v. *State of Maharashtra,* it was held that even if the court was a 'State' a writ under article 32 cannot be issued to a High Court of competent jurisdiction against its judicial orders because such orders

1. *K.M. Thomas* v. *Cochin Refineries Ltd.,* AIR 1982 Ker 248: 1982 Ker LT 553: 1982 (II) LLJ 233.
2. *Tekraj Vasandi* v. *Union of India,* AIR 1988 SC 469: (1988) 1 SCC 236: 1988 (I) LLJ 341.
3. *Chander Mohan Khanna* v. *National Council of Educational Research and Training,* AIR 1992 SC 76: 1991 AIR SCW 2749: (1991) 4 SCC 578.
4. *Unni Krishnan, J.P.* v. *State of Andhra Pradesh,* AIR 1993 SC 2178: 1993 AIR SCW 863: (1993) 1 SCC 645.
5. (2002) 5 SCC 111: JT 2002 (4) SC 146.
6. AIR 1966 SC 1316.

cannot be said to violate the fundamental rights and no action lies against the judge or the court which passes it. The decision only purports to settle the dispute between the parties. The aggrieved can prefer an appeal against the judgment.[1]

A *quasi* judicial body does not infringe a fundamental right merely by misinterpreting a law. But if it acts under an *ultra vires* law or outside its jurisdiction or ignores mandatory rules of procedure laid down under a statute and thereby affects the fundamental rights – then its action can be challenged.

F. Article 13 – Laws inconsistent with the fundamental rights

Article 13 deals with the prospects and consequences of laws which are inconsistent with fundamental rights contained in Part III of the Constitution. It deals with the effect of:

a) the Pre-Constitutional laws which are inconsistent with the fundamental rights under article 13(1) and
b) the Post-Constitutional laws which are inconsistent with fundamental rights under article 13(2).

(1) Pre-Constitutional law

If the laws in force in the territory of India immediately before the commencement of the Constitution are inconsistent with the provisions of Part III- they are void to the extent of inconsistency. [Article 13(1)]
'Laws in force' includes laws passed or made by a Legislative or other competent authority in the territory of India before the commencement of the Constitution and not previously repealed. It does not matter that any such law or any part thereof may not be then in operation either at all or in particular areas. [Article 13(3)(a)]

(2) Post-Constitutional law

The State shall not make any law which takes away or abridges the rights conferred by this Part and if it makes a law taking away or abridging the fundamental rights under Part III they shall be void to that extent. [Article 13(2)]

(3) Meaning of 'law'

The law under article 13 is given a very wide meaning. Unless the context otherwise requires- law includes – any Ordinance, order, bye-law, rule, regulation, notification, custom or usage having the force of law in the territory of India.

Thus, if the fundamental rights are taken away or curtailed by any of these things it can be questioned before the court of law.

(4) Delegated legislation

Order, bye-law, rule, regulation, notification are terms used to indicate a delegated legislation which are made by the administrative authorities.

(5) Custom

Customs and usages prevailing before the Constitution came into force continue to have the force of law. But if the existing custom or usage is

1. *Naresh Shridhar Mirajkar* v. *State of Maharashtra*, AIR 1967 SC 1: 1966 (2) SCA 363: (1966) 3 SCR 744.

inconsistent with fundamental rights it is void to that extent[1]. The custom is a valid one if it is ancient in origin, reasonable, not against public policy, immemorial. In *Sant Ram* v. *Lalbagh Singh* that Supreme Court ruled that right of pre-emption by vicinage[2] is void as infringing the fundamental right to property under article 19(1)(f). Question that arose was- whether tribal customs also are subject to article 13. Though the majority of the judges agreed that tribal women should succeed to the estate of their male relations – it ruled that male succession is subject to the right of livelihood of the females. They did not declare the custom to be void to avoid a chaotic situation.

(6) Legal status of a personal law inconsistent with the fundamental rights

An interesting and a sensitive question that has arisen is- whether 'law' under article 13 includes 'personal law' like Hindu law and Mohammedan law, Parsi and Christian law of marriage and divorce. By and large personal laws are closely linked to religions and religious beliefs and religious dictum. They are non-statutory in nature. Being ancient in origin they relate back to a period of a non-egalitarian society and were prejudicial and discriminatory mainly against the women folk. Hence, we find them incompatible with the fundamental rights in Part III which are based on the principle of equality. So the question is – are personal laws covered under article 13. In *Narasu Appa Mali*- the Supreme Court has held that they are not covered because – the framers of the Constitution were aware of the discriminations under the personal laws; if they had intended that the personal laws should be challenged under article 13- they could have expressly mentioned personal laws as being included under the meaning of 'laws in force'. Hence the courts have refused to hold the personal laws as unconstitutional under article 13. *For example*- polygamy is allowed amongst Muslims whereas for Hindus, monogamy was introduced by the Hindu Marriage Act, 1955 - replacing polygamy which was prevalent in the Hindu community; property rights also were not in favour of the women under their personal laws. When the question arose whether personal laws are laws under article 13 – the courts have held that they either do not violate fundamental rights or that personal laws are not 'laws' within the meaning of article 13. Personal laws is a sensitive area. Hence courts have refrained from interfering on the ground that it is a matter for Legislative action involving policy matters, expediency and practicality and not an area for judicial intervention. In *Ahmedabad Women Action Group* v. *Union of India*[3] Supreme Court refused to declare polygamy recognized under the Muslim Personal Law as void as it is a question of legislative policy and not for judicial decision.

Under section 17 of the Indian Divorce Act – a woman has to prove both adultery and cruelty on the part of the husband to claim a divorce. The court agreed that section 17 of the Act is discriminatory against the women but it refused to declare it as void because personal laws are not 'laws' within the meaning of article 13.[4]

1. *Gazula Dasaratha Rama Rao* v. *State of Andhra Pradesh*, AIR 1961 SC 564: (1961) 2 SCR 931.
2. *E.g.*, A and B have their lands adjoining each other. If A wants to sell it- he must give the first offer to B and only then he can sell to someone else- Pre-emption by vicinage.
3. AIR 1997 SC 3614: 1997 AIR SCW 1620: (1997) 3 SCC 573.
4. *P.E. Mathew* v. *Union of India*, AIR 1999 Ker 345: ILR (1999) 2 Ker 751: 1999 (1) Ker LJ 824.

It will thus, be noticed that though the court has agreed that the provisions challenged were in fact violative of the fundamental rights – in view of the sensitive nature of the issues involved the courts have avoided interfering with the personal laws. On a strict legal construction the matter squarely falls under article 13 but the courts have exercised constraint on the ground of expediency stating that it is a matter of Legislative policy; that only the Legislature can step in to change the law.

(7) Doctrine of severability

Article 13 says that if the law is inconsistent with the fundamental rights *'it is void to that extent'*. So the question is – what about the remaining portion of the law- should it continue to remain in force or should it also become void. The Constitution devised the doctrine of severability as an answer to tackle this problem. It means that if the offending provision is severable, separable from the other portion and the other portion can stand as valid on its own – that other portion continues to remain in operation.

In *RMDC* v. *State of Bombay* section 2(d) of the Prize Competition Act was held to be wide enough to include skill based competitions and gambling based competitions. The latter was held to be severable whereas the former could still continue as valid under the Act. Hence the whole Act was not declared to be void. Following propositions have been laid down concerning the doctrine:

Illustrations of the doctrine:

(a) The test is whether the Legislature would have enacted the valid portion if it had known that the rest of the portion is invalid. Thus , the intention of the Legislature is the determining factor.

(b) If the valid and the invalid portions are so inseparably mixed up that they cannot be separated from one another then the whole Act is invalid.

(c) If both the portions are separate and distinct then they can be severed if what survives can stand independently and is workable it operates as an independent code by itself and will continue to remain valid.

Section 14 of the Preventive Detention Act was held severable from the rest of the Act. The omission of section 14 does not change the nature and structure of the Act.

(8) Constitutional amendment not law under article 13

Nothing contained in article 13 shall apply to any amendment of the Constitution made under article 368.

Note that the Constitution can be amended under article 368. The restrictions contained in article 13 regarding prohibition against making laws taking away the fundamental rights is not applicable in case of Constitutional amendments. In simple words, it means that by a Constitutional amendment the fundamental rights can be curtailed or taken away. However it cannot be so amended as to change the basic structure of the Constitution as laid down in *Keshwanand Bharati* case.

It is to be thus, noted that fundamental rights are given a special status under our Constitution. This is because fundamental rights are "express Constitutional provisions limiting legislative power and controlling the temporary will of a majority by a permanent and paramount law settled by the deliberate wisdom of the nation."[1] State cannot take away the fundamental rights by a law or by an administrative action. This operates as a *limitation on the State's power.* The limitation is one that is imposed by a permanent law- *i.e.,* the Constitutional law, which in turn is the paramount law, a law of all laws, the *grund norm.* The fundamental rights have been placed on a higher footing under the Constitution because they are designed not only for individual benefit but as a matter of public policy. Hence the citizens also cannot waive them *i.e.,* they cannot agree not to exercise their fundamental rights.

(9) Article 13—A source of judicial review

If the law takes away the fundamental rights – to that extent they are void. It is the courts which have to declare them as void under our Constitutional scheme. Thus article 13 gives to the judiciary- the power of judicial review of all laws in India whether passed before or after the Constitution came into force. The power of judicial review is given to the High Court under article 226 and the Supreme Court under article 32. They can declare the law as unconstitutional if inconsistent with the provisions of Part III of the Constitution. Thus article 13 makes the judiciary – more specifically the Supreme Court and the High Court of different States in India the guardian, protector and interpreter of the fundamental rights.

(10) Power-cum-duty of judicial review imposed on the courts

Article 13 imposes a power and also a duty/obligation on the courts to ascertain in a most scrupulous manner if the law or the administrative action is inconsistent with the fundamental rights and only then declare it to be void. This does not mean that the courts very lightly declare the laws as void. By and large not many statutes are hit by article 13. Comparatively a large number of administrative actions have been held to be inconsistent with the fundamental rights.

Judicial review has been held to be the basic feature of the Constitution in *L. Chandra Kumar* v. *Union of India*[2]. In *Keshavanand Bharati* it has been held that the basic feature of the Constitution cannot be curtailed or evaded by any Constitutional amendment. It was realized that power corrupts and absolute power corrupts absolutely leading to tyranny, anarchy (lawlessness) and chaos (disorder, confusion). Hence checks and balances over Legislative and Administrative powers are provided through the instrument of judicial review.

It is interesting to note that in USA the doctrine of judicial review had to be propounded by the Supreme Court of USA in the historic case of *Marbury* v. *Madison*[3]. The doctrine of judicial review in India is on a more solid footing than

---

1. *A.K. Gopalan* v. *State of Madras,* AIR 1950 SC 27: 51 Cr LJ 1383: 1950 SCR 88.
2. AIR 1997 SC 1125: 1997 AIR SCW 1345: (1997) 3 SCC 261.
3. 2L Ed. 60.

in USA. However the courts would never declare the laws unconstitutional "out of a desire to tilt at Legislative authority and a crusader's spirit but in discharge of duty plainly laid upon it."[1]

Pre-constitution laws

Laws in force immediately before the Constitution came into force are known as Pre-Constitutional laws. They are valid and operative and continue to remain in force until repealed or amended. But if they are inconsistent with fundamental rights under Part III of Constitution they are void to the extent of inconsistency as laid down in article 13(1). But they do not automatically become void. They have to be challenged before the court on the ground of inconsistency with the fundamental rights and the court must declare them to be void. They become void with prospective effect. They are not retrospective in operation. Hence they do not affect the transaction or acts or liabilities incurred before the Constitution came into force. In *Keshav Madhav Menon* v. *State of Bombay*[2] prosecution was started against the petitioner under Press Emergency Power Act, 1931 in respect of pamphlet published in 1949. Constitution came into force during the pendency of proceedings. *Keshav* contended that the Act violated the freedom of speech and expression and hence was void and so the proceeding had to be dropped. Supreme Court held that the rights, liabilities which have arisen before the Constitution came into force remain intact because fundamental rights are prospective in operation and not retrospective. But if the pre-constitution procedure by which the case is to be tried is inconsistent with fundamental rights- the procedure is void. That is, the person cannot be tried by a pre-constitution procedure which is inconsistent with the fundamental rights in Part III.

Restriction on fundamental rights can be imposed only through statute, statutory rule, but not by administrative direction not having the force of law.[3]

(11) Waiver of fundamental rights

Can a person waive his fundamental rights? If he is permitted to waive his fundamental rights it would be like saying- "Go ahead- you may discriminate against me and I will not oppose or protest" or say, agreeing not to claim the protection guaranteed against illegal arrest and other protections under article 20 and 21 or say, agreeing not to practice a lawful profession guaranteed under article 19. The rule laid down by the courts is that fundamental rights cannot be waived. Following are the relevant rulings on the point:

(a) In *Behram* v. *State of Maharashtra*[4] the Supreme Court has ruled that the citizen cannot waive his fundamental rights. Fundamental rights are inserted in the Constitution not only for individual benefit but as a matter of public policy. Hence the doctrine is not applicable.

---

1. *State of Madras* v. *V.G. Row*, AIR 1952 SC 196: 1952 Cr LJ 966: 1952 SCR 597.
2. AIR 1951 SC 128: 1951 SCR 228: 52 Cr LJ 860.
3. *Bishan Das* v. *State of Punjab*, AIR 1961 SC 1570: (1962) 2 SCR 69: 1963 (1) SCJ 405.
4. AIR 1955 SC 123: 1955 Cr LJ 215: 1955 SCR 613.

(b) In *Basheshar Nath* v. *IT Commissioner*[1] the Supreme Court has expressed the following views regarding the doctrine of waiver:

- Article 14 is an admonition against the State as a matter of public policy. Its object is to attain equality before the laws and equal protection of the laws. It is the responsibility of the State to ensure equality. No person can relieve the State of this obligation to ensure equality either by any act or conduct.
- A view broader than the first is that none of the fundamental rights can be waived by a person. All fundamental rights are mandatory. Constitution does not categorize fundamental rights – into the ones for the benefit of the individual and ones for public policy.

There is poverty and educational backwardness in the country. People are not politically conscious; nor are they aware of their rights. Individually and even collectively they cannot be pitted against the State. Hence Judiciary must protect their rights.

In this case – *Baseshar* was liable to pay huge income tax as decided by the IT Investigation Commission under section 5(1) of the Act. He agreed to pay 3 lakhs installment by way of full and final settlement of tax and penalty. Later the Supreme Court declared the section as *ultra vires* under article 14. He challenged the settlement. Income tax authorities invoked the doctrine of waiver. In *Olga Tellis* v. *Bombay Municipal Corporation*[2] the Supreme Court held that even if a person says – under a mistake of law or otherwise that he will not enforce any particular fundamental right it cannot create an estoppel against him. In this case the pavement dwellers had given an undertaking that they would not claim any fundamental rights to put up their huts on pavements or public roads and would not obstruct for demolition of huts after certain date. Later when they were sought to be demolished they invoked article 21. State claimed doctrine of waiver. Supreme Court rejected State's contention.

In *Nar Singh* v. *Union of India*[3] Supreme Court held that acceptance of Retrenchment benefit does not mean that the workman has surrendered his Constitutional right. He can still challenge his termination. Supreme Court quashed his termination order and directed reinstatement.

In *Anuj Garg* v. *Hotel Assn of India*[4] it was held that while deciding Constitutional validity of a law court has to keep in mind the societal conditions prevailing at the relevant times changed social psyche and expectations. The court made the observation while quashing prohibition on employment of women in hotels and Bars serving liquor saying that it violates gender equality.

G. Doctrine of Eclipse related to laws which violate the Fundamental Rights

(1) *Formulated by the judiciary in Bhikaji Narayan* v. *State of Madhya Pradesh*

The doctrine has been evolved, formulated by the Supreme Court in *Bhikaji Narayan* v. *State of Madhya Pradesh*. The doctrine is based on the principle that

1. AIR 1959 SC 149: 1959 SCJ 1207: (1959) Supp 1 SCR 528.
2. AIR 1986 SC 180: (1985) 3 SCC 545: 1985 (2) Bom CR 434.
3. AIR 2000 SC 1401: 2000 AIR SCW 1141: (2000) 3 SCC 588.
4. AIR 2008 SC 663: 2007 AIR SCW 7772: (2008) 3 SCC 1.

a law which violates fundamental rights is not *void ab-initio,* it is not a nullity, it only remains unenforceable as long as the fundamental right remains in the Constitution. This doctrine has the following consequences:

(2) Law violating Fundamental right remains dormant but is not dead

The law violating the Fundamental right remains in a *moribund* condition. It is over–shadowed by the Fundamental right and remains dormant, inactivated, but is not dead as held in *Bhikaji Narayan* v. *State of Madhya Pradesh.*[1]

(3) It exists for past transactions

Such laws exist for all the past transactions. The rights, liabilities arising before the Constitution came into force remain intact.

(4) Applicability of such laws to the non-citizens

Such laws violating the Fundamental rights are relevant as regards persons who do not enjoy those Fundamental rights at all. *e.g.,* non-citizens. It is only as regards the citizens that they remain *moribund.*

(5) Such laws can be revived by an amendment to the Constitution

A law which has become unenforceable because it violates the Fundamental rights under the Constitution can be revived and made effective by an amendment to the Constitution. In *Bhikaji Narayan* v. *State of Madhya Pradesh,* C.P. Berar Motor Vehicles (Amendment) Act, 1947 authorised the State Government to create a monopoly in its favour by taking the entire motor transport business and exclude the motor transport operators from the business. This provision was valid when enacted as there was no fundamental right to practice a profession before the Constitution came into force. After the Constitution came into force it violated the Fundamental right to practice any profession under article 19(1)(g) and therefore remained eclipsed- shadowed by the Fundamental right. But then in 1951, the Constitution was amended by the Constitution (First Amendment) Act, 1951 and it authorized the Government to monopolise any business. Now the Motor Vehicles Act regained its original vigour and it was reactivated. Supreme Court held that the effect of the amendment was to 'remove the shadow and to make the impugned Act free from all blemishes and infirmities'.

(6) Doctrine of eclipse – Not applicable to post-constitutional law

The doctrine of eclipse is not applicable to the post-constitutional law. Supreme Court has held in *Deep Chand* v. *State of Uttar Pradesh,*[2] a post-Constitution law which contravenes a Fundamental right is nullity from its very inception. It is a still-born law. Hence there is no question of it being revived as in the case of pre-constitutional law. A pre-constitution law is not void from its inception and hence it is revived when the hindrance is taken away. It has been held in *Mahendra Lal Jain* v. *State of Uttar Pradesh*[3] that the doctrine of eclipse is applicable to a pre-constitutional law and not a post-constitutional law.

---

1. AIR 1955 SC 781: (1955) 2 SCR 589: 1956 SCJ 48.
2. AIR 1959 SC 648: 1959 SCA 377: 1959 SCJ 1069.
3. AIR 1963 SC 1019: (1963) 1 SCR Supp 912.

(7) Doctrine made applicable to post-constitution laws also

In *State of Gujarat* v. *Ambica Mills*[1] - the above view has been modified. It held that a post-constitution law which is inconsistent with a Fundamental right is not an absolute nullity. It is still operative as regards non-citizens who are not entitled to the Fundamental right. In *Ambica* it was held that the Bombay Labour Welfare Fund Act, 1953 was valid in respect of the non-citizens. Hence the Company- *i.e.,* Ambica Mills - being a non-citizen could not contend that the law abridges the right to property without the authority of law and hence is not applicable to it.

(8) In *Dulare Lodh* v. *3rd Additional District Judge, Kanpur*[2] Supreme Court applied the doctrine of eclipse to a post-constitutional law also.

(9) Thus, there has been a shift in the applicability of the doctrine. It is now being applied in respect of post as well as pre-constitutional laws. A landlord got a decree of eviction against the tenant under a post–constitution law. He could not get the decree executed due to some amendments which made the decree non-executable. Later an amendment to the Act was passed with retrospective effect which made the decree executable. By then 13 years had lapsed after the decree was passed in his favour. The land lord was allowed to get the decree executed as the decree which was lying dormant and could not be executed became executable.[2]

---

1. AIR 1974 SC 1300: (1974) 4 SCC 656: (1974) 3 SCR 760.
2. AIR 1984 SC 1260: (1984) 3 SCC 99: 1984 All LJ 555.

CHAPTER 6
RIGHT TO EQUALITY

(Article 1 4)

SYNOPSIS

A. Introduction

Articles 14 to 18 of the Constitution guarantee right to equality. Articles 14 will be dealt with in this Chapter. Articles 15 to 18 in Chapters 7 to 9.

Article 14 lays down that State shall not deny to any person equality before law and equal protection of the laws. It is one of the pillars on which our democratic Republic is based. It is a tool through which the Preambular goals are to be realised. The concept of equality has an important role to play. "Equality is morally necessary because it compels us to care about how people are treated in relation to one another. Equality is analytically necessary because it creates a presumption that people should be treated alike and puts the burden of proof on those who wish to discriminate. Finally the principle of equality is rhetorically necessary because it is a powerful symbol that helps to persuade people to safeguard rights that otherwise would go unprotected.

Article 15-18 refer to specific application of the principle of equality. Article 15 refers to prohibition of discrimination on grounds of religion, race, caste, sex or place of birth. Article 16 guarantees equality of opportunity in public employment. Article 17 abolishes titles. Article 14 is all encompassing. It embodies the holistic concept of equality. Cases not specifically covered by articles 15-18 are covered by article 14. This is in tune with article 17 of United Democratic and Human Rights Convention, 1948 that all are equal before law and are entitles to equal protection of law without any discrimination. Article 14 is declared to be a basic feature of the Constitution.

B. Equality before Law

Article 14 lays down that "State shall not deny equality before law and equal protection of the laws within the territory of India." It has 2 concepts/parts:

(a) Equality before law like to be treated alike
(b) Rule of law-Dicey's concept
(c) Equal protection of the laws

(1) Like to be treated alike

It has its origin in English Common Law. It is a negative concept. It means that the State must not give any special privilege to any person ; that all are equal in the eyes of law; that "be you ever so high, the law is above you". It means that 'like should be treated alike" (Ivor Jennings). This also means that unlike should not be treated alike. There cannot be one law for the rich and the powerful and the influential and another for the poor, uninfluential and an illiterate common man.

(2) Rule of law—Dicey's concept

The guarantee of equality before law is an aspect of what Dicey calls the rule of law in England. It means that no man is above law and that every person is subject to the jurisdiction of ordinary Courts. **Prof. Dicey gives three meanings of Rule of law**

(a) Absence of arbitrary power or supremacy of law

It means absolute supremacy of law as opposed to the arbitrary powers of the Government. That is, it is the rule of law and not the rule of man which will prevail. Men only administer the law.

(b) Equality before law

This means that no one is above law except the monarch who can do no wrong. This is a concept which is recognised in England but not in our country.

(c) The Constitution is the result of the ordinary law of the land

It means that the source of the right of the individuals is not the written Constitution but the rules as defined and enforced by the courts. This is the position in England. For a country like India where there is a written Constitution. It is the *grund norm.* The written Constitution is the supreme law of the land. The laws are framed, executed and enforced and interpreted according to the written Constitution. All laws and all interpretation of laws have to conform to the Constitution.

(3) Equal protection of the laws

This concept owes its origin to the American Constitution. It is a positive concept. Both the phrases together aim at attaining equality. But equality before law is a negative concept because it prohibits the State from giving special privilege to any individual; "equal protection of laws is a positive concept because it directs the State to give equal treatment to those who are in equal circumstances.

Equal protection of laws does not mean that the same law shall be applicable to all throughout India without regard to differences of circumstances. It means that the same laws are applicable to those who are similarly placed. It means amongst equals treat equally without distinction of race, religion, wealth, social status, or political influence. It means that it is an obligation on the State to bring about "a more equal society through the machinery of law".[1]

In *State of West Bengal* v. *Anwar Ali Sarkar,* AIR 1952 SC 75:.1952 Cr LJ 510: 1952 SCJ 55, Patanjali Shastri J. has aptly observed that "the 2nd expression 'equal protection of the laws is a corollary of the 1st expression- 'equality before laws'. It is difficult to imagine a situation in which the violation of equal protection of laws will not be the violation of the equality before law. Thus, in substance both the expressions mean the same.

Equal protection of laws means equality in privileges conferred and the liabilities imposed.[2]

C. Doctrine of classification

(1) Pragmatic justice

Equality is a laudable concept but the truth as seen through facts is that all men are not born equal, there are differences in circumstances and situations. Article 14 does not advocate mechanical equality or equality with mathematical accuracy. This would result in injustice. Hence the State has the powers to distinguish the circumstances and situations and classity persons and things upon which laws would operate. Supreme Court has held in several cases that 'like should be treated alike and not unlike alike'[3] this reasoning has led to the doctrine of classification.

(2) Doctrine evolved by the Judiciary

The Doctrine of classification is one evolved by the Judiciary in order to meet out pragmatic and practical justice having regard to the existing realities in life namely that because men are not born equal; because people are not universally similarly placed- different laws may be required for different set of persons or things. To take a very simple example for more clarity— a second standard kid

---

1. *Sri Srinivas Theatre* v. *Governor of Tamil Nadu,* AIR 1992 SC 1004.
2. *Charanjeet Lal* v. *Union of India,* AIR 1951 SC 41: 1950 SCR 869: ILR 1951 Hyd 461.
3. *Gauri Shanker* v. *Union of India,* AIR 1995 SC 55: (1994) 6 SCC 349: JT 1994 (5) SC 634; *Ashutosh Gupta* v. *State of Rajasthan,* (2002) 4 SCC 34: AIR 2002 SC 1533: 2002 AIR SCW 1419.

cannot be treated on the same lines as a tenth standard student. They cannot be made to compete for the same race or appear for the same examination. Thus the varying needs of the different people, varying circumstances and situations in which people are placed, require different treatment. The courts have evolved the principle that if such differentiation is based on rational classification it is not regarded as discrimination.

It is for the legislature to determine what classification must be made. The classification must have a just and a reasonable relation to the subject of particular legislation.[1]

Akhila Bharatiya Upabhokta Congress v. *State of Madhya Pradesh,*[2] it was held that allotting land on the basis of individual applications or applications by institutions or bodies without any invitation or advertisement by the State of its agency violates article 14. The State cannot exclude other eligible persons from lodging competing claims. Allotment of land or other form of largesse by the State treating it as a private venture is arbitrary, discriminatory and an act of favouritism. Allotting lands to the institutions is not barred under article 14 but the allotment must be done in a manner consistent with the doctrine of equality-like advertisement along with eligibility conditions etc., must be brought to the notice of the public.

(3) Class legislation prohibited

Article 14 permits classification and prohibits class legislation. As observed above article 14 does not direct universal application of laws for all. Rather justice requires different laws for different situations and persons differently placed. Hence reasonable classification is not just permitted but also necessary in the interest of actual justice.[3]

Thus, article 14 permits reasonable classification but prohibits class legislation. When privileges are conferred on a class of persons arbitrarily or a class of persons arbitrarily selected from a large number of persons on whom privileges are conferred, it amounts to class legislation. Class legislation is not permitted.

(4) Test of reasonable classification

(a) Classification must not be arbitrary

Classification must not be arbitrary, artificial and evasive. It should be based on an intelligible differentia. There must be a real and substantial distinction which distinguishes persons or things grouped together from those left out.

(b) Rational nexus with object of the statute

The differentia must have a rational or reasonable nexus with object sought to be achieved by the statute.[4] That is, there must be reasonable relation between basis of classification and the object sought to be achieved. Article 14 is violated

1. *F.N. Bulsara* v. *State of Bombay,* 52 BLR 820.
2. (2011) 5 SCC 29.
3. *Jagjit Singh* v. *State of Hyderabad,* AIR 1954 Hyd 28: ILR 1953 Hyd 648.
4. *Laxmi Khandsari* v. *State of Uttar Pradesh,* AIR 1981 SC 873: (1981) 2 SCC 600: (1981) 3 SCR 92; *Budhan Choudhry* v. *State of Bihar,* (1955) 1 SCR 1045: AIR 1955 SC 191: 1955 Cr LJ 371.

if the 'differentiation is unreasonable or arbitrary or does not rest on any rational basis having regard to the object of the legislation.[1]

Other important rules regarding classification as evolved by the Judiciary:

(5) Doctrine of classification not to replace the doctrine of equality

Doctrine must not be over-emphasised. The doctrine is only a subsidiary rule evolved to give practical content to the doctrine of equality. Doctrine of classification must not be replaced by the doctrine of equality. Thus doctrine of equality should remain superior to the doctrine of classification. Supreme Court has held in *Mohd. Shujat Ali* v. *Union of India*[2] that an anxious and sustained effort to discover some basis for classification may gradually deprive the guarantee of equality of its spacious content. However note that the Supreme Court has not followed this laudable principle many a times in its anxiety to discover some remotely hidden legislative policy in order to uphold classification. This has resulted in equality principle taking a back seat in many cases.

The content, scope and meaning of article 14 has come up before the courts in a number of cases.

(6) Propositions in* Dalmia case *regarding classification doctrine

The propositions laid down in *Dalmia case* in 1958 serve as a useful guide even today:

(a) *Single individual – A class:* A single individual may be treated as a class by himself on grounds of special circumstances applicable to him and not others.

(b) *Constitutionality of statute-presumed:* Presumption is in favour of constitutionality of the Statute. Person alleging unconstitutionality takes the burden of proving the same.

(c) *Rebuttable presumption:* Presumption may be rebutted by showing that there is no real classification at all and no difference peculiar to any individual or class.

(d) *Presumption that discriminations are on reasonable grounds:* It is presumed that the Legislature understands and correctly appreciates the needs of its own people. It is presumed that laws are made in order to solve the problems which are revealed through experience and that its discriminations are based on adequate grounds. The presumption is rebuttable.

(e) *Matters of common knowledge considered by the courts:* In order to sustain the presumption of constitutionality the court may take into consideration matters of common knowledge, reports, history of the times and assume facts existing at the time of the legislation.

(f) *Whether classification needed – Legislature decides:* Legislature is free to recognise the degrees of harm and may confine its restrictions to those cases where the need to classify is the clearest. That is, it is for the Legislature to decide whether there is a need to make a classification

1. *K. Thimmappa* v. *Chairman, Central Board of Directors, SBI,* AIR 2001 SC 467: 2001 AIR SCW 62: (2001) 2 SCC 259.
2. AIR 1974 SC 1631: (1975) 3 SCC 76: (1975) 1 SCR 449.

and enact a provision to tackle any harm. The court cannot step into the shoes of the Legislature and replace its wisdom in place of the wisdom of the Legislature.

(7) Good faith of Legislature rebuttable presumption

Good faith and knowledge of the existing conditions on the part of the Legislature is to be presumed. Yet if there is nothing on the face of the law or the surrounding circumstances brought to the notice of the court on which classification may reasonably be regarded as based presumption of constitutionality may get watered down and the Court may hold the law as violative of article 14.

(8) Various basis of classification

Classification may be on different basis like- geographical, residential; objects, occupation, age etc.

Classification made by the legislation need not be scientifically accurate and mathematically correct.

(9) Reason for presumption of Constitutionality

Supreme Court explained the rationale in favour of the constitutionality of the provision: a provision would be challenged on the ground that the provision is discriminatory because it singles out a single individual for hostile treatment while leaving out others similarly placed. Whether he has been singled out and whether others are similarly placed is a question of fact. Hence the burden of proving these facts rest on the petitioner. But if discrimination is writ large on the face of the legislation, onus of proving the validity of the provision shifts to the State.

(10) Classifications that have been upheld or quashed

1. Military or naval canteens exempt from restrictions on use of liquor etc., having regard to their mode of life – valid

2. State law permitted killing of buffaloes, sheep, goats but totally banning killing of cows, bulls and calves held valid because classification was based on the utility of animals.[1] Differentia between Indian and Foreign prisoners on matters of treatment and diet violates article 14[2]. Bihar Hindu Religious Trust Act excludes Sikhs from its purview and provides for separate trust Board for Hindus and Jains valid because religious practices and faith of Hindus, Jains and Sikhs differ in important aspects.[3] Under Land Acquisition Act, Government can acquire land for Government company but not for private company – held valid because profits from Government company go to a few hands resulting in concentration of wealth in those hands.[4] Special provision for protection and preserving the economic interests of Scheduled castes/Scheduled Tribes and to

---

1. *Mohd. Hanif Quareshi* v. *State of Bihar,* AIR 1958 SC 731: 1958 SCA 783: 1959 SCR 629.
2. *Madhu Limaye* v. *Superintendent, Tihar Jail, Delhi,* AIR 1975 SC 1505: (1970) 1 SCC 525: 1975 Cr LJ 1319.
3. *Mahant Ram Saroop Dasji* v. *S.P. Sahi,* AIR 1959 SC 942: 1959 SCJ 1144: 1959 (2) SCA 432.
4. *R.L. Arora* v. *State of Uttar Pradesh,* AIR 1964 SC 1230: 1965 (1) SCA 12: (1964) 6 SCR 784.

prevent their exploitation is valid.[1] Kerala Agrarian Relations Act, 1961 fixed a land ceiling on tea, coffee, rubber plantations but not on areca and pepper-but there was no rational basis for this distinction; term 'family' was given an artificial definition which did not conform to the type of families in the State; for lands in excess of ceiling limit different cuts were made if the amount of compensation was over Rs. 15000, this was discrimination because two persons having the same kind of land were paid different compensation just because of difference in the extent of land.

D. The New Doctrine of Equality under article 14—The Doctrine of Non-Arbitrariness

(1) Equality—A dynamic concept – Cannot be cribbed and cabined in the classification doctrine

In *E.P. Royappa* v. *State of Tamil Nadu*[2] the Supreme Court questioned the traditional concept of equality based on the doctrine of classification and laid down a new proposition popularly known as the New Doctrine of Equality. P.N. Bhagwati J. delivered the judgment on behalf of himself, *Chandrachud* and *V.R. Krishna Iyer JJ.* and propounded the new doctrine in the following words:

"equality is a dynamic concept with many aspects and dimensions and it cannot be imprisoned within traditional and doctrinaire limits. Article 14 strikes at arbitrariness in State action and ensures fairness and equality of treatment. The principle of reasonableness which legally as well as philosophically is an essential element of equality or non-arbitrariness pervades article 14 like a brooding omnipresence."

The principle was reiterated in *Maneka Gandhi* v. *Union of India* and held that "Article 14 strikes at arbitrariness in State action and ensures fairness and equality of treatment. The principle of reasonableness which legally and philosophically is an essential element of equality or non-arbitrariness pervades article 14 like a brooding omnipresence"[3]

(2) New doctrine settled in R.D. Shetty case

The doctrine got finally settled in *International Airport Authority* case[4]. P.N. Bhagwati J. made the following important observations some of which attempted to displace the time tested 'doctrine of classification:

(1) *Article 14 -Strikes at arbitrariness:* It is now well settled that article 14 strikes at arbitrariness. Therefore an arbitrary action negates equality.

(2) *Classification doctrine gives a formula to find out whether the action is arbitrary - it is not an end-all:* Doctrine of classification evolved by the courts is not a paraphrase of article 14. It is not the objective or end of article 14. The content and reach of article 14 is not determined by the doctrine of classification. It is only a formula evolved by the courts to find out whether legislative/executive action in question is arbitrary

1. *Sri Manchegowda* v. *State of Karnataka,* AIR 1984 SC 1151: (1984) 3 SCC 301: (1984) 3 Kant LJ 1.
2. AIR 1974 SC 555: (1974) 4 SCC 3: (1974) 2 SCR 348.
3. AIR 1978 SC 597: (1978) 1 SCC 248: (1978) 2 SCR 621.
4. *Ramana Dayaram Shetty* v. *International Airport Authority of India,* AIR 1979 SC 1628: (1979) 3 SCR 1014: (1979) 3 SCC 489.

and therefore amounts to denial of equality. If the classification does not satisfy the dual test (intelligible differentia and rational relation between the object sought to be attained) the impugned legislation or executive action would plainly be arbitrary and the guarantee of equality under article 14 would be breached.

(3) Article 14 has activist magnitude

Article 14 has an activist magnitude. If the State action is arbitrary it cannot be justified even on the basis of the doctrine of classification.

Illustrations

1. In *Nakara* liberalised pension scheme was applicable only to the retired Government servants who retired after March 31st 1979 but those retired before the date were left out. Classification violated article 14.[1]
2. *Nakara* ruling was considered in *Krishna Kumar* v. *Union of India* and Supreme Court held that the option given to employees covered by Provident Fund Scheme to switch over to pension scheme with effect from specific cut-off date was not violative of article 14. *Nakara* did not lay down that all retirees form a single class. Provident Fund retirees and pension retirees do not form a homogeneous class. Rights of Provident Fund retirees crystalise on their retirement. Right of pension retirees continues until their death.[2]

   There is a shift from *Nakara* position. Under an Office memorandum a portion of the Dearness Allowance was to be treated as salary for the purpose of retirement benefits with effect from a cut-off date (30-9-1977). Those who had retired before this date challenged it as violative of article 14. Supreme Court rejected the contention.

   Thus, the position now is that post retirement benefits with effect from cut-off dates is legal and valid under article 14.
3. A Regulation terminating the services of Air Hostess in Air India International on her first pregnancy was held to be arbitrary and violative of article 14[3].
4. Wages paid lower than minimum wages under Minimum Wages Act – violates article 14 (*Sanjit Roy* v. *State of Rajasthan*)[4]
5. What was once a non-discriminatory piece of legislation may in course of time become discriminatory for example, Andhra Pradesh Buildings (Lease, Rent and Eviction) Act exempted buildings constructed after August 16th 1957 from operation of the Act as an incentive to build. With lapse of time this incentive did not provide a reasonable nexus to the object sought to be attained. Hence the provision was struck down as discriminatory and all landlords including those who constructed the buildings after 26th August, 1957 were brought within the purview of

---

1. *D.S. Nakara* v. *Union of India*, AIR 1983 SC 130: (1983) 1 SCC 305: 1983 (1) SCJ 188.
2. AIR 1990 SC 1782: 1990 Lab IC 1490: (1990) 4 SCC 207.
3. *Air India* v. *Nargesh Meerza*, AIR 1981 SC 1829: (1981) 4 SCC 335: 1981 (II) LLJ 314.
4. AIR 1983 SC 328: (1983) 1 SCC 525: 1983 (I) LLJ 220.

the Act. However exemption can be granted to the newly constructed buildings for a limited time. This would not violate article 14. (*General Motors Traders* v. *State of Andhra Pradesh*)[1]

6. Article 14 cannot be extended to cases where wrong orders are issued in favour of some. Others cannot insist that same wrong orders be issued in favour of them in order to attain equality. (*Gurusharan Singh* v. *New Delhi Municipal Commissioner*) [2]
7. Preferential treatment to public sector undertakings is not discriminatory.
8. Discrimination in favour of State as against private enterprise is valid because State and private undertakings do not stand on same footing, for example Government claims are barred in a much shorter period. Classification is valid.
9. Principle of classification is applied liberally in case of taxing statutes.
10. Rate of tax and object of taxing is determined by the Legislature. Courts intervene only if it is found to be extremely unreasonable. This is in order to accommodate an inherent complexity of fiscal adjustment of diverse elements. (*Khandige Sham Bhai* v. *Agricultural I-T Officer*)[3] it is not for the courts to examine the justness of tax. (*Hoechst Pharmaceuticals Ltd* v. *State of Bihar*)[4] Taxation is a tool to reduce inequalities hence no tax scheme can be totally free from discriminatory impact. Hence it can be struck down only in case of palpable arbitrariness. (*Kerala Hotel and Restaurant Assn* v. *State of Kerala*)[5]
11. Special Bearer Bonds Act (Immunities and Exemption), 1981 was held valid in *R.K. Garg* v. *Union of India*[6]. Object of the Act was to unearth black money and put it back into circulation for productive purposes. Bearer Bond holders did not have to disclose the source of funds for acquisition of those bonds and no action could be taken against them in the proceedings under the tax laws.
12. Fourteen Banks were acquired by the Central Government and they were prohibited from doing any banking business whereas other Banks could do banking business and new Banks could be floated. This was held to be discriminatory as there was no reasonable basis for taking over some banks while leaving out the others.[7]

---

1. AIR 1984 SC 121: (1984) 1 SCC 222: (1983) 2 Ren CR 579.
2. AIR 1996 SC 1174: 1996 AIR SCW 748: (1996) 7 SCC 757.
3. AIR 1963 SC 591: 1963 Ker LJ 196: (1963) 3 SCR 809.
4. AIR 1983 SC 1019: (1983) 4 SCC 45: (1983) 3 SCR 130.
5. AIR 1990 SC 913: JT 1990 (1) SC 324: (1990) 2 SCC 502; *State of Gujarat* v. *Ambica Mills Ltd., Ahmedabad*, AIR 1974 SC 1300: (1974) 4 SCC 656: (1974) 3 SCR 760.
6. AIR 1981 SC 2138: (1981) 11 Tax Caw Rev 277 (SC): (1981) 4 SCC 675.
7. *Rustom Cavasjee Cooper* v. *Union of India (Bank Nationalisation* case), AIR 1970 SC 564: (1970) 1 SCC 248: (1970) 3 SCR 530.

13. Geographical considerations may form a valid basis for classification if it bears 'reason and just relation to the matter in respect of which differential treatment is accorded. (*Clarannce Pais* v. *Union of India*)[1]
14. Under the State's Reorganisation Act, 1956, territories from one State passed over to territories in another State. The Act laid down that existing laws would continue in force in these areas in order to avoid dislocation in the legal system. The result was that different laws prevailed in different areas of a State in these areas. It was held that it was valid because differentiations arose due to historical reasons.
15. Under Income Tax Act arrears of income can be recovered according to Land Revenue Recovery Laws prevalent in each State. Thus procedures for recovery were harsher in some States than in others. It was held to be valid because defaulters were classified State-wise on geographical groups.
16. Article 14 is applicable to substantive and also procedural laws. Thus all persons similarly situated are entitled to protection of similar procedural laws. Any special procedure if laid down must satisfy the dual test. *For example,* prescribing a stringent procedure for a new offence is not discriminatory. Offences of serious nature can be tried with a stringent procedure different from one prescribed for ordinary offences. Article 14 is not violated.
17. Under section 27 of the Indian Evidence Act statements made by the accused in custody when it leads to discovery of fact is admissible. It was held that classification between accused in custody and not in custody in the context of admissibility of statements made by them concerning offence charged was not arbitrary.
18. Under the Supreme Court rules no security is required to be given for filing a writ under article 32 for enforcing the fundamental rights whereas it is required for filing a review petition. It was held to be valid because in a Review Petition a matter which was closed after hearing is again re-opened. In an article 32 writ it is the most valuable Fundamental right which is challenged to have been violated. That brings out the difference between filing a writ petition and filing a review petition.
19. Even a single person can form a class by himself on account of special circumstances applicable to him and not applicable to others. Parliament enacted an Act and empowered its own directors to take over the control and management of the company and its property. Supreme Court held that facts of the case *viz.,* mismanagement prejudicially affecting the production of an essential commodity (cotton); mass unemployment thereby justified the company being transferred as it formed a class by itself.

---

1. AIR 2001 SC 1151: 2001 AIR SCW 890: (2001) 4 SCC 325.

20. Prime Minister forms a class by himself. His use of Indian Air Force aircraft for non-official purpose including election does not offend article 14 though the leaders of other political parties are not extended this privilege. (*P.V. Sastri* v. *Union of India*).[1]
21. Nationalisation of only one institution in a phased manner is valid. (*Lalit Narayan Mishra Institute of Economic Development and Social Change Patna* v. *State of Bihar)*.[2]
22. In *K.A. Abbas* v. *Union of India* the Supreme Court held that motion pictures being treated differently from other forms of art and expression is valid. Hence categorisation of 'A' & 'U' films according to suitability for adults or unrestricted exhibition is valid. Motion pictures have instant appeal, realism and has co-ordination with visual and real senses. It can stir up emotions more deeply than other forms of art. Its effect particularly on children and adolescent is immense having regard to their immaturity.[3]
23. In *Nishi Maghu* v. *State of Jammu and Kashmir*[4] classification for admission to MBBS was based on regional imbalance. It was held invalid because areas suffering from such imbalance was not identified.
24. Under an admission scheme to PG in medicine in Kerala, only 2% of the seats were reserved for candidates from other Universities in the State of Kerala. It was struck down as unconstitutional. It was held that a mere 2% of the total seats for candidates from the rest of the country is not sufficient fulfilment of articles 14 &15. (*Charles Karia* v. *Dr. C. Mathew*).[5]
25. In *Ajay Hasia* v. *Khalid Mujib*[6] high percentage of marks (1/3rd of the total) were allocated for oral interview which lasted only for 2-3 minutes. It was held to be arbitrary and unreasonable. It is based on subjective satisfaction and based on the first impression capable of abuse. It can only be an additional test but not exclusive test. It suggested allocation of more than 15% for oral interview will be arbitrary and unreasonable.
26. But in *D.V. Bakshi* v. *Union of India*[7] the Supreme Court held that in selection of professionals like Customs House Agents (under Regulation 8 and 9 of Customs House Agents Licensing Regulation, 1984 under section 146 Customs Act) allocation of higher marks for oral test is reasonable. Ruling in *Ajay Hasia* is relevant in case of educational institutions where candidates are young and personality still to be developed. Therefore greater weight must be given to oral examination. But it cannot be applied to matters of grant of licence as a custom

1. AIR 1974 Del 1.
2. AIR 1988 SC 1136: JT 1988 (1) SC 635: (1988) 2 SCC 433.
3. AIR 1971 SC 481: 1972 (1) SCA 1: (1971) 2 SCR 446.
4. AIR 1980 SC 1975: (1980) 4 SCC 95: (1980) 3 SCR 1253.
5. AIR 1980 SC 1230: (1980) 2 SCC 152: 1980 SCC (Lab) 305.
6. AIR 1981 SC 487: (1981) 1 SCC 722: (1981) 2 SCR 79.
7. AIR 1993 SC 2374.

House agent while duties are more demanding and high degree of probity and integrity is needed.

27. In *Pradeep Jain* v. *Union of India*[1] The Supreme Court held that wholesale reservation of seats in MBBS and BDS courses by Karnataka, Uttar Pradesh, and Union Territory of Delhi based on 'domicile or residence' within State at qualifying examination is unreasonable because it totally disregards merit. Object of any scheme of admission must be to select the best candidate or else it would be detrimental to Nation's interest. However Court directed a maximum limit of 50% of seats might be reserved on the basis of institutional preference for admission in the same medical college or University.

28. 33% reservation for post-graduate course in Medicine in AIIMS in favour of students graduating from their own college was struck down. The petitioners had scored more than the in-house students but still could not get a seat for the PG course. The reservation scheme failed to satisfy the twin test of intellible differentia and there was no reasonable nexus between the reservation and the object sought to be attained. (*AIIMS Students Union* v. *AIIMs*).[2]

29. In *Indian Council of Legal Aid and Advice* v. *Bar Council of India*,[3] Rule 9 of Bar Council of India Rules which barred person who have completed 45 years on the date of application for enrolment as advocate as discriminatory, unreasonable and violative of article 14 as there was no material to show that those above 45 years indulge in activities derogative of the profession as alleged.

30. In *State of Maharashtra v. Manubhai Bagaji Vashi* denial of Grant-in-Aid to recognised private colleges while extending it to Arts, Science, Commerce faculties is discriminatory.[4]

31. Court has consistently refused to review economic policy of the Covernment

32. In *Rasila S. Mehta* v. *Custodian Nariman Bhavan Mumbai*[5] section 3(2) of the Special Courts (Trial of Offences Relating to Transactions in Securities) Act, 1992 confers power to the Custodian to notify a person in the official Gazette on being satisfied on information received that such person was involved in any offence relating to transactions in securities during the period 1-4-1991 to 6-6-1992. There is no right of pre-decisional hearing before notification but it contains a fair and a just post-decisional hearing. Absence of pre-decisional hearing is not opposed to principles of natural justice because the decision to notify does not *ipso-facto* take away any right of the person thus notified or impose any duty on him.

---

1. AIR 1984 SC 1420: (1984) 3 SCC 654: (1984) 3 SCR 942.
2. JT 2001 (8) SC 218.
3. (1995) 1 SCC 732: AIR 1995 SC 691: 1995 AIR SCW 473.
4. (1995) 5 SCC 730: AIR 1996 SC 1: 1995 AIR SCW 3701.
5. AIR 2011 SC 2122.

33. In *Manabjyoti Duarah* v. *Dibrugarh University*[1] on revaluation of the LL.B examination papers - from 48 marks scored in re-valuation it was reduced to 43 after taking an average of the original and the re-valued marks. It was held to be an unreasonable classification between two classes of examinees- those whose answer scripts were not properly scrutinised and the other whose scripts were properly scrutinized by the original examiner. Article 14 was therefore violated. Court directed that the revaluation marks be awarded.
34. There are two classes of Councillors under Orissa Municipal Act – those elected directly from every Ward and those nominated by the State Government. Person nominated has no voting right but has the right to attend every meeting except certain meetings. The classification is based on intelligible differentia hence is not arbitrary under article 14.[2]

E. Doctrine of legitimate expectation

Under the doctrine the decision maker can normally be compelled to give effect to his representation in regard to the expectation based on previous practice or past conduct unless some over riding public interest comes in the way. Doctrine requires that reliance must have been placed on the said representation and the representee must have thereby suffered detriment. This normally happens when there is a change of policy because of which the decision taken in the earlier cases cannot be applied in later cases. The question is whether the court can go into the question whether the decision-maker has properly balanced the legitimate expectation as against the need for change? It is for public authority to decide whether there is an "overriding public interest" which justifies change in policy. But change of policy must not transgress Wednesbury principles (rationality of policy makers conclusion).

Courts do not question the policy of the policy makers. It only sees whether there has been fairness in his decision. The principle is applicable in India.

Wednesbury principles have their roots under the English law. Judicial review of administrative action has been a traditional function of the courts. The courts followed maximum judicial restraint during the Second World War. After the war they became more vigilant and demanded they would demand from the administrative authorities that they must satisfy the courts that they had considered all relevant matters and that no irrelevant matter was taken into consideration. But they would not substitute their decision for that of the administrative authority. This is known as *wednesbury principle.*[3]

In *Navjyoti Co-operative Group Housing Society* v. *Union of India*[4] policy for determining the seniority of societies for allotment of land was altered. Under the Previous policy it was based on the date of registration of society with registrar. From 20-1-1990 seniority was determined from the date of approval

1. AIR 2011 Gau 9.
2. *Sarat Chandra* v. *Mohan Naik,* AIR 2011 Ori 78.
3. S.P. Sathe: (New Delhi: Oxford University Press) Judicial Activism in India p. 15, 139-140.
4. AIR 1993 SC 155: 1992 AIR SCW 3075: (1992) 4 SCC 477.

of the final list by the Registrar. It was held that the Society was entitled to a legitimate expectation that the past consistent practice in the matter of allotment will be followed even if there was no right in private law for such allotment. There has to be some overriding public policy reason for change in the earlier criterion.

In this case *Union of India* v. *Hindustan Development Corporation*[1] tenders were called for supply of cast steel bodies to the railways. The bigger manufacturers quoted less than the smaller ones. The Railway then adopted a dual pricing policy giving counter offers of a lower rate to the bigger manufacturers and higher offer to the others to enable healthy competition. This was challenged by the bigger manufacturers that they were also entitled to a higher rate. Supreme Court held that dual policy of the Railways was based on reasonable grounds and hence valid. The court has held that legitimate expectation is not the same thing as anticipation. It was different from a mere wish or desire or hope. It is not a claim or a demand based on right. A mere disappointment does not give rise to legal consequences.

Arbitrary State action entails payment of compensation- every limb of the State machinery is people oriented. Arbitrary actions are quashed by the court and compensation awarded to 2011 case.

F. Rules of natural hearing are implicit in article 14

In *Maneka Gandhi* v. *Union of India*[2] The courts have held that the party adversely affected must be given an opportunity of being heard. This would control arbitrary action on the part of the administration. This is the *'audi alterem partem rule"*. The rule is applicable not only to *quasi*-judicial bodies but also to administrative orders adversely affecting the party in question.

A welfare State has wide powers to regulate and distribute its largesse like leases, licenses, contracts etc. While conferring State benefits on an individual the State has to comply with the provisions of article 14.

In *State of Karnataka* v. *B. Suvarna* regularisation of part time lecturers was held valid by the Supreme Court as it was a one-time legislative measure and the lecturers were required to have the essential educational qualifications. They form a class by themselves. However the court directed that the State Government must insist that the candidates must pass the NET test prescribed by the UGC.[3] (Rule 2(B)(iii) of Karnataka State Civil Services (Absorption of Persons Working as Part-time Lecturers in Karnataka Education Department of College Education Special Rules, 1996).

Rules of natural justice are applicable to Judicial and *quasi* functions also. Substantive and procedural laws and action taken under them has to pass the test of article 14 because in both the cases aim is to arrive at a just decision. Hence even while exercising the right to terminate due to absence from work without leave or prior information or permission from the management- the

1. AIR 1994 SC 988: 1994 AIR SCW 643: (1993) 3 SCC 499.
2. AIR 1978 SC 597: (1978) 2 SCC 248: (1978) 2 SCR 621.
3. AIR 2001 SC 606: 2001 AIR SCW 231: (2001) 1 SCC 728.

management has to give an opportunity of being heard to the employee or else it violates article 14. (*D.K. Yadav* v. *J.M.A. Industries*)[1].

In *Revathi* v. *Union of India*[2] section 198(2) Cr.P.C. and section 497 of IPC were upheld. Under these provisions a wife is disabled from prosecuting her husband for adultery. The right to prosecute the adulterer is given only to the husband of the adulteress. However article 14 is not violated because the object of the provision is to give space to the husband and the wife to make up or break up the matrimonial tie rather than drag the husband to the court for the offence of adultery. They can even condone the offence and forgive and forget and live together.

Under the new Railway policy all employees – general merit, Scheduled Castes/ Scheduled Tribes were to be promoted after 16 years of service but in the other Government offices the SC's and ST's could be promoted after 10-12 years. This was held to be discriminatory under article 14.

(*P&T* Scheduled Castes/ Scheduled Tribes *Employees Welfare Association* v. *Union of India*)[3].

Bhopal Gas Leak Disaster (Processing of Claims) Act, 1985 under which the Central Government took over the conduct of all litigations on behalf of the victims of Bhopal Gas Tragedy was held to be valid. The State in its capacity as *parents patriae* –(parent of the country) is competent to represent the victims.

Equal pay for equal work is a fundamental right under article 14. (*Randhir Singh* v. *Union of India*)[4].

---

1. (1993) 3 SCC 259: 1993 AIR SCW 1995: JT 1993 (3) SC 617.
2. AIR 1988 SC 835: JT 1988 (1) SC 419.
3. AIR 1989 SC 1618.
4. AIR 1982 SC 879: (1982) 1 SCC 618: 1982 (I) LLJ 344.

CHAPTER 7

RIGHT TO EQUALITY (PROHIBITION OF DISCRIMINATION ON RELIGION, ETC.)

Article 15

SYNOPSIS

A. Introduction

Article 15 deals with prohibition of discrimination only on the grounds of religion, race, caste, sex, place of birth. Article 15 is an instance of particular application of article 14.

The purpose of article 15 is to foster national identity[1] and to set right the wrong and misplaced social practices in our country.

B. The five principles

It lays down the following five principles:

(1) the State shall not discriminate against any citizen on grounds *only* of religion, race, caste, sex, place of birth or any of them [article 15(1)];

(2) no citizen shall only on the above mentioned grounds be subject to any disability, liability, restriction or condition with regard to

(a) access to shops, public restaurants, hotels and places of public entertainment, or

---

1. *Valsamma Paul* v. *Cochin University*, AIR 1996 SC 1011 (1019): 1996 AIR SCW 492: (1996) 3 SCC 545.

(b) the use of wells, tanks, bathing ghats, roads and places of public resort maintained wholly or partly out of State funds or dedicated to the use of the general public; [article 15(2)]

(3) the State shall not be prevented from making special provisions for the women and children; [Article 15(3)]

(4) Article 15 or article 29(2) shall not prevent the State from making any special provision for the advancement of any socially and educationally backward classes of citizens (SEBC) or for the Scheduled Castes or Scheduled Tribes (SCs &STs); [article 15(4)][1]

(5) Article 15 or article 19(1)(g) shall not prevent the State from making any special provision by law for the advancement of SEBC and SCs & STs relating to their admission to educational institutions including aided or unaided private educational institutions.

But no such special provision can be made in a minority educational institution mentioned in article 30(1) of the Constitution. [Article 15(5)[2]]

C. Limitations of Article 15

(1) It is applicable only to the citizens. It is not applicable to the aliens and non-citizens.

(2) The prohibition under 15(2) is only in respect of public wells etc., or wells maintained by Government funds. Thus, the owner of a private swimming pool or a private road in his land – will not be violating article 15 by restricting the use or entry into his property.

(3) Religion, race etc., coupled with some other reasonable grounds can be a ground of discrimination.

D. Implication of Articles 14 and 15

Article 14 speaks generally of equality and article 15 speaks of specific equality. Both articles 14 and 15 permit reasonable classification. Reading articles 14 and 15 together the Constitution mandates that there shall be no unequal laws but if unequal laws are made—

- They must satisfy the twin test laid down in article 14, and
- Religion, race, caste, sex, place of birth *alone* cannot be grounds for discrimination. In other words, religion, race etc., coupled with some other reasonable grounds can be a ground of discrimination.
- To determine the validity of the enactment – the effect of the impugned enactment on the fundamental rights is to be determined. If the effect is to discriminate amongst the citizens on the prohibited grounds mentioned in article 15(1) or 15(2) of the Constitution – it is an invalid law.

E. Commentary on Article 15(1) to (4)

(1) Discrimination on the grounds of religion etc. [article 15(1)]

The scope of this clause is very wide. It ropes in all State actions relating to the citizen's rights. Several other Constitutional provisions ensure the guarantee

1. Added by Constitution (First Amendment) Act, 1951.
2. Added by Constitution (93rd Amendment) Act, 2005 –w.e.f. 20-1-2006.

of this right – *for example*- adult suffrage[1]; equality in employment; eligibility for contesting the elections; occupying high level constitutional posts like that of the President; Election Commissioner; MP etc.

Under the Uttar Pradesh Court and Wards Act, 1912 a male proprietor could be declared as incompetent to manage his property on one of the 5 grounds mentioned after giving him an opportunity of being heard; but a female proprietor could be so declared incompetent on any of the grounds without any show cause notice. The provision was held unconstitutional as discrimination was based only on the grounds of sex.[2]

A law providing for elections to municipalities on the basis of separate electorates for members of different religious communities or delimitation of panchayat circles for purposes of election to a panchayat on the basis of castes offends article 15(1).[3]

Residence and place of birth are different. Discrimination on the place of birth is prohibited but on the grounds of residence is allowed. Supreme Court has upheld exemption of capitation fee to the Madhya Bharat residents in a State Medical College while charging capitation fee from the non-residents. Education is a State subject. States spend a huge amount of money on education with a hope that the doctors will settle in the State and render services to the residents of the State.[4]

(2) Discriminations in relation to access to public shops etc. [article 15(2)]

The prohibition is of a general nature and not confined only to the State as under article 15(1). Thus, if a section of the public claims for an exclusive use of a public well, it must establish that the well was dedicated to its exclusive use and not to the use of the general public. Such a custom is not a reasonable one.[5] India has a system of personal laws under which Hindus, Muslims are governed by their personal laws which in turn are based on their religious tenets. Some of these laws have been amended by the statutes and also upheld on the ground that they give effect to article 25(2)(b) of the Constitution. *For example* – Hindu Marriage Act introduced monogamy for the Hindus whereas the Muslims are to this date allowed to take 4 wives. The Supreme Court did not entertain the challenge because personal laws fall outside the scope of the fundamental rights[6]. As held by the Bombay High Court community governed by the given personal

---

1. Article 326.
2. *Rani Raj Rajeshwari Devi* v. *State of Uttar Pradesh*, AIR 1954 All 608.
3. *Nain Sukh Das* v. *State of Uttar Pradesh*, AIR 1953 SC 384: 1953 SCJ 546: 1953 SCR 1184.
4. *D.P. Joshi* v. *State of Madhya Bharat*, AIR 1955 SC 334: 1955 SCJ 298: 1955 SCA 511; *Kumari N. Vasundara* v. *State of Mysore*, AIR 1971 SC 1439: (1971) 2 Civ App J (SC) 32: (1971) Supp 1 SCR 381.
5. *Arumugha Konar* v. *Narayana Asari*, AIR 1958 Mad 282: 71 Mad LW 128.
6. *Krishna Singh* v. *Mathura Ahir*, AIR 1980 SC 707: 1980 All LJ 299: (1981) 3 SCC 689; *Sarla Mudgal, President, Kalyani* v. *Union of India*, AIR 1995 SC 1531: 1995 AIR SCW 2326: 1995 Cr LJ 2926; *Madhu Kishwar* v. *State of Bihar*, (1996) 5 SCC 125: AIR 1996 SC 1864: 1996 AIR SCW 2178; *Ahmedabad Women Action Group (AWAG)* v. *Union of India*, AIR 1997 SC 3614: 1997 AIR SCW 1620: (1997) 3 SCC 573.

law itself forms a recognized class of persons. Hence a given legislation must be examined in the light of the principles of their personal laws.[1]

Section 9 of the Hindu Marriage Act dealing with Restitution of Conjugal Rights was held valid in *Saroja Rani* v. *Sudarshan Kumar*[2] it was held that the right of the husband or the wife to the conjugal company of the other is not merely a creature of the statute but it is inherent in the very institution of marriage itself.

In *Daniel Latif* v. *Union of India*[3] Muslim Women (Protection of Right on Divorce) Act, 1996 was held valid. It did not agree that compared to section 125 Cr.P.C.[4] the Act was unfavourable to the Muslim divorced women. It held that under the MWA – in addition to the *mehr* and maintenance during the *iddat* period, the husband must also make a 'reasonable and fair provision under section 3(3)' consistent with the needs of the divorced woman. Hence the scheme for maintenance is equally beneficial to the Muslim women – if bit more beneficial than section 125 Cr.P.C.

(3) Special Provisions for women and children, [Article 15(3)]

Articles 15(3) and (4) are exceptions to arts. 15(1) and (2).

It recognizes that women and children in India have been socially and economically handicapped for centuries and hence they need special provisions in their favour to equalise the inequalities. In addition, "women's physical structure and the performance of maternal functions place her at a disadvantage in the struggle for subsistence and her physical well being becomes an object of public interest and care in order to preserve the strength and vigour of the race."[5]

Reading article 15(1) and 15(3) together it appears that only special provisions favouring women can be made and not *vice versa*.[6]

(4) Illustrations of Article 15(3)—Applications

(1) Maternity Benefit Act which gives special benefits to the women workers like maternity leave and payment during such leave. Maternity Benefit Act has been amended to make a provision for paternity leave in view of the nuclear families taking the place of joint families.

(2) Under section 497 IPC a woman cannot be punished as an abettor of the offence of adultery.

(3) Under section 497 Cr.P.C. 1898 a woman or a child below 16 years accused of a capital offence crime could be released but not any other person.

(4) Under the Punjab Government Jail Rules, women were ineligible to be posted as Jail Superintendents in men jails. Held- it was valid

1. *Sonubai Yeshwant Jadhav* v. *Bala Govinda Yadav*, AIR 1983 Bom 156: (1983) 1 Bom CR 632: (1983) 2 Civ LJ 58.
2. AIR 1984 SC 1562: (1984) 4 SCC 90: 1984 Mat LR 306.
3. AIR 2001 SC 3958: 2001 AIR SCW 3932: 2001 Cr LJ 4660.
4. Dealing with maintenance for divorced women.
5. *Muller* v. *Oregon*, 52, L.Ed. 551.
6. *Anjali* v. *State of West Bengal*, AIR 1951 Cal 563.

restriction. For similar reasons men would be prohibited from being posted in jails meant for women inmates.[1] Having regard to the nature of duties to be discharged in the Institute for destitute women, only females were held to be eligible for appointment as the Head of the Institute.[2]

(5) *Government of Andhra Pradesh* v. *P.B. Vijay Kumar*[3] is an important decision where the Supreme Court has held the State can fix a quota for appointment of women to the extent of 30% of the posts under article 15(3). It observed that gender equality also requires that equal job opportunities be created for women. Hence making special provisions for their employment under the State is an integral part of article 15(3).

The Supreme Court has held the expression 'special provision' under article 15(3) means the special provision which the State may make to improve women's participation in all activities under the supervision and control of the State. It can be either an affirmative action or reservation. It said that fixing a quota for appointment for women is not reservation, it is only an affirmative action. It operates at the initial appointment stage when men and women are equally meritorious. Supreme Court held that article 15 deals with every kind of State action including the one under article 16 dealing with equality of opportunity in public employment. In dealing with employment provisions both articles 15 and 16 are applicable. Article 15 is of general nature and article 16 is more specific. Article 16 does not touch upon any special provision for women, hence it is to be read as supplementary to the special provision clause in favour of women under article 15(3).

6. In *Prema* v. *Nanje Gowda*[4] it was held that when during the pendency of a suit for partition Hindu Succession Act was amended and section 6A was inserted giving equal rights to daughters in coparcenary property- the preliminary decree can be varied and in final decree proceedings an unmarried daughter can claim equal share in suit property in terms of the amendment. (Article 15(3)]

(5) *Special Provisions in favour of Socially and Educationally Backward Class of Citizens (SEBC) and Scheduled Castes and Scheduled Tribes, Article 15(4)*

Article 15(4) is another exception to article 15(1) & (2). It was added by the Constitution (First Amendment) Act, 1951 in order to overcome the decision in *State of Madras* v. *Champakam Dorairajan*[5]. Madras Government had issued what is popularly known as a communal GO. It had reserved seats in Medical and Engineering Colleges on the basis of religion, race and caste to promote social justice for all sections of the society as required under article 46 which

1. *Raghubans Saudagar Singh* v. *State of Punjab*, AIR 1972 P&H 117: (1971) 1 Serv LR 688.
2. *B.R. Acharya* v. *State of Gujarat*, 1988 Lab IC 1465.
3. AIR 1995 SC 1648: 1995 AIR SCW 2586: (1995) 4 SCC 520.
4. AIR 2011 SC 2077.
5. AIR 1951 SC 226: 1951 SCR 525: 1951 SCJ 313.

is a Directive Principle. The Supreme Court struck it down because it classified students on the basis of caste and religion irrespective of merit. In addition Directive Principles cannot override the fundamental rights.

In *Jaswant Kaur* v. *State of Maharashtra*[1] land was acquired by the State for the construction of a Harijan Colony. The Supreme Court held it void as being discriminatory under article 15(1) because there were other members of the public equally in need of such facilities and as such like were being treated unlike.

Article 15(4) was enacted in order to overcome these rulings. Thus, as the position stands today a provision can be made for the advancement of SEBC and SC and ST. It is an enabling provision. That is, it is not mandatory for the State to make such a provision, but it is within the discretionary powers of the State to do so.[2]

Under the eligibility criteria for Common Law Admission Test (CLAT) OBC category candidates above 20 years of age were debarred from appearing in examination. The University aimed at a high degree of professional commitment of students immediately passing 12th examination for maintaining discipline in college. Maintaining discipline was becoming problematic due to the elder age students' domination. It was held that fixation of 20 yrs. age limit for CLAT exams to enter any of the National Law Schools is not violative of article 15(4) of the Constitution. Section 18 of the Rashtriya Vidhi Sansthan Vishwa Vidyalaya Adhiniyama, 1997 deals with reservations of seats for Scheduled Caste/Schedule Tribes/Other Backward Classes. It does not deal with the age limit. Hence it was open to the University to lay down age criteria for the Other Backward Classe candidates. Rule 28 of Legal Education Rules, 2008 is not violated.[3]

Identification of Scheduled Caste and Schedule Tribes is to be done with reference to articles 341 and 342.

The major difficulty under this article has been the determination of who are 'socially and educationally backward class of citizens'. Article 15(4) is silent as to the determination of SEBC.

The Supreme Court has considered this question in many number of cases. Observations made under article 16(4) also are relevant for the purpose.

6. Propositions emerge on the determination of SEBC

(a) Backward and more backward classification

M.R. Balaji v. *State of Mysore*[2] case was the first to come up after the First Amendment to the Constitution. The Mysore Government reserved seats for admission to the State Medical and Engineering Colleges for Backward and more Backward classes which were designated on the basis of castes and communities. This was in addition to reservation of seats for the Scheduled Caste 15% and Scheduled Caste 3%. The Supreme Court held the order bad and held that article 15(4) is an exception to articles 15(1) and 29(2). The order was based solely on caste without regard to other factors. Sub-classification into backward and more

1. AIR 1952 Bom 461: (1952) 54 Bom LR 678: ILR (1933) Bom 44.
2. *M.R. Balaji* v. *State of Mysore*, AIR 1963 SC 649: 1963 (2) SCA 1: (1963) Supp 1 SCR 439.
3. *Smriti Patel* v. *State of Madhya Pradesh*, AIR 2011 MP 87.

backward is not valid classification. In *Mandal*[1] case while dealing with article 16(4) the Supreme Court has held that sub-classification into backward and more backward classes is valid. This observation is equally applicable to article 15(4). (On this count *Balaji* case stands overruled)

(b) Caste as factor to determine backwardness-more prominent

In *Balaji* the Supreme Court sensed the danger in treating caste as the sole criterion for determining social and educational backwardness. It suggested economic backwardness as a more reliable yardstick for determining social backwardness. In course of time caste as a factor to determine backwardness has been given more prominence. *For example* in *P. Rajendran* v. *State of Madras*[2] the Supreme Court has observed that "... but it must not be forgotten that if a caste is also a class of citizens and if the caste as a whole is socially and educationally backward reservation can be made in favour of such a caste on the ground that it is a socially and educationally backward class of citizens within the meaning of article 15(4). Likewise in *Balram* v. *State of Andhra Pradesh*[3] a list prepared by the Backward Classes Commission only by the names of the castes was held valid because it was prepared after a detailed enquiry and applying tests like general poverty, occupations etc. It is submitted that this approach has kept the caste system in India alive and also makes it manipulative.

(c) Test is social and economic backwardness

Article 15(4) contemplates both social and economic backwardness and not social or economic backwardness. In *Balaji* the court equated social and economic backwardness to that of the Schedule Caste and Schedule Tribe.

(d) Poverty alone not the test of backwardness

Poverty alone cannot be the test of backwardness. With the poverty across the length and breadth of our country, the whole object of reservation would be defeated if poverty alone could be the test of backwardness. In *K.S. Jayshree* v. *State of Kerala*[4] Kerala Government appointed a Commission to inquire into and report as to what sections of the people in Kerala should be treated as SEBC. The Government directed that candidates belonging to families whose annual income was 10000 or above were not entitled to seats reserved for backwards. Supreme Court upheld the direction.

(e) Backwardness is result of several factors

Poverty, occupations, place of habitation all contribute to backwardness and they must all be taken into consideration in determining backwardness. Backwardness should be comparable to that of Schedule Caste and Schedule Tribe. Caste cannot be the sole or even the dominant criteria for defining backwardness.

(f) Caste and class are not synonymous

Caste and class are not synonymous. Article 15(4) speaks of class and not caste. Hence backwardness can be defined without reference to caste.

1. AIR 1993 SC 477: 1992 AIR SCW 3682: JT 1992 (6) SC 273.
2. AIR 1968 SC 1012: 1968 (2) SCJ 801: (1968) 2 SCR 786.
3. AIR 1972 SC 1375: 1972 (1) SCA 214: (1972) 3 SCR 247.
4. AIR 1976 SC 2381: (1976) 3 SCC 730: (1977) 1 SCR 194.

(g) Once a backward class it cannot always be a backward class

SC has held that classification of backward classes on the basis of caste would be permissible only if it is shown to be socially and educationally backward. But once a class is considered as backward it should not continue as such for all times. It would defeat the very purpose of reservation.

(h) Special provision must be less than 50%

In *Balaji* case the court held that special provision should be less than 50% so that the paramount rule of equality is not defeated. How much less depends upon the relevant circumstances prevailing in the case on hand. In principle the Supreme Court has been asserting that concept of reservations must not eat up the rule of equality and hence reservations must be kept lower than the open merit quota.

(i) Relaxation of minimum qualifying marks

Reservations in admissions to educational institutions has become a very knotty issue.

In *State of Madhya Pradesh* v. *Nivedita Jain*[1] the minimum qualifying marks in Pre-Medical exams for selection of students to Medical Colleges of the State were completely relaxed for SCs and STs. It was relaxed from 40% for SC and 30% for STs. As the required number did not qualify – it was further relaxed by 5% for each category. When seats remained unfilled even after second relaxation – minimum qualification was *totally relaxed* for these two categories. The High Court (very rightly – I submit) struck it down as violative of article 15(4). But the Supreme Court held it as valid on the ground that under the Medical Council of India Regulations – minimum qualifying marks was merely directory and not mandatory. It also over-ruled a Full Bench decision of the Patna High Court *Amalendu Kumar* v. *State of Bihar*[2] that relaxing the minimum qualification because the seats reserved for these categories were not filled up was violative of article 15(1). It is submitted that the Supreme Court decision was not in tune with the constitutional value system – it has destroyed the rule of equality; over-emphasised on the concept of reservation; provided a gateway to lower the standard of higher education and in its ultimate analysis divided the population by perverting the very concept of justice.

Supreme Court held[3] that cut-off marks referred to the minimum marks – whether qualifying or eligibility marks required for admission to a course and it is notified to candidates in advance. It said that the seats reserved for the OBC cannot be converted into the general GM candidate seats. Under the procedure adopted by the Jawaharlal Nehru University for the years 2008-2010 – it would fix the minimum eligibility marks for the GM candidates and for the OBC it would decide the marks after all the GM seats were filled by fixing the 10% below the marks of the GM candidate admitted. The procedure was held

1. AIR 1981 SC 2045: (1981) 4 SCC 296: (1982) 1 SCR 759.
2. AIR 1980 Pat 1: 1979 Pat LJR 337: 1979 BBCJ (HC) 677.
3. The Hindu dt 19-8-2011.

to be arbitrary and discriminatory. Minimum eligibility marks must always be declared and known to the applicant before he makes the application. Supreme Court upheld the Delhi High Court decision quashing this procedure.

(j) High caste girl marrying Scheduled Tribe boy is not entitled to reservation of a seat for M.Sc. course.[1] Similarly a female belonging to a high caste on marriage with an SC is not entitled to contest election from a seat reserved for Scheduled Caste.[2]

(k) A Five Judge Bench of the Supreme Court has held that a Scheduled Caste/Scheduled Tribe candidate is entitled to reservation benefit only in the State of his origin and not in other States where he/she migrates.

---

1. *D. Neelima* v. *Dean of P.G. Studies, A.P. Agricultural University,* (1993) 1 Andh LT 458: AIR 1993 AP 229.
2. *Meera Kanwaria* v. *Sunita,* AIR 2006 SC 597: 2005 AIR SCW 6243: (2006) 1 SCC 344.

CHAPTER 8

EQUALITY OF OPPORTUNITY IN PUBLIC EMPLOYMENT

(Article 16)

SYNOPSIS

A. Introduction

B. Articles 15 and 16—A comparison
   - (1) Article 16 mandates equality whereas article 15 prohibits discrimination
   - (2) Article 15(1) prohibits discrimination generally, 16(2) prohibits discrimination under article 16(2) in public services
   - (3) Prohibited grounds of discrimination under Article 16(2)—Wider than those under Article 15(2)
   - (4) Article 16(1) is wider than Article 16(2)
   - (5) Emphasis of article 16(2) is on the word 'only'
   - (6) Term 'special provision' used in article 15 includes a 'reservation' under article 16
   - (7) Articles 14 to 16 aim at equalisation measures
   - (8) Equal opportunity available before and after employment
   - (9) Employment
   - (10) Promotion
   - (11) Seniority
   - (12) Pension

C. Exceptions to Article 16
   - (1) Residence as an exception
   - (2) Religion as an exception
   - (3) Inadequate representation as an exception

D. Two conditions are to be satisfied for making special provisions under article 16(4)
   - (1) 16(4) to be read with Article 335
   - (2) Backward Class of Citizens
   - (3) As to amount of salary etc.—No special provision
   - (4) Backwardness a condition precedent

E. Some important trend-setting and trend-changing cases
   - (1) *Balaji* v. *State of Mysore—Special provision should be less than 50%*
   - (2) Devadasan—Carry-forward rule was struck down
   - (3) *Mandal* case—Over-ruled *Devdasan*
   - (4) *State of Kerala* v. *N.M. Thomas* case
   - (5) *A.B.S.K.* v. *Union of India*—Reservations in promotions valid
   - (6) *Rangachari*—Inadequate representation in promotional posts justifies reservation
   - (7) Guidelines in *Vasanth Kumar* case
   - (8) *Indira Sawhney* v. *Union of India*—A momentous case
   - (9) Constitution amended to provide for reservations in promotions

F. Cases which have evolved new concepts to balance the concepts of reservation and equality
   - (1) Concept of running account—Post based and not vacancy based reservation
   - (2) Concept of 'no accelerated seniority'
   - (3) *Ajit Singh Januja* v. *State of Punjab*—Reiterated that there is no accelerated seniority
   - (4) *85th Amendment provided for accelerated promotion*
   - (5) Article 16(4A) and (4B) flow from Article 16(4)

A. Introduction

Article 16 is an application of the rule of equality laid down under article 14. Article 14 lays down the general rule that no person shall be denied equality before law and the equal protection of the laws. Articles 15 and 16 provide for a specific application of the rule of equality laid down in article 14. Under all the three articles reasonable classification is permissible. Article 14 is applicable to all 'persons' but articles 15 & 16 are applicable only to the 'citizens'. In this sense article 14 is general and broader in its nature.

Article 16 has undergone important amendments in the year in 1956, 1995, 2000, 2001.

Article 16 is to be studied under the following clauses:

(1) There shall be equality of opportunity for all citizens in matters relating to employment or appointment to any office under the State. [Article 16(1)]

(2) No citizen shall on grounds only of religion, race, caste, sex, descent, place of birth, residence or any of them be ineligible for or discriminated against in respect of any employment or office under the State. [Article 16(2)]

Clauses (3), (4), (4A), (4B), (5) provide for 5 exceptions to the rule of equality of opportunity in public employment.

(3) Enables the Parliament to make a law prescribing residence prior to employment or appointment in Government or local authority within the State or a Union territory.

(4) Clause (4) enables the Government to make reservations of posts in Government jobs in favour of backward class of citizens which in the opinion of the State is not adequately represented in the State services.

(5) Likewise clause (4A) enables the State to make reservations in matters of promotion for SC and STs which in the opinion of the State are not adequately represented. Clause (4A) ends the 50% limit for reservations in favour of SC and STs in filling up backlog vacancies.

(6) Under Clause (5) a law which prescribes that a governing body member of a religious institution shall be one professing a particular religion or belonging to the religious denomination shall not violate the article 16(1)(2).

The principle of recruitment by open competition prevailed in India even before it was introduced in England. Article 16(1) *does not provide a right to obtain employment* but it gives a right to equality of opportunity for being considered for such employment. It does not prohibit selection by merit, tests and interviews, laying down of minimum educational qualifications, physical fitness etc. The tests must be reasonable and not arbitrary.

B. Articles 15 and 16 – A comparison

As between articles 15 and 16 – Article 15 is more wide and more general in its character.

(1) Article 16 mandates equality whereas article 15 prohibits discrimination

Article 15(1) prohibits the State from discriminating against any citizen on the grounds only of religion, race, caste, sex, place of birth or any of them.

Article 16(1) mandates the State to provide equal opportunity in public employment to all the citizens. *Article 16 mandates equality whereas article 15 prohibits discrimination.* Word 'discrimination' involves an element of 'unfavour' or a negative or a prejudicial effect.

(2) Article 15(1) prohibits discrimination generally; 16(2) prohibits discrimination in public services

Article 16(2) is restrictive than article 15(1) because 16(2) prohibits discrimination in services under the Central and State Government and their instrumentalities; whereas article 15(1) prohibits discrimination generally on other grounds also.

(3) Prohibited grounds of discrimination under article 16(2)—Wider than those under article 15(2)

The prohibited grounds of discrimination under Article 16(2) are somewhat wider than those under article 15(2). It covers additional grounds of *descent and residence* apart from religion, race, caste, sex and place of birth mentioned under article 15(2). Article 16 deals only with equality of opportunity in public employment. Article 15 covers the entire range of State activities. It also includes within its ambit discriminations in matters of employment.

(4) Article 16(1) is wider than article 16(2)

Article 16(1) is wider than article 16(2) and the grounds of discrimination mentioned under article 16(2) are not exhaustive.

(5) Emphasis of article 16(2) is on the word 'only'

That is discrimination *only* on ground of religion etc. is prohibited but if it is coupled with some other reasonable ground it could be valid.

(6) Term 'special provision' used in article 15 includes a 'reservation' under article 16

Under both the articles reservations can be made in favour of specified categories. However note that the Constitution uses the specific word 'reservation' only under article 16 and not under article 15. But *the term 'special provision' used in article 15 includes a reservation also.*

(7) Articles 14 to 16 aim at equalisation measures

Articles 14 to 16 is 'neither dull uniformity nor specious talentism'. It is a process of producing quality by extending better facilities to the latent capabilities of the lowly. It is not to be mistaken for a method to substitute..."mediocres for intelligent cadres".[1] Public services in India has been the major instrument available to the Government to carry on its multifarious activities. Hence, public services have been the major source of employment and a new form of property. It was thus, held in *State of Maharashtra* v. *Chandraban Tale* that public employment opportunity is a national wealth and all citizens are equally entitled to a share in it.[2]

---

1. *State of Jammu and Kashmir* v. *Triloki Nath Khosa,* AIR 1974 SC 1: (1974) 1 SCC 19: (1974) 1 SCR 771.
2. (1983) 3 SCC 387: AIR 1983 SC 803: 1983 (II) LLJ 256.

(8) Equal opportunity available before and after employment

The equality under article 16 is available in all stages of service. As observed by P.N. Bhagwati J. the concept of equal opportunity "permeates the whole spectrum of an individual's employment through promotion and termination to the payment of gratuity and pension" *i.e.,* both prior to and after the employment. It includes all matters incidental to the employment for example- salary, promotion, termination etc.

However equality cannot be attained with mathematical accuracy. Reasonable classification is permissible. But the courts have warned against 'mini-classifications based on micro-distinctions'.[1]

The term 'office' under article 16 means a subsisting, permanent, substantive position having an existence independent of the person who occupies the office. That is it is an office to be filled up by succession when it falls vacant due to any reason.[2]

(9) Employment

Under article 309 rules regulating service conditions of Government servants can be made by the Government subject to the constitutional principles under articles 14 and 16. In the absence of such rules service conditions may be prescribed by executive instructions in the exercise of its executive power or administrative directions.[3] If statutory rules are made then the executive power to make appointments must be exercised in accordance with such rules. Executive power can only supplement the rules but not supplant them. *For example,* if the rule requires that before appointment to a post it should be suitably published, appointment made without publicity is invalid.[4]

Only the number of posts advertised to be filled up – must be filled up, or else article 16 is violated. Only in an exceptional case this rule can be deviated on reasonable grounds.[5]

Higher pay-scales for employees with higher educational qualification is valid.[6]

When a large number of posts are to be filled up by interview, a rational basis has to be adopted to shortlist the candidates in order to avoid manipulations and a casual approach to the selection process.[7] Supreme Court refused to regularise the appointment of *ad- hoc* appointees who had been working for 13 years. It held that regular appointments were to be made by the Public Service Commission

1. *State of Jammu and Kashmir* v. *Triloki Nath Khosla,* AIR 1974 SC 1: (1974) 1 SCC 19: (1974) 1 SCR 771.
2. *State of Uttar Pradesh* v. *Sri Bhola Nath Srivastava,* AIR 1972 All 460: 1972 All LJ 457: 1972 Serv LR 477.
3. *State of Uttar Pradesh* v. *Ram Gopal Shukla,* AIR 1981 SC 1041: (1981) 3 SCC 1: 1981 (I) LLJ 494.
4. *B.S. Minhas* v. *Indian Statistical Institute,* AIR 1984 SC 363: (1983) 4 SCC 582: 1984 (I) LLJ 67.
5. *Surinder Singh* v. *State of Punjab,* AIR 1998 SC 18: 1997 AIR SCW 3961: (1997) 8 SCC 488.
6. *V. Markendeya* v. *State of Andhra Pradesh,* AIR 1989 SC 1308: JT 1989 (2) SC 108: (1989) 3 SCC 191.
7. *M.P. Public Service Commission* v. *Navnit Kumar Potdar,* AIR 1995 SC 77: 1994 AIR SCW 4088: (1994) 6 SCC 293.

only. Hence *ad hoc* appointments were only temporary appointments without any right for confirmation or regularisation of services.[1]

Appointments based on hereditary principles are bad because 'descent' is a prohibited ground of discrimination under article 16(2).[2]

1. In *Union of India* v. *Bhaskarendu Datta Majumdar*[3] – Respondent was selected by the Selection Board and placed at first place for the post of Director (Marketing) in State Trading Corporation. His name was cleared by the Vigilance Commissioner. But the Appointment Committee refused to appoint him without any reasons being recorded. It was held to be violative of article 16.
2. Laches under article 16: Relief against refusal of promotion on the ground of medical unfitness sought after 2 decades was rejected on the ground of laches. It would upset the settled position of seniority and promotions granted to others. Even if no limitation period is prescribed the petition under article 16 is liable to be rejected as held in *Union of India* v. *Durairaj.*[4]

Article 16(1) mandates equality of opportunity amongst the seekers of the same employment or who are already in the same employment. In other words what is contemplated is that like shall be treated alike and not equality between members of separate independent classes. *For example,* a rule enabled Guards to be promoted to higher grade Station Masters but not the road-side Station Masters. It was held not violative of article 16(1) as Roadside Station Masters and Guards were recruited and trained separately and had separate avenues for promotion. They stood on two different footings and hence there could be no equality of opportunity between them.[5]

Muthamma was denied promotion to Grade I of the Indian Foreign Service on the ground that she had not obtained the permission of the Government in writing before her marriage was solemnised as was required under the Service Rules. The Rules were held to be unconstitutional. But the court made it clear that this does not mean that men and women are equal in all occupations and in all situations. Thus, differentiation can be made based on the sensitivities of sex and other handicaps of either sex.[6]

In *Anuj Garg* v. *Hotel Assn of India,*[7] It was held that while deciding constitutional validity of a law court has to keep in mind the societal conditions prevalent at relevant times, changed social psyche and expectations. The court made the observation while quashing prohibition on employment of women in Hotels and Bars serving liquor saying that it violates gender equality.

The eligibility conditions for the selection for the post of a teacher Grade III Secondary was changed during the selection process. This was held to be

1. *Dr. Surinder Singh Jamwal* v. *State of Jammu and Kashmir,* AIR 1996 SC 2775: 1996 AIR SCW 3481: (1996) 9 SCC 619.
2. *Gazula Dasaratha Rama Rao* v. *State of Andhra Pradesh,* AIR 1961 SC 564: (1961) 2 SCR 931.
3. AIR 2011 SC 196.
4. AIR 2011 SC 1084.
5. *All India Station Masters Assn.* v. *General Manager,* AIR 1960 SC 384: (1960) 2 SCR 311.
6. *C.B. Muthamma* v. *Union of India,* AIR 1979 SC 1868: 1979 Lab IC 1307: (1979) 4 SCC 260.
7. AIR 2008 SC 663: 2007 AIR SCW 7772: (2008) 3 SCC 1.

unconstitutional because once an advertisement is given selection process must continue as per the advertisement. In this case the change was necessitated due to the amendment to rule 266 which was made while the selection process under the previously issued advertisement had begun.[1]

Under the Air India Regulations the air hostesses could retire at the age of 35 years or on first pregnancy. The provision was held to be invalid as it violated gender equality. The Regulations provided that if they got married within 4 years of their service they would have to retire. This provision was held to be valid.

Teachers employed in privately managed aided school in State of Haryana are entitled to the same salary and dearness allowance as is paid to teachers employed in Government schools.[2]

'Matters relating to employment' in article 16 extends to matters subsequent to appointment also *e.g.*, promotions to selection posts[3], termination of employment; salary, increments, leave gratuity pension and the age of superannuation etc.

In *Indira Sawhney (Mandal)* Supreme Court has held that there can be no reservation in promotions to selection posts and has thus overruled Rangachari's case on the point. The judgment was to come into operation after a period of 5 years of the judgment. The Government amended the Constitution and added clause 4A to article 16 which enables the Parliament to make reservations for SC/STs in promotional posts also. The amendment is designed to please a section of the people. It disturbs the rule of equality; the SC/ST have already had the benefit of reservation at the appointment stage; merit could be compromised; it could result in heart burns.

Probationer is also entitled to the protection of this article if his termination is punitive in nature.[4]

Viva voce test cannot be the sole test for appointment.[5] Upon completion of the written examination test selection can be made on the basis of the *viva voce* test as provided in *Ashok* v. *State of Karnataka*[6]. Supreme Court has held that interview brings out the overall intellectual and personal qualities like alertness, resourcefulness, dependability, capacity for discussion, ability to take decisions, qualities of leadership etc, which are so essential for a judicial officer. Supreme Court upheld the Kerala High Court Rules for the selection of judicial officers which fixed a minimum marks for interview for selection of Munsiff Magistrate.[7]

---

1. *Madan Mohan Sharma* v. *State of Rajasthan*, AIR 2008 SC 1657: 2008 AIR SCW 1850: (2008) 3 SCC 724.
2. *State of Haryana* v. *Rajpal Sharma*, AIR 1997 SC 449: 1996 AIR SCW 3833: (1996) 5 SCC 273.
3. *General Manager, Southern Railway* v. *Rangachari*, AIR 1962 SC 36: 1961 (2) SCA 460: (1962) 2 SCR 586.
4. *Dipti Prakash Banerjee* v. *Satvendra Nath Bose National Centre for Basic Sciences, Calcutta*, AIR 1999 SC 983: 1999 AIR SCW 605: (1999) 3 SCC 60.
5. *Praveen Singh* v. *State of Punjab*, AIR 2001 SC 152: 2000 AIR SCW 4024: (2000) 8 SCC 633
6. (1992) 1 SCC 28: 1991 AIR SCW 2764: AIR 1992 SC 80.
7. *K.H. Siraj* v. *High Court of Kerala*, AIR 2006 SC 2339: 2006 AIR SCW 3136: (2006) 6 SCC 395.

Appointment of candidates by 'pick and choose' method without preparing any merit list is an arbitrary exercise of power.[1]

An applicant for a particular post does not get a right to be enforced by *mandamus* unless and until he is selected in the process of selection and gets the letter of appointment.[2] A candidate whose name appears on the waiting list does not get a right of being appointed to any post. It remains in force for a reasonable time and not *'in infinitum'* so that other qualified persons are not deprived of their chance of applying for the post in the succeeding years.[3] A candidate put on the waiting list cannot be appointed to a post arising subsequently without notifying the same for recruitment. No one can be appointed without due notification of vacancies and selection according to the rules.[4]

Appointment cannot be denied to a person due to his past political affinities unless such affinities are likely to affect the integrity and efficiency of the individual's service.[5]

Appointment on compassionate ground[6] has been held to be valid in *Balbir Kaur* v. *Steel Authority of India Ltd.*[7]. No such appointment can be claimed if no post is available. It is submitted that to tide over the hardship there is provision for pension/provident fund and other death related benefits. To appoint a person in a Government post because of the chance that his parent dies in harness amounts to treating the post – so to say – as a hereditary post. It also takes away the fundamental right of every other eligible person waiting in the queue for a Government job.

(10) Promotion

No person has a vested right to be promoted but has a right to be considered for promotion. But if a rule confers a right of actual promotion then it is a service rule.[8] Inequality of opportunity of promotion among members of a single class which is based on no rational criteria is not valid under article 16.[9]

How far distinctions are permissible within the same class of employees for promotion from the lower to the higher grade has engaged judicial attention. The Supreme Court has held that as a general rule differentiating between persons belonging to the same single class is invalid both under article 14 and article 16. However seniority-cum merit has been held to be valid.[10]

---

1. *State of Bihar* v. *Kaushal Kishore Singh*, AIR 1997 SC 2643: 1997 AIR SCW 2605: (1998) 9 SCC 104.
2. *Union of India* v. *Tarun K. Singh*, AIR 2001 SC 2196: 2001 AIR SCW 1928: (2003) 11 SCC 768.
3. *Babita Prasad* v. *State of Bihar*, (1993) Suppl 3 SCC 268: 1992 (Supp) JT 135.
4. *Surinder Singh* v. *State of Punjab*, AIR 1998 SC 18: 1997 AIR SCW 3961: (1997) 8 SCC 488.
5. *State of Madhya Pradesh* v. *Ramashanker Raghuvanshi*, AIR 1983 SC 374: (1983) 2 SCC 145: 1983 (I) LLJ 299.
6. (X – an employee in Government service dies in harness- while still in service. His son/daughter/wife is given an appointment in order to tide over the hardship due to the sudden loss of the bread winner in the family).
7. AIR 2000 SC 1596: 2000 AIR SCW 1745: (2000) 6 SCC 493.
8. *K. Jagadeesan* v. *Union of India*, AIR 1990 SC 1072: (1990) 2 SCC 228: 1990 Lab IC 839.
9. *Mohd Shujat Ali* v. *Union of India*, AIR 1974 SC 1631: (1975) 3 SCC 76: (1975) 1 SCR 449.
10. *State of Jammu and Kashmir* v. *Triloki Nath Khosla*, AIR 1974 SC 1: (1974) 1 SCC 19: (1974) 1 SCR 771.

Degree holders and diploma holders have been differentiated for a long time. Their designations are different; the degree holders are given a higher pay-scale, higher educational qualification has a relevance to the higher promotional post in view of the nature of the functions and duties attached to the post.

However the Food Corporation of India had fixed the eligibility criteria at 3 years of service for graduates and five years of service for matriculates. The Supreme Court struck it down because the nature of work performed was the same and the FCI did not place on record any material to justify the classification.[1]

Two tests are generally applied for the purposes of promotion. Seniority-cum-merit – where more emphasis is given on seniority and minimum required merit for efficiency of administration is considered. The second test is that of merit-cum-seniority where merit is given more emphasis.

The name of the employee against whom disciplinary proceedings are pending cannot be left out from being considered for promotion to the next higher post because he is presumed to be innocent until proved guilty. Mere suspicion is not a substitute for proof.

(11) Seniority

The rule making authority determines what rules should govern the *inter se* seniority and ranking of employees working in a department. Such rules must necessarily be just, fair and reasonable. Seniority of an officer is determined with reference to the date of his regular appointment. Appointment in accordance with the rules is a condition precedent to count seniority.[2] Temporary, *ad hoc* and fortuitous appointment cannot be counted for the purpose of calculating seniority.[3]

A University has directly recruited Readers and Professors and those promoted on merit on the yardstick of continuous officiation. They form independent classes by themselves. Their *inter-se* seniority cannot be determined treating them as one class.[4] An *ex cadre* employee cannot be treated as a cadre employee for determining their *interse* seniority as it amounts to treating unlike alike.[5]

(12) Pension

In *U. Raghvendra Acharya* v. *State of Karnataka*[6] the appellants were retired teachers of the University and private colleges to whom UGC pay-scales were applicable. The revised pay scales including basic, DA were admissible on

1. *Food Corporation of India* v. *Om Prakash Sharma*, AIR 1998 SC 2682: 1998 AIR SCW 2725: (1998) 7 SCC 676.
2. *Direct Recruit Class-II Engineering Officers' Association* v. *State of Maharashtra*, (1990) 2 SCR 900: 1991 AIR SCW 2226: AIR 1990 SC 1607.
3. *V. Sreenivasa Reddy* v. *Government of Andhra Pradesh*, AIR 1995 SC 586: 1994 AIR SCW 4868: JT 1994 (6) SC 461.
4. *Rashmi Srivastava* v. *Vikram University*, AIR 1995 SC 1694: 1995 AIR SCW 2442: (1995) 3 SCC 653.
5. *Direct Recruit Class-II Engineering Officers' Association* v. *State of Maharashtra*, (1990) 2 SCR 900: 1991 AIR SCW 2226: AIR 1990 SC 1607.
6. AIR 2006 SC 2154.

1-1-1996. The Karnataka Government extended the revised UGC pay scales w.e.f. 1-1-1996. But in case of pensioners Karnataka Service Rule 296 provided that it shall be computed w.e.f. 1-4-1998. The same was challenged as violating article 16. The challenge was upheld. Supreme Court held that pension is not a bounty but a deferred salary. The benefit of revised pay scales once given cannot be withdrawn or reduced by an executive order.

Provision for compulsory retirement in public interest does not infringe articles 14 and 16.

C. Exceptions to Article 16

(1) Residence as an exception

Nothing contained in article 16 shall prevent the Parliament from making a law prescribing residence in a State or Union territory in respect of class of employment or appointment to an office – prior to such employment or appointment. Article 16(3)

Such a power is given to the Parliament and not the State Legislature.

The Parliament has passed Public Employment (Requirement as to residence) Act, 1957. It provides that no one will be disqualified on the ground that one is not the resident of a particular State. However due to backwardness of Himachal Pradesh, Tripura, Manipur, Telangana the Act permits prescription of residential requirement up to March 21, 1974.

Article 16(3) is an exception to clause 16(2) which forbids discrimination on the ground of residence.

(2) Religion as an exception

A law may prescribe that the incumbent of an office in connection with the affairs of a religious or denominational institution or a member of the governing body thereof shall belong to a particular religion or denomination. [Article 16(5)]

(3) Inadequate representation as an exception

It empowers the State to make special provision for the reservations of appointments or posts in favour of any 'backward' class of citizens which in the opinion of the State is not adequately represented in the public services under the State. Article 16(4)

Article 16(4) is an important exception to Article 16(1) and a most contentious part of the Article.

D. Two conditions are to be satisfied for making special provisions under article 16(4)

(1) The class of citizens is backward,

(2) It is not adequately represented in the services of the State.

Both the conditions must be cumulatively satisfied. Article 16(4) is an enabling provision.[1] It confers a discretionary power on the State to make special

1. *Mohan Kumar Singhania* v. *Union of India,* AIR 1992 SC 1: 1991 AIR SCW 2646: 1991 Lab IC 2334.

provisions. It imposes no duty on the State to make reservations nor does it confer a right to demand for reservations.[1]

(1) 16(4) to be read with article 335

Article 16(4) must be read with article 335 which lays down that the claims of the Scheduled Castes and Scheduled Tribes must be taken into consideration consistently with the maintenance of efficiency of administration. Reservations necessarily means choosing less meritorious when more meritorious are available. Hence the policy of reservations must be such that efficiency of the administration is not hampered.

On one hand article 14 and article 16(1) lay down the rules of equality which is a paramount rule under which every citizen has the fundamental right of equal opportunity in public employment. Equality is necessary for an integrated India. On the other hand article 16(4) makes provisions for reservations in favour of a specified class of persons. Both have to be balanced in such a way that the rule of reservations does not eat away the rule of equality or *vice-versa.*

Reservations under articles 15 and 16 have given to a lot of discontent resulting in reservations being challenged before the judiciary. As observed by Shri H.M. Seervai "law on the co-relation of articles 15 and 16 has been in an untidy state because cases decided under article 16 refer to principles laid down in article 15 and *vice-versa.*"[2]

(2) Backward Class of citizens

For article 16(4) to be applicable – the class must be a backward class. It has been held by a series of cases that 'backward class of citizens' under 16(4) means the same as 'socially and educationally backward class of citizens under article 15(4).[3]

(3) As to amount of salary etc.—No special provision

It should be noted that as regards conditions of service relating to employment such as salary increment, gratuity pension and age of superannuation – article 16(4) is not applicable. In other words, as regards these matters there can be no special provisions made in favour of the backward class of citizens. These matters are absolutely protected by the concept of equality.

(4) Backwardness a condition precedent

Under article 16(4) there can be no reservations independent of backwardness. Hence when posts were reserved in favour of harijans, backward Hindus, Hindu Brahmins, non-Brahmins and Christians. It was held that it was distribution of posts on the basis of community, which was prohibited by article 16(2). To determine whether a section of the population forms a 'class' a test solely based on caste, community, race, religion, sex, descent, place of birth or residence cannot be adopted.

1. *Indira Sawhney* v. *Union of India,* AIR 1993 SC 477: 1992 AIR SCW 3682: 1993 Lab IC 129; *Ajit Singh* v. *State of Punjab,* (2000) 1 SCC 430.
2. Seervai H.M.: Constitutional Law of India, p.387, (Bombay: N.M. Tripathi Pvt. Ltd., 3rd Ed. Vol I).
3. *Janki Prasad Parimoo* v. *State of Jammu and Kashmir,* AIR 1973 SC 930: (1973) 1 SCC 420: 1973 Lab IC 565.

E. Some important trend-setting and trend-changing cases

(1) Balaji v. *State of Mysore—Special provision should be less than 50%*[1]

The court struck down a GO by which 68% of the seats in educational institutions were reserved for Scheduled Castes and Schedule Tribes and other Backward Classes. It was held to be excessive and a fraud on the Constitution. It also held that a *special provision should be less than 50%*. How much less than 50% depends upon the relevant prevailing circumstances in each case. This 50% rule is an important rule valid to this date except for the 81st Amendment in 2000 which incorporated article 16(4B) under which for filling back-log vacancies, 50% rule is not applicable.

(2) Devadasan – *Carry-forward rule was struck down*

Carry-forward rule was struck down in this case. 17 ½ % posts were to be reserved for Schedule Caste/Schedule Tribe. If all the reserved posts were not filled up in a given year, then the shortfall was to be carried forward to the next year and added to the reserved quota for that year and this could be done for the next two years. The result was that in an year out of 45 vacancies 29 went to the reserved categories and only 16 were left for the general merit. This amounted to 65% reservations in the 3rd year. This was in excess of 50% limit laid down in *Balaji* and hence it was held unconstitutional. Court held that *article 16(4) was an exception to article 16(1).* It should remain smaller than the rule and not be allowed to destroy the rule of equality or else the rule of equality would become illusory and meaningless. In making reservations the State cannot ignore the fundamental rights of the rest of the citizens. In addition keeping the qualified candidates out was also detrimental to the administrative efficiency mandated by article 335.

(3) Mandal case—Over-ruled Devadasan

In *Mandal* case[2] the Supreme Court has over-ruled *Devdasan* and held that carry-forward rule is valid as long as it does not exceed 50%.

(4) State of Kerala v. *N.M. Thomas case*[3]

It is a trend-changing case. It has been subject to much criticism "the law was reasonably certain till the judgments in *State of Kerala* v. *N.M. Thomas* introduced considerable confusion in the law"[4] Hither to it was a settled law that article 16(4) is an exception and that the quantum of reservations shall not exceed 50%. But *Thomas* brought a change in the settled law.

Facts in brief:

The case dealt with promotional concessions to reserved categories. The Kerala State and Subordinate Service Rules, 1955 (Rules) prescribed a unified test for the promotion of the lower division clerk to an upper division clerk. All were given two years time to pass the test under R 13A. The Schedule Caste/Schedule Tribe were given an extra two years time to pass the test. Further R 13A provided that a member of the Service who had not passed the test but was

1. AIR 1963 SC 649: 1963 (2) SCA 1: (1963) Supp 1 SCR 439.
2. *Indra Sawhney* v. *Union of India*, AIR 1993 SC 477: 1992 AIR SCW 3682: JT 1992 (6) SC 273.
3. AIR 1976 SC 490: 1976 Lab IC 395: (1976) 2 SCC 310.
4. Seervai H.M.: Constitutional Law, 3rd Edn., Vol. I, p. 387.

otherwise qualified and suitable for the post could be appointed temporarily but had to pass the test within 2 years of the introduction of the test or else he would be reverted back to the category from which he was appointed. A large number of Schedule Caste/Schedule Tribe were facing an immediate reversion from their post. Therefore Rule 13AA was passed exempting them from appearing the test for a specified period. Out of 51 lower division clerks promoted as upper division clerks 34 belonged to the Scheduled Caste/Scheduled Tribe *i.e.,* 68%. Hence *Thomas* filed a petition under article 226 that Rule 13AA is violative of article 16. High Court held the rule as void as it violated article 16(1)(2). It also held that promotion of 34 persons out of 51 even though they had not passed the necessary tests was not conducive to maintenance of efficiency of administration. It is to be noted that the Advocate General acting for the State had contended that rule was valid under article 16(1) (2) and that he did not rely on article 16(4) to urge the validity of the rule.[1]

The ruling on the case

(i) *Article 16(4) is not an exception* to article 16(1) but a facet of article 16(1). Article 16(1) in turn is a facet of article 14. Therefore article 16(1) itself permits reasonable classification for attaining equality of opportunity assured by it. Note that the majority ruling in *Devadasan, Balaji* and *Rangachari* that article 16(4) is an exception has been overruled. *Thomas* ruled that even without article 16(4) reservations in favour of backward class of citizens is permissible under article 16(1)

(ii) *Classification on the basis of backwardness permissible:* Classification on the basis of backwardness is not prohibited under articles 16(2), 16(1) or 14.

(iii) Extended period of 2 years to the Scheduled Caste/Scheduled Tribe for passing the tests is a just and a reasonable classification having a rational nexus to the object of providing equal opportunity for all citizens in matters of employment in public offices.[2]

(iv) Krishna Iyer J. held that the post was only of a clerk and not that of a Scientist or a Magistrate. Hence it was designed only for 'better performance and not basic proficiency' to relax on basic qualification is to compromise on minimum administrative efficiency but to relax on additional test qualification is only to take a calculated and controlled risk. Hence efficiency contemplated under article 335 is not compromised.

(v) *Reservations not to exceed 50% – a rule of caution:* The rule that reservations shall not exceed 50% is only a rule of caution and not meant to be exhaustive of all categories.[3]

It is submitted that the decision has opened up a *pandora's box* specially with the observation that article 16(4) is not an exception. The delicate balance

---

1. In this sense any observation by the court on article 16(4) is *obiter dicta- i.e.,* only a passing observation in the course of giving the judgment. But then as it happens – even an *obiter* coming from the Highest Court has not only a high persuasive value but also a tendency to become a ratio of the case.
2. Per Subba Rao C.J. in *Thomas.*
3. Per Fazl Ali J. in *Thomas.*

between the reservation rule and the equality of opportunity rule – so neatly maintained by the earlier rulings of the Supreme Court have been disturbed leading to unrest amongst various sectors of the society.

A meaningful criticism of the judgment is made by Marx Gallanter[1] he opines "*Thomas* does not offer any hope of breaking out of the pattern of patronage and dependence. ... the judgments visualise the Scheduled Castes as a passive recipients of Government largesse rather than as active participants in their own improvement. ...*Thomas* enlarges State power in a way that may jeopardise the future of compensatory preference for backward classes." It is a false victory for the Scheduled Caste – court attempts to make the legal doctrine yield up benefits that it cannot yield. Therefore the Scheduled Castes are mesmerised into thinking that much is being done for them.[2]

Dr. Ambedkar too had opined "...we have to safeguard two things, *viz* the principle of equality of opportunity and at the same time satisfy the demand of communities which have not had so far representation in the State then I am sure they will agree that unless you use some such qualifying phrase as 'backward' the exception made in favour of reservations will ultimately eat up the rule altogether."[3]

(5) A.B.S.K. v. Union of India—Reservations in promotions valid

Reservations for SCs/STs in promotions and various other concessions was held valid under article 16(4), applying the ruling in Thomas. It held that SCs/STs are not castes within the ordinary meaning of the word caste. They are a backward class of human groups. The carry-forward rule for 3 years which amounted to 66% was held valid though it exceeded the 50% limit laid down in *Balaji* and *Devdasan*. Likewise reservations in promotion posts based on seniority-cum-suitability in selection as well as non-selection posts were held valid. The observation of the court was that if reservations in selection posts is valid it is *a fortiori* valid in non-selection posts.

(6) Rangachari—Inadequate representation in promotional posts justifies reservation

In *Rangachari* the court held that inadequate representation contemplated under article 16(4) as a mandatory condition for reservations is not only numerical inadequacy but also qualitative inadequacy of representation. Thus adequate representation means not only reservations in the lowest rungs of service at the appointment stage but also in selection posts. This case was relied upon in *Thomas*.

(7) Guidelines in Vasanth Kumar case

In *K.C. Vasanth Kumar* v. *State of Karnataka*,[4] following guidelines were laid down by the Supreme Court:

1. "Symbolic activism: A judicial encounter with the contours of India's compensatory discrimination policy" 229 published in "Judges and the Judicial Power' essays in honour of J. V.R. Krishna Iyer (Bombay: N.M. Tripathi Pvt. Ltd, 1985).
2. For a detailed criticism of the article 16(4) being read as not an exception – see- Dr. Veena M. Tonapi: A Seminal Approach To Constitutional Philosophy – contributions of P.N. Bhagwati J. and V.R. Krishna Iyer J. (Bangalore: Karnataka Institute For Law And Parliamentary Reforms) pp. 95-102.
3. CAD Vol 7 No.16, p. 702.
4. AIR 1988 SC 2287.

(i) Reservations without applying the means test (economic backwardness) must continue for SCs/STs until 2000 AD – a period sufficiently long to overcome the baneful effects of social oppression.

(ii) Even after 2000 AD the means test is to be applied even to the SCs/STs.

(iii) As far as other backward classes are concerned- two tests are to be applied- their backwardness must be comparable to that of the SCs/STs & they must satisfy the means test.

(iv) Reservation policy must be reviewed every 5 years.[1]

(8) Indira Sawhney v. Union of India[2]—A momentous case

It is a momentous case which reflects the reaction of the non-reserved classes to the concept of reservations. 27% seats were reserved for backward classes in Government services based on the recommendations of the Mandal Commission. This threw the Nation into turmoil and a violent anti-reservation movement rocked the nation for nearly three months resulting in a huge loss of persons and property. The matter was ultimately decided by a 9-judge Bench. Judgment was pronounced on several important aspects relating to reservations:

(i) 27% reservations in Government jobs for backward classes was valid but the creamy layer *i.e.,* the socially advanced persons had to be left out.

(ii) Reservations shall be confined only to initial appointments but not to promotions.

(iii) Total reservations shall not exceed 50%.

(iv) Backward class of citizens can be identified on the basis of caste and not only on economic basis.

(v) Article 16(4) is not an exception to article 16(1) but an instance of classification.

(vi) Backward class of citizens contemplated under article 16(4) is wider than 'socially and educationally backward class of citizens' under article 15(4). Thus certain classes which may not qualify for reservations under article 15(4) may qualify for reservations under article 16(4).

(vii) Creamy layer must be excluded from backward classes. The decision can be implemented only when the creamy layer is eliminated.

(viii) Article 16(4) permits classification of backward classes into backward and more backward classes.

(ix) A backward class cannot be identified only and exclusively with reference to economic criteria.

(x) Reservations can be made by an executive order.

(xi) A permanent statutory body must be appointed to examine complaints of over inclusion or under inclusion of groups in the list of backward classes.

---

1. AIR 1985 SC 1495: (1985) Supp 1 SCR 352: (1985) Supp SCC 714.
2. AIR 1993 SC 477: 1992 AIR SCW 3682: JT 1992 (6) SC 273.

(xii) On Mandal Commission Report- no opinion was expressed.

(xiii) All disputes regarding new criteria evolved by Central or State Government to exclude socially advanced persons, creamy layer etc., can be raised only in the Supreme Court and not before the High Court.

(xiv) Total reservations of 50% is divided into 'vertical' and 'horizontal' reservation. Reservations in favour of SC/ST, OBC is vertical reservations whereas reservations in favour of physically handicapped (under 16(1) is horizontal, for example if 3% vacancies are reserved for physically handicapped. Such a person will be placed in the appropriate quota depending on whether he is an SC or an ST etc.

Under the judgment reservations in promotions would be unconstitutional after 16-11-1997. Reservations have become such a manipulative game of the political power that in order to continue with reservations in promotions and to overcome the *Mandal* ruling the Parliament amended the Constitution.

(9) Constitution amended to provide for reservations in promotions

The State may make reservations in matters of promotions, (with consequential benefits)[1] to any class or classes of posts in the services under the State in favour of SCs/STs which in the opinion of the State are not adequately represented in the services of the State. Article 16(4A)

It has been inserted by Constitution 77th Amendment. The evil of reservations in promotions which was attempted to be set at naught by the *Mandal* judgment has been perpetuated by this amendment.

It laid down that the unfilled vacancies of the previous years which could not be filled due to non-availability of eligible candidates belonging to SC/ST/BC will be considered as a separate class and be filled up in any succeeding year. Such class of vacancies would not be considered together with the vacancies of the current year in which they are being filled up for determining the 50% rule. Thus the vacancies in subsequent years can go even beyond 50%. Article 16(4B) inserted by The Constitution (81st Amendment) Act, 2000.

After the introduction of article 16(4A) & (4B) many cases have come up before the Supreme Court which have evolved new concepts to make the reservations concept more meaningful and balance it with the paramount principle of equality.

F. Cases which have evolved new concepts to balance the concepts of reservation and equality

(1) Concept of running account—Post based and not vacancy based reservation

R.K. Sabharwal v. *State of Punjab*[2] it was held that reservations must be *post based and not vacancy based*. The concept of 'vacancy' has no relevance in operating the percentage of reservations. The concept of running account is to see that SCs and STs and Backward Classes get their percentage of reserved posts. The account must be so operated that it does not result in excessive reservations. As and when there is vacancy whether permanent or temporary in

1. Inserted by Constitution 85th Amendment Act, 2001.
2. (1995) 2 SCC 745: AIR 1995 SC 1371: 1995 AIR SCW 1371.

a particular post the same has to be filled from amongst the category to which the post belonged.

(2) Concept of 'no accelerated seniority'

Union of India v. *Virpal Singh Chauhan*[1] was a case which came up soon after article 16(4A) was introduced. It was held that persons promoted due to roster system are given accelerated promotions and not accelerated seniority. Hence when a GM candidate who was senior to the reserved candidate in the feeder category is promoted such GM candidate regains his seniority over the reserved candidate who has been promoted earlier than[2] the GM candidate. In this case reservations in the higher grades of Railway Guards were based on vacancies and not on posts. The net result was that the SC/ST representation rose to 70% instead of 22.5%. The Supreme Court observed that this happened due to the faulty implementation of the rule of reservations. Reservations were being made on vacancy basis and not on post basis, not following the running account system laid down in *Sabharwal*. It is submitted that the process of reservations exceeding the limit has begun gradually when reservations in promotions were upheld without protecting the service seniority of the general category candidates.

(3) In Ajit Singh Januja v. State of Punjab*[3]*—Reiterated that there is no accelerated seniority

The ruling in *Virpal Singh* was followed – *i.e.,* there is accelerated promotion and not accelerated seniority. The court held that if accelerated seniority also were to be allowed– a stage should be reached where majority of the posts would be held by persons who have not only entered in service on the basis of reservations but have excluded the general category candidates from being promoted to the posts reserved for general category merely on the ground of their initial accelerated promotions.

(a) This point was overruled in *Jagdish Lal* v. *State of Haryana*[4] it was held that the normal rule of seniority must prevail in the reservations field also.

The matter was referred to the Constitutional Bench in *Ajit Singh II.*[5] It overruled *Jadgish Lal* and restored the 'accelerated promotion; no accelerated seniority' rule.

(4) 85th Amendment provided for accelerated promotion

To overcome the politically inconvenient yet a sane and a rational ruling the Constitution was amended in 2001 by 85th Amendment to provide for not only accelerated promotion but also consequential seniority with retrospective effect.

In *M.G. Badappanavar* v. *State of Karnataka*[6] the Supreme Court confirmed its ruling in *Ajit Singh II* and directed that the seniority lists as between the general and reserved promotees and promotions be reviewed in the light of the

1. AIR 1996 SC 448: 1995 AIR SCW 4309: (1995) 6 SCC 684.
2. AIR 1996 SC 1188: 1996 AIR SCW 1178: (1996) 3 SCC 332.
3. (1996) 2 SCC 775: AIR 1996 SC 1189: 1996 AIR SCW 1196.
4. AIR 1997 SC 2366: 1997 AIR SCW 2257: (1997) 6 SCC 538.
5. AIR 1999 SC 3471: 1999 AIR SCW 3460: (1999) 7 SCC 209.
6. AIR 2001 SC 260: 2000 AIR SCW 4340: (2001) 2 SCC 666.

ruling in that case. The Court directed that the seniority of the GM candidates be restored accordingly.

(5) Article 16(4A) and (4B) flow from article 16(4)

The 85th Amendment was challenged in *M. Nagraj* v. *Union of India*[1]. In this landmark judgment a five judge Bench unanimously held that the Constitutional Amendment by which article 16(4A) & (4B) have been inserted flow from article 16(4) and do not alter the basic structure of article 16(4) laid down in *Keshavanand Bharati* v. *State of Kerala.* They also said that providing reservations in promotion with consequential seniority impairs administrative efficiency contemplated under article 335. Hence they do not dilute the Constitutional requirements of 50% ceiling on reservations , creamy layer concept etc. In other words the 50% ceiling rule is still applicable.

(a) *Mandal case* had laid down that 50% ceiling limit shall apply to current as well as to backlog vacancies. To overcome the political hardship created by such rulings the Constitution was amended in 2000 by 81st Amendment and article 16(4B) was introduced. In its ultimate analysis it exempted the 50% ceiling limit from being applicable while filling up backlog vacancies and that the backlog vacancies form a class by themselves. Thus, the vacancies in subsequent years can go even beyond 50% and may even touch 100%. This is the fallout of the 81st Amendment.

(b) It is submitted that it would not be exaggeration to say that article 16 is a political history of cunning and shrewd political manoeuvrings in the field of public employment with an eye on the vote bank. Probably the *Mandal* kind of agitation has been avoided because of the Information Technology revolution and the private employers due to which the youngsters are not that lured by Government jobs. They have taken recourse to private employments.

SBI SC/ST Employees Assn. v. *State Bank of India*[2]

(a) SBI framed a reservation policy in promotions under which 22 ½ % was reserved in favour of SCs/STs. The vacancies which could not be filled up were to be carried over for three years. But in any one year the maximum reservations was not to exceed 50%. If at the end of 3 years the vacancies could not be filled up it was to be treated as lapsed and it could not be revived and filled up retrospectively. Supreme Court upheld the policy and observed that article 16(4) is an enabling provision. It gives discretion to the State to make reservations in favour of backward class of citizens who are not adequately represented in State services. It neither imposes a duty to make reservations nor does it confer a right to demand reservation.

Ashok Kumar Thakur v. *State of Bihar*[3] Supreme Court quashed the criteria for determination of the creamy layer laid down by the Bihar and UP Government

1. AIR 2007 SC 71: 2006 AIR SCW 5482: (2006) 8 SCC 212.
2. (1996) 4 SCC 119: AIR 1996 SC 1838: 1996 AIR SCW 2138.
3. AIR 1996 SC 75: 1995 AIR SCW 3731: (1995) 5 SCC 403.

for it contravened the *Mandal Judgment* and also the criteria laid down by Central Government[1] under which being a son or a daughter of an IAS or IPS Officer or a Class I Officer in Government service constituted creamy layer. But the two State Governments had laid down additional criteria like "and the wife or husband is at least a graduate; salary is Rs. 10000 or more etc". The result was that in spite of being in All India Service if additional criteria was not satisfied his children could avail the benefit of reservations. This violated article 16(4) and article 14 as it was arbitrary and defeated the very object of creamy layer concept.

State of Bihar v. *Bal Mukund Sah*[2] —Bihar Reservations of Posts and Services for SCs and STs and other OBCs Act, 1991 was held violative of articles 233 to 235 and article 309. It provided reservations for direct recruitment to the posts in the Subordinate Judicial Service of the State and the posts of District Judges and of the lower Judiciary. The proposal of the Bihar Government to provide for reservations of posts in Subordinate Judicial Service was turned down by the High Court in 1991 and the High Court proceeded as per the 1951 Rules which did not provide for reservations. However the Government issued an advertisement reserving 50% of the judicial posts. The High Court quashed the advertisement. The Governor then issued an Ordinance to the same effect which later became an Act. It was held invalid. The recruitment to the Judicial Services of the State is governed by articles 233, 234, 235. The said articles are not subject to laws made by the State or the Centre. Hence these articles override any law made by the appropriate Legislature in exercise of power under article 309. In addition article 16(4) must be read with article 335. Efficiency in administration in the making of appointments to services and posts is a *sine qua non* before making reservations in judicial services.

Chattar Singh v. *State of Rajasthan*[3] *SCs & STs are a different category from OBCs*: Supreme Court held that SCs and STs are a different category from OBCs. Though they are also eligible for reservations under article 16(4) they are a distinct class. Though they are socially and educationally backward they do not suffer the same social handicaps inflicted upon the SCs and STs. Hence excluding them from the 5% relaxation for cut off marks for admission to the Public Service Commission Main Examinations does not violate article 16(4)

P.G. Institute of Medical and Research Chandigarh v. *Faculty Assn.*[4] – *No reservation in a single post cadre:* A Five Judge Bench held that there could be no reservations in a single post cadre either directly or by rotation of roaster point. Such total exclusion of General Merit candidates amounts to 100% reservations which violates article 16(1) & (4A) of the Constitution.

State of Karnataka v. *K. Govindappa*[5] reservation was not available for a single post of lecturer in History – court held that in the absence of duality of posts

1. In Para 2(b)(c)(i) of Column 3 of Schedule to Government of India Memorandum dt 8-9-1993.
2. AIR 2000 SC 1296: 2000 AIR SCW 1180: (2000) 4 SCC 640.
3. AIR 1997 SC 303: 1997 AIR SCW 52: (1996) 11 SCC 742.
4. AIR 1998 SC 1767: 1998 AIR SCW 1553: (1998) 4 SCC 1.
5. AIR 2009 SC 618: 2008 AIR SCW 7774: (2009) 1 SCC 1.

if the rule of reservations is applied it amounts to 100% reservations which is not permissible.

Indira Sawhney v. *Union of India II*[1] Kerala Government passed an Act in 1995 that there were no creamy layers in the State of Kerala and gave retrospective effect to the Act from 1992. This was in order to overcome the politically inconvenient judgment of the Supreme Court in *Mandal* – given in 1992 – that reservations to backward classes in Government jobs could be given only after excluding the creamy layer "the declaration is a mere cloak and is unrelated to facts in existence" said the Supreme Court and the Act was held unconstitutional.

---

1. AIR 2000 SC 498: 1999 AIR SCW 4661: (2000) 1 SCC 168.

CHAPTER 9

ABOLITION OF UNTOUCHABILITY, TITLES

(Articles 17-18)

SYNOPSIS

(A) Abolition of Untouchability

Articles 14-18 deal with right to equality. Articles 14-16 have been dealt with in the earlier chapters.

Article 17 lays down that untouchability is abolished and its practice in any form is forbidden. The enforcement of any disability arising out of 'untouchability' shall be an offence.

(1) Untouchability – Not defined

Untouchability is neither defined in the Constitution nor in the Act. It is not to be understood in its grammatical sense. It is to be understood as the 'practice as it had developed historically in this country. It is the product of the Hindu caste system under which a particular section of the Hindu section was looked down by other sections.

(2) Protection of Civil Rights Act, 1955

In exercise of article 35 Parliament has enacted the Untouchability (Offences) Act, 1955. It has been made more stringent by the Amendment in 1976, it is now renamed as Protection of Civil Rights Act, 1955. Term 'civil right is defined as any right accruing to a person by reason of abolition of untouchability by article 17 of the Constitution. Under the amended Act any discrimination on the ground of untouchability shall be considered an offence. It imposes a duty on public servants to investigate such offences. It provides that if a public servant wilfully neglects the investigation of any offence punishable under this Act he shall be deemed to have abetted an offence punishable under this Act. The punishment prescribed is imprisonment up to 6 months and also a fine up to Rs. 500

People's Union for Democratic Rights v. *Union of India*[1] the Supreme Court has held that Fundamental right under article 17 is available against private individuals. It is the Constitutional duty of the State to take necessary steps to see that these Fundamental rights are not violated. Article 15(2) also helps in the eradication of untouchability. Thus on the grounds of untouchability no person can be denied access to shops, public restaurants, use of wells, places of

1. AIR 1982 SC 1473: (1982) 2 SCC 494: 1982 (II) LLJ 454.

entertainment, tanks, bathing ghats public resorts maintained wholly or partly out of State funds or dedicated to the use of general public.

(B) Abolition of titles under Article 18

Article 18 prohibits State to confer titles on anybody whether a citizen or a non-citizen. Military and academic distinctions are exempted from the prohibition. They are an incentive for further efforts in perfection.

Conferment of titles of Bharat Ratna, Padmavibhushan and Padmashree are not prohibited under article 18 as they denote State recognition of good work as citizens in various fields of activity. National awards do not amount to titles within the meaning of article 18.[1]

---

1. *Balaji Raghavan* v. *Union of India*, AIR 1996 SC 770.

CHAPTER 10

PROTECTION OF FREEDOM OF SPEECH ETC.

(Article 19)

SYNOPSIS

A. Introduction

B. Five heads of right to freedom (Articles 19-22)

C. Protection of certain rights regarding freedom of speech etc., (Article 19)

D. Restrictions under Article 19(2) to (6)

E. Tests of reasonable restrictions in *Chintamani Rao* case

Tests laid down in Chintamani Rao v. State of Madhya Pradesh

F. Direct effect of law on Fundamental right—A true test

G. Freedom of speech and expression

- (1) Need for the freedom of speech and expression
- (2) Meaning and scope of article 19(1)
- (3) Includes rights not expressly included under Article 19(1)(a)
- (4) Freedom of Press

H. Freedom to Assemble—Articles 19(1)(b) and 19(3)

I. Freedom to form Associations and Unions—Article 19(1)(c)

- (1) No hearing given before banning the association - void
- (2) Right to strike - Not Fundamental right
- (3) Object of the association - Not protected under Article 19(1)(c)
- (4) Imposition of members—Unconstitutional
- (5) Unlawful Activities Prevention Act, 1967
- (6) Includes right not to join an association
- (7) Special provisions for police and Armed Forces

J. Freedom of Movement—Article 19(1)(d) and 19(5)

K. Freedom of residence under article 19(1)(e) and 19(5)

L. Freedom to acquire, hold and dispose of property—Article 19(1)(f) and (5)

M. Freedom of profession, occupation, trade or business—Article 19(1)(g)

- (1) Condition of service & restriction
- (2) Protection of livelihood
- (3) Trading in liquor
- (4) Trading on pavements
- (5) Pursuing 2 professions
- (6) Lottery business
- (7) Sale of eggs
- (8) Ban on paan masala
- (9) Ban on transport of sand
- (10) Ban on cow slaughter
- (11) Ban on bidi manufacture
- (12) Nationalisation of text books
- (13) Right to work—Not protected
- (14) Protection from fraudulent financial establishments
- (15) Conditional licences

A. Introduction

Our Constitution guarantees right to freedom as a Fundamental right. Fundamental rights occupy a place of pride in the Constitution. The State cannot take away or abridge the Fundamental rights as is laid down in article 13.

B. Five heads of right to freedom (Articles 19-22)

The fundamental right to freedom is covered under five heads.

(1) Protection of certain rights regarding freedom of speech etc., (Article 19).
(2) Protection in respect of conviction of offences (Article 20)
(3) Protection of life and personal liberty (Article 21)
(4) Right to education (Article 21A).
(5) Protection against arrest and detention in certain cases (Article 22).

C. Protection of certain rights regarding freedom of speech etc. (Article 19)

Freedoms relating to speech etc., are valuable freedoms available to every citizen. They are not available to non-citizens. Corporation, or a company cannot claim this right as they are not natural persons. But in *Bank Nationalisation* case the court has held that though a company cannot claim a right under article 19 its shareholder can claim the right guaranteed by article 19 if by the State action the right of the company and that of the shareholders is impaired.

Article 19 guarantees to the citizens of India six Fundamental freedoms. None of these freedoms are absolute. They are subject to reasonable restrictions laid down from article 19(2) to (6). They lay down the purposes for which these rights can be restricted.

Though article 19(1) guarantees the six freedoms expressly, it has been held that it also takes within its fold – rights not specifically mentioned but which are implicit[1] *for example* – freedom of speech and expression includes right to information; right to know; etc., though right to information is not specifically mentioned in article 19(1)(a) – it has been read into it.

The rights are not made absolute because they have to be balanced against the rights of the others and of the community as a whole. "Man as a rational being desires to do many things but in a civil society his desires have to be controlled, regulated and reconciled with the exercise of similar desires by other individuals."[2]

D. Restrictions under Article 19(2) to (6)

The following chart shows the Fundamental rights under article 19(1)(a) to (g) alongwith the *restrictions under Article 19(2) to (6)*

Fundamental freedoms (Article 19)	Reasonable restrictions in the interest of:
Freedom of speech and expression (19)(1)(a)	(i) Sovereignty and integrity of India (ii) Security of the State (iii) Friendly relations with (i) foreign State (iv) Public order

1. *Maneka Gandhi* v. *Union of India*, AIR 1978 SC 597: (1978) 1 SCC 248: (1978) 2 SCR 621; *Kharak Singh* v. *State of Uttar Pradesh*, AIR 1963 SC 1295: (1963) 2 Cr LJ 329: (1964) 1 SCR 332.
2. *A.K. Gopalan* v. *State of Madras*, AIR 1950 SC 27: 1950 SCJ 174: 51 Cr LJ 1383.

	(v) Decency (vi) Morality or In relation to (vii) Contempt of court (viii) Defamation (ix) Incitement of an offence Article 19(2)
Freedom to assemble peaceably and without arms (19)(1)(b)	(i) Sovereignty and integrity of India (ii) Public order Article 19(3)
Freedom to form associations or unions (19)(1)(c)	(i) Sovereignty and integrity of India (ii) Public order (iii) Morality Article 19(4)
Freedom to move freely throughout the territory of India (19)(1)(d) Freedom to reside and settle in any part of the territory of India (19)(1)(e)	(i) in the interest of general public (ii) for the protection of the interests of any Scheduled Tribe Article 19(5)
Freedom to practice any profession, occupation trade or business (19)(1)(g)	(i) general public (ii) prescribing professional or technical qualifications for practising any profession etc. (iii) carrying on of any business by the State to the complete or partial exclusion of citizens Article 19(6)

Freedom to acquire, hold and dispose of Property (19)(1)(f) – deleted by 44th Constitution Amendment Act

E. Test of reasonable restrictions in *Chintamani Rao Case*

Restrictions must be—(a) reasonable and not arbitrary and (b) must be for the purposes mentioned in the Constitution under article 19(2) to (6).

Restrictions can be imposed only by law; not by executive: Restrictions can be imposed only by a law and not by executive or departmental instructions. They must not be arbitrary or excessive in nature *i.e.,* beyond that which is required in the interests of the public.

Tests laid down in Chintamani Rao* v. *State of Madhya Pradesh

The Supreme Court has laid down the following tests[1] for determining the reasonableness of the restrictions.

(1) Courts to determine the reasonableness of the restriction

It is for the courts to determine the reasonableness of the restriction and not for the Legislature; If it is unreasonable the court strikes it down as void. The restriction must be reasonable both from the viewpoint of the substantive law and procedural law.[2] The word 'reasonable' thus widens the scope of judicial review.

1. *Chintamanrao* v. *State of Madhya Pradesh,* AIR 1951 SC 118: 1950 SCJ 571: 1950 SCR 759.
2. *N.B. Khare* v. *State of Delhi,* AIR 1950 SC 211.

(2) Word 'reasonable' means intelligent care and deliberation

(3) Reasonableness to be decided on the facts of the case

There is no absolute test for determining the reasonableness of the restriction. It has to be decided based on facts and circumstances of the case.

(4) Restriction to secure objects of Directive Principles

A restriction imposed for securing the objects laid down in the Directive Principles may be regarded as reasonable.

(5) Test of a reasonable man applied

Court must determine the reasonableness of restriction by objective standard and not by subjective one. That is – it is to be seen whether a normal reasonable man would regard the restriction as reasonable. The judges must not bring in their philosophy and ideology in the determination of the reasonableness.[1]

(6) Reasonableness of the restriction to be determined

Court must determine the reasonableness of the restriction and not that of the law. Mere possibility of the abuse of power by the executive authority is not the test for determining the reasonableness of restriction.

(7) Restrictions may also amount to prohibition under certain circumstances

(8) Freedom of speech and expression of legislators is wider than under Article 19

Freedom of speech available to an MP or an MLA under articles 105(1) and 194 is wider than the freedom of speech and expression available to other citizens under article 19(1)(a) as the former is not subject to limitations under article 19(2). Thus, freedom of speech under article 19 is subject to Parliamentary privileges under the Constitution.

F. Direct effect of law on Fundamental right—A true test

The court held that the direct effect of the law on the Fundamental right is the true test to determine the question whether the law violates article 19 or other Fundamental right and not the subject-matter of the legislation in *Bennet Coleman* v. *Union of India*[2] the Central Government argued that increasing the cost of paper was to ration the imported commodity and not to restrict or take away freedom of speech and expression. The court did not agree with the Government that the substance of law must be taken into consideration and not its effect to determine whether the law infringes article 19. The 'effect' test has been applied in *Maneka Gandhi* case, *Bank Nationalisation* case and *Gopalan case* and many other cases.

G. Freedom of speech and expression

(1) Need for the freedom of speech and expression

Freedom of speech and expression is the foundation on which a successful democracy is based. For a successful democracy people need to know the facts; form opinion and express the same. It is the first condition of liberty. So many other rights depend for their meaningfulness on the freedom of speech and expression. It is described as a bulwark of democratic Government. It facilitates

1. *State of Madras* v. *V.S. Roo*, AIR 1952 SC 196: 1952 SCR 597: 1952 Cr LJ 966.
2. AIR 1973 SC 106: (1972) 2 SCC 788: 1973 (1) SCJ 177.

in participative Government and in the discovery of truth and proper human right relations. A major source of information and an avenue for expression of opinion and communicate the same to the country, rather the world at large is newspaper. Hence the Government should be cautious while levying taxes on matters concerning newspaper industry than while levying taxes on other matters.[1]

(2) Meaning and scope of article 19(1)

- Right to express one's own convictions and opinions freely by words of mouth, writing, printing pictures or any other mode
- It includes expression of ideas through any communicable medium or visible representation such as gesture signs
- It connotes publication and freedom of the press. Liberty of circulation
- To propagate one's own views and also that of other's.
- Liberty to form one's own opinion, belief and to communicate to others through whatever means

The importance and relevance and the wide scope of freedom of speech and expression is stated in a gist in the following cases:

In *Maneka Gandhi* "democracy is based essentially on free debate and open discussion, ... every citizen must be entitled to participate in the democratic process and in order to enable him to intelligently exercise his right of making a choice, free and general discussion of public matters is absolutely essential".[2]

In *Whitney* v. *California*[3] Louis Brandeis made the classic statement equally applicable in India: "those who won our independence believed that the final end of State was to make men free to develop their faculties...they believed liberty to be the secret of happiness and courage to be the secret of liberty. They believed that the freedom to think as you will and to speak as you think are means indispensable to the discovery and spread of political truth: that without free speech and Assembly discussion would be futile ... that public discussion is a political duty and that this should be the fundamental principle of the American Government "

Associated Press v. *United States*, 326 US 1 (1945) "it is the purpose of the First Amendment to preserve an uninhibited market place of ideas in which truth will ultimately prevail rather than to countenance monopolisation of that market- whether it be by the Government itself or a private licensee,"

What is to be noted is that what has been given to us as a Fundamental right of speech and expression from the inception of the Constitution itself- was brought by way of an Amendment in America.

(3) Includes Rights not expressly included under article 19(1)(a)

Freedom of speech and expression has been interpreted very broadly by the Judiciary so as to include rights not expressly covered by article 19(1)(a).

---

1. *Indian Express Newspapers (Bombay) Private Ltd.* v. *Union of India*, (1985) 1 SCC 641: AIR 1986 SC 515: (1985) 2 SCR 287; *Reliance Petrochemicals Ltd.* v. *Proprietors of Indian Express Newspapers Bombay Pvt. Ltd.*, AIR 1989 SC 190: (1988) 4 SCC 592: 1988 Cr LJ 778.
2. AIR 1978 SC 597: (1978) 1 SCC 248: (1978) 2 SCR 621.
3. (1926) 274 US 357: 71 Law Ed 1095: 47 S. Ct. 641.

(1) *Right to information:* The Parliament has passed the Right to Information Act in 2005, which makes it mandatory for the public authorities covered under the Act to disclose the information requested for by any citizen. But that does not mean that until 2005 the doors of information regarding the functioning of the Government were totally closed.

(2) *Right to know the facts about administration:* In *S.P. Gupta* v. *Union of India*[1] – the question was whether correspondence between the Law Minister, the CJ of Delhi and the Chief Justice of India was protected from disclosure. The Supreme Court emphasized that citizen's right to know the true facts about administration of the country is one of the pillars of a democratic State. It said that it failed to see how when non-appointment of Additional judge and the transfer of a High Court Judge is challenged- how the disclosure of correspondence between the CJs of the State and of India and the Law Minister could be said to be injurious to public interest. Rather they would shed light on the question whether there was a full and effective consultation as contemplated under the Constitution. Harm caused to public interest in justice by non-disclosure would far outweigh the injury which may possibly be caused by their disclosure. Hence in order to maintain public confidence in the independent functioning of judiciary people should know whether Constitutional requirements were complied with before decision was taken not to continue the additional judge.

(3) *Freedom of speech includes right to acquire and disseminate information: Secy., Ministry of Information and Broadcasting, Government of India* v. *Cricket Assn. of India, Bengal*[2] it was held that freedom of speech and expression includes right to acquire information and to disseminate it . It enables people to contribute to debates of social and moral issues. It is the best way to find a truest model of anything since it is only through it that the widest possible range of ideas can circulate. In this case Supreme Court has held that the Government has no monopoly on electronic media and a citizen has a right to telecast and broadcast to the viewers/listeners through electronic media. Restrictions can be based only on grounds mentioned in article 19(2). State monopoly on electronic media is not mentioned as a reasonable restriction.

In this case *Cricket Assn of Bengal* was allowed to telecast the Six Nations International Cricket Tournament to be held in India and also upheld the agreement with TWI (Trans World International) for telecasting all the matches out of India and asked the DD to provide signals to the foreign TV for telecasting the matches to the foreign viewers.

(4) *Commercial speech – advertisement is a part of freedom of speech and expression:* In this case, Mahanagar Telephone Nigam published telephone directories. It contained white pages and yellow pages. Yellow pages consisted of advertisements procured by the contractors to whom the printing, publication and distribution of telephone directories was outsourced.

1. AIR 1982 SC 149: 1982 Raj LR 389: 1981 Supp SCC 87.
2. AIR 1995 SC 1236: 1995 AIR SCW 1856: (1995) 2 SCC 161.

Now Tata Press Ltd., published 'Tata Press Yellow pages' comprising paid advertisements from businessmen, traders and professionals. The Nigam contended that it had the monopoly to publish the same. Supreme Court held that it had no monopoly over the yellow pages. Advertising is 'commercial speech' it is dissemination of information regarding the product advertised. Public also has a right to receive it.[1]

In *Hamdard Dawakhana* v. *Union of India*[2] Drug and Magic Remedies (Objectionable Advertisements) Act put restrictions on advertisement of certain drugs and prohibited advertisements of magical qualities of the drugs for curing diseases. It was challenged as violating article 19(1)(a). Supreme Court did not agree and held that though advertisement is a form of speech every advertisement is not a matter of dealing with the freedom of speech and expression of ideas. In this case it was trade and not propagation of ideas. Advertisement of prohibited drugs is not protected under article 19(1)(a). After the *Tata Nigam case* Hamdard Dawakhana has a limited application. That it prohibits obnoxious advertisement and cannot be applied to general advertisement as such.

(5) *Voters' right to know about the contesting candidates:* Mafia links with bureaucrats: *Dinesh Trivedi, MP* v. *Union of India*[3]. The Vohra Committee Report had exposed the criminalization of politics. It had established mafia links with the bureaucrats, Judiciary, NGO etc. Dinesh Trivedi – a Rajya Sabha MP filed PIL seeking for disclosure of the material based on which Report was given and to reveal the names of bureaucrats, etc., who were named therein. Court did not direct such disclosures. The Report was so sensitive that Mr. Vohra had himself drafted and alone signed the Report and made only 3 copies (MOS, HM and one for himself). It was information gathered from Heads of various Intelligence Agencies. Disclosures would cause great harm to agencies involved and to conditions of assured secrecy and confidentiality under which they function.

(6) *Information about contesting candidates: Union of India* v. *PUCL.*,[4] The court directed Election Commission to secure to the voters – information about whether the contesting candidate is accused of an offence punishable with imprisonment, disclosure of assets, facts giving insight to candidate's competence, capacity and suitability, educational qualifications etc. But having regard to increasing criminalization of politics in order to equip the citizens to vote for a competent candidate it was held the people have a right to know about educational qualification and about criminal cases filed/convicted etc.

---

1. (1995) 5 SCC 139: AIR 1995 SC 2438: 1995 AIR SCW 3602.
2. AIR 1960 SC 554: (1960) 2 SCR 671: 1960 Cr LJ 735.
3. (1997) 4 SCC 306: JT 1997 (4) SC 237.
4. AIR 2002 SC 2112: (2002) 5 SCC 294: 2002 AIR SCW 2186.

(7) *PUCL* v. *Union of India and Assn. for Democratic Reforms* v. *Union of India*[1] under the amendment to the Representation of People Act, 2002 a candidate was required to disclose whether he was accused/convicted of any crime etc. but not his assets and liabilities. The provision (section 33B) was challenged as the candidate was not liable to disclose any other information other than those mentioned in the Act notwithstanding any judgment, order, or direction of any court or of the Election Commission. The court held that it amounted to blatantly asking the candidates not to obey the court decisions and hence was unconstitutional as being beyond the legislative competence. It was argued by the Union of India that voters' right to know the antecedents of the candidate is not a fundamental right but only a derivative fundamental right on the basis of the interpretation of article 19(1)(a). The contention was rejected by the court saying that there is no such thing as a derivative fundamental right; that fundamental rights have no fixed content, most of them are empty vessels into which each generation must pour its content in the light of its experience;

The court quoted from *Sakal Papers' case*: "the faith in the popular Government rests on the dictum: 'let the people have the truth and the freedom to discuss it all will go well'. Thus the right of the voter to know the bio-data of a candidate is the foundation of democracy.

Right to interview the undertrial by the Press is not an unfettered right. Competing interests of the Press and the jail authorities who are refusing permission must be weighed by the court.[2]

(8) *LIC* v. *Manubhai Shah*[3] the respondent published a research Paper titled – "Fraud on Policy Holders – A Shocking Story'. An LIC member published a counter in a magazine called 'Yogakshema' an in-house magazine. Manubhai requested the LIC to publish his rejoinder in the same magazine. LIC refused to do so because 'yogakshema' was an in-house magazine in which the members express their views regarding their activities; and that it is not sold in the open market. Court did not agree with the contentions of the LIC. It held that LIC is a 'State' under article 12 and it must function in the best interest of the community. The community is entitled to know about the functioning of LIC; 'yogakshema' is printed out of public money. Manubhai is entitled to get his rejoinder printed as it is his Fundamental right of speech and expression

In another case- Doordarshan had refused to telecast a documentary on Bhopal Gas tragedy as its contents were outdated. High Court held that Doordarshan's refusal was based on an executive order and not law within the meaning of article 19(2). Doordarshan is a State funded agency and controlled by the State. The public too has an interest in knowing what has happened and what is happening in connection with the Bhopal Gas Tragedy. The court directed the Doordarshan to telecast it. It explained

1. AIR 2003 SC 2363: 2003 AIR SCW 2353: (2003) 4 SCC 399.
2. *State* v. *Charita*.
3. (1992) 3 SCC 637: AIR 1993 SC 171: 1992 AIR SCW 3099.

the scope of freedom of speech and expression – it includes freedom to circulate one's views by words or in writing or through audio-visual instrumentalities. The print media and the radio and the screen plays – play an important role towards the growth of a healthy democracy. Any attempt to stifle this right would sound the death knell of democracy. Freedom to air one's views is the lifeline of democracy. Hence, denial can be based only on the prescribed reasonable restrictions under article 19(2). The burden of proving that the restriction is reasonable and justified under article 19(2) is on the State. Freedom to communicate and also to receive information is a Fundamental right guaranteed under article 19(1)(a). This freedom of speech and expression must be exercised so as not to trench on the rights of other citizens or to jeopardise public interest.

(9) In *M. Hassan* v. *Government of Andhra Pradesh*[1] it was held that denial by the jail authorities to a journalist and a videographer to interview the condemned prisoners in jail amounts to deprivation of their Fundamental right of freedom of speech and expression under article 19(1)(a). The reasons for denial were that the public may campaign for reducing the sentence; it may lower the position of the court; it may jeopardise safety and security; the prisoner had not asked to be interviewed. Court held that these restrictions were not mentioned under article 19(2). If there is any objectionable element in it under the Cinematograph Act, 1952 there are checks and counter checks to set them right. Jail manual permits the prisoner to be interviewed by others including friends- a friend includes a journalist. Hence the interview by the Press was allowed.

(10) In *State of Uttar Pradesh* v. *Raj Narain*[2] the Supreme Court held that freedom of speech and expression takes within its fold the right of the citizens to know and receive information regarding matters of public importance. The citizens have a right to know every public transaction and every public act that is done in a public way by their public functionaries using public fund.

(11) Anti-defection law was passed by the Government to improve and strengthen the democratic fabric of the country. Hence prohibition of defection of MLAs &MPs could not amount to infringement of freedom of speech and expression under article 19(1)(a).[3]

An exhibitor of Video films cannot claim protection of article 19(1)(a) because he is not propagating ideas. It is just a commercial activity. But circulation of newspapers and magazines continues with the publisher but the film after production goes out of the producer's hands for being exhibited by such persons as are totally unconnected with production.[4]

(12) *Marriage beyond caste*: Article 19 right to marry a person of one's choice outside one's caste is a right under article 19 – freedom of expression

---

1. AIR 1998 AP 35: 1997 (6) Andh LD 826: 1997 (6) Andh LT 209.
2. AIR 1975 SC 865: (1975) 4 SCC 428: (1975) 3 SCR 333.
3. *Shri Kihota Hollohon* v. *Zachilhu*, AIR 1993 SC 412: 1992 AIR SCW 3497: (1992) 1 SCR 686.
4. *Sitar Video* v. *State of Uttar Pradesh*, AIR 1994 All 25: 1994 All LJ 136: 1994 (2) Civ LJ 558.

and of conscience. The police has no right to interfere in their conjugal affairs.[1]

(13) *Banning of "Bandit Queen': Bobby Art International* v. *Om Pal Singh Hoon*[2] the Supreme Court held that restriction of the exhibition of the film 'Bandit Queen' is unreasonable. It said that 'nakedness does not always arouse the baser instincts. Bandit Queen tells a powerful human story and to that story the scenes of Phoolan Devi's enforced naked is central. It helps to explain why she became a dacoit. Her rape and vendetta against the society that had heaped indignities upon her forced her to revolt against the society.

(14) *A. Raja* v. *P. Srinivas – violation of right to privacy:* Publishing family photographs of Cabinet Minister including that of a minor child amounts to violation of the right of the child by exposing identity and family relationship of minister; publication of the photos of the wife who is neither a public figure nor in public domain infringes her right to privacy.[3] It amounts to violation of article 19(1)(a).

(4) Freedom of Press

A free Press is the Fourth Estate in a democracy- the other three being – the Executive, the Legislature, Judiciary. The democratic credentials of a State are judged by the extent of freedom enjoyed by the Press. J. Douglas said "acceptance by Government of a dissident (dissenting) Press is a measure of the maturity of the nation."[4]

(1) *No specific mention in Constitution:* In India, there is no specific provision laying down the freedom of the Press. It is a part and parcel of the freedom of speech and expression and implicit under article 19(1)(a)[5]; "a species of which freedom of expression is a genus"[6]. Press enjoys no special privilege apart from what the ordinary citizens enjoy. Dr. Ambedkar said[7]: "press has no special rights which are not given to or exercised by the citizen in his individual capacity. The editor of the Press or the manager is merely exercising the right of expression, and therefore no special mention is necessary of the freedom of the Press." Press is a great source of information. Facts, opinion, articles, views and editorial published therein enlightens the citizens about the functioning of the administration and helps them to form a considered opinion based on reliable information. During the internal emergency in 1976, the way Press was censored that the Indian Express had on an occasion left its editorial space blank. Editorial in a newspaper is a space where the editor takes the readers beyond the facts and expresses his free, frank and a studied opinion on the burning affairs of the State and makes the readers ponder

1. *Ashok Kumar Todi* v. *Kishwar Jahan,* AIR 2011 SC 1254.
2. (1996) 4 SCC 1: AIR 1996 SC 1846: 1996 AIR SCW 2156.
3. *A. Raja* v. *P. Srinivasan,* AIR 2010 Mad 77: 2009 (8) Mad LJ 513: 2009 (5) Mad LW 117.
4. *Terminiello* v. *Chicago,* (1949) 337 US 1: 93 Law Ed 1131.
5. *Printers (Mysore) Ltd.* v. *Asst. Commercial Tax Officer,* (1994) 2 SCC 434: 1995 AIR SCW 204.
6. *Sakal Newspaper* v. *Union of India,* AIR 1962 SC 305: 1962 (2) SCJ 400: (1962) 3 SCR 842.
7. CAD Vol VII, 980.

over the point discussed. Editorial space being left blank spoke volumes about the low ebb at which the freedom of speech and expression was placed during emergency. It was a unique way of communicating through silence.

(2) *Newspaper: 2 aspects-commercial aspects and freedom of speech*: volume of circulation: Freedom of the Press includes freedom of circulation of a publication because without circulation publication is of little value.[1] In *Sakal Newspaper*, An Act and a Government Order[2] regulated the number of pages according to the price charged; prescribed the number of supplements to be published and regulated the size and area of advertisements in relation to other matters contained in a newspaper. The result was that it reduced circulation of some newspapers by making their price unattractively high. Reduction of advertisements would reduce the incoming revenue leading to raising the prices of the newspaper and reduced circulation. This violated article 19(1)(a) for it includes the right of publication and the volume of circulation.[3] The court did not agree with the Government that the object of the Act was to regulate commercial aspects of the newspaper and not the freedom of speech because commercial aspects fall under article 19(1)(g) read with restrictions under article 19(6); and freedom of speech falls under article 19(1)(a) read with article 19(2). Hence as far as freedom of speech is concerned reasonable restrictions have to be justified under article 19(2) and when freedom to carry on business is alleged to be violated it has to be justified under article 19(6).

(3) *Volume of news and views: Bennet Coleman & Co.* v. *Union of India,* AIR 1973 SC 106: (1972) 2 SCC 788: 1973 (1) SCJ 177 newsprint quota was fixed by the Government because of the shortage of newsprint. The actual consumption for 1970-71 or 1971-72 which ever was less was taken as the base. For dailies with a circulation of 100000 copies 10% increase and for larger circulations 3% increase was allowed. The policy of the Government was to curtail the circulation of big newspapers which could not increase the number of pages, page area or periodicity by reducing circulation to meet their requirements even within their admissible quota of newsprint. Supreme Court declared the policy as void and unconstitutional. The Government could not in the garb of regulating distribution of newsprint control the growth and circulation of newspapers. It became the newspaper control policy. Newsprint quota could be fixed on a reasonable basis but post-quota restrictions was not permissible. The policy of limiting all papers – small and large; whether in English or vernacular language to 10 pages was held to be discriminatory as it treated unequals as equals. Freedom of speech lies not only in the volume of circulation but also in the volume of news and views.

---

1. *Romesh Thappar* v. *State of Madras,* AIR 1950 SC 124: 1950 SCR 594: 1950 Cr LJ 1514.
2. The Newspaper (Price and Circulation) Act, 1956 & The Daily Newspaper (Price & Page) Order, 1960.
3. *Sakal Newspaper* v. *Union of India,* AIR 1962 SC 305: 1962 (2) SCJ 400: (1962) 3 SCR 842.

(4) *Newsprint – not totally exempt from taxes*: Expression is the soul of article 19(1)(a) – newsprint-its body: In *Indian Express Newspaper (Bombay) Pvt. Ltd*. The petitioners challenged levy of customs duty on imported newsprint on the ground that it was excessive and it led to increase in the price of newspaper resulting in reduction of their circulation and hence it violated the freedom of speech and expression. Supreme Court accepting the contention held that imposition of excessive tax on newsprint amounted to tax on knowledge and would virtually amount to a burden on a man for being literate and for being conscious of his duty as a citizen to inform himself on the world around him. Court directed the Government to reconsider the taxes levied. It did not agree that the newsprint is totally exempt from taxes because the petitioners were using the State amenities like post, communication etc, for which they also had to bear the common fiscal burden like the others. If expression is the soul of freedom of speech, newsprint is its body. Hence the court has to reconcile social interest in the freedom of speech with the public interest in the fiscal levies. Working Journalists (Conditions of Service) and Miscellaneous Provisions Act, 1955 enacted to regulate conditions of service of the newspaper employees does not violate article 19(1)(a). Labour and service laws Amendment also applicable to them.

(5) In *Express Newspaper Pvt. Ltd* v. *Union of India*[1] Government of India had allotted plots of land to the Express on lease for construction of buildings. Express Buildings were constructed. Later Lt. Governor of Delhi served a notice for re-entry and building demolition. Court held that the impugned notices were an immediate and direct treat to the freedom of the Press intended to silence the voice of Indian Express and was unconstitutional.

(6) In *Ajay Goswami* v. *Union of India*[2] when art and obscenity are mixed – what is to be seen is whether art outweighs obscenity or *vice versa*. A blanket ban on publication of obscene material to shield juvenile innocence cannot be imposed.

(7) In *Odyssey Communications Pvt. Ltd* v. *Lokvidyan Sanghatana*[3] Supreme Court refused to restrain the telecasting of the serial *'Hony Anhony'*. The petitioners contended that the serial spreads false or blind beliefs and superstition amongst the members of the public. Court did not agree. It held that freedom of speech could be curtailed only on the grounds mentioned under article 19(2). The telecast was not likely to endanger public morality nor was it prejudicial to the community.

(8) In *Brij Bhushan* v. *State of Delhi*[4] Supreme Court held that pre-censorship of a journal is a restriction on the liberty of the Press. The printer, publisher

---

1. (1986) 1 SCC 133: AIR 1986 SC 872: 1986 (29) DLT 131.
2. AIR 2007 SC 493: 2007 AIR SCW 15: (2007) 1 SCC 143.
3. (1988) 3 SCC 410: AIR 1988 SC 1642: JT 1988 (3) SC 66.
4. AIR 1950 SC 129: 1950 SCR 605: (1950) 51 Cr LJ 1525.

editor of an English Weekly Organiser was directed to submit for scrutiny in duplicate before publication all communal matters and news and views about Pakistan including photographs and cartoons.

(9) In *Romesh Thappar* v. *State of Madras*[1] under the Maintenance of Public Order Act, 1949 Madras Government banned the entry of an English Weekly- 'Cross Road' which was published and printed in Bombay on grounds of 'public safety and maintenance of public order.' Court held that it was not a ground on which restriction could be imposed under article 19(2).

(10) Publication of private aspects gathered from public records: In *Auto Shanker case*[2] auto Shanker was sentenced to death for 6 murders. While inside the Jail he wrote his autobiography disclosing his close nexus with IAS, IPS officers – some of them were his partners in crime. He sought to get this published in a Weekly Magazine *'Nakheeran'*. The petitioners publicised that they would be coming up with a serial publication of the sensational life history of Auto Shanker. This sent shock waves among several police and prison officials. He was tortured and made to deny that he had written any such book. It was held that

- the petitioners had a right to publish the autobiography insofar as it appears from the public records even without his consent. That is publication of private aspects based on public records is not objectionable. Once a matter becomes a matter of public record the right to privacy no longer subsists and it is open for publication and comments.
- It is enough for the Press to prove that they published it after a reasonable verification of the facts. It is not necessary for the Press to prove that what is published is true.
- publishing his life story may invade his right to privacy
- prior restraint upon the publication of the alleged autobiography cannot be imposed. Remedy of the affected officials is after the publication.

(11) Film censorship is valid. *K.A. Abbas* v. *Union of India,* AIR 1971 SC 481: 1972 (1) SCA 1: (1971) 2 SCR 446 is the first case where the question of prior censorship arose. Under the Cinematograph Act, 1952 films are divided into U and A category-U-for unrestricted exhibition and A for adults. 'Tale of Two Cities' was refused U certificate. The petitioner contended that there were other forms of speech and expression besides the films and none of them were subject to prior restraint. It was held to be justified under article 19(2) because a motion picture was able to stir up emotions more deeply than any other product of art. Hence the classification was valid.

---

1. AIR 1950 SC 124: (1950) 51 Cr LJ 1514: 1950 SCR 594.
2. *R. Rajagopal* v. *State of Tamil Nadu,* AIR 1995 SC 264: 1994 AIR SCW 4420: (1994) 6 SCC 632.

(12) In *Ramesh* v. *Union of India*[1] the court refused to restrain the telecast of the serial 'Tamas' on the ground that the serial- viewed in its entirety could create a lasting impression of the message of peace and co-existence.

(13) *Orderly demonstration – valid:* Demonstrations are protected under freedom of speech and expression as long as they are not disorderly and violent. A demonstration is a visible manifestation of the feelings or sentiments of an individual or a group. It is thus a communication of one's ideas to others and is hence a form of speech and expression. Court struck down Bihar Government's order banning demonstration by Government servants in connection with their conditions of service. It held that the Government servants do not lose their Fundamental right under article 19 by virtue of the Government post.

(14) *Bandh-unconstitutional; compensation for loss*: Kerala High Court has held in a landmark decision in *Bharat Kumar Palicha* v. *State of Kerala*[2] that Bandh organised by political parties is unconstitutional. It violates the Fundamental right of the citizen. When a bandh is called people are expected not to travel, not to trade or attend to their work. A threat is held out weather expressly or impliedly that any attempt to go against call for Bandh may result in physical injury. While dismissing the appeal by the Communist Party of India the Supreme Court observed that a Bandh interferes with the Fundamental rights of other citizens and causes national loss in many ways. The Fundamental right of the people cannot be regarded as subservient to a claim of Fundamental right of an individual.[3] The Patna High Court held[4] that the Government is bound to pay compensation to those who suffer loss of life, liberty or property due to Bandh as it is the duty of the Government to protect the citizens. In appropriate cases even the organisers of the Bandh can be directed to pay compensation.

(15) In *Maneka Gandhi case*[5] question was whether right to travel abroad was a part of freedom of speech and expression under article 19(1)(a) and the freedom to practice profession under article 19(1)(g). Bhagwati J. held that freedom of speech can be exercised outside India as well. Hence impounding of the passport may restrict the exercise of this right abroad. The same is true of the freedom to practice a profession. However right to go abroad is not an essential part of article 19(1)(a) and article 19(1)(g). It is only a peripheral right. Hence, section 10(3)(c) Passport Act under which restrictions can be imposed cannot be held to be void under article 19(1)(a) or (g).

(16) Telephone tapping also is an infringement of the freedom of speech and expression

---

1. AIR 1988 SC 775: (1980) 2 SCR 315: (1980) Tax LR 303.
2. AIR 1997 Ker 291.
3. *Communist Party of India (M)* v. *Bharat Kumar*, AIR 1998 SC 184: 1997 AIR SCW 4147: (1998) 1 SCC 201.
4. *Ranchi Bar Association, Ranchi* v. *State of Bihar*, AIR 1999 Pat 169: 1999 (2) BLJ 731: 1999 (1) Pat LJR 922.
5. AIR 1978 SC 597: (1978) 1 SCC 248: (1978) 2 SCR 621.

Grounds of restriction under Article 19(2) to (6)

'in the interest of': Reasonable restrictions can be imposed 'in the interest of' public order etc., 'in the interest of' gives a larger leeway to the Legislature to curtail freedom of speech and expression. *For example* it can penalise activities having a 'tendency' to cause public disorder – though it may not have actually caused a public disorder. In other words the State can take preventive actions if the activities have a potential to create public disorder etc.

(a) *Security of the State*: in *Romesh Thappar* v. *State of Madras*, AIR 1950 SC 124: (1950) 51 Cr LJ 1514: 1950 SCR 594 – the Supreme Court held that every public disorder does not threaten 'security of the State'. The term 'security of the State' refers only serious and aggravated forms of public disorder like rebellion, waging war against the State, insurrection and not ordinary breaches of public order and public safety like unlawful assembly, riot.

(b) *Friendly relations with foreign State*: added by Constitution (1st Amendment) Act, 1951. Object is to prohibit unrestrained malicious propaganda against a foreign State which may prejudice friendly relations with a foreign country. In India, Foreign Relations Act provides punishment for libel by Indian citizens against foreign dignitaries. Foreign Recruiting Act empowers the Executive to prohibit recruitment of any citizen of India to the army of foreign States. Note that members of the Commonwealth including Pakistan is not a foreign country.

(c) *Public order:* Is a term introduced by the First Constitutional Amendment in 1951 to overcome the ruling in *Romesh Thappar* that 'ordinary breaches of public order' are not sufficient to impose restrictions on freedom of speech and expression. Public order is different from public tranquillity. *For example* a person playing loud music at night may disturb public tranquillity but not public order. In *Kishori Mohan* v. *State of West Bengal*[1] the Supreme Court explained that the three concepts of 'law and order; public order; and security of the State; are like three functional concentric circles – the largest representing 'law and order'; the next 'public order'; and the smallest 'security of the State'. Every infraction of law necessarily affects law and order but not necessarily public order and an act may affect public order but not necessarily security of the State. Anything that disturbs public peace disturbs public order. *For example,* communal disturbances are offences against public order. Public order implies absence of violence and on orderly state of affairs in which people can peaceably pursue their normal avocation in life.[2]

In *Supdt. Central Prison* v. *Ram Manohar Lohia*[3] section 3 of UP. Special Powers Act, 1932 punished a person if he incited a single person not

---

1. AIR 1972 SC 1749: 1972 SCD 805: 1973 SCC (Cri) 30.
2. *Basudeva* v. *Rex*, AIR 1949 All 513: 50 Cr LJ 798: 1949 ALJ 397.
3. AIR 1975 SC 633: (1974) 2 SCC 738: 1975 (I) LLJ 256.

to pay or defer the payment of Government dues was held invalid because there was no proximate nexus between the speech and public order. Court said that Fundamental right cannot be controlled on such imaginary considerations. In *Babulal Parate* v. *State of Madras*[1] Court upheld the validity of section 144 Cr.P.C. as an anticipatory action to prevent disorder. Under section 144 if a Magistrate is of the opinion that there is sufficient ground for immediate danger of breach of peace he can by a written order direct a person or persons to abstain from certain acts if he considers that such direction will prevent a riot, disturbance of public tranquillity.

(d) *Decency and morality*: Are of wide meaning. The words are identical with the word 'obscene' under the English law, the test of obscenity laid down in *Re* v. *Hicklin* is 'whether the tendency of matter charged as obscene is to deprave and corrupt those whose minds are open to such immoral influences and into whose hands a publication of this sort is likely to fall.[2] Our Supreme Court has accepted this test because the Indian Penal Code has not laid down any test for determining obscenity.

Sections 292 to 294 of the Indian Penal Code provide instances of restrictions on the freedom of speech and expression in the interest of decency and morality. They prohibit the distribution and sale of or exhibition of obscene matters in public places. In *Ranjit Udeshi* v. *State of Maharashtra*[3] the book seller was prosecuted for selling the book 'Lady Chatterley's Lover'.

(e) *Contempt of court*: If the freedom of speech exceeds a reasonable and fair limit it amounts to contempt of court under the Contempt of Courts Act, 1971. Contempt may be either civil or criminal contempt. Civil contempt means wilful disobedience of any Judgment, decree, direction, order, writ or the process of a Court or wilful breach of an undertaking given to the Court. Criminal contempt means publication whether by words spoken or written or by signs or by visible representations or otherwise which

- scandalises or tends to scandalise or lowers or tends to lower the authority of the courts;
- prejudices or interferes or tends to interfere with the due course of any judicial proceedings
- interferes or tends to interfere with or obstructs or tends to obstruct the administration of justice in any manner.

Following are not contempt:

- Innocent publication and distribution of any matter
- Publication of fair and accurate report of Judicial proceedings
- Fair criticism of Judicial acts

---

1. AIR 1961 SC 884: (1961) 3 SCR 423: (1961) 2 Cr LJ 16.
2. LR 3 QB 360.
3. AIR 1965 SC 881.

- Complaints against Presiding Officers made in good faith
- Publication of fair information relating to proceedings in chambers or in camera.

Contempt of court is punishable with simple imprisonment for a term of 6 months or with fine extending to Rs. 2000 or both. A judge or a Magistrate acting judicially also is liable under the Act.

In *Baradakanta* v. *Registrar of Orissa High Court*[1], Baradkanta was a senior judicial officer. He was suspended after a disciplinary proceeding. He wrote 3 letters to the High Court and one to the Government. He made contemptuous allegations with reference to the administrative functions of High Court amounting to criminal contempt. Supreme Court held that administration of justice is closely associated with the court of justice which has to perform multifarious functions of due administration of justice. The whole set of a Court is for the purpose of justice. Superior court has to be vigilant about the conduct of the subordinate judge. It held that defamatory criticism of a judge functioning as a judge even in purely administrative or adjudicatory matters amounts to criminal contempt.

(f) *Defamation:* A statement which injures a man's reputation is defamation. It consists in exposing a man to hatred, ridicule or contempt. Section 499 IPC deals with criminal contempt. It includes slander (oral defamation) and libel (written defamation). The civil law of defamation is uncodified and is dealt with under the law of Torts.

(g) Incitement to an offence added by First Amendment to the Constitution in 1951. Offence means any act or omission made punishable by any law for the time being in force. What is incitement is a question of facts and circumstances of each case to be decided by the court.

(h) Integrity and sovereignty of India added by 16th Amendment in 1963. Freedom of speech cannot be used to challenge the integrity of India or to preach cessation.

Example sedition section 124A of the IPC "whoever by words spoken or written or by signs or by visible representation or otherwise brings or attempts to bring into hatred or contempt or excite disaffection towards the Government established by law in India shall be punished. Mere comment expressing disapproval of Government actions is no offence if it does not excite or attempt to excite disaffection towards Government established by law. In *Kedar Nath* v. *State of Bihar*[2] the constitutional validity of the provision was upheld.

H. Freedom to Assemble – Articles 19(1)(b) and 19(3)

Right to assemble subject to 3 conditions: Article 19(1)(b) guarantees to its citizens the right of assemble subject to three conditions:

- Assembly must be peaceful and without arms.

---

1. AIR 1974 SC 710.
2. AIR 1953 SC 404: 1954 SCR 30: 1953 Cr LJ 1621.

Reasonable restrictions can be imposed in the interests of public order, sovereignty and integrity under article 19(3).

It includes the right to hold meetings and to take out processions. Meetings, demonstrations etc., are also a part of freedom of speech and expression under article 19(1)(a). Hence the same principles as for freedom of speech and expression are applicable in the case of freedom of assembly.

Meetings on Government land: It does not confer a Fundamental right to hold meetings in Government premises. Right of assembly cannot be exercised on the property of somebody. Right to hold public meetings on Government property like a maidan can be created by usage.[1]

Prohibition of holding or attending of any meeting on the date of polling is valid as being in the interest of public order.[2]

Unlawful assembly: Under section 141 Indian Penal Code – an assembly of five or more persons becomes an unlawful assembly when the common object of the persons composing the assembly is to overpower the Government or any public servant in the exercise of his lawful powers or to take possession of any property, or resist the execution of any law, or compel a person to do what he is legally not bound to do or omit what he is legally bound to do or commit any criminal trespass etc., & this is done or sought to be done by means of criminal force or show of criminal force.

An assembly not unlawful when assembled, may subsequently become unlawful if it becomes violent or is likely to result in disturbance.

Security for breach of peace: Under section 107 Cr.P.C. a Magistrate may obtain security for keeping peace from any person who is likely to commit a breach of peace. Section 144 Cr.P.C. empowers the Magistrate to restrain an assembly meeting or procession if there is a risk of obstruction, annoyance or injury to any person lawfully employed or danger to human life, health or safety etc.

I. Freedom to form Associations and Unions—Article 19(1)(c)

Introduction

All the citizens of India have the freedom to form association or unions. Reasonable restrictions can be imposed in the interest of public order or morality or sovereignty and integrity of India under article 19(4). It is an important right which enables the formation of political parties; trade unions; etc. Such associations are necessary if democracy is to function efficiently and the people are to discuss matters of common interest and grievances and work towards collective good. Right to form an association includes right not to be compelled to join an association. Hence rules making it compulsory for all teachers of elementary schools to become members of an association were void as being in violation of article 19(1)(c).

---

1. *D. Anantha Prabhu* v. *District Collector, Ernakulam,* AIR 1975 Ker 117: 1974 Ker LJ 151: ILR (1974) 1 Ker 422.
2. *Rameshwar Mahton* v. *State,* AIR 1957 Pat 252: ILR 34 Pat 855: 1957 Cr LJ 648.

Some important case laws on Article 19(1)(c) read with Article 19(4)

(1) No hearing given before banning the association – void

The leading case on the point is *State of Madras* v. *V.G. Roo*[1]. The Criminal Law (Amendment) Act, 1908 as amended by the Madras Act provides that if the State Government is of opinion that any association interferes with the administration of law or with the maintenance of law and order or that it constitutes a danger to the public peace it may by a Gazette notification declare such association to be unlawful. The notification is then placed before the Advisory Board. If the Advisory Board is of the opinion that the association was lawful – the Government has to cancel the notification. This Act was challenged in *Row case*.

A Notification declared 'Peoples Education Society' as an unlawful association. The object of the society was broadly 'advancement of knowledge' but the Government alleged that in fact the funds of the society were used for helping the Communist Party of India which was declared as unlawful. Supreme Court held the restriction unreasonable because the matter was left entirely to the subjective satisfaction of the Government. In addition there was no obligation on the Government to give notice to the persons concerned before declaring an association to be unlawful.

(2) Right to strike – Not Fundamental right

It was held in *All India Bank Employees Association* v. *National Industrial Tribunal*, AIR 1962 SC 171 that the right to strike is not a Fundamental right. Right to strike is controlled by appropriate industrial legislation.[2]

(3) Object of the association – Not protected under article 19(1)(c)

Freedom to form association does not carry with it a guarantee that the objects of an association shall not be interfered with except on grounds mentioned in article 19(4). Government took over an educational institute, but there was no interference with the society or its constitution. Held that freedom to form association was not violated.

(4) Imposition of members – Unconstitutional

Freedom to form an association carries with it the right to be associated with only whom they voluntarily agree to associate without any compulsion from the Government. The Hindi Sahitya Sammelan Act, 1962 changed the composition of an association of which the petitioner was a member. It introduced new members in the association in whose membership the other members had no say. Alteration of the constitution of the association is not in the interest of sovereignty and integrity of India or public order or morality. Hence the Supreme Court held that the right to form association under article 19(1)(c) is violated.[3]

A Bombay Act provided that only a representative union having at least 15% of the total employees in an industry could represent the entire body of workers in their relations with the employees. The Fundamental right was not violated.

---

1. AIR 1952 SC 196: 1952 Cr LJ 966: 1952 SCR 597.
2. AIR 1962 SC 171: 1962 (1) SCA 604: (1962) 3 SCR 269.
3. *Damyanti Naranga* v. *Union of India*, AIR 1971 SC 966: (1971) 3 SCR 840: 1971 UJ (SC) 409.

Nothing prevented the other workers from forming an association enrolling a higher percentage so as to acquire right of representation.

(5) Unlawful Activities Prevention Act, 1967

Government can declare by a notification that an association unlawful on grounds mentioned under the Act. The notification is not effective unless the Tribunal consisting of a sitting High Court judge confirms it. The Tribunal has to decide whether or not there is sufficient cause for declaring the association unlawful. In the wake of demolition of Babri Masjid VHP, RSS, Bajrang Dal, Islamic Sevak Sangh and Jammat-e-Islami Hind were declared unlawful. Ban against VHP and Jammat-e-Islam was upheld but quashed as against RSS and Bajrang Dal. Supreme Court set aside the ban with respect to Jammat-e-Islami as there was no factual basis for the Tribunal's ruling. Ban against VHP came to an end on 9-12-1994 and reimposed on 14-1-1995. The Tribunal set it aside because it was based on extraneous grounds.

(6) Includes right not to join an association

A rule made it compulsory for every teacher to become a member of a government sponsored association. Disciplinary action could be initiated if the teacher remained absent from two consecutive meetings. It was held by the Andhra Pradesh High Court that article 19(1)(c) was violated.[1]

Termination order not protected: Services of a Railway employee were terminated because he was a Communist Party of India member. He contended that his termination amounted to restriction from joining an association and hence article 19(1)(c) was violated. Supreme Court did not agree. It held that his termination order did not violate article 19(1)(c) because he could still remain the member of CPI. And that he had no Fundamental right to be continued in Railway employment.[2]

(7) Special provisions for police and armed forces

Police Forces (Restriction of Rights) Act, 1966 which restricts members of the police force from enjoying Fundamental right has been held to be valid in *Delhi Police Non-Gazetted Karmachari Sangh* v. *Union of India.*[3] The Act enacted under article 33 is valid under article 19(1)(c) & 19(4) also. It was held that statutory rules regarding recognition and de-recognition of the association were not violative of article 19(1)(c).

Civilian employees of the Defence Establishment-like cooks, barbers, mechanics, tailors etc., answer the description of members of the Armed Forces under article 33 of the Constitution. Though non-combatants, they are an integral part of the Defence Forces. Hence restriction were reasonable.

J. Freedom of Movement – Article 19(1)(d) and 19(5)

It guarantees to all citizens the right to move freely throughout the territory of India. It is subject to reasonable restrictions in the interest of general public or for the protection of the interest of any Scheduled Tribe.

1. *Sitharamacharya* v. *Dy. Inspector of Schools,* AIR 1958 AP 78.
2. *Balakotiah* v. *Union of India,* AIR 1958 SC 263.
3. AIR 1987 SC 379: (1987) 1 SCC 115: 1987 (1) Supreme 9.

Thus, the whole of India is one unit for the purpose of movement. It does not deal with the general right of locomotion but the right to move from one part of India to another part.[1]

Externment orders: Article 19(1)(d) and (e) have been invoked to challenge externment orders. Supreme Court has held in *N.B. Khare* v. *State of Delhi*, AIR 1950 SC 211: 1950 SCR 519: (1951) 52 Cr LJ 550 that because the order of externment is to be made by the State Government or a District Magistrate whose satisfaction is final does not make the restriction unreasonable. More over in this case, the East Punjab Safety Act was of a limited duration and the petitioner was directed to extern himself for 3 months and return back to Delhi, grounds of externment were to be communicated to the externee; he had a right to make a representation which was to be referred to an Advisory Board constituted under the Act.[2]

In *Hari*[3] though there was no Advisory Board to scrutinise the externment order, there were other safeguards like – though action could be initiated by a police, externment order could be issued only by the Commissioner of Police and an appeal against the order could be made to the State Government. Under the Bombay Police Act the Commissioner of Police could direct a person to remove himself from Bombay upto 2 years – (a) if Commissioner was satisfied that his acts could cause alarm to person or property; or (b) that he was about to commit an offence involving violence or force and (c) in his opinion witnesses were not forthcoming to testify against him in public.

Prem Chand v. *Union of India*[4] viewed externment orders very strictly. It observed that externment orders are 'economic *hara-kiri* and psychic distress'. Externment provisions must be read strictly and that any police apprehension is not enough. There must be a clear and a present danger based upon credible material which makes the movements and acts of the person concerned alarming or dangerous or fraught with violence. Supreme Court quashed the externment proceedings.

It is to be noted that in *Prem Chand's case* restriction could be imposed only in a disturbed area and only on a 'goonda'. In *Hari's case* there were no such restrictions in the Bombay Act under which any person could be externed. The discretion conferred in *Hari* was broader than in *Prem Chand's case*. Yet externment of Hari was held to be valid and that of Prem Chand was held unconstitutional.

Helmets: Compulsory wearing of helmets is valid in the general interest of general public.[5]

In *Kharak Singh* v. *State of Uttar Pradesh*[6] Supreme Court held that police surveillance did not offend the freedom of movement. The purpose of secret

1. *A.K. Gopalan* v. *State of Madras*, AIR 1950 SC 27: (1950) 51 Cr LJ 1383: 1950 SCR 88.
2. *N.B. Khare* v. *State of Delhi*, AIR 1950 SC 211: 1950 SCR 519: (1951) 52 Cr LJ 550.
3. *Hari* v. *Dy. Commr of Police*, AIR 1959 SC 559.
4. AIR 1981 SC 613: 1981 Cr LJ 5: (1980) 1 SCC 639.
5. *Ajay Canu* v. *Union of India*, AIR 1988 SC 2027: JT 1988 (3) SC 523.
6. AIR 1963 SC 1295: (1963) 2 Cr LJ 329: (1964) 1 SCR 332.

picketing was only to identify the visitors to the suspect so that police get an idea of his activities. On the same ground domiciliary visits were upheld. The case was criticised as being a too restricted a view of article 19(1)(d). But in *Govind* v. *State of Madhya Pradesh*[1] Supreme Court has held that police surveillance must be restricted to such persons only against whom reasonable materials exist to show 'a determination to lead a life of crime'. Likewise domiciliary visits must be confined to clear cases of danger to community security and must not be a routine affair of the police.

Deportation of 'any person outside India' does not include 'any citizen': Deportation of Indian citizens out of India is viewed still more strictly by the Supreme Court. Central law authorised the Government to deport any person against whom a reasonable suspicion existed that he has entered India without a permit etc. Supreme Court held that 'any person' did not include a citizen of India. For disloyalty to his country an Indian citizen may be liable for the gravest punishment, but he cannot be deported from the country for it would destroy his citizenship which can be done only under article 11 of the Constitution.

K. Freedom of residence under articles 19(1)(e) and 19(5)

Every citizen of India has the right to reside and settle in any part of the territory of India, reasonable restrictions can be imposed in the interest of general public or for the protection of the Scheduled Tribe. Right to reside and right to move freely go hand in hand. Hence most of the cases referred under article 19(1)(d) are relevant under this head also. *For example* under the Suppression of Immoral Traffic in Women and Girls Act, 1956 a prostitute was directed to remove herself out of the limits of a busy city – the restriction was held to be valid and reasonable.

Under the MP Public Security Act State Government could issue orders to a person reside in such place as specified in the order or to go to another place as selected by authorities in the interests of security of the State or public safety. Restriction was held to be unreasonable- there was no hearing given to the person concerned; place selected may be without any residential accommodation and no means of livelihood etc.

L. Freedom to acquire, hold and dispose of property – Article 19(1)(f) and (5)

It is now deleted by 44th Amendment 1978.

Before 44th Amendment: Before it was deleted the citizens had the Fundamental right to acquire, hold and dispose of the property. The State could impose reasonable restrictions in the interests of the general public or for the protection of the interests of the general public or the Scheduled Tribes.

The right includes the right to possess and enjoy all the benefits attached to the ownership of the property. It includes right to hold a fair in one's own land. Right of pre-emption on the ground of vicinage was held to be void. (*e.g.*, if A and B have lands adjacent to each other. A wants to sell it. It must be first offered to B. Right of pre-emption is recognised amongst Mohammedans).

---

1. AIR 1975 SC 1378: 1975 Cr LJ 1111: (1975) 2 SCC 148. Also see *Malak Singh* v. *State of Punjab and Haryana*, AIR 1981 SC 760: 1981 Cr LJ 320: (1981) 1 SCC 420.

The topic is more specifically dealt with under the Chapter No. 27 dealing with Constitutional right to property.

M. Freedom of profession, occupation, trade or business – Article 19(1)(g)

All the citizens of India have the freedom 'to practice any profession, carry on any occupation, trade or business. Four different expressions are used to make the guarantee as comprehensive as possible to include all avenues through which a citizen makes a living. Article 19(1)(g) protects only if the activity concerned is of a commercial or a trading nature. Thus *for example*, betting and gambling are not trade[1]; prize competitions involving substantial skills are regarded as business. There is no Fundamental right to manufacture, sell fireworks producing sound beyond permissible limits[2] or to deal in adulterated food stuffs.[3] Money lending to the poor villagers is not a business or trade as it is exploitative of the village people. But money lending amongst commercial community is trade as it is integral to trade and commerce[4].

Grounds of restriction: Restrictions can be imposed by law if 2 conditions are satisfied:

Restriction must be reasonable and in the interest of public the State can[5]:

(a) Prescribe professional or technical qualifications necessary for practising any profession or carrying on any occupation, trade or business. For example, the Advocates Act, 1961, the Indian Medical Council's Act prescribes qualifications for a law graduate and for an MBBS examination.

(b) The State can carry on any trade or business to the exclusion of citizens wholly or partially. *I.e.*, a partial or a total monopoly to carry on trade etc in favour of the State is valid.

Reasonable restrictions can be imposed in "the interest of the general public". It is a term of wide amplitude. It comprehends "public order, public health, public security, morals, economic welfare of the community and the objects mentioned in the Directive Principles."[6]

What is a reasonable restriction:

Reasonableness of the restriction must be tested with reference to procedural as well as substantive law. Factors like nature of the business, conditions prevailing in the trade, must be taken into consideration. These factors differ from trade to trade and no hard and

---

1. *State of Bombay* v. *R.M.D. Chamarbaugwala*, AIR 1957 SC 699: 1957 SCJ 607: 1957 SCA 867.
2. *Burrabazar Fire Works Dealers Association* v. *Commissioner of Police, Calcutta*, AIR 1998 Cal 121: 1997 (2) Cal LJ 468: 1998 Cal WN 183.
3. *State of Uttar Pradesh* v. *Kartar Singh*, AIR 1964 SC 1135: (1964) 6 SCR 679: (1964) 2 Cr LJ 229.
4. *Fatehchand Himmatlal* v. *State of Maharashtra*, AIR 1977 SC 1825: 1978 (1) SCJ 1: 79 Bom LR 552.
5. Inserted by the or First Amendment in 1951.
6. *Municipal Corporation of the City of Ahmedabad* v. *Jan Mohammed Usmanbhai*, AIR 1986 SC 1205: (1986) 3 SCC 20: 1986 (2) SCJ 456.

fast rules can be laid down for determining the reasonableness.[1] The word reasonable implies intelligent care and deliberation. Legislation which arbitrarily or excessively invades the right cannot be said to be reasonable. A balance has to be struck between the right to profession and the permissible social control under article 19(6).[2]

Right to carry on a profession includes right to close down at any time he chooses.[3]

India being a 'socialist Republic' – the term 'socialist' being added by the 44th Amendment the question that arises is : whether social control over business and profession should dominate over the right of the private enterprises to carry on business etc. In *Excel Wear* v. *Union of India*[4] the court has held that though there may be greater emphasis on nationalisation and State ownership of industries – private ownership of businesses and industries is still recognised. Private undertaking contribute to the growth of the national economy in addition to personal returns to the entrepreneur. This was the ruling given in 1979. As of now the trend has totally changed specially in view of India having signed the GATT and thrown open its economy to the private players from across the Globe. Emphasis is on LPG – liberalisation, Privatization and Globalization. Government is now more of a facilitator than as a controller of private enterprise. It has been encouraging private entrepreneurship.

(1) Condition of service & restriction

In *Sukumar Mukherjee* v. *State of West Bengal*[5] under the West Bengal State Health Service Act, 1990 *'teacher- doctors'* of *West Bengal* Medical Education Service were prohibited from doing private practice but the *'doctors'* of WB Health Service were not so prohibited. When these services were separated the teachers were given the option to join either WBMES or WBHS. It was challenged as violating article 19(1)(g). Supreme Court held that there was no violation. Restriction is not on the freedom to practise medical profession. It is only a condition of service on those who opt to join Government service.

(2) Protection of livelihood

In *Kerala SMT Federation* v. *Kerala TBO Assn.*[6] Orders under section 4 of the Kerala Marine Fishing Regulation Act, 1980 under which 'bottom trawling' by owners of mechanised boats was prohibited during the monsoon period was held valid. Supreme Court held that it was a reasonable restriction in public interest. It was in order to protect the economic interest of the traditional fishermen and to ensure that they are not deprived of their livelihood.

(3) Trading in liquor

In *Khoday Distilleries* v. *State of Karnataka*[7] law relating to carrying on of the right to carry on the trade in liquor was summarised. It held that there is no Fundamental right to trade in intoxicating liquors and articles that are immoral or obnoxious or injurious to health, safety and welfare of the general

1. *Sreenivasa General Traders* v. *State of Andhra Pradesh*, AIR 1983 SC 1246: (1983) 4 SCC 353: (1983) 3 SCR 843.
2. *Chintamanrao* v. *State of Madhya Pradesh*, AIR 1951 SC 118: 1950 SCJ 571: 1950 SCR 759.
3. *Hathising Manufacturing Co., Ltd., Ahmedabad* v. *Union of India*, AIR 1960 SC 923: 1961 (1) SCJ 22: (1960) 3 SCR 528.
4. AIR 1979 SC 25 (36): (1978) 4 SCC 224: (1979) 1 SCR 1009.
5. (1993) 3 SCC 723: AIR 1993 SC 2335: 1993 AIR SCW 2772.
6. (1994) 5 SCC 28: 1994 AIR SCW 3239.
7. (1995) 1 SCC 574: 1995 AIR SCW 313: AIR 1996 SC 911.

public. The State can prohibit the manufacture, sale and possession, distribution and consumption of liquor in order to give effect to the directive principle of article 47 that the State shall endeavour to bring in total prohibition. State can monopolise in itself or in any other agency, the manufacture, possession, sale and distribution of liquor as a beverage. Exception can be made for its use for medicinal purpose.

Hitherto the Supreme Court had ruled that the citizen has no inherent right to engage in the business of trading liquor because it is dangerous to the community[1]; that it was opposed to the morality standards; that standards of morality taken at a given point of time affords guidance to impose restriction[2]; morality or illegality or otherwise of a deal would not affect the quality or character of the activity though it might be a ground for imposing restriction on the activity; that 'there is police power of the State to enforce public morality to prohibit trades in noxious and dangerous goods[3].

(4) Trading on pavements

Hawkers' right to trade on pavement of roads – in *Sodan Singh* v. *New Delhi Municipal Committee*[4] the Supreme Court held that right to carry on trade on pavements – If properly regulated cannot be denied to the hawkers. It helps small traders and the general public by making ordinary articles of every day use at lesser prices. But they cannot claim to do so on any place of their choice. If the road is not wide enough to conveniently manage the traffic on it no hawking may be permitted at all. The court suggested that hawking and non-hawking zones be created for regulating the hawking business.

(5) Pursuing two professions

In *Dr. Haniraj Chuhani* v. *Bar Council of Maharashtra and Goa*[5] the Maharashtra Bar Council Rules restricted the entry of other professionals into the legal profession if they are already carrying on any other full time profession. "The legal profession required full attention and would not countenance (tolerate) an advocate riding two horses or more at a time." Thus right to practise a profession is not an absolute right. The restriction imposed was a reasonable one.

(6) Lottery business

Uttar Pradess Government banned the sale of lottery tickets of other States in the State of Uttar Pradesh under Validity of Lotteries (Regulation) Act, 1998. It was challenged as[6] violative of articles 19(1)(g) and article 310, 302, 303 of the Constitution. Supreme Court held that lottery contains an element of chance and hence cannot be regarded as a trade or commerce but is gambling. Gambling is a chance with no skill; trade is a skill with no chance.

In *M/s Raunak Agency Mumbai* v. *State of Mizoram*[7] it has been held that restraining persons who have court cases against the State from bidding in the State largesse *viz.*, bidding for on-line lottery business violates right to practise profession under article 19, 14, 21.

1. *Cooverjee B. Bharucha* v. *Excise Commissioner and the Chief Commissioner, Ajmer*, AIR 1954 SC 220: 1954 SCA 256: 1954 SCR 873.
2. *Krishan Kumar Narula* v. *State of Jammu and Kashmir*, AIR 1967 SC 1368: 1967 (2) SCJ 373: (1967) 3 SCR 50.
3. *Nashirwar* v. *State of Madhya Pradesh*, AIR 1975 SC 360: (1975) 1 SCC 29: (1975) 2 SCR 861.
4. AIR 1989 SC 1988: 1989 All LJ 1097: (1989) 4 SCC 155.
5. (1996) 3 SCC 342: 1996 AIR SCW 1913: AIR 1996 SC 1708.
6. AIR 1955 SC 549: 1955 SCA 577: (1955) 2 SCR 225.
7. AIR 2011 Gau 53.

(7) Sale of eggs

In *Om Prakash* v. *State of Uttar Pradesh*[1] prohibition on sale of eggs within municipal limits of Rishikesh was held to be a reasonable restriction on the freedom of trade.

(8) Ban on paan masala

Ban on paan masala and ghutka issued by the State Government was held unconstitutional because they were carrying on the business under a licence issued by Central Government. The power to ban these products is vested with the Central Government under the Cigarettes and Other Tobacco Products (Prohibition of Advertisement and Regulation of Trade and Commerce, Production Supply and Distribution) Act, enacted by the Parliament. Unless the terms of the licence were violated by the licensee the State Government could not ban the manufacture and trade of ghutka by an administrative order.

(9) Ban on transport of sand

In *Santosh Krishna Kalgutkar* v. *State of Karnataka*[2] ban on transportation of ordinary sand outside Karnataka in view of shortage of sand and in the interest of maintaining local environment and conservation of minerals was held to be a reasonable restriction and not a violation of the freedom to practise any trade under articles 19(1)(g) and 301.

(10) Ban on cow slaughter

In *State of Gujarat* v. *Mirazpur Moti Kureshi Kassab Jamat*[3] Gujarat Government banned slaughter of cows, calves and other milch and draught cattles. It was held to be valid as it was not a total ban. The ban was only with respect to a particular class of cattle. The restriction was reasonable as cow and her progeny are the backbone of Indian agriculture and economy. But a ban on the slaughter of bulls, bullocks, she-buffalows below the age of 25 years is an unreasonable restriction because these animals lose their utility value after 15 year and so it involves a wasteful drain on the nation's cattle feed and deteriorates the breed.

Order for closure of slaughter houses for 9 days during religious festival of Jains was valid.[4]

Fixation of a ceiling of 200 quintals on wheat stocks also is valid[5].

(11) Ban on bidi manufacture

Madhya Pradesh State law banned the villagers from engaging in bidi manufacture during the agricultural season. It was in order to ensure adequate supply of labour for agriculture purposes. Even old persons and children were prevented from engaging in the bidi making work during their spare time and in order to supplement their income. The prohibition was held to be unreasonable as it was in excess of object of the Act.[6]

(12) Nationalisation of text books

In *Ram Jawaya Kapur* v. *State of Punjab*[7] nationalisation of school text books was held valid because the private publishers' right to print and publish any book they like and offer the same for sale was not curtailed. The choice of text

1. AIR 2004 SC 1896: 2004 AIR SCW 1652: (2004) 3 SCC 402.
2. AIR 2011 Kar 49.
3. AIR 2006 SC 212: 2005 AIR SCW 5723: (2005) 8 SCC 534.
4. *Hinsa Virodhak Sangh* v. *Mirzapur Moti Kuresh Jamat*, AIR 2008 SC 1892.
5. *P.P. Enterprises* v. *Union of India*, AIR 1982 SC 1016.
6. *Chintamanrao* v *State of Madhya Pradesh*, AIR 1951 SC 118: 1950 SCJ 571: 1950 SCR 759.
7. AIR 1955 SC 549: 1955 SCA 577: (1955) 2 SCR 225.

books for the recognised schools lay with the Government and the publishers have no Fundamental right to get their books prescribed as text books.

A taxing statute is rarely regarded as a restriction on the freedom of profession even if it imposes some hardship on individual cases.

(13) Right to work—Not protected

Article 19(1)(g) does not protect 'right to work'. Hence the contention of the workers of Fertiliser Corporation Kamgar Union that the sale of certain plants and equipment would lead to their retrenchment and hence it was an unreasonable restriction on their Fundamental right under article 19(1)(g) was not accepted by the Supreme Court.[1]

Fixing of minimum wages under the Minimum Wages Act is reasonable as it seeks to protect the workers who may be willing to work on starvation wages.[2]

(14) Protection from fraudulent financial establishments

Tamil Nadu Protection of Interests of Depositors (in Financial Establishments) Act, has the benevolent object of protecting the gullible depositors from unscrupulous financial establishments who defrauds public by offering lucrative returns. Under the Act the properties of such fraudulent establishments and the *mala fide* transferees is to be attached and out of the sale proceeds the innocent depositors are to be paid. Hence it does not violate articles 14, 19(1)(g)[3].

Condition that the shops and establishments shall remain closed for one day in a week is reasonable. It seeks to improve health and efficiency of the workers.[4]

(15) Conditional licences

Cycle Rickshaw Bye laws allowed licences to be issued only to the owners who ply themselves and not to the owners who had more than one rickshaw and hired them out to the rickshaw pullers – it was held valid.[5]

Karnataka State Government Rule that no Talkies would be allowed to exhibit more than 4 shows was a reasonable restriction. It was found that when 5 shows were exhibited in a day it was not possible to take care of health and hygiene requirements.[6]

1. 19(1)(g) under the Tamil Nadu Schools (Regulation of Collection of Fee) Act and Rules the authority has to approve the fee structure proposed by private institution. Purpose was to strike a balance between autonomy of institutions and measures to be taken to prevent commercialisation of education. There are sufficient guidelines in the statute for approving of the fees. The committee is headed by a retired High Court judge hence the Act does not violate article 19(1)(g) or 26 or 30 of the Constitution.[7]

---

1. *Fertilizer Corporation Kamagar Union (Regd.) Sindri* v. *Union of India*, AIR 1981 SC 344: (1981) 1 SCC 568: (1981) 2 SCR 52.
2. *U. Unichoyi* v. *State of Kerala*, AIR 1962 SC 12: (1962) 1 SCR 946: 1963 (1) SCJ 355.
3. *K.K. Bhaskaran* v. *State rep. by its Secy., Tamil Nadu*, AIR 2011 SC 1485.
4. *State of Uttar Pradesh* v. *Basti Sugar Mills Co. Ltd.*, AIR 1961 SC 420: (1961) 2 SCR 330: 1963 (1) SCJ 778.
5. *All Delhi Cycle Rickshaw Operators Union etc.* v. *Municipal Corporation of Delhi*, (1987) 1 SCC 371: AIR 1987 SC 648: 1987 (1) SCJ 114.
6. *Minerva Talkies, Bangalore* v. *State of Karnataka*, AIR 1988 SC 526: 1988 (1) SCJ 208: (1988) 1 Kant LJ 347.
7. *Tamil Nadu Nursery, Matriculation and Higher Secondary Schools Association, Chennai* v. *State of Tamil Nadu*, AIR 2010 Mad 142: 2010 (4) Mad LJ 209: 2010 (2) Mad LW 726.

CHAPTER 11

PROTECTION IN RESPECT OF CONVICTION FOR OFFENCES

Article 20

SYNOPSIS

A. Introduction

Article 20 is a part of the right to freedom dealt with under articles 19 to 22.

Article 20 gives three basic and valuable guarantees connected with conviction of offences—*Ex post facto* law, Double jeopardy, Prohibition against self-incrimination.

B. *Ex post facto* law

(i) No person shall be convicted of any offence except for the violation of a law in force at the *time of the commission of the act* charged as an offence.

(ii) Likewise no person shall be subject to a *penalty greater than* that which might have been inflicted under the law in force at the time of the offence.

(1) Minimum fine prescribed under an Ordinance can be levied

Under section 420 IPC an unlimited amount of fine can be levied; an ordinance laid down a minimum fine to be compulsorily levied on the person convicted under section 420. Supreme Court held that article 20 was not infringed because the minimum fine levied under the Ordinance[1] could not be said to be greater than what could be levied under section 420.

(2) Ex post facto law can be applied to reduce the punishment

However note that an *Ex- post facto law can be applied to reduce the punishment.* A 16-year-old boy had committed an offence and awarded a rigorous imprisonment. Later Probation of Offenders Act came into force which took a lenient view of the offences committed by children below 16 years. Supreme Court held that the boy was entitled to the benefit of the lenient provisions under the Act.[2]

(3) Interpretation of a judgment related back to the date of the law itself

In *Sarla Mudgal* v. *Union of India*[3] the Supreme Court held that a second marriage of a Hindu husband after conversion to Islam without having the marriage annulled is void and the husband is guilty of bigamy under section 494 IPC. Later in *Lily Thomas* v. *Union of India* it was argued that the law declared in *Sarala* could not be given retrospective operation because of article 20(1) and therefore the ruling could not be applied to a person whose second marriage was already solemnised before the date on which judgment was given in *Sarala Mudgal.* Supreme Court held that judgments never lay down a new law. They only interpret the existing law because courts do not legislate. They only interpret. *Interpretation of a judgment related back to the date of the law itself.* Thus ruling in *Sarala was applicable in Lily Thomas.*[4]

An offence is any act or omission made punishable by any law for the time being in force.

That is – if an act is not an offence today- the State cannot make a law after one year making that act an offence and punish a person after one year for what he has done today. Such laws are regarded as unjust and unreasonable. In other words criminal laws cannot be made retrospectively applicable; but civil laws can be retrospective in operation.

For example, section 304B enacted on 19-11-1986 made dowry death punishable as an offence under IPC. A person could not be tried under section 304B for a dowry death which had taken place in 1984. This is because section 304B was not a 'law in force' on the date of the dowry death.

But when an Act was passed in June, 1957 imposing on the employers closing their undertakings a liability to pay compensation to the employees since November 28, 1956, it was held that it could be enforced because it was a civil liability and article 20(1) was not applicable.[5]

1. *K. Satwant Singh* v. *State of Punjab,* AIR 1960 SC 266: (1960) 2 SCR 89: 1960 Cr LJ 410.
2. *Rattan Lal* v. *State of Punjab,* AIR 1965 SC 444: (1965) 1 Cr LJ 360: (1964) 7 SCR 676.
3. AIR 1995 SC 1531: 1995 AIR SCW 2326: 1995 Cr LJ 2926.
4. AIR 2000 SC 1650: 2000 AIR SCW 1760: 2000 Cr LJ 2433.
5. *Hathising Manufacturing Co. Ltd., Ahmedabad* v. *Union of India,* AIR 1960 SC 923: 1961 (1) SCJ 22: (1960) 3 SCR 528.

(4) No Fundamental right to be tried by a particular court or by a particular procedure

It is only a conviction based on *ex post facto* law that is prohibited but not a trial or a change of court. Thus, when there is a procedure different from one that prevailed at the time of the commission of the offence or the court having the jurisdiction at the time of the commission of the offence is changed- article 20(1) is not applicable. This is because no person has a Fundamental right to be tried by a particular court or by a particular procedure.

Under section 5(3) of the Prevention of Corruption Act – If a Government servant has in his possession property wholly disproportionate to his known sources of income and if he cannot explain the same satisfactorily he is guilty of criminal misconduct. The Supreme Court held that this section does not create any new offence. It only lays down a rule of evidence.[1]

(5) Conviction under Ex post facto law is prohibited and not enacting of a new law

What article 20(1) prohibits is conviction and sentence under an *ex-post-facto* law but not the enactment or validity of such law. In other words what it means is, in India there can be 2 sets of laws under which persons may be punished based on what was the law at the time the offence was committed. In America an *ex-post facto* law is itself void.

C. Double jeopardy—*Nemo debet bis vexari*

It is based on the maxim – *Nemo debet bis vexari* – a man must not be put twice in peril for the same offence.

(1) Prosecution and punishment – Must co-exist

No person shall be prosecuted and punished for the same offence more than once. Prosecution and punishment must co-exist. The High Court had quashed the trial under section 161 IPC (illegal gratification) because no sanction was obtained as required. Article 20(2) was no bar for a fresh prosecution after obtaining sanction.[2]

(2) Punishment and not acquittal

In India this rule is applicable only when a person is 'prosecuted and punished and not when he is acquitted.' In other words if he is prosecuted but acquitted- he can be tried again for the same offence.

(3) Identical offence

Article 20(2) is applicable only when prosecution and punishment is for an identical offence. The same set of facts may constitute more than two distinct and separate offences with different ingredients. In such a case double punishment is not barred.[3] Example conviction under section 409 for criminal breach of trust and later on the same facts under section 105 Insurance Act is not barred.[4]

---

1. *Sajjan Singh* v. *State of Punjab*, AIR 1964 SC 464: (1964) 1 Cr LJ 310: (1964) 4 SCR 630.
2. *Mohammad Safi* v. *State of West Bengal*, AIR 1966 SC 69: 1966 Cr LJ 75: (1965) 3 SCR 467.
3. *State of Bihar* v. *Murad Ali Khan*, AIR 1989 SC 1: 1989 Cr LJ 1005: (1988) 4 SCC 655.
4. *State of Bombay* v. *S.L. Apte*, AIR 1961 SC 578: (1961) 1 Cr LJ 725: (1961) 3 SCR 107.

(4) Prosecution must be before a court of law

Departmental enquiry is not a prosecution. Prosecution must be before a court of law. Dismissal after a departmental enquiry does not bar a subsequent prosecution.

Confiscation of goods under Customs Act is not penalty or prosecution. Other examples of distinct offences are under section 161 IPC & section 5(2) of Prevention of Corruption Act.; Customs Act and Gold (Control) Act. In *Maqbool Hussain*[1] gold was confiscated from him at the Indian airport and later he was prosecuted before a criminal court under the Foreign Exchange Regulation Act. Article 20(2) was not attracted. In *Jitendra Panchal* v. *Intelligence Officer N.C.B.*, 2008 Cr LJ 974 the offences for which the appellant was tried and convicted in USA was different from the one being tried in India.[2]

D. Prohibition against self-incrimination

It is fundamental rule of criminal jurisprudence raised to the level of a Constitutional rule. It lays down that no person shall be compelled to be a witness against himself.

Three ingredients are necessary—

(1) Right available only to the accused

It is a right available to a person who is accused of an offence. It is not necessary that actual trial should have begun. A person is said to be an accused when formal accusation has been levelled which may result in his prosecution and conviction. If no case is registered or FIR lodged – but he is only arrested on suspicion and a *panchanama* is prepared – it does not mean that he is accused. Mere issue of notice or pendency of contempt proceedings do not attract article 20(3).[3] If the FIR mentions a person's name as an accused and investigation is ordered- he can claim the protection of article 20(3)

(2) Giving any evidence out of personal knowledge alone is protected

It is a protection 'against compulsion to be a witness'. In *M.P. Sharma's* case it was held that it includes oral documentary and testimonial evidence. But in *State of Bombay* v. *Kathi Kalu*[4] Supreme Court narrowed down the meaning of 'to be a witness' and held that it is not equivalent to giving evidence. Self-incrimination can only mean conveying information based on personal knowledge of the person giving information and cannot include merely the mechanical process of producing documents in court which may throw light on any point in controversy but which do not contain any statement of the accused based on his personal knowledge. Thus, giving of finger prints; or specimen writing or signature for comparison; seizures under search warrant; compulsory taking of photographs – is not giving any evidence out of personal knowledge and hence not protected under article 20(3).

---

1. A leading case on the point.
2. AIR 2009 SC 1938: 2009 AIR SCW 1559: (2009) 3 SCC 57.
3. *Delhi Judicial Services Association* v. *State of Gujarat*, AIR 1991 SC 2176: 1991 Cr LJ 3086: (1991) 4 SCC 406.
4. AIR 1961 SC 1808: (1961) 2 Cr LJ 856: (1962) 3 SCR 10.

Under section 27 Evidence Act if the information given by the accused leads to the discovery of a fact – it is admissible in evidence. Thus where accused charged with murder stated that he had hidden the clothes of the victim in a pit and the police found it in the pit – the statement was admissible in evidence.[1]

(3) Self-incrimination

It is a protection from being compelled to give evidence against himself. The protection is available only when a person is compelled to give evidence 'against himself.'

(4) Can waive the right

He may waive this privilege or may voluntarily give the evidence on request.

(5) Duress

Compulsion means duress. It includes threatening, beating, imprisoning of the wife, parent or child of the person. When confession is made without any inducement or threat or promise article 20(3) is not applicable.

(6) Scope widened

In *Nandini Satpathy* v. *P.L. Dani*[2] scope of this article has been widened. The protection is available right from the stage of police interrogation and not only in the court. In includes mental torture, environmental pressures, tiring interrogatives, intimidatory methods and the like. The right to silence is available not only to the case for which a person is examined but extends to the accused in regard to other offences pending or imminent which may deter him from voluntary disclosure of criminatory matter.[3] In this case, Nandini Satpathy – the Chief Minister of Orissa had refused to answer questions at the Police interrogation. Supreme Court accepted *Nandini* ruling in *Kartar Singh* v. *State of Punjab*.[4]

(7) Tape recorded statement of the accused is admissible

Taped without his knowledge and without force is admissible in evidence. Searching the premises of the accused and recovering a document, taking specimen finger print and handwriting is not protected under this Article.[5]

---

1. *Pershadi* v. *State of Uttar Pradesh*, AIR 1957 SC 211: 1957 Cr LJ 328.
2. (1978) 2 SCC 424: AIR 1978 SC 1025: 1978 Cr LJ 968 note that the views expressed are in the nature of 'obiter' observations *i.e.*, passing observations made by a judge while giving the judgment which are not binding upon the subsequent courts or the subordinate courts, but when they come from the highest court – they are of high persuasive value. In this case, Krishna Iyer J. himself says that "we are not directly concerned with this facet of article 20(3)'.
3. For a critical analysis of the right of silence given to the accused *see* article titled: Right against self-incrimination and presumption of innocence defeats the cause of speedy justice. Cr.L.J. 2002 JS at p. 198. The article is in response to the questionnaire of Justice Malimath where-in one question was relating to the desirability of continuing with the present law where the accused is given a right of silence under article 20(3).
4. AIR 1995 SC 1726: 1994 Cr LJ 3139: (1994) 3 SCC 569.
5. *State through SPE and CBI, A.P.* v. *M. Krishna Mohan*, AIR 2008 SC 368: 2007 AIR SCW 7044: (2007) 12 SCALE 618.

Medical examination by a doctor to find if the accused is intoxicated, compulsory taking of urine and blood samples from the accused, is not protected under article 20.

Confession by an accused while in police custody is not admissible unless made in the immediate presence of the Magistrate. Retracted confession can be used if made voluntarily.

(f) Under section 15 of TADA, 1987 confession made by the accused was held admissible in evidence. It would be admissible only if voluntary because the accused has protection from being compelled to be a witness against himself.[1]

(g) The privilege is available to an incorporated body also.

The protection is not available in civil cases[2], in administrative proceedings like under section 45 of the Banking Companies Act or section 137(5) of the Companies Act, 1913. The accused is not entitled to the assistance of a lawyer during the questioning.[3]

---

1. *Ayyub* v. *State of Uttar Pradesh,* (2002) 3 SCC 510: 2002 AIR SCW 968: AIR 2002 SC 1192.
2. *Shyam Sundar Chowkhani alias Chandan* v. *Kajal Kanti Biswas,* AIR 1999 Gau 101: 1999 (2) Gau LR 529: 2000 (1) Land LR 388.
3. *Poolpandi* v. *Superintendent, Central Excise,* 1992 AIR SCW 2012: AIR 1992 SC 1795: 1992 Cr LJ 2761.

CHAPTER 12

RIGHT TO LIFE AND PERSONAL LIBERTY

(Article 21)

SYNOPSIS

A. Introduction

Right to life and personal liberty under article 21 is one of the four freedoms granted under Part III of the Constitution which deals with fundamental rights. The other three freedoms which come under the category 'Right to freedom' are:—freedom of speech & expression etc., under article 19; protection in respect of conviction of offences under article 20; protection to the persons arrested and protection against detention in certain cases under article 22.

Article 21 lays down that 'No person shall be deprived of his life and personal liberty except according to the procedure established by law'.

It protects both the citizens and the non-citizens alike. It is an extremely valuable right. Take out 'life' and all other rights- whether constitutional, fundamental or otherwise are set at naught; take out 'personal liberty' and so many other rights become meaningless. Yet, compulsions of an orderly society do require the flame of 'life' to be put off and personal liberty to be curtailed at times. Therefore balance must be struck between individual liberty on one hand and social control and social order on the other. Article 21 has generated a heated debate- right from the period the Constitution was in the making. The interpretation has mainly centred round the meaning of the phrase 'personal liberty' and the phrase 'procedure established by law.'

B. Personal Liberty – Restricted approach—*A.K. Gopalan*

Initially the term 'personal liberty' was given a restricted meaning *viz.*, 'freedom from external restraint'. The later phase saw such a liberal interpretation of 'personal liberty', that practically every right under the sun has been linked to 'life and personal liberty.'

The term 'personal liberty' came up for consideration of the court for the first time in *A. K. Gopalan's* case. *Gopalan* was detained under Preventive Detention Act, 1950.[1] He challenged the validity of his detention on the wide ground that the Act was void as it violated articles 19, 21 and 22. Following were the contentions of the detenue and the *rulings of the Supreme Court in Gopalan*:

(1) Personal liberty does not include article 19 freedom

Contention: Personal liberty under article 21 includes the freedoms conferred under article 19. Therefore restrictions under the Preventive Detention Act must be reasonable as specified in article 19(2) to (6).

Supreme Court did not agree. It relied on the Drafting Committee's Report that the word 'liberty' had to be qualified with the word 'personal' in article 21 or else liberty could be very widely construed 'so as to include even the freedoms under article 19. (draft article 13). Hence the intention of the framers of the Constitution was not to read the article 19 freedoms under article 21.

Contention: More particularly, the Preventive Detention Act violated Gopalan's right to move freely throughout the territory of India under article 19(1)(d) because freedom of movement is of the essence of personal liberty and that the impugned Act did not satisfy the requirements of article 19(5).[2]

The contention was rejected. It held that personal liberty under article 21 means 'freedom from arrest and detention without the authority of law'.

---

1. A person can be arrested on an apprehension that he is likely to commit offence leading to law and order problem. He is arrested in order to prevent him from committing the crime.
2. The State can impose reasonable restrictions in the interest of general public or the Scheduled Tribes.

Article 19 freedoms are enjoyed by free men and article 21 is a guarantee against deprivation of personal liberty.

Contention: The word law includes not only enacted law but also the principles of natural Justice.

Supreme Court did not agree because rules of natural justice are vague and indefinite and the Constitution nowhere uses 'law' in the sense of 'natural justice'.[1] The word 'law' was used as 'lex'- State made law; and not *'jus naturale'*- natural justice.

Contention: Procedure established by law means not any procedure but a reasonable procedure as is contemplated under the American law. The courts can see whether the procedure is just, fair and reasonable.

The Supreme Court rejected all these contentions raised by *Gopalan.* The US Constitution lays down that 'no person shall be deprived of his life, liberty or property without the due process of law. Our Constitution does not use the term 'due' and hence reasonableness cannot be tested by the courts. The Draft Constitution had rejected the words 'due process of law'[2]. Hence the intention of the framers of the Constitution was not to introduce the concept of procedural due process in India.

It was held that a law depriving personal liberty must conform to articles 20, 21, 22 because these articles form a comprehensive code.

In effect *Gopalan* laid down that.

(2) Courts to see that Procedure was followed

Article 21 was a restriction only on the Executive and not the Legislature. Thus, the Executive could curtail the liberty of any person. All that had to be done was follow the procedure laid down by the Legislature.[3]

(3) Court not to see whether procedure is reasonable

Whether the procedure for depriving personal liberty was just and reasonable was not for the courts to look into. It was totally left to the good sense of the Legislature. The Legislature could make any drastic law and lay down any drastic procedure and put restraints on personal liberty. Procedural safeguards could not be tested by the courts with the yardstick of reasonableness.

(4) Exclusivity rule—Articles 19, 21, 22 – Mutually independent

Exclusivity rule: Articles 19, 21, 22 were mutually exclusive and independent of each other.

It is submitted that the ruling is a very narrow approach of article 21 as regards 'procedure established by law'. Thus, though *Gopalan* describes due

---

1. J. Fazl Ali gave a dissenting opinion – *viz.,* that law includes the principle of natural justice.
2. For a comment that the framers of the Constitution were in two minds on whether to introduce procedural fairness or not – *see* – Dr. Veena M. : A Seminal Approach to Constitutional Philosophy: A Special Contribution of P.N. Bhagwati J. and V.R. Krishna Iyer J.: (Bangalore: Karnataka Institute of Law and Parliamentary Reforms).
3. *Kharak Singh* v. *State of Uttar Pradesh,* AIR 1963 SC 1295: (1963) 2 Cr LJ 329: (1964) 1 SCR 332; *Satwant Singh Sawhney* v. *D. Ramarathnam, Assistant Passport Officer, New Delhi,* AIR 1967 SC 1836: 1967 (2) SCA 523: 1968 (1) SCJ 178.

process and reasonableness as a vague concept- the very same Constitution under article 19 speaks of reasonableness. There is not much vagueness about the due process clause. It basically means 'fair hearing; which is ingrained in the jurisprudence of any civilised country.[1] However as regards keeping article 21 'personal liberty' and article 19 'liberties' apart it is submitted that the judgment is in tune with the Constitutional intention.[2]

C. Personal liberty – Seeds of liberal view—*Kharak Singh*

Article 19(1) deals with particular attributes of personal liberty; article 21 deals with the residue: In *Kharak Singh* v. *State of Uttar Pradesh*[3], it was held that article 19(1) deals with particular attributes of personal liberty and article 21 deals with the residue. Freedom to move is carved out of personal liberty as understood under article 21. Therefore article 21 excludes article 19(1). Kharak Singh was charged in a dacoity case and released for want of evidence. Domiciliary visits by the police was held to be void because there was no law to justify the domiciliary visits. But in *Govind* v. *State of Madhya Pradesh,*[4] domiciliary visits were held to be constitutional as they had the force of law. It further held that whether domiciliary visits violate right to privacy depend upon the character and antecedents of the person concerned, and the object and limitations under which surveillance is made. The petitioner was a dangerous criminal whose conduct showed that he was determined to lead a criminal life. Hence the restrictions on article 21 were reasonable.

In *Satwant Singh Sawhney* v. *D. Ramarathnam, Assistant Passport Officer, New Delhi*[5] right to travel abroad was held to be a part of personal liberty under article 21. But it excludes ingredients of liberty mentioned in article 21.

D. Exclusivity rule rejected

Bank Nationalisation case; minority view of Kharak Singh accepted: The majority view in Kharak Singh that article 19(1) deals with particular attributes of personal liberty and article 21 deals with the residue was rejected in *R.C. Cooper*'s[6] case. The *minority view* was that life & personal liberty has many attributes and some of them are found in article 19. In other words there is some overlapping between article 19 and 21. Life and personal liberty is like a larger circle within which there is a smaller circle containing the liberties under article 19. Smaller circle also is a part of the larger circle. Hence article 19 liberties is also a part of the article 21 personal liberty. Therefore, if there is an allegation that Fundamental right under article 21 is infringed, the State must sustain its action by the test laid down in article 19(2) so far as the attributes covered by Art 19(1)[7] are concerned. The minority view was accepted as correct in *R.C. Cooper's* case. The exclusivity rule was rejected and it was held that Fundamental rights under Part III are

1. Prof. M.P. Jain: Indian Constitutional Law, p. 1082, (Nagpur: Lexis Nexis Butterworths Wadhwa).
2. For a critical analysis – see Seervai H.M.: Constitutional law of India, p.707, (Bombay: N.M.Tripathi Pvt. Ltd, 3rd Ed. Vol I).
3. AIR 1963 SC 1295: (1963) 2 Cr LJ 329: (1964) 1 SCR 332.
4. (1975) 2 SCC 148: AIR 1975 SC 1378: 1975 Cr LJ 1111.
5. AIR 1967 SC 1836: 1967 (2) SCA 523: 1968 (1) SCJ 178.
6. AIR 1970 SC 564: (1970) 1 SCC 248: (1970) 3 SCR 530. Also known as Bank Nationalisation Case.
7. Article 19(1) guarantees freedom of speech etc., (referred to as the seven lamps of freedom by Bhagwati J. These freedoms are not absolute but subject to restrictions under article 19(2) to (6).

not distinct and mutually exclusive rights but inter-linked. Each freedom has different dimensions. Thus, it is not sufficient if the impugned law steers clear of the restrictions imposed by one freedom. It must also meet the challenge of other guaranteed rights. This case over-ruled *Gopalan*'s case.

E. Personal liberty – Most liberal approach—*Maneka Gandhi*

Maneka Gandhi's case arose out of the Government's decision to impound her passport under section 10(3)(c) of the Passport Act, 1967 'in the interest of general public'. Further the Government turned down her request for the statement of reasons for making the order, again in the name of public interest.

One of the grounds on which she challenged the order was that her freedom of speech and expression and of profession under article 19(1)(a) & (g) respectively was violated and that the procedure for impounding the passport was violative of article 21 because it did not lay down any procedure and the procedure if any, was arbitrary and unreasonable as it did not provide for an opportunity to be heard. Therefore, the question that arose was-whether by restricting the right to travel abroad, was she being deprived of her personal liberty without the procedure established by law under article 21 and was it a violation of the fundamental rights under article 19(1)(a) and (g).[1]

Rulings in Maneka Gandhi's case:

(1) Exclusivity rule rejected—Articles 14, 19, 21 are interlinked

Articles 14, 19, 21 are not mutually exclusive. In other words –they are interlinked.[2] A law prescribing a procedure for deprivation of life and personal liberty must satisfy the test of articles 14, 19, 21. As Krishna Iyer J. puts it- no article in the Constitution pertaining to a Fundamental right is an island in itself. Just as a man is not dissectible into separate limbs cardinal rights in an organic Constitution have synthesis.

(2) Personal liberty has wide scope

The expression personal liberty in article 21 is of the widest amplitude & it covers a variety of rights which go to constitute the personal liberty of man and some of them have been raised to the status of distinct Fundamental Rights and given additional protection under article 19."[3] (emphasis added). "It is indeed difficult to see on what principle we can refuse to give its *plain natural meaning* to the expression 'personal liberty' as used in article 21 and read it in a narrow

---

1. Ultimately, it was held that it was not necessary to formally interfere with the impugned order having regard to the Attorney General's statement that she would be given a hearing and the Passport was to remain in the custody of the Registrar. Further, it was held that section 10(3)(c) of the Passport Act, did not offend articles 14, 19, 21 of the Constitution. The view of the Supreme Court was that the right to go abroad in the circumstances of this case, was not a Fundamental Right.
2. For a critical analysis on article 19 being read into article 21 *see* supra note 2 on p. 132 of this book at pp. 141 to 146, I have urged that there is no reason for article 19 to be read into article 21 though article 14 may be read into it. Sri Sharma also remarks '*Maneka* could have been decided on narrower grounds without endowing article 21 with a sweep of an Alladin's lamp K.M. Sharma: the Judicial Universe of Krishna Iyer J. p. 316 to 319 in Judges and Judicial Power (Bombay: N.M. Tripathi Pvt. Ltd., 1985):
3. *Maneka Gandhi* v. *Union of India,* AIR 1978 SC 597 (622).

and restricted sense so as to exclude those attributes of personal liberty which are specially dealt with in article 19.[1]

(3) Due process read into article 21

Procedure established by law under article 21 must be fair and reasonable and not arbitrary. The principle of reasonableness is an essential element of equality or non-arbitrariness. It pervades article 14 like a brooding omni-presence. Thus, the concept of reasonableness is projected into article 21. According to Krishna Iyer J. procedure means "fair and not formal procedure".

(4) Law must be reasonable

'Law' is reasonable law and not any enacted piece. This makes 'procedure established by law' under article 21 similar to 'procedural due process' under the American law. Ordinarily 'law' is enacted law. But for the purposes of article 21 'law'; takes other forms also. With this interpretation life and personal liberty is better protected. It includes—

(a) An Ordinance which is promulgated by the Executive. It held that our Constitution makes no difference between law made by the Legislature and an ordinance made by the President.[2]

(b) A rule made by the Supreme Court or the High Court under its rule making powers.[3]

(c) Rules made by the State Legislature under article 208 is 'law' under article 21. Article 21 is applicable to the area of Legislative privileges. Hence a person cannot be imprisoned for breach of privilege of legislature except according to the procedure established by law.[4]

(d) Regulations made by Police Act fall under article 21. But departmental instructions is not 'law' under article 21.[5]

In *Maneka Gandhi's* case – though the Passport Act does not expressly mention of *audi alterem partem*[6] - principles of natural justice – more specifically the right to be heard which is a common law principle was read into the Passport Act. The power to impound the passport is a *quasi*-judicial power. Right to be heard was read by implication in the Passport Act.

(5)* Gopalan *overruled

Gopalan case was overruled. It was held that law depriving a person of personal liberty must stand the test of article 21 and also articles 14 and 19.

---

1. I submit that *Gopalan* has been wrongly over-ruled in *Bank Nationalisation* case and an express ruling in of the majority in *Gopalan* has been misread in *Bank Nationalisation* case.

   J. Bhagwati in *Maneka Gandhi* case has relied upon the defective judgment in *Bank Nationalisation* case while analysing personal liberty under article 21 in spite of Kailasam J. having made this point very clear in *Maneka Gandhi* case itself. For a critical analysis see- supra note 2 on p. 132 of this book.
2. *A.K. Roy* v. *Union of India*, AIR 1982 SC 710: 1982 Cr LJ 340: (1982) 1 SCC 27.
3. Article 145 & 225.
4. *M.S.M. Sharma* v. *Sri Krishna Sinha*, AIR 1959 SC 395: 1959 SCJ 925: (1959) Supp 1 SCR 806
5. *Govind* v. *State of Madhya Pradesh*, AIR 1975 SC 1378: 1975 Cr LJ 1111: (1975) 2 SCC 148.
6. Hear the other side.

Ever since the passing of *Maneka* ruling there has been no looking back. Life and personal liberty have been interpreted in the widest possible terms; it has influenced the administration of criminal justice; service matters; it has an impact on the administrative law also. Life and personal liberty have been interpreted in such wide terms that practically every right under the sun is now a part of article 21.

Onus of proof: Under article 14 the onus of proof is on the petitioner because he has to prove that he has been singled out for an unfavourable treatment. It is basically a question of fact and so the petitioner has to prove it. But under article 19, 21 – once the petitioner shows that his right has been taken away it is for the State to prove that the restrictions imposed on the liberties of the petitioner are reasonable or that the procedure is just, fair and reasonable and not arbitrary.[1]

F. Applications of *Maneka Gandhi* judgment

With the new version of 'personal liberty' and 'procedure established by law' the court has entertained challenges to the laws passed by the Legislatures, questioning their reasonableness and justness. Many more liberties have been brought within the fold of article 21 and the list is growing day-by-day.

Following rights are held to be falling under article 21:

(1) Right to live with human dignity

In *Francis Coralie* v. *Union of India*[2] it was held that right to live is more than just animal existence and physical survival. It is not confined to protection of any faculty or limb through which life is enjoyed. It includes the 'right to live with human dignity and all that goes along with it *viz.*, the bare necessaries of life, such as adequate nutrition, clothing and shelter, and facilities for reading, writing, and expressing oneself in diverse forms, freely moving about and mixing and commingling with fellow human beings.

(2) Right to livelihood—Humanistic approach

In Olga Tellis v. *Bombay Municipal Corporation*[3] it was held that 'life' under article 21 includes 'right to livelihood' because no person can live without the means of livelihood. It is an important facet of right to life. Sections 313, 313A, 314, 497 of Bombay Municipal Corporation Act, 1888 empowered the authorities to remove the huts from pavement and public places. It was challenged on the ground that it deprived them of their right to livelihood and hence it was violative of article 21. Court held that it was a reasonable restriction on the right of livelihood of pavement and slum dwellers in the interest of general public. But the court took a humanistic approach and directed that they could be evicted only after the current monsoon season. But in *Sodan Singh* v. *New Delhi Municipal Committee*[4] Supreme Court held that doing business on the pavements is not a right included in article 21.

---

1. *Deena* v. *Union of India*, AIR 1983 SC 1155: 1983 Cr LJ 1602: (1983) 4 SCC 645.
2. AIR 1978 SC 597: (1978) 1 SCC 248: (1978) 2 SCR 621.
3. AIR 1986 SC 180: (1985) 3 SCC 545: 1985 2 Bom CR 434.
4. AIR 1989 SC 1988: 1989 All LJ 1097: (1989) 4 SCC 155.

(3) No fundamental Right to work

In *Delhi Development Horticulture Employees Union* v. *Delhi Administration*[1] Supreme Court rejected the contention that right to livelihood includes right to work, that the country has not attained the capacity to guarantee Fundamental right to work. In this case the daily wagers under the Jawahar Rozgar Yojana had claimed automatic regularisation which was rejected. National Rural Employment Guarantee Scheme guarantees 100 days of assured employment in villages. Even if a villager works on his own field he is paid the prescribed remuneration by the Government. This is to give effect to the right to livelihood and work and earn concept.[2]

(4) Right to shelter is fundamental right

Right to shelter is a Fundamental right under article 21. Right to live as a human being implies right to food, water, decent environment, education and shelter. These are basic human rights without which civil, political and social right cannot be exercised.[3]

(5) Beauty contest violates article 21

Holding of a beauty contest is objectionable under section 3 of Andhra Pradesh Objectionable Performances Prohibition Act, 1956 as it is repugnant to dignity or decency of women and offends article 21.[4]

(6) Hearing before termination

Right to life under article 21 includes right to be heard before termination. Thus, in *D.K. Yadav* v. *J.M.A. Industries*[5] held that fair play requires that the workmen be given an opportunity of explaining his case before he is terminated. Article 21 clubs life with liberty, dignity of person with means of livelihood without which the glorious content of dignity of person is reduced to animal existence.

(7) Telephone tapping violates article 21

In *People's Union for Civil Liberties* v. *Union of India*[6] Supreme Court held that telephone tapping is a serious invasion of an individual, state right to privacy under article 21. The Constitutional validity of section 5 of the Indian Telegraph Act, 1885 which authorises tapping in certain circumstances was challenged when the CBI was alleged to have tapped the telephones of the politicians. The court lamented that no rules were framed by the Government to prevent misuse of the power under section 5. In the absence of a just and a fair procedure to exercise these powers the rights guaranteed under articles 19 and 21 could not be protected. The court laid down exhaustive guidelines to regulate the discretion of the State under section 5. For example – that an order for telephone

---

1. AIR 1992 SC 789: 1992 AIR SCW 616: (1992) 4 SCC 99.
2. It is submitted that the scheme has its adverse impact. The villagers have become too lazy to work; there is shortage of labour because of which agriculture sector is facing grave problems.
3. *Chamelisingh* v. *State of Uttar Pradesh*, (1996) 2 SCC 549: AIR 1996 SC 1051: 1996 AIR SCW 542.
4. *Chandra Raja Kumari* v. *Police Commissioner, Hyderabad*, AIR 1998 AP 302.
5. (1993) 3 SCC 259: 1993 AIR SCW 1995: JT 1993 (3) SC 617.
6. AIR 1997 SC 568: 1997 AIR SCW 113: (1997) 1 SCC 301.

tapping can be issued only by the Home Secretary; it shall be reviewed by the review Committee; it shall be in force only for 2 months; records of intercepted communications shall be kept; the intercepted material shall be used only for the limited purposes under section 5(2) of the Act. Tapping is permissible only if a public emergency has occurred or in the interest of public safety. The judgment goes a long way in protecting right to privacy of the Indian citizens.

(8) Right to LIC policy is right to life

In *LIC of India* v. *Consumer Education and Research Centre*[1] - only the salaried classes could take the LIC policies under Table 58. It was held that right to LIC policies was a right to life and livelihood. It is in order to provide for an economic support to the dependents in case of death or disablement of the policy holder. An appropriate LIC policy within the paying capacity of the insured to pay the premium is one of the social security measures contemplated in the Constitution. Restricting the policy only to the salaried class is violative of article 21. This portion of Table 58 was set aside by the court as it was severable from the rest of the portion.

(9) Section 10 of the Indian Divorce Act is unconstitutional

In *Pragati Varghese* v. *Cyril George Verghese* Bombay High Court struck down section 10 of the Indian Divorce Act as it was violative of articles 21, 15, 14 of the Constitution. A Christian wife had to prove adultery along with cruelty or desertion to get a divorce from her husband. There was no such condition on the husband. He could get a divorce only on the ground of adultery

(10) Right to privacy

(a) Right to privacy – A fundamental right

In *Auto Shanker* case[2] Supreme Court has held that right to privacy or the right to be let alone is guaranteed by article 21. A citizen has the right to safeguard his own privacy and that of his family, marriage, procreation, motherhood, child bearing and education etc.

(b) Easy virtue woman has right to privacy

In *State of Maharashtra* v. *Madhulkar Narain*[3] Supreme Court held that right to privacy is available to a woman of easy virtue also and no one can invade her right to privacy. A police inspector visited the house of one Banubai and demanded to have sexual intercourse. She raised a hue and cry. He contended that as she was a woman of easy virtue her evidence was not reliable. The court rejected his contention and held him liable for violating her right to privacy.

(c) Limitations on right to privacy

A doctor working in a hospital donated blood for a patient. He turned out to be HIV positive. This was disclosed to his would be wife, due to which his marriage broke down. He contended that his right to privacy under article 21 was violated. The information was a confidential information which was

---

1. (1995) 5 SCC 482: AIR 1995 SC 1811: 1995 AIR SCW 2834.
2. *R. Rajagopal* v. *State of Tamil Nadu*, AIR 1995 SC 264: 1994 AIR SCW 4420: (1994) 6 SCC 632.
3. AIR 1991 SC 207: (1991) 1 SCC 57: JT 1990 (4) SC 169.

protected from disclosure under the Rules of Medical Ethics. It was held that though right to privacy is a Fundamental right it is subject to restrictions. Right to marry is an essential element of right to privacy. Marriage is the sacred union of two healthy bodies of opposite sex. Disclosure of this information has saved the would-be wife from the risk of being infected with AIDS. Her right to life includes the right to be told that a person with whom she was to get married is a victim of a deadly disease which was sexually communicable. In this case there was a clash of two Fundamental rights – the doctor's right to privacy and his would be wife's right to lead a healthy life – the right which would advance the public morality or public interest. Court said that moral considerations cannot be kept at bay and the court must keep their fingers firmly upon the pulse of the accepted morality of the day.[1]

(d) Adultery alleged – DNA test – permitted

When adultery is an allegation on which divorce is claimed; and the foetus was preserved in the hospital Lab and is no longer a part of the body- the wife cannot claim that a DNA test to determine whether the husband is the father of the child which was in her womb[2] – violates her right to privacy.

(e) DNA test not to be granted casually

DNA test to determine paternity of a child involves a conflict between the right to privacy and the duty of the court to arrive at the truth. DNA test must not be granted as a matter of course. Court must consider diverse matters including presumption under section 112, the Evidence Act; pros and cons of the order directing the test; and whether it is not possible for the court to reach the truth without use of such a test.[3]

(f) Virginity test unconstitutional

Virginity test to determine whether the marriage was consummated is a violation of the right to privacy. Wife had filed for decree of nullity of marriage as the marriage was not consummated due to the husband's impotency. To allow the virginity test would amount to roving enquiry against a female who is vulnerable even otherwise.[4]

(g) Telephone tapping of wife's conversation

Husband filed a divorce petition and sought to produce telephonic conversation of his wife recorded in US with others. It was held that the very act of the husband tapping the wife's conversation without her knowledge is an infringement of her right to privacy. Even if true these recordings are not admissible in evidence. The wife cannot be asked to undergo a voice test and then compare it with the conversation denied by her.[5]

---

1. *Mr. X* v. *Hospital Z*, (1998) 8 SCC 296: AIR 1999 SC 495: 1998 AIR SCW 3662.
2. *Mrs. X* v. *Mr.Z*, AIR 2002 Del 217: 2002 (2) Hindu LR 32: 2002 (2) Marri LJ 180.
3. *Bhabani Prasad Jena* v. *Convenor Secretary, Orissa State Commission for Women*, AIR 2010 SC 2851: 2010 AIR SCW 4603: (2010) 7 SCALE 582
4. *Surjit Singh* v. *Kanwaljit Kaur*, AIR 2003 P&H 353: 2004 (1) Cur LJ (CCR) 52: 2004 (2) Marri LJ 108.
5. *Rayala M. Bhuvaneswari* v. *Nagaphanender Rayala*, AIR 2008 AP 98: 2008 (64) All Ind Cas 860: 2008 (1) Andh LT 613.

(11) Right to health

(a) in *Parmanand Katara* v. *Union of India*[1] Supreme Court held that it is the professional obligation of all doctors – Government and private – to extend medical aid to the injured immediately without waiting for the legal formalities to be complied with by the police under Cr.P.C. Court also directed that publicity be given to this judgment to create awareness about the right and the duties.

(b) In *Paschim Banga Khet Mazdoor Samiti* v. *State of West Bengal*.[2] The Supreme Court held that denial of medical help to a seriously injured person due to non-availability of beds is a violation of article 21 which imposes an obligation of the State to provide medical assistance to every injured person. In this case the State was directed to pay a compensation of Rs. 25,000 to the petitioner as compensation as he had to take treatment in a private hospital and incur an expenditure of Rs. 17,000.

(c) In *Consumer Education and Research Centre* v. *Union of India*[3] is a historic judgment in which Supreme Court held that the right to health and medical care is a Fundamental right under article 21. It laid down detailed guidelines to promote health, strength and vigour of the workmen during period of employment and leisure and health even after retirement as basic essentials to life with health and happiness. This right was available also against the private industries.[4] Guidelines laid down were for the asbestos industries in the country – like health insurance, compensation in case of occupational health hazards 'membrane filter test, etc. The State employees are entitled to medical reimbursement of expenses for treatment and room rent charges.[5]

(12) Detention in civil prison unconstitutional

In *Jolly Verghese* v. *Bank of Cochin*,[6] it has been held that the arrest and detention of an honest judgment debtor in civil prison who has no means to pay the debt in the absence of *mala fides* and dishonesty- violates article 11 of the International Covenant on Civil and Political Rights and article 21 of the Constitution. Krishna Iyer J. said 'to be poor is no crime'. Hence to recover debts by imprisoning violates article 21 unless there is proof of wilful failure to pay in spite of sufficient means.[7]

(13) Right to die is not a Fundamental right under article 21

In *Gian Kaur* v. *State of Punjab*[8] Supreme Court has held that right to live does not include right to die. It overruled its decision In *P. Rathinam* v. *Union of India*[9] that it includes right to die. The Bombay High Court also had held

1. AIR 1989 SC 2039.
2. (1996) 4 SCC 37: AIR 1996 SC 2426: 1996 AIR SCW 2964.
3. (1995) 3 SCC 42: AIR 1995 SC 922: 1995 AIR SCW 759.
4. *Kirloskar Brothers Ltd.* v. *Employee's State Insurance Corpn.*, (1996) 2 SCC 682: AIR 1996 SC 3261: 1996 AIR SCW 2296.
5. *State of Punjab* v. *Mohinder Singh Chawla*, AIR 1997 SC 1225: 1997 AIR SCW 1260: (1997) 2 SCC 83.
6. AIR 1980 SC 470.
7. AIR 1980 SC 470: (1980) 2 SCC 360: ILR (1980) 1 Kant 273.
8. (1996) 2 SCC 648: AIR 1996 SC 946: 1996 Cr LJ 1660.
9. (1994) 3 SCC 394: 1994 Cr LJ 1605: AIR 1994 SC 1844.

that right to life includes right to die and had declared section 309 IPC which punishes attempt to commit suicide as unconstitutional. In *Gian Kaur* the Court held that right to life includes any aspect of life which makes it dignified but not that which extinguishes it.

(14) Protection of environment

(a) Protection of ecology and environment and Right to get pollution free water and air[1] are fundamental Rights; The court ordered closure of lime stone quarries[2], closure of tanneries near Kanpur to prevent pollution of river Ganga[3] and because there were serious deficiencies regarding safety requirements; shifting of 168 hazardous industries in Delhi as they were causing danger to the ecology.[4] The court has observed that though such industries are of vital importance for the country's progress as they generate foreign exchange and create employment-having regard to pollution caused by them principle of sustainable development has to be adopted as a balancing concept between ecology and development. Precautionary principle and polluter pays principle are an important feature of polluter pays principle.[5]

(b) Shriram Foods and Fertilisers were directed to take all necessary steps to ensure good health and safety of workers working in their company which was manufacturing hazardous and lethal chemicals like oleum. Rs. 20 lakhs was directed to be deposited to be paid as compensation to gas leak victims; 15 lakhs in case of escape of chlorine gas within a period of 3 years from the date of this Judgment.

(c) In *M.C. Mehta (2)* v. *Union of India*[6] Supreme Court agreed with the contentions taken by the environmentalist M.C. Mehta that river Ganga was becoming a public nuisance and the water was getting polluted beyond imagination. It directed the Kanpur Nagar Mahapalika to submit its proposals for effective prevention and control of water pollution within 6 months to the Board constituted under the Water Act; to get the Dairies shifted outside the city and arrange for disposal of accumulated wastes; to construct public urinals and toilets and its use free of charge for the poor; to ensure that dead bodies and half charred bodies are not thrown in the river; licenses for new industries to be given subject to condition that adequate provisions are made for the treatment of trade effluents flowing from the factory.

---

1. *Subhash Kumar* v. *State of Bihar*, AIR 1991 SC 420: 1991 AIR SCW 121: (1991) 1 SCC 598.
2. *Rural Litigation and Entitlement Kendra, Dehradun* v. *State of Uttar Pradesh*, (1985) 2 SCC 431: AIR 1985 SC 652: (1985) 2 Cur CC 70.
3. *M.C. Mehta* v. *Union of India*, (1987) 4 SCC 463: JT 1987 (4) SC 630.
4. *M.C. Mehta* v. *Union of India*, (1996) 4 SCC 750: 1996 AIR SCW 2732: AIR 1996 SC 2231.
5. *Vellore Citizens* v. *Welfare Forum Union of India*, (1996) 5 SCC 650.
6. (1988) 1 SCC 471: AIR 1988 SC 1115: JT 1988 (1) SC 69. It was a public interest litigation filed by a public spirited person. It was held that though Mr. Mehta was not a riparian *i.e.*, living on the river side he had a right to get the various statutory provisions enforced. M.C. Mehta is popularly known as a 'Green lawyer'.

(d) *Indian Council for Enviro-Legal Action* v. *Union of India*[1] is a significant judgment which laid down the principle of 'polluter pays'. An industrial complex had developed in Udaipur District of Rajasthan. Some of the industries produced chemicals like oleum. The industries were run without requisite licences and without installing equipments for treatment of highly toxic effluents discharged by them. Water in the well became unfit for human consumption. It spread diseases, death and disaster in the village and the surrounding areas. The villagers revolted and the industries were closed but the consequences of their action remained in existence and caused damage to the village. 720 out of 2440 tonnes of sludge still remained. It was spread across and covered with mud to conceal it in spite of Court's order to remove the sludge. The Supreme Court directed the Government and the authorities to comply with the various Acts – Environment Protection Act; Water Act; Air Act and Hazardous Waste Disposal Act. The villagers right to life was invaded. Hence the court directed the respondents to pay for all the damage to the soil, to the underground water and to the village in general. Liability of the respondents is determined on the principle of 'polluter pays' – the offending industry must pay for the damage that occurs.

Likewise there are any number of cases wherein the Courts have been moved for the protection of life and liberty. *For example-* to stop the intensive type of prawn farming in the ecological fragile coastal areas.[2]

(15) Noise pollution

Every person has the right to live in a noise free atmosphere. An engineer by profession filed a PIL for a direction to the Government to strictly enforce various laws enacted for restricting the use of loudspeaker and high volume noise producing audio-video systems. The immediate reason for the PIL was that the cries of a 13-year-old rape victim were not heard due to the noise of music in the neighbourhood and she set herself ablaze and died of burn injuries. It was held that freedom from noise is a part of the Fundamental right under article 21. It has to be balanced with the Fundamental right to speech and expression under article 19(1). Nobody can be compelled to listen. Increasing the volume of speech with artificial devices and compelling unwilling persons to hear the noise violates article 21. Compared to the development of laws in developed countries India is lagging behind in enacting adequate laws to contain pollution. However the Judiciary has been contributing its might in containing noise pollution.[3] The Court has issued valuable directions to curtail the menace of noise pollution like – a ban on using microphones after 10 pm; complete ban on bursting sound emitting fire crackers between 10 pm to 6 am.

---

1. (1996) 3 SCC 212: AIR 1996 SC 1446: 1996 AIR SCW 1069.
2. *S. Jagannath* v. *Union of India*, AIR 1997 SC 811: 1997 AIR SCW 635: (1997) 2 SCC 87.
3. For a detailed analysis of noise pollution see 'Noise pollution: Are the laws audible?" by the author: AIR 2005 JS.

(16) Smoking in public places

Smoking in public places is a violation of the Fundamental right of others due to harm caused by passive smoking.[1]

(17) Right to education

It has been held to be a Fundamental right under article 21. Life includes 'education' because education promotes dignified life and makes other Fundamental right meaningful.

(a) *Education at all level is Fundamental right*: In *Mohini Jain* v. *State of Karnataka*[2] -Mohini Jain was not able to pay the heavy capitation fee of Rs. 60,000 for a medical seat and so she was denied admission. The Supreme Court held that right to education at all levels is a Fundamental right under article 21 read with the directive principles under articles 38, 39(a), 41, 45. Charging capitation fee is illegal, it also violates article 14 as it is arbitrary, unfair and unjust. Capitation fee makes the availability of education beyond the reach of poor. Education has never been a commodity for sale. *'vidya daana'* considered as a most revered *'daana'*(gift). Thus the State was cast with heavy obligations.

(b) *Free education up to 14 yrs- Fundamental right*: In *Unni Krishnan, J.P. v. State of Andhra Pradesh*[3] – *Mohini Jain* was put to test. The petitioners contended that without capitation fees- private Medical and Engineering institutions will have to close down their institutes. The court partly overruled *Mohini Jain* and held that right to free education is limited to children upto 14 years of age. After that obligation of the State to provide education is subject to the limits of its economic capacity. It was held that admissions shall be based on merit. But 50% of the seats in all professional colleges may be filled by candidates ready to pay more. There shall be no quota for management, caste etc. Only two categories were provided – free seats and payment seats. Thus more opportunities were provided to the meritorious students who were unable to pay higher fees.

(c) Under the Schools Act, 2009 seats were reserved in private schools for children of poor families and they were prohibited from taking donation or capitation fee. It was to give effect to article 21A – right to education until 6 years. It was held valid.

(18) Prisoners' rights

The convicts are not deprived of all their Fundamental rights by reason of imprisonment. They continue to enjoy them though in a truncated form. Thus, they cannot exercise freedom of movement but they cannot be deprived of their life and liberty without the due process of law. In *D.B.M. Patnaik* v. *State of Andhra Pradesh*[4] – 146 naxalite undertrial prisoners were sought to be prevented from escaping by posting armed guards and live electrical wires fixed on top of

1. *Murli S. Deora* v. *Union of India*, AIR 2002 SC 40: 2001 AIR SCW 4505: (2001) 8 SCC 765.
2. (1992) 1 SCC 645: AIR 1992 SC 1454: 1992 AIR SCW 1535 (capitation fee case).
3. AIR 1993 SC 2178: 1993 AIR SCW 863: (1993) 1 SCC 645.
4. AIR 1974 SC 2092: 1975 Cr LJ 556: (1975) 3 SCC 185.

the jail. It was held that it was a valid restriction on article 21 having regard to the fact that the usual watch and ward was insufficient and that some naxalites had tried to escape.

(19) Right to free legal aid

(a) Fundamental right to copy of judgment

In *M.H. Hoskot* v. *State of Maharashtra*[1] – Hoskot was given the certified copies of the judgment sentencing him to imprisonment was given only after the period of appeal was over and he was imprisoned for the full term awarded by the High Court. It was held that at least a single right of appeal is basic to any civilised jurisprudence. It includes providing free legal aid to the poor and otherwise disabled person and providing him a copy of the judgment. Giving legal aid is 'State's duty and not Government's charity' said Krishna Iyer J.

(b) Grant-in-Aid to law colleges—Fundamental right

In *State of Maharashtra* v. *Manubhai Bagaji Vashi*[2]: To provide free legal aid well trained lawyers are needed; this in turn requires good Law colleges with necessary infrastructure, good teachers. Since the Government is not in a position to start sufficient number of colleges, it is the duty of the Government to give grant–in–aid to the private law colleges on similar lines on which it is given to the Government law colleges to facilitate effective and meaningful functioning. Article 39(A) provides for equal justice and free legal aid so that opportunities for securing justice are not denied to any citizen by reason of economic or other disabilities. In order to fulfil this Constitutional mandate good lawyers trained in good law colleges are needed. Lawyers are needed in large numbers and are needed to be trained in different branches of law. Hence the direction was given to provide Grant-in-Aid to the law colleges. Right to free legal aid at the cost of the Government is a Fundamental right of the accused and is implicit in the requirement of reasonableness and fairness of the procedure.[3]

(c) Right to speedy trial

In *Hussainara Khatoon* v. *Home Secretary State of Bihar*[4] right to speedy trial was held to be a Fundamental right implicit in the guarantee of life and personal liberty under article 21. It was a case where a number of under-trials were languishing in the jails for a period longer than that for which they would be imprisoned if they were convicted of the offence charged. It was held that a procedure which does not ensure a reasonably quick trial cannot be said to be just, fair and reasonable. Right to speedy trial is one aspect of Fundamental right under article 21. But why was the delay caused is a question of fact. When the delay was due to the nature of the case (accused was tried for waging war against the State); and the tactics used by the accused – it was held that there is

---

1. AIR 1978 SC 1548: 1978 Cr LJ 1678: (1978) 3 SCC 544.
2. (1995) 5 SCC 730: AIR 1996 SC 1: 1995 AIR SCW 3701.
3. *Suk Das* v. *Union Territory of Arunachal Pradesh*, AIR 1986 SC 991: 1986 Cr LJ 1084: (1986) 2 SCC 401.
4. AIR 1979 SC 1360: 1979 Cr LJ 1036: (1980) 1 SCC 81.

no violation of Fundamental right.[1] A suit filed for Rs. 7,000 was pending for 60 years. It was directed to be taken up immediately.[2] Proceedings were quashed when the trial was pending for 17 years and no speed up action was initiated in spite of High Court issuing directions to complete the trial in 3 months and the appellant filed a second petition complaining of the delay in investigation.[3] Handcuffing must be only when there is a clear and a present danger of escape.[4] Handcuffing of the petitioners who had staged a dharna for a public purpose, and had refused to come out on bail was violative of article 21. Handcuffing and tying with a long rope the 7 TADA detenues lodged in the hospital was held to be violative of the due process clause under article 21.[5]

(20) Delay in executing death sentence

Undue delay in the execution of the death sentence will justify the sentence being reduced to life imprisonment.[6] When a mercy petition was pending for 7 years it was commuted to life imprisonment.[7] Detenue's right to have interview with lawyer and family member is a Fundamental right.[8]

(21) Death sentence—Constitutional

In *Bachan Singh* case it has been held that death penalty under section 302 IPC is not violative of article 21[9] ; executing the death sentence by hanging by rope is not violative of article 21[10] ; execution by public hanging is barbaric and violative of article 21[11] ; person sentenced to death is also entitled to procedural fairness until the last breath[12]

(22) Illegal arrest etc.

(a) Protection against illegal arrest, detention and custodial death. In *Joginder Kumar* v. *State of Uttar Pradesh*[13] Supreme Court laid down valuable guidelines to protect a person during investigation like – a relative may be informed of the fact of arrest if so desired by the arrested person; arrested person must be told of his rights; an entry must be made regarding who was informed about the arrest. These rights under article 21 and 22 must be strictly enforced. A person

---

1 *Raghubir Singh* v. *State of Bihar,* (1986) 4 SCC 481: AIR 1987 SC 149: 1987 Cr LJ 157.
2. *Moses Wilson* v. *Kasturiba,* AIR 2008 SC 379: 2007 AIR SCW 7058: (2007) 11 SCALE 405.
3. *Vakil Prasad Singh* v. *State of Bihar,* AIR 2009 SC 1822: 2009 Cr LJ 1731: 2009 AIR SCW 1418.
4. *Prem Shankar Shukla* v. *Delhi Administration,* AIR 1980 SC 1535: 1980 Cr LJ 930: (1980) 3 SCC 526.
5. *Citizen for Democracy through its President* v. *State of Assam,* (1995) 3 SCC 743: 1996 AIR SCW 2815: AIR 1996 SC 2193.
6. *Triveniben* v. *State of Gujarat,* AIR 1989 SC 142: 1989 Cr LJ 870: (1988) 4 SCC 574.
7. *Madhu Mehta* v. *Union of India,* AIR 1989 SC 2299: (1989) 4 SCC 62: 1989 Cr LJ 2321.
8. *Francis Coralie Mullin* v. *Administrator, Union Territory of Delhi,* AIR 1981 SC 746: 1981 Cr LJ 306: (1981) 1 SCC 608.
9. *Bachan Singh* v. *State of Punjab,* AIR 1980 SC 898: 1980 Cr LJ 636: (1980) 2 SCC 684 J.Bhagwati dissenting.
10. *Deena* v. *Union of India,* AIR 1983 SC 1155: 1983 Cr LJ 1602: (1983) 4 SCC 645.
11. *Attorney General of India* v. *Lachma Devi,* AIR 1986 SC 467: 1986 Cr LJ 364: 1986 (1) SCJ 166.
12. Triveni ben.
13. (1994) 4 SCC 260: AIR 1994 SC 1349: 1994 Cr LJ 1981.

aged 22 yrs died due to beating in police custody. His mother was awarded Rs. 1,50,000 as compensation.[1]

(b) In *D.K. Basu* v. *State of West Bengal*[2] detailed guidelines were laid down to be followed in all cases of arrest and detention- like the police personnel must have a clear identification; a memo of arrest must be prepared and attested by a witness; friend of the arrested person must be informed; arrested person must be told that he has such a right; medical examination of the arrestee must be done within 48 hours; copies of all these documents must be sent to the nearest Magistrate; he must be allowed to meet his advocate

(23) Compensation for violation of Article 21

Compensation have been awarded in the following cases:

(a) *Rudal Shah* v. *State of Bihar*[3] is a decision of far reaching importance. Rudal Sah remained in jail for 14 years even after acquittal due to the irresponsible behaviour of the State Government officers. Bihar Government was directed to pay Rs. 30,000.

(b) For death in fake encounters.[4]

(c) Labourer taken to police station for work, beaten because he demanded salary and he died.[5] (75,000 compensation)

(d) Death of a 9-year-old due to police beating.[6]

(e) A police officer directed to personally pay compensation to Ravikant- an undertrial prisoner – for handcuffing him and parading him. This violation of duty was directed to be entered in his service register.[7]

(f) Army officer died in service due to negligence of army officers. 6 lakhs awarded as compensation to widow and minor children.[8]

(24) Compensation for rape victims and special directions

Rape is not only a crime against the person of a woman but also against the society. It pushes her into deep emotional crisis. Hence, it is the most hated crime.

(25) Honour killing violative of article 21

Khap Panchayat decrees honour killing of boys intending to marry girls of different castes.[9]

(a) in *Delhi Domestic Working Women's Forum* v. *Union of India*[10] four domestic women servants were raped by 7 army personnels in a running train. Court

1. *Nilabati Behera* v. *State of Orissa,* AIR 1993 SC 1960: 1993 Cr LJ 2899: (1993) 2 SCC 746.
2. AIR 1997 SC 610: 1997 AIR SCW 233: 1997 Cr LJ 743.
3. AIR 1983 SC 1086: 1983 Cr LJ 1644: (1983) 4 SCC 141.
4. *People's Union for Civil Liberties* v. *Union of India,* AIR 1997 SC 1203: 1997 AIR SCW 1234: (1997) 3 SCC 433.
5. *People's Union for Democratic Rights* v. *Police Commissioner,* (1989) 4 SCC 730: (1989) 1 SCALE 598: 1990 SCC (Cri) 75.
6. *SAHELI, a Women's Resources Centre* v. *Commissioner of Police, Delhi,* AIR 1990 SC 513: (1989) Supp 2 SCR 488: (1990) 1 SCC 422.
7. (1991) 2 SCC 373: 1991 AIR SCW 871.
8. *Chiranjit Kaur* v. *Union of India,* (1994) 2 SCC 1.
9. *Arumugam Servai* v. *State of Tamil Nadu,* AIR 2011 SC 1859.
10. (1995) 1 SCC 14.

laid down detailed directions after noting the following defects in the system – complaints are handled roughly; victims are humiliated by the police; rape trials are a bad experience for the victims. The Court laid down detailed guidelines for the trial of rape:

- The victims of rape must be provided with an advocate well acquainted with the criminal justice who should represent her till the end of the case. He must also guide her on how to get assistance from other agencies like medical assistance and psychiatrist assistance.
- legal assistance must be provided at the police station itself.
- police must inform her that she has a right to be represented by an advocate.
- list of advocates willing to represent such victims must be kept at the police station.
- names of the victim of rape must not be disclosed as far as possible.
- Criminal Injuries Compensation Board must be set up. Board will pay the compensation whether or not conviction has taken place. In addition compensation shall be awarded by the court on conviction of the offender.

(b) In *Chairman Railway Board* v. *Chandrima Das*[1], *Hanufa Khatoon* – a Bangladeshi – was gang raped by Railway employees in a railway room. 10 lakhs was awarded as compensation to be paid by the Railway authorities. The court held that in addition to claiming compensation under Private law by filing a suit – when public functionaries are involved and there is violation of a Fundamental right or it deals with enforcement of public duties remedy is available under Public law *i.e.,* the Constitution. It is all the more so in a case of rape which amounts to deprivation of personal liberty guaranteed under article 21. A Bangladeshi is also entitled to this relief as article 21 is available to all 'persons' and not only the citizens. In addition, Universal Declaration of Human Rights, 1948 has the international recognition as the Moral Code of Conduct adopted by the General Assembly of the United Nations.

(c) *Interim compensation to rape victim*: In *Bodhisatwa v. Subhra Chakraborty*[2] accused was a lecturer and the victim – a student. Until the charges of rape were decided by the trial Court Rs. 1000 was awarded as interim compensation to the victim. He had given a false assurance of marriage and gone through fraudulent marriage ceremonies to make her believe that she was a legally wedded wife. Rape is a crime against the basic human rights and violative of the victims most cherished Fundamental right under article 21.

1. AIR 2000 SC 988: 2000 Cr LJ 1473: 2000 AIR SCW 649.
2. (1996) 1 SCC 490: 1996 AIR SCW 325: AIR 1996 SC 922.

(d) *Vishakha* v. *State of Rajasthan*[1] Supreme Court laid down that it is the responsibility of the employer of a public or a private institution to prevent sexual harassment of working women in work places in a PIL filed by Vishakha – an NGO complaining of brutal gang rape of a social worker of Rajasthan. Sexual harassment violates the victim's right under article 19(1)(g) to practice any profession, trade etc. It is also violative of articles 14, 15. Following guidelines were laid down which were to be followed until an Act was passed.

(1) Employer must expressly prohibit by publication and circulation, sexual harassment which includes physical contact, demand or request for sexual favours, sexually coloured remarks; showing pornographic or any other unwelcome physical, verbal or non-verbal conduct of sexual nature.

(2) In case of Government and Public sectors – Conduct and discipline rules must include rules prohibiting sexual harassment and provide for penalties. In case of private sectors - Standing Orders under the Industrial Employment (Standing Orders) Act, 1946 must provide for it.

(3) Appropriate work conditions should be provided in respect of work leisure, health and hygiene to ensure that there is no hostile environment towards women at work place.

(4) Where such conduct amounts to specific offences under the IPC or under any other law the employer shall initiate appropriate action in accordance with law by making a complaint with the appropriate authority.

(5) The victims of sexual harassment must have the option to seek transfer of the perpetrator or their own transfer.

The court held that International Conventions and norms must be read into domestic laws when there is no inconsistency between them and the domestic laws are silent on the point. It relied on CEDAW[2] and the Beijing Declaration. *Vishakha* was followed in *Apparel Export Promotion Council* v. *A.K. Chopra*[3] it was held that the court must examine the broader probabilities of the case and not go into the technicalities of the expression 'molestation' or 'physical assault'.

(26) Amendment in Jail Manual

In *R.D. Upadhya* v. *State of Andhra Pradesh*[4] court directed the Jail Manual to be suitably amended so as to include provisions to take care of the welfare of the children living in jails along with their prisoner mothers.

G. Article 21A

Provides that the State shall provide free and compulsory education to all children of the age of 6 to 14 years in such manner as the State may by law determine.

---

1. AIR 1997 SC 3011: 1997 AIR SCW 3043: (1997) 6 SCC 241.
2. Convention for Elimination of All Forms of Discrimination Against Women, 1979.
3. AIR 1999 SC 625: 1999 AIR SCW 274: (1999) 1 SCC 759.
4. AIR 2006 SC 1946: 2006 AIR SCW 2274: 2006 (3) Supreme 546.

CHAPTER 13

PROTECTION AGAINST ARREST AND DETENTION IN CERTAIN CASES

(Article 22)

SYNOPSIS

A. Introduction

Article 21 lays down that no person can be deprived of his life and personal liberty except according to the procedure established by law. Article 20 provides the safeguards to the person who is accused. Article 22 provides the procedure to be followed on arresting the person and the procedure to be followed in case a person is preventively detained to prevent him from committing crime. These procedural requirements must be incorporated in the procedure laid down by the Legislature by any law.

B. Rights of a person arrested under laws other than preventive detention laws

Article 22(1) and (2) speak of 4 rights available to persons arrested under ordinary laws. These rights are available to citizens and non-citizens

Arrest and detention of a person in police lock-up is a serious infringement of the personal liberty. It has to be justified under the Constitution and the other laws of the land. It can be a traumatic experience. Any arrest has to be justified on strong grounds. With the new interpretation of article 21 the rights of the arrested person are very well protected and can be tested by the courts with reference to the reasonableness of the law and the reasonableness of the procedure.

(1) Information of the grounds of arrest

No person is to be detained in custody without being informed as soon as may be of the grounds of arrest.[1]

The arrestee must be informed of the grounds of arrest to enable him to prepare his defense, apply for bail or file a writ of *Habeas Corpus*. It need not be with full details but it must be sufficient enough for him to understand why he has been arrested.[2] If the information is insufficient his arrest becomes unlawful. In *Joginder Kumar* v. *State of Uttar Pradesh*[3] Supreme Court laid down valuable guidelines to protect a person during investigation like- a relative may be informed of the fact of arrest if so desired by the arrested person; arrested person must be told of his rights; an entry must be made regarding who was informed about the arrest. These rights under articles 21 and 22 must be strictly enforced. A person aged 22 years died due to beating in police custody. His mother was awarded Rs. 1,50,000 as compensation.[4]

(2) Right to consult a lawyer

He shall not be denied the right to consult and to be defended by a legal practitioner of his choice.

After the decision in *Maneka Gandhi case* the arrested person shall be provided with legal assistance if he is not able to engage one due to poverty, indigence of incommunicado situation because right to legal aid is a Fundamental right. It is the State responsibility to provide for free legal aid so that no citizen is denied justice due to economic and other reasons as laid down in article 30A as directive principle. The Legal Services Authorities Act, 1986 also makes provision for free legal aid under section 12 of that Act. This right 'to defend' himself continues even if he is released on bail.[5] The word 'defend' means that the right continues as long as the effect of the arrest continues. This right is also available to a person not actually arrested but to a person who is under circumstances of 'near custodial interrogation. If the accused wishes his lawyer to be by his side during examination this facility should not be denied to him.'[6]

(3) Production of the arrested person before the Magistrate within 24 hours

It is mandatory that the arrested person is brought before the Magistrate within 24 hours of his arrest. It is immaterial whether the Magistrate sits in

1. Article 22(1).
2. *Madhu Limaye* v. *State of Punjab*, AIR 1959 Punj 506: 1959 Cr LJ 1209: ILR 1959 Punj 1111.
3. (1994) 4 SCC 260: AIR 1994 SC 1349: 1994 Cr LJ 1981.
4. *Nilabati Behera* v. *State of Orissa*, AIR 1993 SC 1960: 1993 Cr LJ 2899: (1993) 2 SCC 746.
5. *State of Madhya Pradesh* v. *Shobharam*, AIR 1966 SC 1910: 1966 Cr LJ 1521: 1967 (1) SCA 449.
6. *Nandini Satpathy* v. *P.L. Dani*, (1978) 2 SCC 424: AIR 1978 SC 1025: 1978 Cr LJ 968.

the court or not at the time the arrested person is produced before him.[1] The Magistrate has to apply his mind and see whether the arrest is legal and proper. Production before the Magistrate is not just a formality.[2]

In *Bhim Singh* v. *State of Jammu and Kashmir*[3] the Magistrate had remanded the accused to police custody without the accused having been produced before the Magistrate. The Supreme Court held that there was either collusion between the Magistrate and the police or the Magistrate had acted very casually. The State was directed to pay a compensation of Rs. 50,000 to the arrested person.

If the arrested person is released on bail – he need not be produced before the Magistrate but his right to be defended by a lawyer continues.[4]

(4) Detention beyond 24 hours only with Magistrate's authority

No person must be detained in custody beyond 24 hours without the authority of a Magistrate.

This means that if detention beyond 24 hrs is necessary- it is possible only under judicial custody.

In *CBI* v. *Anupam J. Kulkarni*[5] Supreme Court laid down important guidelines regarding arrest of an accused when investigation is not completed within 24 hours. Beyond 24 hours and up to 15 days the Magistrate can order detention in police custody; but beyond 15 days – detention can be only in judicial custody. When the investigation is not complete within 90 days or 60 days then the accused has to be released on bail under section 167(2) of Cr PC.

(5) Exceptions

Rights given to arrested person under clauses (1) and (2) are not available to an *enemy alien*[6] and a person arrested and detention under preventive detention law. Thus, these Articles are not applicable where arrest is not connected with an accusation of an offence *e.g.*, arrest of a defendant before judgment; arrest of a judgment debtor in execution of a decree under CPC.

C. Preventive Detention

(1) Gist of Articles 22(4) to (7)

The said articles deal with the safeguards provided to the detenue detained under a preventive detention law. No preventive detention law shall provide for detention for a period longer than 3 months. (Article 22(4)). If detention is to be for a period longer than 3 months the Constitution provides two alternatives:

(a) The Advisory Board has to report its opinion that there is sufficient cause for such detention beyond 3 months [Article 22(4a)]. However proviso to article 22(4a) provides that 'nothing in article 22(4a) shall authorise the

---

1. *Prabhakar Nath Dwivedi* v. *District Magistrate, Allahabad,* AIR 1960 All 467: 1960 All Cr R 122: 1960 Cr LJ 1049.
2. *In Re Madhu Limaye.*
3. AIR 1986 SC 494: 1986 Cr LJ 192: (1985) 4 SCC 677.
4. Supra note 5.
5. (1992) 3 SCC 141: 1992 AIR SCW 1976: AIR 1992 SC 1768.
6. A citizen of a country which is at war with India.

detention of any person beyond the maximum period prescribed by any law made by Parliament under sub clause (b) of clause 7.

(b) The second way to deta in beyond 3 months is to detain the person in accordance with the provisions of any law made by the Parliament under article 22(7)(a) & (b). That is a law prescribing the circumstances under which and the class of cases under which a person may be detained for a period longer than 3 months under a Preventive Detention law without obtaining the opinion of the Advisory Board under article 22(4a) and article 22(7b) prescribing the maximum period for which any person may in any class of cases be detained under any law providing for preventive detention.

Preventive detention and punitive detention distinguished: Preventive detention means detention of a person without trial, in such circumstances that the evidence in possession of the authority is not sufficient to make a legal charge or to secure the conviction of the detenue. Object of punitive detention is to punish a person for what he has done; object of preventive detention is to prevent him from doing something likely to be injurious to the security and safety of the State.

The distinguishing feature in India is that persons can be kept in preventive detention even during normal times. In other democratic countries preventive detention is allowed only during emergencies. Hence the court has been cautioning time and again against the indiscriminate use of preventive detention laws and laying down safeguards to protect the personal liberty of the people. Hence though preventive detention is a *necessary evil* it has to be in strict adherence of the Constitution and the preventive detention laws.[1]

The courts can examine the validity of the preventive detention order. But they are not competent to enquire into the truth of the facts mentioned as grounds for preventive detention. They cannot go into the question whether on merits the detaining authority was justified in making the preventive detention order.[2]

In *A.K. Roy* v. *Union of India (NSA Case)*[3] - *detention order valid*

Supreme Court upheld the Constitutional validity of National Security Act which provided for detention on grounds of –*'acting in a manner prejudicial to the security of India or a State, defence of India, relations with foreign power, maintenance of public order, maintenance of supplies and services essential to the community'*. These grounds were held to be not vague or arbitrary. Directions were issued to protect the detenues – like the kith and kin should be immediately informed of the place of detention of the detenue; he is entitled to his book etc; he must be kept separate from those convicted; no treatment of a punitive character must be meted out to him.

Principles for protection of misuse of preventive detention provisions: Following are the principles evolved by the judiciary from article 22(4) to (7) to protect

1. *State of Punjab* v. *Jagdev Singh Talwandi,* AIR 1984 SC 444: 1984 Cr LJ 177: (1984) 1 SCC 596.
2. *Bhim Sen* v. *State of Punjab,* (1952) SCR 18: AIR 1951 SC 481: 1952 Cr LJ 75.
3. AIR 1982 SC 710: 1982 Cr LJ 340: (1982) 1 SCC 27.

the personal liberty of the detenue from insensitivity and a casual approach to preventive detention:

1. Communication of the grounds of detention. 'Grounds' are different from 'facts'.
2. Right to make representation & Consideration of representation
3. Advisory Boards.
4. Confirmation of detention order.
5. Parliament's power to dispense with advisory Boards.
6. Maximum period of detention.

Communication of the grounds of detention:

There is a difference between grounds of detention and facts. Grounds are the conclusions drawn by the Government which must be communicated to the detenue. They indicate the kind of prejudicial acts suspected to be done by the detenue. Facts are the reasons for arriving at the conclusion.

There are two safeguards:

(1) Grounds of detention must be communicated 'as soon as possible' *i.e.*, within a reasonable time. What is reasonable time is for the court to decide[1]. If the Act prescribes a period then the grounds must be communicated within that time[2] and

(2) Detenue must be given the earliest opportunity of making a representation against the order of detention

(2) Grounds of detention

(i) All basic facts to be disclosed

In *Khudiram Das* v. *State of West Bengal*[3] Bhagwati J. held that 'grounds' mean all the basic facts and materials which have been taken into consideration by the detaining authority and on which the order of detention is based. In short grounds mean those grounds which are the 'cause of detention'. In this case the whole history sheet was before the Magistrate, but only 3 of the grounds were communicated to the detenue. Magistrate filed an affidavit that he had considered only the 3 grounds that were communicated. Detenue challenged the order of detention on the ground that other grounds were not disclosed. Supreme Court quashed the order of detention with an observation that the undisclosed material was of highly damaging character; human mind takes decisions based on the totality of the impressions and it is not possible to dissect the information which went into the making of the decision. Detention order under COFEPOSA has been set aside for non-supply of documents which were considered by the detaining authority.[4]

---

1. *Ujagar Singh* v. *State of Punjab,* AIR 1952 SC 350: 1952 Cr LJ 146: 1952 SCR 756.
2. *E.g.,* under COFEPOSA- ordinarily not later than 5 days.
3. AIR 1975 SC 550: 1975 Cr LJ 446: (1975) 2 SCC 81.
4. *Prakash Chandra Mehta* v. *Commissioner and Secretary, Government of Kerala,* AIR 1986 SC 687: 1986 Cr LJ 786: (1985) 3 SCR 697.

(ii) Rational relation between grounds of and purpose of detention

There must be a rational connection between the grounds of detention and the purpose of the preventive detention statute.

(iii) Communication in one lot and not vague

All the grounds of detention must be communicated in one instalment in clear terms[1]. It should not be vague. Even if one ground is vague and others are clear- detention will be illegal.[2] No fresh 'grounds' can be added later on because detention must be based on the grounds then existing[3] but 'additional facts' to support the ground already conveyed can be communicated within a reasonable time[4]. Detenue is a man of 'desperate habits and dangerous character' is held to be vague and not clear.[5]

(iv) Refusal to disclose in Public interest

Under article 22(6) grounds which the detaining authority considers not desirable to be disclosed in public interest – need not be disclosed.

(v) Grounds of detention to be disclosed as soon as possible

Grounds of detention must be communicated 'as soon as possible' *i.e.*, within a reasonable time. What is reasonable time is for the court to decide[6]. If the Act prescribes a period then the grounds must be communicated within that time.[7]

(3) Right to make representation and consideration of representation

Article 22(5) does not say to whom the representation must be made. Supreme Court has held that the *Government* must consider the representation. Representation must be made to the authority having the power to rescind the order.[8] Right to make representation is a valuable right. It must be considered speedily. Representation to the Government is different from 'referring to the Advisory Board'.[9] If on consideration of the representation the Government decides to release the detenue there is no question of referring to the Advisory Board. If the representation is made after the matter is referred to the Advisory Board – the Government must consider it after the Board gives its Report, but it must be considered independently of the Report.[10] The detention can be declared to be bad if the Government does not justify its delay in considering the representation.[11]

---

1. *Piyush Kantilal Mehta* v. *Commissioner of Police, Ahmedabad City,* AIR 1989 SC 491: 1989 Cr LJ 956: JT 1988 (4) SC 703.
2. *Prem Nath Bazaz* v. *Union of India,* AIR 1957 Punj 235: ILR (1956) Punj 374: 1957 Cr LJ 1168.
3. *State of Bombay* v. *Atma Ram Shridhar Vaidya,* AIR 1951 SC 157: 52 Cr LJ 373: 1951 SCJ 208.
4. *Hansmukh* v. *State of Gujarat,* AIR 1981 SC 28: (1981) 1 SCR 353: 1980 Cr LJ 1286.
5. *Sasthi Keot* v. *State of West Bengal,* AIR 1974 SC 525: 1974 Cr LJ 464: (1974) 4 SCC 131.
6. *Ujagar Singh* v. *State of Punjab,* AIR 1952 SC 350: 1952 Cr LJ 146: 1952 SCR 756.
7. *E.g.,* under COFEPOSA- ordinarily not later than 5 days.
8. *Amir Shad Khan* v. *L. Hmingliana,* AIR 1991 SC 1983: 1991 Cr LJ 2713: 1991 AIR SCW 2214.
9. *Vimal Chand Jawantraj Jain* v. *Pradhan,* AIR 1979 SC 1501: 1979 Cr LJ 1131: (1979) 4 SCC 401
10. *Union of India* v. *Manish Bahal,* AIR 2001 SC 2685: 2001 Cr LJ 3311: 2001 AIR SCW 2493.
11. *S.M. Jahubar Sathik* v. *State of Tamil Nadu,* AIR 1999 SC 1945: 1999 Cr LJ 2881: 1999 AIR SCW 1628.

(4) *Advisory Board*

To confirm if detention is beyond three months

If detention is up to three[1] months no reference to the Advisory Board is necessary. The Board consists of persons who are, or who have been, or who are qualified to be High Court judges.

Beyond three months – the Board must confirm the detention and the Government also must confirm and extend the period of detention within the three months time limit. If the Government fails to do so the detention order lapses as soon as the three month period is over.

(5) Parliaments' power to dispense with Advisory Boards

Article *22(7)(a) was held to be an exception to article 22(4)(a):* Under article 22(7) (a) Parliament may prescribe the **circumstances under which *'and'* the class of cases under which a person can be detained beyond 3 months** without referring it to the Board and prescribing a maximum period for which any person may in any class of cases be detained under any law providing for preventive detention.

The question that has come up before the court, in short - is whether the term ***and'*** in article 22(7)(a) is to be used as 'and' or as 'or'. In other words whether the Parliament must prescribe *'both the circumstances and the class of cases'* under which a person can be detained without reference to the Advisory Board— or it can prescribe *'either the circumstances or the class of cases'* . In *Gopalan* it was held that the Parliament may prescribe either the circumstances or the class of cases. But in *Sambhu Nath Sarkar* v. *State of West Bengal*[2] it was held that the Parliament must prescribe both the circumstances and the class of cases. Only then, a person can be detained beyond three months without referring it to the Advisory Board. *Shambhu Nath* was a case that came up under MISA. It narrated 5 out of the 6 heads mentioned in the Constitution for which a law of preventive detention could be made without reference to the Advisory Board. The court declared the section unconstitutional because it had *not mentioned 'class of cases'* in which alone the case was not required to be referred to the Advisory Board Thus, article *22(7)(a) was held to be an exception to article 22(4)(a).* As a rule, if detention was to be for more than three months – reference to the Advisory Board was a must. As a law under article 22(7)(a) was by its very nature, a drastic law- it had to strictly comply with the constitutional provisions. *Hence the word 'and' was read conjunctively as 'and' and not as 'or'.*

Following are the laws authorising preventive detention

National Security Act; Conservation of Foreign Exchange and Prevention of Smuggling Act, 1974; PBMSECA- Prevention of Blackmarketing and Maintenance of Supplies of Essential Commodities Act, 1980. The States also have enacted preventive detention laws. MISA.

---

1. 44th amendment to the Constitution reduced the period of detention without referring to the Advisory Board from three months to two months. But it has not yet been brought into force.
2. AIR 1973 SC 1425: (1973) 1 SCC 856: 1973 Cr LJ 1155.

CHAPTER 14

RIGHT AGAINST EXPLOITATION

(Articles 23-24)

SYNOPSIS

A. Introduction

Article 23 protects the people from being exploited either by the State or the private citizens. It is aimed at ensuring human dignity.

B. Right against exploitation

Right against exploitation is dealt with under two heads:

(a) Prohibition of traffic in human beings and forced labour (Article 23)

(b) Prohibition of employment of children in factories etc. (Article 24)

C. Prohibition of traffic in human beings and forced labour (Article 23)

Traffic in human beings and *begar* and other similar forms of forced labour are prohibited and any contravention of this provision is made an offence punishable in accordance with law.

But the State can impose compulsory service for public purposes (*e.g.*, Military or social service) and there shall be no discrimination only on the grounds of religion, race, caste, class or any of them in imposing such compulsory service. (Article 23)

Traffic in human beings means 'buying and selling' men and women and includes immoral trafficking in women and children for immoral or other purposes. The Parliament has passed the Immoral Traffic (Prevention) Act, 1956 for punishing for acts resulting in traffic in human beings.

It is a provision which is applicable to all persons. The State is under an obligation to see that traffic in human beings and forced labour is abolished. In *People's Union for Democratic Rights* v. *Union of India*[1]'*begar*' means forced work without payment. Making a person to work, against his will- when he is legally entitled not to work is 'forced or involuntary work.'

Article 23 is very wide. It strikes at traffic in human beings, forced labour and other forms of forced labour wherever they are found. 'Force' includes not only physical or legal force but also force arising from the compulsion, Fundamental right, economic circumstances which leaves a person without any choice. When labour is provided for less than the minimum wage it is forced labour within the meaning of article 23. In *People's Union for Democratic Rights* v. *Union of India*[1] deduction of Re. 1 per worker per day by the Jamadars from the wages paid to the Asiad Project workers was held to be violative of article 23. Forced labour as a punishment for an offence is not prohibited.

1. AIR 1982 SC 1473: (1982) 2 SCC 494: 1982 (II) LLJ 454.

Following have been held to be violative of article 23:

Payment of wages lower than minimum wages to persons employed on Famine Relief Work,[1] unreasonably low wages to prisoners for their work;[2] bonded labour system;[3] customary offering of free labour to the Headman of a village;[4] Sarpanch's order of fine for any person who violates his command that one person from every family must come with a spade and a pan for embankment of a village tank;[5]

Following are not violative of article 23:

In *Dubar Goala* v. *Union of India*[6] the petitioners-licenced porters had voluntarily agreed to work for two hours extra under an agreement with the Railways. They were paid extra remuneration, they had the benefit of reduced licence fee, they were allowed the free use of Railway premises for earning their livelihood. The court did not agree that they were doing forced labour within the meaning of article 23. Their voluntary agreement itself dispels the contention of 'forced labour'.

D. Prohibition of employment of children in factories etc. (Article 24)

Article 24 prohibits employment of children below 14 years in factories, mines or any hazardous employment.

This is in tune with the directive principles under article 39 that the State is under an obligation to ensure the health and strength of workers, men and women and the tender age of the children are not abused and that citizens are not forced to take up work unsuited to their age or strength due to poverty.

Construction industry has been held to be hazardous for the children to work even if construction industry is not mentioned in the schedule to Employment of Children Act, 1938.[7] Child Labour (Prohibition and Regulation) Act, 1986 in pursuance of the constitutional provision. Article 24 does not prohibit employment in any innocent or harmless job.

In *M.C. Mehta* v. *State of Tamil Nadu*[8] in a public interest litigation filed by the advocate Mehta Supreme Court has laid down exhaustive guidelines for the protection of the rights of millions of children working in public and private sectors. It was more specifically in connection with the employment of children in Shivkasi Cracker Factories. The court directed setting up of Child Labour Rehabilitation Centre. The offending employer had to pay a compensation of Rs. 20,000 to be deposited in a Fund. When a child was removed from service an adult member was to be offered a job in a factory or elsewhere.

---

1. *Sanjit Roy* v. *State of Rajasthan*, AIR 1983 SC 328: (1983) 1 SCC 525: 1983 (I) LLJ 220.
2. *Deena* v. *Union of India*, AIR 1983 SC 1155: 1983 Cr LJ 1602: (1983) 4 SCC 645.
3. *Bandhua Mukti Morcha* v. *Union of India*, AIR 1984 SC 802: 1984 Lab IC 560: (1984) 3 SCC 161.
4. *Ruiweinao Kahaosan Tangkhul* v. *Ruiweinao Simirei Shailei Khullakpa*, AIR 1961 Mani 1.
5. *Chandra* v. *State of Rajasthan*, AIR 1956 Raj 188: 1956 Raj LW 311: ILR (1956) 6 Raj 797.
6. AIR 1952 Cal 496.
7. *People's Union for Democratic Rights* v. *Union of India*, AIR 1982 SC 1473: (1982) 2 SCC 494: 1982 (II) LLJ 454.
8. AIR 1997 SC 699: 1997 AIR SCW 407: (1996) 6 SCC 756.

CHAPTER 15
RIGHT TO FREEDOM OF RELIGION

(Articles 25-28)

SYNOPSIS

A. Introduction

India is a secular State. Religion is a matter of faith and belief. The State treats all religions and religious denominations alike. Secularism is not anti-God. In matters of religion the State is neutral and treats all religions equally.

India is a country of diverse religions and faiths and ideologies. The Constitution protects religions and religious practices from State interference. India has always believed in secularism. Hence it has been not just tolerant but has welcomed all other religions and faith with an open mind. The term 'secular' has been inserted by the 42nd Amendment. It does not mean that it is an atheist State but that it treats all religions equally; there shall be no State religion. It means respect for all religions and faiths.

B. Freedom of religion

Freedom of religion is covered under the following four heads:

1. Freedom of conscience and free profession practice and propagation of religion (Article 25).
2. Freedom to manage religious affairs (Article 26).
3. Freedom as to payment of taxes for promotion of any particular religion (Article 27).
4. Freedom as to attendance at religious instruction or religious worship in certain educational institutions (Article 28.).

(1) *Freedom of conscience and freedom of practice and propagation of religion (Article 25)*

Article 25(1) guarantees to every citizen the 'freedom of conscience and the right to freely profess, practise and propagate religion.' This right is subject to *public order, health, morality* and other provisions relating to Fundamental right.

Exception: However article 25 does not prevent the State from making any law.

(a) Regulating or restricting any economic, financial, political or other secular activity which may be associated with religious practice.

(b) Providing for social welfare and reform or the throwing open of Hindu religious institutions.

Thus the State can over-ride or regulate an economic activity connected with the religious practices; or may make a law contrary to the religious tenets in the interest of social reform. *For example,* polygamy was practised amongst Hindus as a part of their religion, but then monogamy was introduced as a measure of social reform. It is submitted that fundamentalist lobbying has hampered the passing of such socially reformative laws amongst Muslims where polygamy still prevails. Under these provisions the State has thrown the temples and other religious institutions open to all irrespective of their caste and sub-caste.

Secularism – a basic feature: in *S.R. Bommai* v. *Union of India* it is held that secularism is a basic feature[1] of the Constitution. It has been held in *Keshwanand Bharati's case* that the State cannot amend the basic structure of the Constitution. This means that the Constitution cannot be amended to make India a non-secular State or a theocratic State – like a Hindu or a Muslim country. 'Religious tolerance and equal treatment of all religious groups and protection of their life and property and places of their worship are an essential part of secularism enshrined in our Constitution.'[1] It is not a passive attitude of religious tolerance. It is a positive concept of equal treatment of all religions. The Constitution does not define the term 'secular' as it is not capable of being defined. Articles 25-28; 29-30; 14, 15, 16, 44, 51A promote the idea of secularism and by implication prohibit establishment of a theocratic State.[2]

"State tolerance of religion does not make it either a religious or a theocratic State. Secularism represents faith born out of the rational faculties and it enables to see the imperative requirements for human progress in all aspects. Secularism is neither anti-God nor pro-God as it treats alike the devout, agnostic[3] and the atheist.[4]'

Religion: 'Religion' is that which binds a man with his creator. Religion is not merely an opinion or a belief. It includes outward expression[5] of acts and Religious practices or performance of acts in pursuance of religious beliefs. It is considered to be conducive to their spiritual well-being. It may lay down a code of ethical conduct, may prescribe rituals and ceremonies; it is a matter of personal faith and belief. Freedom of conscience is absolute inner freedom to shape his relation with God in whatever manner he likes. When this freedom becomes articulate and is expressed in an outward form it takes the form of 'to profess and practise religion.' To practice religion is to perform the prescribed

1. (1994) 3 SCC 1: 1994 AIR SCW 2946: AIR 1994 SC 1918.
2. *Santosh Kumar* v. *Secretary, Ministry of Human Resources Development,* AIR 1995 SC 293: 1994 AIR SCW 4459: (1994) 6 SCC 579.
3. Idol breaker.
4. Non-believer in God.
5. In *Commissioner, Hindu Religious Endowments, Madras* v. *Lakshmindra Thirtha Swamiar of Sri Shirur Mutt,* AIR 1954 SC 282: 1954 SCA 415: 1954 SCR 1005.

religious duties, rites etc. To 'propagate' means to spread and publicise his religious views. Propagation must be without any co-ercion. It does not give the right to convert any person to his own faith. In *Rev. Stainislaus* v. *State of Madhya Pradesh.*[1] The Supreme Court held that 'to propagate' does not mean the right to convert another person to one's own religion.[2]

Religious practices: The court decides what constitutes an essential part of religion or religious practice by taking into consideration the religious tenets. Some religious practices may have sprung from superstitious belief and hence may be unessential additions to the religion. Such practices are not protected and the State can disallow them, *for example-* the practise of *Sati,* the practice of tonsure can be legally prohibited. Hence what is to be seen is whether the practice for which protection is claimed is an integral part of the said religion or is merely 'secular' or 'superstitious' in nature.[3] The court has to strike a balance between the freedom of the citizen to practice a religion or religious practices which are an essential part of the religion and those which are not essential and integral and the need for the State to regulate or control in the interest of the community.

It was held that a non-Brahmin can be appointed as *Pujari* in a temple if he is properly trained and well versed with rituals.

Sanskrit language- not anti-secular: *Santosh Kumar* is a landmark judgment in which the Supreme Court has held that introduction of Sanskrit as a subject for Central Board of Secondary Education is not against secularism. Sanskrit is a mother of all Aryan languages. It held that for without Sanskrit it is not possible to 'decipher' Indian philosophy, culture and heritage as *Vedas, Puranas* and *Upanishads* are in Sanskrit. The Court rejected the argument that introducing Sanskrit alone would be anti-secular and Arabic and Persian also would have to be introduced.

Secularism – Sarva dharma sambhava: Study of religions (under The New Education Policy) in school education was held[4] to be not anti-secular. It provided for value based education on the basis of all religions. Secularism means developing, understanding and respecting all religions. It is *'sarva dharma sambhava'* – *i.e.,* equal treatment and respect for all religions.

In the *National Anthem Case: right of silence:*[5] The children of 'Jehovah's Witnesses' from the Christian community refused to sing National Anthem, because their faith did not permit them to join any rituals except prayer to Jehovah. However they stood in silence without showing any disrespect. It was held no person can be compelled to sing the National Anthem if he has a genuine conscientious religious objection. The Kerala High Court had held that it is the fundamental duty under the Constitution to show unqualified respect to the National Anthem; the trend would endanger the security of the Nation, it will

1. AIR 1977 SC 908.
2. AIR 1977 SC 908: 1977 Cr LJ 551: (1977) 1 SCC 677.
3. *Supra* note l.
4. *Aruna Roy* v. *Union of India,* AIR 2002 SC 3176: 2002 AIR SCW 3670: (2002) 7 SCC 368.
5. *Bajoe Emmanual* v. *State of Kerala,* (1984) 3 SCC 615.

develop a tendency to ignore mandates of the Constitution. If religious practices run counter to public order, morality, health or policy of the Government to uphold the unity of the nation – the religious practice cannot be protected. But the Supreme Court overruled the well – meaning Kerala High Court ruling saying that the Constitutional right under article 25 cannot be regulated by an executive instruction which had no force of law. This was a decision given in 1952. It is opined that after the introduction of Fundamental Duties in 1976, this decision should be treated as overruled because it is now the fundamental duty under article 51 to respect the National Flag, National Anthem and the National Song- something that is even otherwise implicit in any country. It is submitted that 'respect for the National Flag' has a positive and a pro-active element in it. It is not 'absence of disrespect' but 'manifestation of the respect by a positive act like singing the National Anthem'.

A letter treated as a writ sought for directions to the State to educate its citizens in the matter of fundamental duties and questioned the correctness of a decision of the court in the National Anthem case in *Hon'ble Shri Rangnath Mishra* v. *Union of India*[1]. By the time matter was taken up for hearing the National Commission for review of the Constitution submitted its Report stating that strong steps must be taken to sensitise the people in discharging their fundamental duties. Hence with the directions that proper steps be taken for implementation of the Report, the writ was disposed.

In *Ismail Faruqui* v. *Union of India*[2] the Supreme Court has held that the State can acquire places of worship like mosques etc., if it is necessary for maintenance of law and order. It does not violate articles 25 and 26. A mosque is not an essential part of the practice of the religion of Islam and Namaz can be offered anywhere, even in open. The ruling was given in the famous Babri Masjid Demolition case when the Government had acquired the whole property surrounding the mosque.

Religious freedom subject to the rights of others

Rights of a Hindu wife: A Hindu convert taking a second wife under Muslim law during the subsistence of the first marriage violates the personal freedom and religious rights of the Hindu wife.[3]

Loudspeakers in prayers: No religion prescribes practice of religion by the use of loudspeakers. Use of loudspeakers is subject to the provisions of the Environment (Protection) Act, 1986. Restriction on the use of loudspeakers at the time of Azan is not violative of article 25[4], use of loudspeakers to offer prayers leads to noise pollution and is violative of the rights of personal liberty[5] of the public.

---

1. JT 2003 (7) SC 206.
2. (1994) 6 SCC 360: 1994 AIR SCW 4897: AIR 1995 SC 605.
3. *Lily Thomas* v. *Union of India,* AIR 2000 SC 1650: 2000 AIR SCW 1760: 2000 Cr LJ 2433.
4. *Moulana Mufti Syed Md. Noorur Rehman Barkati* v. *State of W.B.,* AIR 1999 Cal 15: 1999 Cal WN 323: 1998 (2) ICC 590.
5. *Church of God (Full Gospel) in India* v. *K.K R. Majestic Colony Welfare Association,* AIR 2000 SC 2773: 2000 AIR SCW 3089: 2000 Cr LJ 4022.

Restriction on freedom of religion

Freedom subject to public order, morality and health – the Police Act prohibits the slaughter of cattle or indecent exposure on one's person in a public place. In the name of religion untouchability or traffic in human beings like the *devdasi* system cannot be tolerated.

Two children norm

Two children norm for elective post is not violative of the personal law of the Muslims under which 4 wives is permissible. It was held that practices which encourage bigamy or polygamy can be regulated by law.

Regulation of economic, financial, political, and secular activities associated with religious practices

Cow sacrifice: Cow sacrifice is not an obligatory overt act for a Muslim to exhibit his religious beliefs.[1] Performance of *tandava dance*[2] by Anand Margis in procession is not an essential religious rite[3]. Collection and distribution of the offerings among temple sevaks is purely a secular activity. The system of hereditary *archakas* is not an essential and integral part of Hindu religion.

Taking over of Aurobindo Society under the Auroville (Emergency Provisions) Act, 1980 due to economic mismanagement of the society was not violative of article 25 because the utterings of Sri Aurobindo made it clear that neither the Society nor Auroville constituted a religious denomination and the teachings of Sri Aurobindo did not constitute a religion.[4]

Social welfare and social reforms: An act which prohibited polygamy and introduced monogamy was held valid. Polygamy is not an essential part of the Hindu religion. Right of the Sikhs to wear and carry *Kirpans* is recognised as a religious practice. But he cannot keep more than one *Kirpan* without a licence.

(2) Freedom to manage religious affairs (Article 26)

Subject to public order, morality and health every religious denomination or any section of it shall have the following rights:

(a) To establish and maintain institutions for religious and charitable purposes.

Terms 'establish and maintain' must be read together. Aligarh University was not established by Muslim minority and therefore could not claim the right to maintain it. It was established under the Statute passed by the Parliament. It was held valid as it was a secular aspect.[5]

(b) To own and acquire movable and immovable property.

(c) To administer such property in accordance with law.

---

1. *Mohd. Hanif Quareshi* v. *State of Bihar,* AIR 1958 SC 731: 1958 SCA 783: 1959 SCR 629.
2. It is a dance which Lord Shiva is supposed to have danced with immense anger in his 'Roudravtara'.
3. *Acharya Jagdishwaranand Avadhuta* v. *Commissioner of Police, Calcutta,* AIR 1984 SC 51: 1983 Cr LJ 1872: (1983) 4 SCC 522.
4. *S.P. Mittal* v. *Union of India,* AIR 1983 SC 1: (1983) 1 SCC 51: (1983) 1 SCR 729.
5. *Raja Bira Kishore Deb* v. *State of Orissa,* AIR 1964 SC 1501: 1964 (2) SCA 782: (1964) 7 SCR 32.

Note that the right to manage its religious matters is a Fundamental right subject to restriction under article 25 but Right to 'own acquire and administer' the religious property is subject to the regulations issued by the State.

Freedom of religion becomes meaningful when there is a right to manage the religious affairs. This right is available to a religious denomination or a section of it. 'Religious Denomination' is a collection of individuals having a system of belief considered to be conducive for their spiritual well being, having a common organisation, and designated by a distinct name. Thus followers of *Dwaita* (dualism); *Advaita (monism)*, *Vishista-adwaitas* and *Shaivaites* are a denomination. Ramkrishna Mission,[1] Shirur Math, Raghvendra Math is a denomination.

(3) Freedom from taxes for promotion of any religion (Article 27)

No person shall be compelled to pay any tax for the promotion or maintenance of any particular religion or religious denomination.

Thus, taxes collected from the public cannot be spent for promoting any particular religion because taxes are compulsory payments made by the public to the State for public purpose. This is because India is a secular State. The prohibition is against giving aid to any one religion. Thus if aid is given to all religions it would not be violative of article 27.

(4) Freedom as to attendance at religious instruction or religious worship in certain educational institutions (Article 28)

Article 28 prohibits religious instructions in the following 4 kinds of educational institutions:

(a) Institutions wholly maintained out of State funds.	No religious instruction can be imparted.
(b) Institutions recognised by the State.	Religious instruction can be imparted only with consent of the individuals.
(c) Institutions that are receiving aid out of State fund.	Religious instruction can be imparted only with consent of the individuals.
(d) Institutions administered by the State but are established under any trust of endowment.	There is no restriction on religious instructions.

Study of Gurunanak's life and teaching and doing a research on it was provided under section 4 of the Guru Nanak University Act. Court held the provision valid as it did not amount to religious instruction in State aided educational institution but it was to encourage an academic study of the teachings of Guru Nanak.[2]

In *Aruna Roy* v. *Union of India*[3] Supreme Court has held that article 28 does not ban study of religions.[3]

---

1. (1995) 4 SCC 646.
2. *D.A.V. College, Jullundur* v. *State of Punjab*, AIR 1971 SC 1737: 1971 (Supp) SCR 688: (1971) 2 SCC 269.
3. AIR 2002 SC 3176: (2002) 7 SCC 368.

CHAPTER 16

CULTURAL AND EDUCATIONAL RIGHTS

Articles 29-30

SYNOPSIS

A. Introduction

India being a country with various religions and faiths the founding fathers have taken care to see that persons professing different religions etc., are given constitutional right to maintain their culture and establish educational institutions.

B. Cultural and educational rights

Cultural and educational rights fall under two categories:

1. Protection of interests of Minorities. (Article 29)
2. Rights of Minorities to establish and administer educational institutions. (Article 30)

These articles guarantee cultural & educational rights to various cultural, religious and linguistic minorities located in India.

C. Protection of interests of Minorities

(1) Conserving language etc.

It provides that any section of the citizens residing in any part of India having a distinct language, culture, or script of its own has the right to conserve the same. Article 29(1).

What is required for the applicability of article 29(1) is that the section of the citizens must have a *distinct* language script or culture of its own. If so, they have a right to preserve the same.

It includes right to agitate for the protection of a language. Promise by a contesting candidate to work for the conservation of a language is not corrupt electoral practice. But appeal by a candidate to vote or refrain from voting on the ground of religion is a corrupt practice under section 123(3) of the Representation of People Act, 1951. Section 123(3) must be read with Article 29(1).[1]

1. *Jagdev Singh Sidhanti* v. *Pratap Singh Daulta*, AIR 1965 SC 183: 1965 (1) SCA 72: (1964) 6 SCR 750.

The purpose and object of the linguistic States is to provide greater facility for the development of the people of the area educationally, socially and culturally in the regional language. In addition, it is opined that language is closely related to culture. India is a land of diverse rich culture. Protecting the language is necessary to protect the culture. It was held that provisions to promote studies and research in Punjabi language by the Guru Nanak University does not infringe article 29(1). But this does not mean that minority institutions affiliated to the Guru Nanak University also must teach only in Punjabi. Thus, promotion of a majority language does not mean stifling the minority language.[1]

(2) State funded educational institution

No citizen shall be denied admission to any educational institution maintained by the State fund or receiving aid out of State funds on grounds only of religion, race, caste, language or any of them. [Article 29(2)]

Differences between articles 29(2) & 15(1)

Articles 29(2) & 15(1) prohibit discrimination on the same grounds of religion, race, caste, sex or place of birth. Yet following are the differences:

Article 29(2)	Article 15(1)
Protection is against the State or any others.	It protects the citizens against discrimination by the State.
Protection is against a particular class of wrongs-*i.e.*, denial of admission into State aided educational institutions.	It protects all citizens from discrimination generally on the grounds mentioned.
Discrimination on the ground of sex or place of birth are not mentioned. It prohibits discrimination only on the ground of religion, race, caste or language.	Discrimination on the ground of language is not mentioned. It prohibits discrimination only on the ground of religion, race, caste, sex or place of birth.

Article 29(2) is applicable to all groups- whether minority or majority. What is to be seen is whether the school or the college is run by the State or with State funding.

In *State of Bombay* v. *Bombay Educational Society*[2]– Bombay Government banned admissions of those whose language is not English into English medium schools. The order was quashed though it was for the promotion of vernacular languages.

D. Right of Minorities to establish and manage Educational Institutions (Article 30)

The right is provided to the linguistic and religious minorities.

(1) Establish and manage

It is the right to establish and manage educational institutions of their choice. Unless it is 'established' and 'managed' it cannot claim the protection of article 30. *For example,* an institution was not established as a minority institution though

1. *D.A.V. College, Jullundur* v. *State of Punjab,* AIR 1971 SC 1737: 1971 (Supp) SCR 688: (1971) 2 SCC 269.
2. AIR 1954 SC 561: 1955 SCR 568: 1954 SCA 784.

it was being managed by a minority community.[1] Since both the conditions were not satisfied it could not claim the benefit of article 30.

The Supreme Court has held in *St. Xaviers case* that this right is not an absolute right; Government has the power to regulate minority run educational institutions.

(2) Abolition of Fundamental right to property—Does not affect minority right

Article 30(1A) introduced by 1978 Amendment states that while making a law to compulsorily acquire any property of a linguistic or a religious minority institution the State must ensure that the amount fixed by such law or determined by such law is such as would not restrict or abrogate the right guaranteed under these articles.[2]

In *Society of St. Joseph's College* v. *Union of India*[3] the Supreme Court has held that article 30(1A) mandates that when property belonging to minority educational institution is acquired – the amount payable for acquiring the property must be such that it will not impair the functioning of the educational institution.

(3) No discrimination

While granting aid to educational institutions, the State shall not discriminate on the ground that it is a minority educational institution.[4]

Thus, the linguistic and the religious minorities have a right to 'establish' *i.e.,* start an educational institution and to 'administer' it *i.e.,* manage the affairs of the institution without any control so that they have the freedom to decide how best to manage and run it so that it would promote their idea of 'how the interest of the community in general and the institution in particular' will be served.[5] The purpose is to 'conserve their religion, language and culture and to impart education to their children in their own language.

What is minority: The term is not defined in the Constitution. Who are Minorities must be determined with reference to the population of the State whose law is under a challenge. If it is less than 50% of the State population – then it is a minority. *For example* – Malyalees in Karnataka are linguistic minorities because their population is less than 50% of the State population. Arya Samjists in Punjab are a *religious minority,* so they can claim the benefit under article 30(1). But Arya Samaj in Union Territory of Delhi is a *religious denomination* for the purpose of article 26 and may claim certain rights under article 25, 28, 29, but it is not a minority based on religion for the purpose of article 30(1) because Arya Samaj is a reformed Hindu sect. Minority based on

---

1. *Yogendra Nath Singh* v. *State of Uttar Pradesh,* AIR 1999 All 356: 1999 All LJ 2458: 1999 (2) All WC 1563.
2. Article 1-A added by Constitution (44th) Amendment 1978. By the same amendment right to property as a fundamental right has been taken away. Article 1-A has been inserted so that the right of the minorities to administer and manage their educational institutions is not affected.
3. AIR 2002 SC 195: 2001 AIR SCW 4813: (2002) 1 SCC 273.
4. Article 30(2).
5. *Ahmedabad St. Xavier College Society* v. *State of Gujarat,* AIR 1974 SC 1389: (1974) 1 SCC 717: (1975) 1 SCR 173.

religion is restricted only to those religious minorities *i.e.,* Muslims, Christians, Jains, Buddhists, Sikhs etc. Though Sikhs, Jains and Buddhists are subject to Hindu personal law, their religions are different from that of Hindus and hence they are religious minorities.[1]

E. Differences between articles 29(1) and 30(1)

Differences between articles 29(1) and 30(1) were elaborately examined in *Ahmedabad St. Xavier College Society* v. *State of Gujarat,* AIR 1974 SC 1389: (1974) 1 SCC 717: (1975) 1 SCR 173.

Article 29(1).	Article 30(1).
The right is conferred on every section of the society.	The right is conferred only on the religious and linguistic minorities.
The right is to conserve a distinct 'language, script, culture' of any section.	The right is to establish and manage an educational institution.
The article does not deal with education as such. It deals with conservation of a distinct language etc.	It deals only with the establishment and administration of an educational institution.
It may be wholly unconnected with educational institution.	It may be unconnected with the purpose of protecting language, script, culture.

St. Xaviers College case is an important case in which the State had contended that the College was not founded for the conservation of language, script or culture as mentioned in article 29(1) hence it was not entitled to the protection available to the minorities under article 30. After reviewing earlier rulings,[2] it held that – Article 30 covers institutions imparting general secular education also. It is not limited to institutions which are established for conserving its own language script or culture. The purpose is to enable the children of minorities to go out in the world fully equipped.

It is submitted that allowing a linguistic or a religious educational institution to run a general educational institution and giving special facilities which are not afforded to other educational institutions amounts to discrimination. It has no reasonable nexus with the object of the Constitutional provision. The object is to ensure that culture as ingrained in the religion or the language is not watered down or lost in the midst of the majority religion or the majority language/culture. Hence the benefit of the protection must be limited only to educational institutions imparting religious education. It is opined that minority linguistic and religious institutions running English medium schools or medical and engineering colleges stand on no different footing than the other institutions running like schools and colleges. Hence unless they are treated alike it violates article 14.[3] It also deepens the majority-minority divide. In addition article 30(1A) coupled with the interpretation in *Society of Joseph College* adds to the injustice done to the majority run institutions. In effect it simply means that when a

1. *Arya Samaj Education Trust, Delhi* v. *Director of Education, Delhi Administration, Delhi,* AIR 1976 Del 207: ILR (1976) 2 Del 93.
2. *In re The Kerala Education Bill, 1957,* AIR 1958 SC 956: 1959 SCJ 321: 1959 SCR 995; *Sidhrajbhai* v. *State of Bombay,* AIR 1963 SC 540.
3. For further critical comments see M.P. Jain: Indian Constitutional Law: (Nagpur: LexisNexis Butterworths Wadhwa) 5th Ed. P.1249.

minority run educational institution is compulsorily acquired amount paid must be reasonable so that it will not impair the running of the institution; but the amount paid for acquiring a majority run institution need not stand the test of 'not impairing the running of the institution'. The law on this point needs to be reviewed both by the law makers and the law interpreters.

F. Establishing and managing educational institutions

(a) *Punjabi language- medium of instruction:* A Panjab University circular making Punjabi the sole medium of instruction was held to be violative of the rights of Hindi speaking minorities to have instructions in Hindi (*DAV College, Bhatinda* v. *State of Punjab*).[1]

(b) *Appointments in minority institutions:* Appointment in minrity institutions does not require prior approval of the Vice-Chancellor and the persons appointed will be entitled to aid from the Government in view of article 30(2).

(c) *Ram Krishna Mission Case:* In *Bramhachari Sidheshwar* v. *State of West Bengal*[2] Supreme Court held that the Ram Krishna Mission established by Swami Vivekanand to propagate Vedanta values as expounded by Ramkrishna is not a minority religion. It is a denomination of Hindu religion and hence not entitled to the benefit of Fundamental right under article 30(1).

Power of the Government to regulate minority run educational institutions:

State regulations must not abrogate minority right: It has been held in *St. Xaviers* case and in *RE Kerala* Education Bill that the Fundamental right of the minorities is not an unregulated one. However the power to regulate must be so exercised that it does not destroy its character as a minority institution. The regulations must be reasonable and must be conducive to making the institution an effective vehicle for minority education.

Unaided Minority Educational Institution is one with 75% minority students – Says a Cabinet decision CNIE—

G. Important rulings pertaining to regulatory provisions

(a) *Pay protection:* Conditions designed to protect the ill paid teachers who were in fact rendering service to the Nation. (*Re Kerala Education Bill* case)

(b) *Healthy surroundings:* Regulations to prevent educational institutions in unhealthy surroundings or insisting on qualified teachers (*Sidhrajbhai* v. *State of Bombay*)[3]

(c) *Applicability of Industrial Disputes Act:* In *Christian Medical College Hospital Employees Union* v. *Christian Medical College, Vellore Assn.*[4] it was held that the Industrial Disputes Act, 1947,(IDA) is a social security measure enacted for the welfare of the workers; it deals with the machinery for settling disputes. The reference of the industrial dispute raised on account of dismissal of the cook, clerk and a packer working in the Christian Hospital was held not to violate article 30. The contention was that the

1. AIR 1971 SC 1731: 1971 (Supp) SCR 677: (1971) 2 SCC 269.
2. (1995) 4 SCC 646.
3. AIR 1963 SC 540: 1963 (2) SCA 394: (1963) 3 SCR 837.
4. AIR 1988 SC 37: (1987) 4 SCC 691: JT 1987 (5) SC 129.

provisions [1] were not applicable to the Hospital because it was an integral part of the college run by the Christian minority. The court did not agree as the IDA is applicable to all industries irrespective of who is running it.

(d) *Threat to withhold grants:* Order threatening to with hold grant-in-aid and recognitions of college unless 80% seats in minority run institutions were reserved to the nominees of the Government (*Sidhrajbhai* case) was held unconstitutional.

(e) *Taking over management:* Power to take over the management of the minority institution if it fails to carry out the State Government directions was held to be invalid. (*State of Kerala* v. *Very Rev. Mother Provincial*[2])

(f) *Total control of Government body:* The provisions of the Gujarat University Act were such that in effect it displaced the Managing Committee of the College itself because every college had to be under the management of a Government body consisting of representatives of the university, teachers, students etc. In appointments and dismissals also the University played a decisive role (section 51A).

These provisions were held to be not applicable to the minority institutions because they curtail their right to administer their institutions.

(g) *Right of affiliation:* Right of affiliation to the university or of recognition is not a Fundamental right of the minority educational institution. Affiliation is for the purpose of regulating the educational character and content of the minority institution. Conditions like qualifications for appointment of teachers, library facilities etc., are for the purpose of uniformity and efficiency and excellence in educational courses and hence not violative of minority rights under article 30.

(h) *Right of admission in its community school:* A Roman Catholic Mission School was refused permission to admit girl students in their school as the school was a boys school and because within a radius of one mile there was a Muslim Girls School where girls could take admission. In effect it amounts to the girl students not being able to take admission in a school belonging to their community. This violated the right of the minority educational institution under article 30. (*Rt. Rev. Magr. Mark Netto* v. *Govt. of Kerala*)[3]

(i) *Rules to maintain educational standards:* The Supreme Court has held in *Frank Anthony Public School Employees Assn.* v. *Union of India*[4] that the statutory measures regulating the terms and conditions of service of teachers and other employees of minority educational institutions for maintaining educational standards are not violative of the Fundamental right of the minorities under article 30. It provided that the pay and

1. (Section 9A, 10, 11, 12, 33).
2. AIR 1970 SC 2079: 1970 Ker LT 630: (1970) 2 SCC 417.
3. AIR 1979 SC 83: (1979) 1 SCC 23: (1979) 1 SCR 609.
4. (1986) 4 SCC 707: (1986) 4 SCC 707: 1987 Lab IC 427.

conditions of service of the recognised private school shall not be less than those of the Government schools of Delhi. Supreme Court held the provision valid. Under the guise of a minority school the management cannot be allowed to exploit its employees.

(j) *Dissolution of the Managing Committee:* Under section 7(2)(n) of the Bihar State Madarsa Education Board Act, the Managing Committee of the Respondent's Madarsa was dissolved because they had failed to follow the directions regarding payment of salary to teachers. Supreme Court held that in the guise of regulating the institution the management of the minority institution cannot be taken over. It violates article 30(1).

(k) *Admission procedure:* In St. Stephen's college the college prospectus provided for an interview before the final selection for admission to the college. The University circular directed admission of students on merit based on the marks in the qualifying examination. It was held in *St. Stephen College* v. *University of Delhi*[1] that selection of students was an important facet of administration; College was not bound to follow the University directions as it would take away their right under article 30(1).

In *TMA Pai Foundation* case eleven Judge Bench rendered an important decision. 6 of them have given a majority Judgment and 3 have concurred:

1. Religious and linguistic minorities must be determined by taking into consideration the population of the State.
2. Religious and linguistic minorities can establish educational institutions 'of their choice'. It includes professional educational institutions also.
3. Minority educational institutions are of 2 kinds- aided and unaided Minority educational institutions. The aided one's enjoy greater autonomy.
4. The unaided educational institutions cannot be regulated by the State or the University except for providing qualifications and minimum conditions of eligibility in the interest of academic standards. In professional institutions provision can be made for merit based selection and the management can be given sufficient discretion to admit students.
5. An aided minority educational institution must admit non-minority students also. The percentage is to be notified by the State Governments.
6. Observance of *inter se* merit amongst the minority students could also be ensured. CET can be made compulsory. Merit must be observed by unaided minority educational institution also.
7. It may have its own reasonable procedure for selection.
8. Right to administer can be subject to regulatory measures.
9. Grant giving agency can put restrains on the freedom of administration and management for proper maintenance of the high standard of education.

---

1. (1992) 1 SCC 558: 1992 AIR SCW 1792: AIR 1992 SC 1630.

10. Fees charged by unaided institutions cannot be regulated but no capitation fee can be charged. In aided institutions fees must be so charged that there is no profiteering. But excess fees to meet infrastructural development etc., is allowed.
11. All citizens have a right to establish and administer educational institutions under articles 19(1)(gj) & 26(a).

This case has partly overruled *Unnikrishnan* case in which it was held that private unaided and aided recognised and affiliated educational institutions conducting professional courses could charge fees subject to a maximum limit fixed by the State. Commercialisation is not allowed.

In *Islamic Academy of Education* v. *State of Karnataka*[1] – Court added certain conditions as clarification to *TMA Foundation* judgment. Two committees were to be set up in each State -one to give effect to *TMA Pai* and to approve the fee structure charged by Minorities institutions and second Committee to see the tests to be conducted by the institutions.

In *P.A. Inamdar* v. *State of Maharashtra*[2], it was held that reservations in private educational institutions – (minorities and majority) is violative of articles 30 and 19(1)(g). Reservations of seats in unaided private professional institution – aided and unaided- violates articles 30 and 19(1)(g). 15% seats can be reserved for NRI subject to condition that seats must be used for NRI only and the money collected from them be utilised for benefit of economically backward students. Common Entrance Test is valid. Subject to no profiteering each institution is free to devise its own fee structure. Capitation fee not permitted to be charged.

In *Bal Patil* v. *Union of India*[3] following the decision in *T.M.A. Pai* case the Supreme Court held that Jain community is not a Minority in State of Maharashtra. It held that Minority Group has to be identified not merely on the recommendation of the Commission but on consideration of the social, cultural, religious conditions of the community in each State. Numerical minority as shown by Statistical data is not sufficient. If it is shown that the majority of the members of the community belong to the affluent class of industrialists, professionals and propertied class it may not be necessary to notify them as Minority and extend any special treatment to them as minority.

It is submitted that the decision goes against the intention of the framers of the Constitution. Intention was to protect the religious and linguistic distinctness and to give special privileges to educational institutions established for the purpose of protecting this limited distinctness. It was never intended to extend the privileges to institutions imparting general/secular education like Arts, Science, Engineering, Medicine etc. That would be blatantly treating 'like unlike' and hence violative of articles 14 and 15. Looking at the time frame in which the Constitution was framed – *viz.*, in the midst of partition of the country – intention was to send a message of 'we care for you, your religion and your culture' to the persons professing a minority religion. It is high time that the

1. (2003) 3 SCC 697.
2. AIR 2005 SC 3226: 2005 AIR SCW 3923: (2005) 6 SCC 537.
3. AIR 2005 SC 3172: 2005 AIR SCW 3762: (2005) 6 SCC 690.

Constitution be amended to make it more egalitarian and provide to the effect that "all citizens have the freedom to establish institutions to impart religious education whether in their own language or otherwise in order to conserve their religion script, language".

CHAPTER 17

RIGHT TO CONSTITUTIONAL REMEDIES

(Articles 32-35)

SYNOPSIS

A. Introduction

Article 32 dealing with Constitutional remedy is described as the very soul of the Constitution and the very heart of it. A right is a recognised and a protected interest. Fundamental rights are both recognised and protected by the Constitution. They are intended to protect not only the individual rights but it is a matter of high public policy. It is the very essence of the democratic way of life adopted by the Constitution and is the privilege and the duty of the court to uphold these rights.[1] A right becomes ineffective and hence meaningless unless there is a remedy in the event of its infringement. It is based on the maxim: *Ubi jus ibi remedium* – no right without a remedy.

B. Summary of Article 32

Article 32 can be summarised as under:

(1) Right to move the Supteme Court for enforcement of Fundamental right

Constitution guarantees the right to move the Supreme Court for the enforcement of the Fundamental right (article 32(1)).

---

1. *Daryao* v. *State of Uttar Pradesh,* AIR 1961 SC 1457: (1962) 1 SCR 574: 1962 (1) SCJ 702.

(2) Power to issue writs

The Supreme Court has the power to issue directions or orders of writs including writs in the nature of *habeas corpus, mandamus, prohibition, quo warranto, and certiorari* as may be appropriate for the enforcement of the Fundamental right mentioned in Part III of the Constitution. Article 32(2)

(3) Power of other Courts

The powers mentioned in article 32(2) can be exercised by any other court empowered by the Parliament by law. Article 32(3)

(4) Article 32 cannot be suspended

The right to move the Supreme Court for the enforcement of Fundamental rights shall not be suspended excepted as may be provided by the Constitution.

C. Uniqueness of Article 32

Right to enforce Fundamental right is a Fundamental right: The unique feature of our Constitution is that the right to enforce a Fundamental right is itself a Fundamental right and hence cannot be taken away by a law. Article 32 provides a quick and a summary remedy for the enforcement of Fundamental right because a person can go straight to the Supreme Court without approaching the lower courts as he does in ordinary litigations.

Violation of Fundamental right – a sine qua non: The writ jurisdiction under article 32 can be invoked only if there is a violation of a Fundamental right. Hence violation of a Fundamental right is a *sine qua non* (condition precedent) for invoking article 32. The Supreme Court has the power to issue writs and also declaratory orders or give directions as may appear to it necessary to give proper relief to the petitioner. It is a basic structure of the Constitution.

D. Curative petition

Final orders can be reviewed by a curative petition: In a judgment of high significance in *Rupa Ashok Hurra* v. *Ashok Hurra*[1] Supreme Court has held that in case there is a gross miscarriage of justice in the final Judgment there can be a second review of final order known as 'curative petition'. Curative petitions can be filed only when there is a legal and a moral obligation of the Court to rectify the error. As a normal rule final decisions of the Supreme Court are not allowed to be challenged. It is submitted that when the Constitution has provided for a single review under article 137 – providing for a second review goes beyond the intention of the framers of the Constitution. And in addition there must be an end to the litigation process.

E. *Locus standi* rule

Who can apply Public Interest Litigation (PIL)? Normally only the aggrieved party who has suffered a personal injury to property, body, mind or reputation due to violation of a legal right can seek judicial redress. But this is "a rule of ancient vintage which arose when private law dominated the scene and public law was not yet born"[2] This is the traditional approach to the concept of *locus*

1. AIR 2002 SC 1771: 2002 AIR SCW 1730: (2002) 4 SCC 388.
2. S.P. Gupta at p. 1192.

standi. Locus standi pertains to 'whether the petitioner is a proper party to request for adjudication of the issue.'

(1) Interpretation of 'appropriate proceeding' in article 32 leads to PIL

The court interpreted article 32 in an innovative fashion so as to expand the reach and ambit of article 32 by liberalising the *locus standi* concept. It centred round the interpretation of the term 'appropriate proceeding' under article 32. It held that what article 32 requires is that 'Supreme Court may be moved for enforcement of the Fundamental rights by an *appropriate proceeding.'*

It does not lay down

(a) in which specific manner the court shall be moved; or

(b) who shall move it.

So having regard to the length and breadth of illiteracy and poverty in our country, even a letter written by any public spirited person is an *appropriate proceeding within the meaning of article 32.* However two basic conditions must be satisfied – *viz.*, there must not be an ulterior motive in approaching the court and the rights of the disadvantaged group or someone in an incommunicado situation must be involved. This interpretation gave birth to public interest litigation in India which is 'judge made and judge induced and a product of juristic and judicial activism in our country.' PIL therefore is now used not only to get redress to the disadvantaged individuals but also to get redressal for public grievances where the whole society is involved – *for example* in case of noise pollution, water pollution, right to know about the antecedents of the contesting candidate etc.

Thus, the courts have liberalised the rule of *locus standi* and have permitted public interest litigations by public spirited citizens who approach the court for the enforcement of Constitutional or other rights of any person or a group of persons who because of their poverty, illiteracy or socially or economically disadvantaged position are unable to approach the court for relief. What is important is that the petition must not be filed with any ulterior motive. Thus an unregistered association can file a petition for a common cause.[1] The concept of public interest litigation took firm roots in *S.P. Gupta* v. *President of India*[2]. P.N. Bhagwati J. observed that where a legal wrong or a legal injury is caused to a person or to a determinate class of persons by reason of violation of any Constitutional or legal right and such person or determinate class of persons is by reason of poverty, helplessness or disability or socially or economically disadvantaged position unable to approach the court for relief – any member of the public can maintain an action under article 32. PILs on behalf of under trial prisoners languishing in jails; or inmates in Protective Home in Agra or the exploited labour class working for Asiad Games, etc., were entertained by the court and appropriate relief given. The court also entertained post cards as writ petition. Jurisdiction exercised based on letters written to the court or the judge is known as writ jurisdiction. The court has to verify that the person applying

1. *Akhil Bharatiya Soshit Karamchari Sangh (Railway)* v. *Union of India,* AIR 1981 SC 298: (1981) 1 SCC 246: (1981) 2 SCR 185.
2. AIR 1982 SC 149: 1982 Raj LR 389: 1981 Supp SCC 87.

has 'sufficient interest' and is not acting *mala fide* or with political motives. This decision is a 'golden master key' which has given access to the court for the poor and the downtrodden'[1]. The concept worked quite well for some time. PILs have been effectively used to protect inmates of Protective Home in Agra from flesh trade; to protect children in jails, to give effect to various labour laws,[2] for abolition of bonded labour[3], for protection of environment and ecology.

P.N. Bhagwati J. observed in *Bandhua Mukti Morcha* case[4] PIL is not in the nature of an adversary litigation but is a challenge and an opportunity to the Government and its officers to make basic human rights meaningful to the deprived and the vulnerable sections of the community and to assure them social and economic justice which is the signature tune of our Constitution. Pathak and Sen JJ. however warned that PIL must be entertained very cautiously after considering all materials produced by the petitioner. They suggested that letters be addressed to the entire Court and not to an individual judge. P.N. Bhagwati J. held in *M.C. Mehta* v. *Union of India*[5] that even a letter can be treated as a writ. It need not be accompanied by an affidavit also. P.N. Pathak J. opined that letters must not be written to individual judges but only to the court. But P.N. Bhagwati J. did not agree as people may be more comfortable writing to judges from their areas whom they know rather than to the court. Even compensation can be granted in appropriate cases where Fundamental rights of the poor and disadvantaged are violated or the violation is unduly harsh or oppressive or 'gross and patent'. But article 32 cannot be used as a substitute for claiming compensation for the infringement of Fundamental right through the ordinary process of the Civil Court. With this judgment the doors of the highest Court were thrown open to the poor, disadvantaged and the illiterate.

Scope of PIL was further widened in *M.C. Mehta* v. *Union of India*.

(2) Misuse of PIL and limitations imposed by Courts

But later people started misusing the public interest litigation concept.

In *Janata Dal* v. *H.S. Chaudhari*[6] the PIL was filed to protect all the named and unnamed accused in the Bofors kickback deal. Supreme Court re-examined the scope of PIL and laid down several guidelines to see that it is not misused. Thus it laid down that anonymous PILs would not be entertained; it expressed anguish that PIL petitions were very poorly drafted without even a second look at what was written; it warned that specially in Constitutional law matters – persons having absolutely no knowledge of the subject must not file the PIL etc. Likewise in *Simaranjit Singh Mann* v. *Union of India*[7] the conviction of the assassins of General Vaidya was sought to be challenged through PIL. It was not entertained. Appointment of a person likely to be appointed as a judge was

1. *Janata Dal* v. *H.S. Chowdhary*, AIR 1993 SC 892: 1993 Cr LJ 608: (1992) 4 SCC 305.
2. *People's Union for Democratic Rights* v. *Union of India*, AIR 1982 SC 1473: (1982) 2 SCC 494: 1982 (II) LLJ 454.
3. *Bandhua Mukti Morcha* v. *Union of India*, AIR 1984 SC 802: (1984) 3 SCC 161: 1984 Lab IC 560.
4. *Ibid.*
5. AIR 1988 SC 1087: JT 1988 (2) SC 8: (1988) 2 SCC 470.
6. (1992) 4 SCC 305.
7. (1992) 4 SCC 605: AIR 1993 SC 1407: (1992) 4 SCR 53.

challenged in a PIL; the petitioner had no personal knowledge of the allegations against the person. The PIL was dismissed and exemplary cost of Rs 10000 was imposed on the petitioner.

In *Guruvayur Devasawom Managing Committee* v. *C.K. Rajan*[1] the scope of PIL was re-examined to check its misuse. In this case one Mr. C.K. Rajan wrote a letter to the Kerala High Court judge complaining of corrupt practices in the Sri Krishna temple and the High Court directed the management of the temple to be taken over. The temple managing committee approached the Supreme Court. It was held that PIL cannot be used to solve disputes of private nature. It cannot replace the traditional litigation.

In *Gaurav Jain* v. *Union of India* demand of a separate school and hostels for children of prostitutes made through PIL was rejected as it was not in the interest of the children and it is a policy matter for the law makers.[2]

(3) Criticisms against PIL

1. The court will be flooded with cases and there will be a delay in deciding other important cases and traditional litigations.
2. Issuing directions which actually fall in the realm of the Executive or the Legislature disturbs the doctrine of separation of powers.
3. Many of the directions issued are non-enforceable.

F. Instances of directions issued by the court

1. Directions were issued to the State to ban smoking in public places and public transports, railways.
2. Writ of *habeas corpus* was issued for protecting the prisoners from inhuman treatment (*Sunil Batra* v. *Delhi Administration*[3]).
3. Prisoners who were cured of insanity but still detained were directed to be released based on a letter written to the court. *Veena Sethi* v. *State of Bihar,* AIR 1983 SC 339: 1983 Cr LJ 675: (1982) 2 SCC 583.
4. A letter complained of malpractices by some social organisation as regards adoption of the Indian children by foreigners. In the guise of adoption they were exposed to long dreadful journey and risk to life and if they survived they were not provided any shelter and in course of time they became beggars or prostitutes. Bhagwati J. laid down detailed guidelines for giving the children in adoption. *Lakshmikant Pandey* v. *Union of India.*[4]
5. In *Sheela Barse* v. *Union of India*[5] the petitioner personally visited different parts of the country to verify whether the information about children detained in jails is correct. She was awarded 10,000 as compensation.
6. In *D.C. Wadhwa* v. *State of Bihar*[6] while doing a research on political science the petitioner found that Bihar was being run not by laws enacted by the

---

1. 2003 (3) KLT 618.
2. AIR 1990 SC 292: 1990 Supp SCC 709.
3. AIR 1978 SC 1675: 1978 Cr LJ 1741: (1979) 1 SCR 392.
4. AIR 1984 SC 469: (1984) 2 SCC 244: (1984) 2 SCR 795.
5. (1986) 3 SCC 596: AIR 1986 SC 1773: 1986 Cr LJ 1736.
6. AIR 1987 SC 579: 1986 (4) Supreme 465: (1987) 1 SCC 378.

Legislature but by Ordinances[1] made by the Executive. He filed a PIL arguing that the people have a right to be governed not by laws made by the Executive but those made by the Legislature and that it amounts to subverting the Constitutional process. He was awarded Rs. 10,000 by way of compensation.

7. In *Rudal Saha* v. *State of Bihar*[2] the petitioner was kept in jail for 14 years after he was acquitted in a criminal trial. Court said if damages were not awarded it would be doing only a lip service to the concept of enforcing Fundamental right.
8. A raped woman was awarded Rs. 1000 per month to be paid by the rapist, in *Bodhisatwa* v. *Subhra Chakraborty*[3].
9. Guidelines have laid down in the following cases:
   (a) *Lakshmi Kkant Pandey* v. *Union of India*[4]: For adoption of minor children by foreigners
   (b) In *Supreme Court Advocates on Record* v. *Union of India*[5] guidelines were laid down for the appointment and transfer of High Court judges
   (c) In *Visakha* v. *State of Rajasthan*[6] guidelines were laid down for protection of working women from sexual harassment in work places.
   (d) In *Vineet Narain* v. *Union of India*[7] directions were laid down to ensure independence of the Vigilance Commission and to reduce corruption in Government offices. The judgment runs like a legislation and is quite an encroachment in the legislative field.
   (e) In *Union of India* v. *Association for Democratic Reforms*[8] based on a PIL directions were issued to the Election Commission to issue a notification that the contesting candidates must disclose their assets and liabilities and criminal antecedents if any. People in jail cannot contest elections.[9]

Article 32 cannot be restricted by a legislation: Under section 14 of the Preventive Detention Act, 1950, the detenue was forbidden from disclosing the grounds of his detention communicated to him by the detaining authority. But then unless the grounds of detention were disclosed it was not possible for the court to decide whether the detenu's Fundamental right was infringed. Hence article 32 became nugatory (non-functional). Section 14 was held unconstitutional.[10]

Res judicata is applicable to article 32: Under the doctrine of *res judicata* a case once decided cannot be agitated again on the same cause of action. (All those

1. When the legislature is not in session and there is an urgent matter on which a law is needed the Governor – who is the head of the Executive promulgates a law which is known as an Ordinance.
2. AIR 1983 SC 1086: 1983 Cr LJ 1644: (1983) 4 SCC 141.
3. (1996) 1 SCC 490: 1996 AIR SCW 325: AIR 1996 SC 922.
4. AIR 1984 SC 469: (1984) 2 SCC 244: (1984) 2 SCR 795.
5. (1993) 4 SCC 441: AIR 1994 SC 268: 1993 AIR SCW 4101.
6. AIR 1997 SC 3011: 1997 AIR SCW 3043: (1997) 6 SCC 241.
7. AIR 1998 SC 889: 1998 AIR SCW 645: 1998 Cr LJ 1208.
8. AIR 1997 SC 83: 1996 AIR SCW 4239: (1996) 10 SCC 642.
9. *Ajit Chopra* v. *Sadhu Ram*, AIR 2000 SC 212: 1999 AIR SCW 4308: (2000) 1 SCC 114.
10. *A.K. Gopalan* v. *State of Madras*, AIR 1950 SC 27: 51 Cr LJ 1383: 1950 SCR 88.

bundle of facts which the party has to prove in order to succeed in his case). It is in order to give finality to the litigation. The doctrine is applicable to writ proceedings. It is not applicable to the *habeas corpus* (produce the body of the person) writ because it deals with the personal liberty of a person.

Laches: Laches or inordinate delay may disentitle the petitioner from moving a petition under article 32 to enforce article 32.[1] But In *R.S. Deodhar* v. *State of Maharashtra*[2] the court entertained the petition even after 10 years. It was held that the rule of laches is not a rule of law but a rule of practice based on proper exercise of discretion and there is no hard and fast rule that in all cases where there is a delay the court must necessarily reject the petition. Each case must be viewed on the facts and circumstances.

Against whom writ can be issued: Fundamental rights are enforceable against the State as defined under article 12. Articles 17, 21, 23, 24 are available against private persons also.

G. Reliefs under article 32

Wide jurisdiction: The wordings of article 32 are very wide. Supreme Court can issue 'orders, directions, writs *including* writs in the nature of *habeas corpus, quo warranto*, prohibition, *certiorari* and *mandamus* as it considers appropriate in the circumstances of the case to give proper relief to the petitioner. Thus the power of the court is not restricted only to the five writs as indicated by the term 'inclusive'[3]. It is wide as to include any other writ or direction as may be necessary to give proper relief to the party. What is proper relief varies from case to case. And for this purpose it can devise any procedure appropriate for giving relief. It can declare a particular enactment to be *ultra vires* or beyond the competence of the Legislature.[4]

Fundamental right are enforced by awarding damages.

H. Difference between Articles 32 and 226

Article 32	Article 226
The right under article 32 can be exercised only for the enforcement of Fundamental right.	Can be exercised for the enforcement of Fundamental right and any other purpose.
Narrower than under article 226.	More wider powers than under article 32
Jurisdiction of the Supreme Court constitutes the 'basic structure' of the Constitution.	Order under article 32 supersedes order under article 226.
Application under article 32 can be made without first making an application to the High Court under article 226.	

1. *Tilokchand Motichand* v. *H.B. Munshi, Commissioner of Sales Tax, Bombay*, AIR 1970 SC 898: (1969) 2 SCR 824: (1970) 1 SCJ 859.
2. AIR 1974 SC 259: (1974) 1 SCC 317: (1974) 2 SCR 216.
3. Note the difference between the use of the term 'inclusive' and 'means'. When it is said that the court can issue writs *including habeas corpus* etc., it means that writs which are named are only illustrative and the court can add to the list by including certain other writs which fit within the type/genus of the one's already mentioned. But when you say 'industrial dispute' means the dispute between the employer and the employee; or the employer and the employee or the employee and the employee- it means that list is exhaustive and no other inclusion is possible.
4. *Bodhisatwa* v. *Subha Chakravorty*, (1996) 1 SCC 490: 1996 AIR SCW 325: AIR 1996 SC 922.

I. Restriction of Fundamental rights of certain categories of persons (Article 33)

Article 33 restricts the Fundamental right of certain categories of persons. It empowers the Parliament to restrict or abrogate by law Fundamental rights in their application to:

(a) Members of the armed forces.

(b) The forces charged with the maintenance of public order.

(c) Persons employed in Intelligence Bureau.

(d) Persons employed in connection with the telecommunication system set up for purposes of any Force, Bureau or organisation referred to above.

This power can be exercised only by the Parliament and not by the State.

Article 33 cannot be challenged under article 13 which lays down that the law which takes away the Fundamental right is void to that extent.

J. Restrictions on Fundamental right during Martial law

Under article 34 while Martial law is in force there can be restrictions on the Fundamental rights. The Parliament can indemnify any person in the service of the Union or a State for any act done by him for the maintenance or restoration of order in an area where Martial law was on force. The indemnity validates any sentence passed, punishment inflicted, forfeiture ordered or other act done under Martial law in such area. Martial law is defined as the suspension of ordinary law and the Government of the country or a part of it by Military Tribunals.

Emergency and Martial Law

Emergency is different from Martial law. The following are the—

Martial law	Emergency
Martial law has its origin in common law. It is implicit in the text of article 34 under which Martial law can be declared in any Part of India.[1]	The basis is the Constitutional provision under article 352.
The basis for martial law is actual rebellion or insurrection.	An emergency can be proclaimed only when the security of India is threatened by war, external aggression or armed rebellion.
No Proclamation by the President is necessary for enforcement of martial law. Yet the President can issue a Proclamation if he so desires under article 53(2) as a Commander of defence forces. But the Court can enquire whether a rebellion in fact exists or not because a proclamation is only an evidence of and not proof of rebellion.	Can come into existence only with a Presidential Proclamation
Is operative only in the actual area of rebellion and not throughout the country. Fundamental right of citizens outside the troubled areas is not affected.	Until the 42nd Amendment it used to be in operation throughout the country and the Fundamental right of all the citizens used to be affected.

1. *Additional District Magistrate, Jabalpur* v. *Shivakant Shukla*, AIR 1976 SC 1207: (1976) 2 SCC 521: 1976 Cr LJ 945.

As soon as martial law situation arises, civil Court's power to interfere with military action automatically comes to an end until martial law situation ceases. But there is no impact on federalism or legislative powers of the State or the Centre.	Maintenance of law and order and also the Governmental aspects like federalism, legislative powers and reservations are . affected
Depends upon the factual existence of a state of rebellion etc.	Depends upon the 'subjective satisfaction' of the President that there is threat to the security of India by war, external aggression or armed rebellion. It can be declared even when there is only a threat without actual war etc.

In order to fight terrorism note that of late some drastic laws have been enacted. *For example* Armed Forces (Assam and Manipur) Special Powers Act – which has been held by the Supreme Court to be within the competency of the Parliament to enact. Terrorist and Disruptive Activities (Prevention) Act, 1985 was enacted to fight terrorism. It prescribed capital punishment for terrorist act; designated courts were established for speedy trial of the cases. The Act was replaced by POTA – Prevention of Terrorist Activities Act.

K. Legislation to effectuate certain Fundamental rights

(a) Under article 35(a)(1) Parliament and not the State Legislature has the power to make legislation to give effect to the following Fundamental rights:

(1) Prescribe residence within the State as qualification for employment in the State. {Article 16(3)}

(2) Empowering Courts other than the Supreme Court and the High Court to issue writs and orders to enforce Fundamental rights. {Article 32(3)}

(3) Abrogate or restrict the Fundamental rights of the members of the Armed Forces and the Police in the interest of discipline and efficiency of forces. Article 33

(4) Pass an Act of Indemnity after operation of martial law in any area. Article 34.

(b) Under article 35(a)(ii) the Parliament and not the State Legislature has the power to prescribe punishments for those acts which are declared offences under the Fundamental rights. These are:

(1) Prescribing punishment for enforcement of any disability arising out of untouchability. Article 17

(2) Prescribing punishment for traffic in human beings and imposition of *begar* and other forms of forced labour. Article 23(1) *e.g.*, SITA Suppression of Immoral Traffic in Women and Girls Act, 1956.

L. WRITS

(1) *Writ of Habeas Corpus*

It is the most important writ to protect personal liberty of the people. It protects against wrongful detention. *Habeas corpus* means 'produce the body of the person.' It orders the detainer to produce the detained person before the court and issues a show cause why he must not be released. The court finds out under what authority he has been detained. Thus, the object of the writ is remedial and not punitive.

Who can apply: normally it is the person illegally detained who must apply. But in *Kanu Sanyal* v. *Dist. Magistrate Darjeeling*[1] it was held that the legality of the detention can be examined even without the person detained being produced before the court. Kanu Sanyal- a Naxalite leader was arrested and detained without trial in Vishakapatnam jail. His advocate contended that the essence of writ of *Habeas Corpus* was that the prisoner must be produced before the court. The court did not agree and observed that the age old British practice was no longer applicable. The writ is not issued if the court is satisfied that the prisoner is not under unlawful restraint. It is for the detaining authority to show that the detention was legal. The detention is legal if (1) the law is valid and the procedure in article 21 is strictly followed. (2) the detention is lawful if, the condition laid down in article 22 is complied with. If the arrested person is not produced within 24 hours of his arrest the arrest, is illegal.

Procedures relaxed: Procedural technicalities in the issue of *habeas corpus* have been kept at a minimum by the Supreme Court because personal liberty is the most cherished Fundamental right and having regard to illiteracy and poverty in our country. Even a post card by a detenue from jail is treated as a writ. In England strict rules of pleading are applicable. Where persons picked up by the army or the police have disappeared without a trace, his relatives can move the court.

Extended application of the writ: The writ has been used even to protect the prisoner from ill treatment within the jails.

A foreigner who comes to India secretly cannot claim freedom of movement and his detention with a view to expel him is not illegal.[2]

(2) *Mandamus*

Writ of *mandamus* is an order by a superior court commanding a person or a public authority to do or forbear to do something in the nature of public duty or in certain cases of statutory duty. It is a high prerogative writ remedial in nature. Original form of it was a command issued in the name of the King by the King's Bench Division of the High Court of Justice and directing any person, corporation or inferior court of Judicature – to do the things stated therein.

1. AIR 1974 SC 510: 1974 Cr LJ 465: (1974) 4 SCC 141.
2. *Anwar* v. *State of Jammu and Kashmir*, AIR 1971 SC 337: 1971 (1) SCA 519: (1971) 1 SCR 637.

Today it is used principally for public purposes and to compel the performance of public duties.

The object of the writ of *mandamus* is to keep the authorities concerned within the limits of their jurisdiction.

Following are the important characteristics of the writ of *Mandamus*:

1. It lies against the executive, judicial and *quasi*-judicial authorities. It does not lie against private individuals or a private organisation.
2. The petitioner must show that he has a legal right to demand the performance of a public/legal duty by the authority concerned.
3. Such a duty must be one imposed by the Constitution or any other law but not a contract. It should not be a private duty but a public duty.
4. The performance of the duty must be mandatory and not discretionary. Whether the duty is discretionary or mandatory is to be determined by the scheme of the statute in which the duty is set out. Even if the duty is not clearly set out it may be implied as co-relative of the right. For example- the directive principles of State policy are goals to be attained by the State; they are not justiciable. There is no legal duty to make a law in accordance with the directions in Part IV of the Constitution. No writ of *mandamus* can lie against the State or any other authority directing it to pass a law in accordance with the directive principles of State policy. Likewise no *mandamus* can lie to direct the Government not to pass a law. In *Ahmedabad Women's Assn* v. *Union of India* Supreme Court refused to direct the Government not to enact the Muslim Women's (Protection of Rights on Divorce) Act, 1986.
5. The right should be a judicially enforceable right.
6. There must be a demand by the party and a refusal by the authority.[1]
7. The High Courts under article 226 and the Supreme Court under article 32 has the power to issue a writ of *mandamus* when the Government or a public authority has failed to exercise or has wrongly exercised the discretion conferred upon it by a statute or a rule or a policy diction of the Government or has exercised such discretion *mala fide* or on irrelevant consideration or by ignoring the relevant considerations and material or in such manner as to frustrate the object of conferring such discretion of the policy for implementing such discretion.
8. Government decision taken on purely political considerations without any material can be quashed by the writ court.[2]

---

1. *Saraswati Industrial Syndicate Ltd.* v. *Union of India*, AIR 1975 SC 46: (1974) 2 SCC 630: 1975 (2) SCJ 332.
2. *Mansukhlal Vithaldas Chauhan* v. *State of Gujarat*, AIR 1997 SC 3400: 1997 Cr LJ 4059: 1997 AIR SCW 3478.

9. *Mandamus* can be issued to restrain the executive from acting under a void law.[1]
10. *Mandamus* is not granted against the President or the Governor; High Court or High Court judge acting in judicial capacity; Legislature; Parliament; a Company registered under the Companies Act unless is in an instrumentality of the State.

Limitations on the court in granting the writ of mandamus: In the modern era the executive is conferred with lot of discretionary powers. The court cannot direct the authority to exercise its discretion in a particular manner. It can only direct it to exercise the discretion according to law.[2]

The court does not sit in appeal over the order and consider the correctness or satisfactoriness of the reasons given. It only directs that the authority must act according to law.

Examples: Under section 6 of Prevention of Corruption Act, 1947 a public servant cannot be prosecuted for certain specified offences without the sanction of the Government. Supreme Court held that the grant of sanction is a solemn affair. It must not be done mechanically. When sanction was given without application of mind the Court quashed the same.[3]

University cancelled an examination and directed reasonable-examination due to question paper leakage. No *mandamus* could be issued for that would amount to substituting its opinion for that of the University's.

***(3) Prohibition and* Certiorari**

(a) Practically the same grounds: The writ of Prohibition and *Certiorari* are issued on practically the same grounds. The only difference between the two is that *Certiorari* is issued to quash a decision after the decision is taken by a lower court while Prohibition is issued before the proceedings are completed.

(b) Both writs issued: At times the court may issue both the writs- Prohibition to prohibit the body from proceeding further and *Certiorari* to quash what has already been done.

(c) To whom issued: These writs are issued to a body acting in an adjudicatory capacity and according to natural justice and not to one acting in a purely administrative capacity. Whether the body is needed to act according to natural justice and give a hearing is not usually expressed as a specific provision. It has to be inferred/implied from the statute.

Differences: The object of *Certiorari* is curative. It quashes the decision already given by the lower court or the Tribunal. It is issued by a Superior Court (High Court or Supreme Court) to an inferior court or body exercising judicial or *quasi*

---

1. *Dwarka* v. *State of Uttar Pradesh,* (1993) 2 SCR 70.
2. M.P. Jain: Constitution Law 2009 ED. At p. 425.
3. *Mansukhlal Vithaldas Chauhan* v. *State of Gujarat,* AIR 1997 SC 3400: 1997 Cr LJ 4059: 1997 AIR SCW 3478.

judicial functions to remove a suit from such inferior court and adjudicate upon the validity of the proceedings.

The object of Prohibition is preventive. It prevents the lower court from taking a decision. *For example* a Tribunal can be restrained from acting under an unconstitutional law.

The jurisdiction to issue *Certiorari* is a supervisory jurisdiction and the court exercising it is not entitled to act as an appellate court. *Certiorari* cannot be used to question the Constitutional validity of a legislation. The proper relief is to ask for declaration that a particular law is unconstitutional and void.

Writ of *Certiorari* can be issued on the following grounds:

1. When the judicial or *quasi*-judicial body acts without or in excess of its jurisdiction.
2. Fails to exercise its jurisdiction.
3. There is an error of law apparent on the face of the record in the impugned (challenged) decision of the body concerned. It cannot be issued for correcting an error of fact. What is an error on the face of the record has to be decided on the facts of the case. It is one that is self-evident and requires no further argument to establish it.
4. The findings of fact reached by the inferior tribunal are based on no evidence.
5. It proceeds to act in violation of the principles of natural justice. The two basic principles are:
   (a) *Audi alterem partem* –no person shall be condemned unheard, and
   (b) Rule against bias- *i.e.,* no person shall be a judge in his own cause and that justice must not only be done but must be seen to be done.
6. It means that the judge should be disinterested and unbiased; judge should be neutral; that a person interested in one of the parties to the dispute should not even formally take part in the adjudicatory proceedings. Actual existence of bias is not necessary. The test of bias is 'real likelihood of bias'. If a reasonable man thinks that the judge is likely to be biased based on the facts of the case – it is sufficient to quash the decision.[1] If he has a pecuniary interest in the matter before him- howsoever small the interest may be – the proceedings are liable to be quashed. For example in *Kraipak* case a candidate selected was himself the member of the Selection Board. His selection was cancelled. A senior officer expresses appreciation of the work of his junior in his confidential report. This does not bar the officer from being a member of the Promotion Committee. If it is rational and

1. *S. Parthasarathi* v. *State of Andhra Pradesh,* AIR 1973 SC 2701: (1973) 2 SCWR 464: 1973 Lab IC 1607; *Amar Nath Chowdhury* v. *Braithwaite and Co. Ltd.,* AIR 2002 SC 678: 2002 AIR SCW 295: (2002) 1 SCALE 173.

unaccompanied by considerations of personal interest, pecuniary interest or otherwise, it would not vitiate the decision.[1]

7. It proceeds to act under a law which is itself invalid, *ultra vires* or unconstitutional.
8. It proceeds to act in contravention of the Fundamental right.

Examples:

1. Want of jurisdiction may arise from the nature of subject matter – because the court has no authority to adjudicate on the matter. Courts have pecuniary jurisdiction, territorial jurisdiction and jurisdiction with respect to the subject matter. If the Small Cause court takes up a suit regarding partition of immovable property it is exceeding its jurisdiction and a *Certiorari* can be obtained.
2. Absence of jurisdictional fact will entitle a writ of *Certiorari*. Where the jurisdiction of a body depends upon a preliminary finding of fact in a writ of *Certiorari* the court can determine whether or not that finding of fact is correct. By wrongly deciding the fact the Court cannot give itself the jurisdiction.
3. In *Ranjit Singh* v. *Ravi Prakash*[2] the District Court allowed the appellant's suit for possession of the premises that he had lent out as it was *bona fide* required for his personal use. But the High Court reversed the ruling. Supreme Court reversed the High Court ruling with an observation that the High Court should not reasonably appreciate the evidence in its *Certiorari* jurisdiction as though it was exercising appellate jurisdiction.

(4) Quo Warranto

It means 'what is your authority'. Under this writ the holder of the office is called upon to show under what authority he is holding the office. Object is to prevent a person from holding an office to which he is not entitled. If he is found not entitled to the office, he is directed to vacate the office and the office is declared to be vacant.

Who can apply: it can be applied by any person by showing that—

(a) The office is a public post.

(b) It is held by a person without legal authority.

(c) It is not issued in respect of a private office like the members of the working committee of the Bihar Arya Samaj Sabha.[3]

(d) The applicant need not be personally aggrieved.

(e) If the statute prescribes certain qualifications for the appointment of a public office under the writ of *Quo Warranto* the court can examine whether the qualifications have been satisfied or not.

---

1. *G.N. Nayak* v. *Goa University*, (2002) 2 SCC 712: AIR 2002 SC 790: 2002 AIR SCW 442.
2. AIR 2004 SC 3892: 2004 AIR SCW 4221: (2004) 3 SCC 682.
3. *Jamalpur Arya Samaj* v. *D. Ram*, AIR 1954 Pat 297: ILR 33 Pat 157.

(f) The writ has been moved to challenge the appointment of a mayor of a municipal corporation, appointment of Chief Minister, of Chief Justice of India, Advocate General of India, public prosecutor, University teachers, University Syndicate etc.

(g) No *quo warranto* can be issued against the Council of Ministers as they do not command majority support in the House. This is because under article 164 of the Constitution there are no conditions regarding minority or majority party.

(h) This writ cannot be issued to seek the dismissal of a Chief Minister of a State for non-performance of a Constitutional duty.

CHAPTER 18

DIRECTIVE PRINCIPLES OF STATE POLICY

(Articles 36-51)

SYNOPSIS

A. Introduction

Fundamental rights and directive principles are basic to our Constitution. We have dealt in detail with the Fundamental rights in the preceding chapters.

Directive principles of State Policy are laid down under Part IV of the Constitution from articles 36 to 51. They lay down the goals to be attained by the State in its discharge of the duties of a welfare State. They are pious obligations of the State.

B. Classification of the directive principles

They can be classified into following three categories:

(1) Social and Economic Charter (Articles 38, 39).

(2) Social Security Charter (41, 42, 43, 43A, 45, 46, 47, 39A).

(3) Community Welfare Charter (Articles, 40, 44, 48, 48 A 49, 50, 51).

C. Social and Economic Charter (Articles 38, 39)

(1) Promote welfare of people

Article 38 provides that the State shall strive to promote the welfare of the people by securing and protecting as effectively as it may a social order in which justice social economic and political shall inform all the institutions of national life.

(2) Minimise inequalities

State shall in particular strive to minimise inequalities in income and endeavour to eliminate inequalities in status, facilities and opportunities not only amongst individuals but also amongst groups of people residing in different areas or engaged in different vocations. 38(2).

Social justice is the signature tune of our Constitution. Social justice is a categorical imperative. Social justice is not a Constitutional claptrap but a fighting faith which enlivens legislative texts with militant meaning.[1] Concept of social justice vary with age and time.[2] It is a dynamic devise to mitigate the sufferings of the poor, weak, dalits, tribals and deprived sections of the society and raise them to the level of equality to live a life with dignity of person.[3]

Under article 39 the State is required to direct its policy for securing the following principles:

(a) Equal right for men and women to adequate means of livelihood.

(b) Distribution of ownership and control of the material resources of the community to the common good.

(c) To ensure that the economic system does not result in concentration of wealth and means of production to the common detriment.

(d) Equal pay for equal work for men and women *e.g.,* Under the Equal Remuneration Act there can be a reasonable classification based on rational nexus is permissible. Different salaries for different nature of work in the same cadre is permissible.

(e) To protect health and strength of workers and tender age of children and to ensure that they are not forced by economic necessity to enter a vocation unsuited to their age or strength.

(f) That children are given opportunities and facilities to develop in a healthy manner and in conditions of freedom and dignity and that childhood and youth are protected against exploitation and against moral and material abandonment. For *e.g.,* employment of children in match factories is hazardous.[4] In *M.C. Mehta* v. *State of Tamil Nadu,*[5] detailed guidelines

1. *Captain Ramesh Chander Kaushal* v. *Veena Kaushal,* AIR 1978 SC 1807: (1978) 4 SCC 70: 1978 Cr LJ 3.
2. *Rajendra Prasad* v. *State of Uttar Pradesh,* AIR 1979 SC 916: 1979 Cr LJ 792: (1979) 3 SCC 646.
3. *Air India Statutory Corporation* v. *United Labour Union,* AIR 1997 SC 645: 1997 AIR SCW 430: (1997) 9 SCC 377.
4. *M.C. Mehta* v. *State of Tamil Nadu,* (1991) 1 SCC 283: AIR 1991 SC 417: 1991 AIR SCW 60.
5. AIR 1997 SC 699: 1997 AIR SCW 407: (1996) 6 SCC 756.

were given for child labour abolition. It laid down that the employer must not employ children below 14 years in hazardous employment; offending employer must pay 20,000 as compensation to be deposited in the Child Welfare Deposit Rehabilitation Welfare Fund etc.

Articles 38 and 39 embody jurisprudential principles of distributive justice.[1]

D. Social Security Charter

(1) Workers' participation in management

Participation of workers in management of industries is provided under 43A. State shall take steps to secure the participation of workers in the management of undertakings and establishments or other organisations engaged in any industry by suitable legislation or in any other way.

(2) Right to work, assistance and education

Right to work, education, and public assistance in certain cases. Article 41 directs the State to ensure the people within the limits of economic capacity and development a) employment b) Education, and c) public assistance in cases of unemployment, old age, sickness and disablement and in other cases of undeserved want.

(3) Just and humane conditions of work

Article 42 directs the State to make provision for securing just human conditions and for maternity relief.

(4) Living wage for workers

Article 43 – State must try to secure by suitable legislative or economic organisation or in any other way to all workers agricultural, industrial or otherwise a living wage conditions of work ensuring a decent standard of life and full enjoyment of leisure and social and cultural opportunities and in particular the State shall endeavour to promote cottage industries on an individual or co-operative basis in rural areas.

It refers to 'living wage' and not just a 'minimum wage'. Living wage includes the bare necessities of food, clothing, shelter and also provisions for education of children and insurance etc.

(5) Early childhood care

The State shall endeavour to provide for early childhood care and education to children until they complete the age of 6 years. This provision has been substituted for the earlier one in 2002 by 86th Constitutional Amendment. The now repealed article 45 required the State to make provision within 10 years for free and compulsory education for all children until they complete the age of 14 years. The same has been raised to the status of a Fundamental right under article 21A (inserted by the 86th Amendment) which provides that the State

---

1. **Note** – Distributive justice as distinguished from corrective justice. Distributive justice is where laws are made by the Legislature for the distribution of social goods (benefits and burdens) amongst the members of the society. Corrective justice is where – there is an unequal distribution of the social goods – the aggrieved person goes to the court – and the court corrects the injustice. What the Court is administering is corrective justice.

shall provide free and compulsory education to all children of the age of 6 to 14 years in such manner as the State may by law provide. In order to ensure that the parents also are made pro-active a fundamental duty has been imposed on the parents under article 51A(k) to provide opportunities for education to their child between the age of 6 and 14 years.

In *Unni Krishnan, J.P.* v. *State of Andhra Pradesh,* (1993) 1 SCC 645: 1993 AIR SCW 863: AIR 1993 SC 2178, the Supreme Court has held that the right to education up to the age of 14 years is a Fundamental right within the meaning of article 21 of the Constitution but thereafter the obligation of the State to provide education is subject to the limits of its economic capacity.[1]

(6) Duty to raise the standard of living

Duty to raise the standard of living and improvement of health: Article 47 imposes duty upon the State to raise the level of nutrition and the standard of living of its people and the improvement of public health. In particular the State must bring about prohibition of the consumption except for medicinal purposes of intoxicating drinks and of drugs which are injurious to health.

(7) Promotion of educational and economic interest of weaker sections

Under article 46 the State must promote with special care the education and economic interests of the Scheduled Castes and Scheduled Tribes and to protect them from social injustice and of all forms of exploitation.

(8) Equal justice and free legal aid to economically backward classes[2]

Article 39 provides that the State shall ensure that the operation of the legal system promotes justice on the basis of equal opportunities and shall in particular provide free legal aid by suitable legislation or schemes or in any other way to ensure that opportunities for securing justice are not denied to any citizen by reason of economic or other disabilities. In pursuance of this article the Parliament has enacted Legal Services Authority Act, 1986 which has made provisions for free legal aid to certain categories of persons mentioned therein.

This is a very important provision having regard to the high cost involved in litigations and the length and breadth of poverty in the country.

Following are the important cases in connection with this article:

(a) Legal aid and speedy trial are held to be Fundamental right under article 21 available to all prisoners.[3]

---

1. In *Unnikrishnan* case the question was whether right to higher education is a fundamental right but the court gave a judgment that right to primary education is a fundamental right. Later the Parliament acted upon the judgment and made right to education upto 6 years a fundamental right. When comments are made by the court which are not essential for passing the judgment – such comments or passing observations are known as *obiter dicta* which are not authoritatively binding on the subordinate courts but coming from the Highest Court of the land they are of high persuasive value.
2. Inserted by 42nd Amendment Act, 1976
3. *Hussainara Khotoon* v. *Home Secretary, State of Bihar,* AIR 1979 SC 1360: 1979 Cr LJ 1036: (1980) 1 SCC 81.

(b) Voluntary organisations must be encouraged and supported in operating the legal aid programme.[1]

(c) In *State of Maharashtra* v. *Manubhai Bagaji Vashi*[2] it was held that right to speedy justice is a Fundamental right; if this right is to be realised there is a need for competent lawyers; to produce competent lawyers we need good law colleges; which in turn needs good infrastructure and good teachers who are properly paid. And hence the law colleges are entitled to be covered under the Grant-in-Aid as sole Government colleges cannot cater to the needs of legal education. It should facilitate private law colleges.

E. Community Welfare Charter

(1) Uniform Civil Code

Article 44 requires the State to secure for the citizens a Uniform Civil Code throughout the territory of India. Following are the important cases:

(a) In *Sarla Mudgal, President, Kalyani* v. *Union of India*[3] the Supreme Court directed the Union Government to file an affidavit by August, 1995 indicating steps taken and efforts made by the Government to secure a uniform Civil Code. In the four petitions that were filed the common point was that the Hindu husbands were misusing the Mohammedan law of marriage; converting themselves into Islam and then marrying another Muslim woman under the Mohammedan law leaving the Hindu wife in distress. In one of the cases both the Hindu husband and the Hindu paramour got converted into Islam faith and then got married, the court held that a Hindu marriage continues to exist even after one of the spouse converted to Islam. There is no automatic dissolution of Hindu marriage it can only be dissolved by a decree of divorce. Hence second marriage after conversion to Islam is void and the husband can be prosecuted for bigamy under article 494 IPC.

(b) In *Pragati Verghese* v. *Cyril George Verghese*[4] it was held that section 10 of the Indian Divorce Act which requires a Christian wife to prove cruelty or desertion along with adultery to get a divorce is unconstitutional as it violates her Fundamental right to live with human dignity and in addition this condition was not applicable to the Christian husband and hence article 14 also was violated.

(c) In *Noor Saba Khattoon* v. *Mohd Kasim*[5] Supreme Court held that a divorced Muslim woman is entitled to claim maintenance for her children till they become major; that both under 125 Cr. P.C. and under the Muslim Personal Law the obligation of the father was absolute when the children were living with the divorced wife. The court rejected the

1. *Centre of Legal Research* v. *State of Kerala*, AIR 1986 SC 1322: (1986) 2 SCC 706: 1986 (3) Supreme 223.
2. (1995) 5 SCC 730: AIR 1996 SC 1: 1995 AIR SCW 3701.
3. AIR 1995 SC 1531: 1995 AIR SCW 2326: 1995 Cr LJ 2926.
4. AIR 1997 Bom 349.
5. AIR 1997 SC 3280.

plea of the husband that the liability of the father to maintain his minor child ceased after the expiry of *iddat* period (three months)

(d) In *Daniel Latif* v. *Union of India*[1] the Supreme Court held that a Muslim husband is liable to make a reasonable and fair provision for the future of the divorced wife which clearly extends beyond *iddat* period in terms of section 3(1)(a) of the Muslim Women (Protection of Rights on Divorce) Act, 1986.[2]

(e) In *John Vallamatton* v. *Union of India,* 2003 AIR SCW 3536: JT 2003 6 SC 37: AIR 2003 SC 2902 the Supreme Court again expressed regret as Uniform Civil Code has not yet been enacted. In this case section 118 of the Indian Succession Act was held discriminatory. Under the section a Christian having a nephew or a niece or even an adopted son or any other near relative cannot bequeath his property for charitable or religious purpose without following the strict conditions laid down under the Act. But the wife was not a 'near relative' within the meaning of the Act. This provision was held to be unconstitutional.

(2) Protection and improvement of forests and wild life

Article 48A provides that the State shall endeavour to protect and improve the environment and safeguard the forests and wildlife of the country. Environment Protection Act, Water and Air Act, Wild Life Protection Act, have been passed in pursuance of this directive.

(3) Protection of monuments and places and objects of national importance

The State shall be under an obligation to protect every monument or place or object of artistic or historic interest declared to be of national importance from spoilation (looting, plundering etc.), disfigurement, destruction removal, disposal or export as the case may be.

(4) Separation of judiciary and executive

Article 50 mandates the State to take steps to separate the Judiciary from the Executive in the public services.

(5) Promotion of international peace and security

The State shall endeavour to:

(a) Promote international peace and security.

(b) Maintain just and honourable relations between nations.

(c) Foster respect for international law and treaty obligations in the dealings of organised peoples with one another. And

(d) Encourage settlement of international disputes by arbitration.

The Parliament has enacted the Protection of Human Rights Act, 1993 to give effect to the direction in article 51 of the Constitution and International Commitments. National Human Rights Commission and Human Rights Courts have been constituted under the Act.

---

1. AIR 2001 SC 3262: 2001 AIR SCW 3143: (2002) 1 SCC 428.
2. For a critical analysis of the Muslim Women Act *see* the Article of this author titled: 'Muslim Women's Act – an illustration of legislative supremacy over the Judiciary'; AIR 1997 SC 135.

(6) Organisation of Village Panchayats

Article 40 directs the State to take steps to organise village panchayats and endow them with such powers and authority as may be necessary to enable them to function as units of self Government. 73rd and 74th Constitutional Amendments have been passed in 1992 to provide for grass root level administration by introducing Part IX and IX A. 73rd Amendment provides for a three tier of Panchayat Raj system – at the village, intermediate and district levels. It envisages Gram Sabha as the foundation of the Panchayati Raj system. 74th Amendment Act provides for three types of municipal corporations for urban areas- Nagar Panchayats, Municipal Councils and Municipal Corporations according to population.

F. Relationship between Directive principles and Fundamental rights

Difference between the Fundamental right and the directive principles

1. Fundamental rights are contained in Part III of the Constitution and Directive Principles are contained in Part IV.
2. Fundamental rights mandate that the State shall not make a law to take away the rights laid down by it. Hence they are by and large negative obligations imposed by the State. Directive principles lay down the principles to be taken into consideration while making laws and hence they are described as the 'positive obligations' of the State.
3. The Fundamental rights are justiciable *i.e.,* enforceable in the Courts of law but the Directive principles are non-justiciable *i.e.,* not enforceable by the courts. Yet they are 'fundamental in the governance of the country'[1]. In the Constituent Assembly the question was "which of the fundamental principles must be made justiciable and which must be made non-justiciable." This shows that both the Fundamental rights and the Directive principles were considered to be fundamental by the framers of the Constitution. But because the State was in its formative stage – the framers did not want to load the Government with the obligation of making all these fundamental principles enforceable through litigations in the courts of law.
4. Fundamental rights are described as the *Magna Carta of India.*[2] Directive Principles were criticised as being only 'pious obligations' as they are not enforceable by Courts. But Dr. Ambedkar did not agree. He said that 'Directive principles are like the Instrument of Instructions which were issued to the Governor-General and the Governors of the Colonies. They are instructions given to the Legislature and the Executive. Such instructions are necessary whenever there is a grant of power in general terms for good governance because they regulate the exercise of this power. Whichever political party may come to power it has to respect these ideals and frame laws keeping them in mind.

---

1. Article 37.
2. In 1214 the English people exacted an assurance from King John for respect of the then ancient liberties. *Magna Carta* is the evidence of their success. It is written document.

5. Granville Austin describes Parts III and Part IV of the Constitution as the 'Conscience of the Constitution.' The core commitment to social revolution lies in the Fundamental right and the Directive Principles taken together.
6. Directive Principles aim at making the Indian masses free in the positive sense – free from degrading physical conditions which prevented their full fledged development. They lay down the "kind of India that politicians must create for children and the poor and the manner in which the country's resources are to be used".[1]

G. Relationship between the Fundamental right and Directive Principles—Judicial decisions

1. In *State of Madras* v. *Champakam Dorairajan*[2] the Supreme Court held that Chapter III dealing with Fundamental right is sacrosanct and they override the provisions in Part IV dealing with Directive Principles because the Fundamental rights are enforceable whereas the Directive Principles are not enforceable in the courts of law. Fundamental rights cannot be abridged or curtailed except to the extent provided by in Part III itself. Hence in case of a conflict between Fundamental right and Directive Principles the former prevails over the latter.
2. In *State of Bihar* v. *Kameshwar Singh*[3] the court modified its approach. It relied on the Directive Principles in article 39 and held that Zamindari Abolition Act was passed for a public purpose within the meaning of article 31 and was valid though it violated the Fundamental right to property under article 19. (Fundamental right to property deleted in 1976).
3. In *Re Kerala Education Bill, 1957*[4] and in *State of Kerala* v. *N.M. Thomas*[5] it was held that the Court must adopt a harmonious construction and should attempt to give effect to both Fundamental right and the Directive Principles as far as possible. Thus, in determining the scope and ambit of Fundamental right – Directive Principles must be taken into consideration.
4. In *Mohd Hanif Quareshi* v. *State of Bihar*[6] the State law which prohibited slaughter of cows and calf capable of work was held valid though it violated the Fundamental right of profession under article 19 as it gave effect to the Directive Principles under article 48
5. In *Ranjan Dwivedi* v. *Union of India*[7] the court changed its trend in the later years and held that there is no conflict between the Fundamental right and the Directive Principles. They supplement each other in aiming at a social revolution and establishment of a welfare State.

---

1. Krishan Mahajan: Directive Principles: the Supreme court Breaks New Ground' Indian Express dt 11-9-1995.
2. AIR 1951 SC 226: 1951 SCR 525: 1951 SCJ 313.
3. AIR 1952 SC 252: 1952 SCR 889: 1952 SCJ 427.
4. AIR 1958 SC 956: 1959 SCJ 321: 1959 SCR 995.
5. AIR 1976 SC 490: 1976 Lab IC 395: (1976) 2 SCC 310.
6. AIR 1958 SC 731: 1958 SCA 783: 1959 SCR 629.
7. AIR 1983 SC 624: 1983 Cr LJ 1052: (1983) 3 SCC 307.

6. In *Kesavanand Bharati* v. *State of Kerala*[1] Supreme Court has held that Fundamental right and Directive Principles are supplementary and complementary to each other. They aim at the same goal of attaining social revolution and hence can be applied and interpreted together.
7. The same is reiterated in *Unni Krishnan* v. *State of Andhra Pradesh*[2].
8. In *State of Bombay* v. *Balsara*[3] it was held that Directive Principles are relevant to decide what is 'reasonable restriction' under the Fundamental rights Chapter. It relied on article 47 which directs the State to bring about prohibition of consumption of intoxicating drinks except for medical purposes. It held the restriction imposed by Bombay Prohibition Act as reasonable.
9. In *Bijay Cotton Mills* it upheld the validity of Minimum Wages Act, 1948 as it was enacted to give effect to Directive Principles of State Policy in article 43. It did not violate freedom of trade under article 19(5).[4]

H. Article 31C and the Directive Principles

(1) Article 31C is a tug of war between the Judiciary and the Legislature

The legislature attempting to give primacy to the Directive Principles and the Judiciary insisting on primacy to the Fundamental rights and then the Legislature amending the law to override the decision.

(2) Article 31C was added by 24th Amendment, 1971

First part of article 31 C provides that no law which is intended to give effect to the Directive Principles contained in article 39(b) (c) shall be deemed to be void on the ground that it is inconsistent or takes away or abridges any of the rights conferred by articles 14 or 19 or 31. It was held valid in *Keshwanand Bharati (Fundamental right case).*

(3) Judicial scrutiny barred under article 31C—Held void

The second part of article 31C provided that 'no law containing a declaration that it is for giving effect to such policy can be called in question on the ground that it does not in fact give effect to such policy. It was held void as it barred judicial scrutiny of such laws.

(4) Primacy to all directive principles by 42nd amendment

By the 42nd Amendment, article 32C was further widened to give primacy to all the Directive Principles in Part IV and not just article 39(b)(c).

***(5) Minerva Mills* v. *Union of India—42nd amendment struck down*[5]**

The Supreme Court struck down the 42nd Amendment as destroying the basic features of the Constitution relying on *Keshwananda Bharati*. None of the laws enacted to give effect to any of the Directive Principles could be challenged as violating the Fundamental right under articles 14, 19, 31. It held that to give

---

1. AIR 1973 SC 1461: (1973) 4 SCC 225: 1973 Supp SCR 1.
2. AIR 1993 SC 2178: 1993 AIR SCW 863: (1993) 1 SCC 645.
3. AIR 1951 SC 318: 52 Cr LJ 1361: 1951 SCR 682.
4. *Bijay Cotton Mills Ltd.* v. *State of Ajmer*, AIR 1955 SC 33: 1955 SCR 752: 1955 SCJ 51.
5. AIR 1980 SC 1789: (1980) 2 SCC 591: (1981) 1 SCR 206.

absolute primacy to one over the other disturbs the harmony of the Constitution which is the essential feature of the Constitution. The goals set out in the Directive Principles must be attained without abrogation of Part III. It held that the Constitution is founded on the bedrock of the balance between Part III and IV and so it has to be harmoniously interpreted. Fundamental rights are not an end itself but are a means to an end. P.N. Bhagwati J. gave a dissenting ruling giving primacy to the Directive Principles over the Fundamental rights.

(6) Sanjeev Coke Manufacturing Company—Doubted Minerva decision

Supreme Court expressed a doubt on the validity of *Minerva Mills* case. It held that validity of section 4 of the 42nd Amendment was not in issue directly in *Minerva*. So striking down 42nd Amendment was uncalled for and an obiter (passing observation in a judgment while deciding the case). It held that nationalisation of coke oven plants of the petitioner was done in order to realise the Directive Principles contained in article 39(b)(c) and hence valid even if it violated article 14 or 19. Further it was held that the industry as a whole must be nationalized. It is a matter of State policy to decide whether the whole industry will be nationalised or only a part of the industry.

In *State of Gujarat* v. *Mirzapur Moti Kureshi Kassab Jamat,* AIR 2006 SC 212: 2005 AIR SCW 5723: (2005) 8 SCC 534, the butchers challenged the Constitutional validity of the Bombay Animal Act, 1994 as it violated their Fundamental right to carry on business. Gujarat State had imposed a total ban on the cow slaughter. It was held that Directive Principles are relevant in considering the reasonability of restriction imposed on the Fundamental rights. It held that restriction will be valid if two conditions are satisfied – (i) it should not conflict with the Fundamental right and (ii) the Legislature must be competent to enact it. It was held that the prohibition on the slaughter of cows and calves is not a total ban on the business activity. Only part of their activity was prohibited. Cow and her progeny is the backbone of Indian agriculture and rural economy having regard to the cattle products. Hence the restriction is in the interest of general public within the meaning of article 19(6) of Constitution.

(7) Directive Principles raised to the status of Fundamental Right

The dissenting ruling of Bhagwati J. in *Minerva Mills* giving primacy to the Directive Principles has taken off and being implemented by the subsequent Courts. For example, in *Unni Krishnan, J.P.* v. *State of Andhra Pradesh,* AIR 1993 SC 2178: 1993 AIR SCW 863: (1993) 1 SCC 645, the Directive Principles in article 45 was raised to the level of Fundamental right and it was held that children between 6 and 14 years have a Fundamental right to education; equal pay for equal work raised to Fundamental right in *Randhir Singh* v. *Union of India*[1]; in *Hoskot* v. *State of Maharashtra,* AIR 1978 SC 1548: 1978 Cr LJ 1678: (1978) 3 SCC 544, held that legal aid and speedy trial are fundamental rights under article 21 available to prisoners.

---

1. AIR 1982 SC 879: (1982) 1 SCC 618: 1982 (I) LLJ 344.

CHAPTER 19

FUNDAMENTAL DUTIES

Article 51A

SYNOPSIS

A. Fundamental Duties
   (1) Basis for 'duties' lies in our tradition
   (2) Fundamental duties introduced during emergency

B. Sources of fundamental duties in other countries

C. Enforcement of Fundamental Duties

A. Fundamental Duties

Part IVA consisting of article 51A was added by the Constitution 42nd Amendment 1976. It specifies 10 fundamental duties of the citizens. It says that it shall be the duty of every citizen of India:

(a) To abide by the Constitution and respect its ideals, institutions, the National Flag and the National Anthem.

(b) To cherish and follow the noble ideals which inspired our national struggle for freedom.

(c) To uphold and protect sovereignty, unity and integrity of India.

(d) To defend the country and render the national service when called upon to do so.

(e) To promote harmony and the spirit of common brotherhood amongst all the people of India transcending religious, linguistic and regional or sectional diversities; to renounce practices derogatory to the dignity of women.

(f) To value and preserve the right heritage of our composite culture.

(g) To protect and improve the natural environment including forests, lakes, rivers and wild life, and to have a compassion for living creatures.

(h) To develop the scientific temper, humanism and the spirit of inquiry and reform.

(i) To safeguard the public property and to abjure violence.

(j) To strive towards excellence in all spheres of individual and collective activity so that the nation constantly rises to higher levels of endeavour and achievements.

(k) Who is the parent/guardian to provide opportunity or education to child, (or the ward as the case may be,) between age of 6-14 years. (Added by 86th Amendment 2002.)

(1) Basis for 'duties' lies in our tradition

Our Constitution provided for *fundamental rights* at the time it was framed but it did not make any mention of the *fundamental duties*. It is believed that the framers of our Constitution did not make specific mention of the fundamental duties as they were brought up in a culture where duties were ingrained in the rich tradition of this country. The *Bhagavad Gita* itself provides for *"Karamanye Vadhikaraste" i.e.,* Your right is to perform your duties. Thus duty was placed at such high level that "if a person is prohibited from performance of duties, it would amount to violating his right to perform his duties."

(2) Fundamental duties introduced during emergency

It is ironical that the chapter of Fundamental duties was introduced during the internal emergency in our country when the rights of thousands of citizens were infringed because the person at the apex of the country's administration had forgotten the duties attached to her office. It is now history that internal emergency was the darkest phase in the history of Independent India. It was an Emergency which was imposed on the country to cater to the political and personal ambitions of the then Prime Minister Smt. Indira Gandhi. Life and personal liberty of thousands of people were curtailed and people were put behind bars without reasons being disclosed. Laws were amended to suit the Smt. Gandhi's idiosyncrasies. Learning by the mistakes during the emergency period and in an attempt to set right the wrongs done by the 42nd Amendment during emergency— the 44th Amendment to the Constitution was passed after the Janata Party came to power.

B. Sources of fundamental duties in other countries

It is significant to note that none of the Constitutions of Western countries specifically provide for the duties and obligations of citizens. Among the democratic Constitutions of the world, we find mention of certain duties in the Japanese Constitution. Britain, Canada and Australia are governed largely by common law and judicial decisions. The French Constitution makes only passing reference of the duties of the citizens. The American Constitution provides only for Fundamental Rights and does not refer to duties. However the Constitution of Socialist countries lay great emphasis on citizens, duties.

Under Yugoslavian Constitution: Article 36 of the Yugoslavian Constitution is unique. It says "right to work and freedom to work are guaranteed and whoever will not work, though he is fit to do so, shall not enjoy the rights and the social protection that man enjoys on basis of work." Article 66 lays down that "every citizen shall consciously discharge any public or social duties vested in him and shall be personally accountable for discharging it."

Note that in our country right to work is not a fundamental right and personal accountability has been now introduced emphatically under the Right to Information Act, 2005. The Soviet Constitution contains a comprehensive chapter on the citizens duties and imposes punishment for its non-compliance. Military services is made compulsory under article 63.

Constitution of China also gives the citizens right to work and payment in accordance with quantity and quality (Article 118).

C. Enforcement of Fundamental Duties

The Constitution does not provide for enforcement of Fundamental duties the way it provides for enforcement of fundamental rights. Hence these duties are to be enforced by the law made by the Parliament. Thus, they would be enforced as statutory duties having a base in the Constitution. However it has been held in *AIIMS Students Union* v. *AIIMS*[1] that though fundamental duties are not made enforceable like fundamental rights they cannot be overlooked as "duties in Part IVA are prefixed by the same word "Fundamental" with which the 'rights' in Part III are prefixed.

These duties are best enforced by an intensive education and by making the people sensitive to the performance of their duties *suo motu*.

In *M.C. Mehta (2)* v. *Union of India*[2] the Supreme Court has held that it is the duty of the Central Government under article 51A(g) to introduce compulsory teaching of lesson for one hour in a week on protection and improvement of natural environment in all educational institutions of the country.

Fundamental duties though not enforceable by writs, provide a valuable guide and assist in the interpretation of Constitution and legal issues. They also guide in moulding the reliefs to be given by the courts.

In *Aruna Roy* v. *Union of India*[3] the National Curriculum Framework for School Education provided for imparting value development education relating to basics of all religions. It was challenged as violating article 28 of the Constitution and as being anti-secular. The court held that NCFSE does not mention of imparting religious instructions which are prohibited under article 28. What is sought to be promoted is "harmony and the spirit of common brotherhood amongst the people of India" surpassing religious, linguistic and other diversities as provided in fundamental duties in article 51A(e). It is also in tune with Preambular goals of promoting brotherhood. Hence the court held that such education is not violative nor anti-secular. It is in furtherance of fundamental duties.

In *State of Gujarat* v. *Mirazpur Moti Kureshi Kassab Jamat*[4] The Supreme Court held that the ban imposed under Bombay Animal Act, 1994 on cow slaughter was not violative of right to carry on business under article 19(1)(g). The ban was held to be a reasonable restriction "in the interest of general public" under article 19(6). They promoted the Directive Principles in article 48 and the fundamental duties under article 51A.

---

1. AIR 2001 SC 3262: 2001 AIR SCW 3143: (2002) 1 SCC 428.
2. (1988) 1 SCC 471: AIR 1988 SC 1115: JT 1988 (1) SC 69.
3. AIR 2002 SC 3176: 2002 AIR SCW 3670: (2002) 7 SCC 368.
4. AIR 2006 SC 212: 2005 AIR SCW 5723: (2005) 8 SCC 534.

CHAPTER 20

UNION AND STATE EXECUTIVE

(Articles 52-78; 152-167)

SYNOPSIS

A. Introduction

Provisions pertaining to the Union Executive and the State Executive are almost parallel. Hence they have been dealt with in a single chapter and the differences pointed out for a more comprehensive understanding of the Constitutional provisions. Provisions pertaining to Union Executive, President, Vice President and Council of Ministers is dealt with from articles 52 to 78 and 123. Provisions pertaining to the State Executive, Governor and Council of Ministers at the State are dealt with under Articles 153 to 167, 213.

The Constitution has established a Parliamentary form of Government based on British model. The essence is that the President is the constitutional head of the country. He is the head of the Executive. But he exercises his powers with the aid and advice of the Council of Ministers and is bound by such aid and advice. Council of Ministers is headed by the Prime Minister. Prime Minister is the head of the Council of Ministers. Thus in reality – real powers vest in the Council of Ministers headed by the Prime Minister. Members of the Council of Ministers are all elected by the people and they are members of the Parliament. The same is true at the State level with Governor as the head of the Executive and the Council of Ministers to aid and advice him but the Governor is not bound to act in accordance with such aid and advice; the Chief Minister is the head of the Council of Ministers.

B. Similarities and differences between the Centre and the State Executive

The following chart brings out the similarities and differences between the position at the Centre and the State—

President of the Union	**Governor of the State**
1. Status of the President: President is the Constitutional Head of India under article 52.	**Status of the Governor:** Governor is the Constitutional Head of the State under article 153.
2. Council of Ministers There shall be a Council of Ministers with the Prime Minister at the head to aid and advice the President *who shall act in accordance with such advice.* President may require the Council of Ministers to reconsider the advice and the President *shall act* in accordance with the advice tendered after such reconsideration. (Article 74).	**Council of Ministers:** There shall be a Council of Ministers with the Chief Minister at the head to aid and advice the Governor in the exercise of his functions, *except* insofar as he is by or under the Constitution required to exercise his functions or any of them *in his discretion.* If a question arises whether a matter is in his discretion or not, the decision of the Governor is final and the validity of anything done by him shall not be called in question on the ground that he ought or ought not to have acted in his discretion. (Article 163)
3. Election of the President: President is elected not directly but by an electoral college consisting of a) The elected members of both the Houses of the Parliament and *Elected* members of the Legislative Assemblies of the State. The nominated members of the LA and the members of the Legislative Council are not within the electoral college.	**Appointment of the Governor:** (a) The President of India appoints the Governor by warrant under his hand and seal. He is neither elected directly nor indirectly by any electoral college as in the case of the President. He is the nominee of the Union Government.
4. Qualifications: (a) Must be a citizen of India; (b) Completed 35 yrs of age; (c) Must be qualified for election as a member of the House of People; (d) Must not hold office of profit under Government of India or of the State or under any local or other authority subject to control of the Governments. (e) The President, Vice-President, Governor of any State, Minister of the Union or of the State are not deemed to hold any office of profit and hence are qualified to contest for Presidentship. (f) He cannot be a member of LS or RS or an MLA. If he is elected as a member of either House of the Parliament or State legislature he is deemed to have vacated his seat on the date on which he enters the office. 1997 Amendment now provides that the name of a Presidential candidate must be proposed by 20 electors and seconded by at least 50 electors. In case of vice Presidential elections by 20 to propose and 20 to second the proposal. The candidate has to deposit 15,000 rupees as security deposit.	**Qualifications: (Article 157)** (a) Must be a citizen of India; (b) completed 35 yrs of age; (c) Must not hold office of profit under Government of India or of the State or under any local or other authority subject to control of the Governments; (d) Must not hold any office of profit (Article 158).
5. Emoluments etc: Entitled to official residence free of rent. Entitled to emoluments allowances and privileges as determined by the Parliament by law until then as specified in the Second Schedule. Salary raised to *1,50,000* per month[1] Emoluments etc. shall not be diminished during his term of office.	**Emoluments etc.:** Entitled to official residence free of rent. Entitled to emoluments allowances and privileges as determined by the Parliament by law until then as specified in the Second Schedule. Salary raised to *1,25,000* per month[1] When the same person is appointed as the Governor of two or more States- the emoluments etc., are allocated amongst different States in such proportion as may be decided by the President. Emoluments etc., shall not be diminished during his term of office.

1. Presidents (Emoluments, Allowances and Privileges) Act, 2008.

6. Term of office of President (Article 56)

1. President holds office for a term of *5 yrs* from the date on which he enters upon his office.
2. He continues after the expiry of his term until his successor enters upon his office.
3. He is eligible for re-election.
4. He may resign before expiry of 5 years by writing to the Vice-President. He must communicate the same to the Speaker of the LS immediately.
5. He can be removed from his office for the violation of the Constitution by the process of impeachment under article 61.

Term of office of the Governor

1. Holds office during the *pleasure of the President*. Subject to this provision he holds office for a term of *5 years* from the date on which he enters upon his office.
2. He may resign by writing under his hand to the President.
3. He continues after the expiry of his term until his successor enters upon his office. (Article 156).

7. Extent of Executive Powers of the Union- (Article 73)

(a) He has executive, Legislative, Ordinance-making, pardon powers and *military, Diplomatic, Emergency* powers.

(b) Executive powers vest in the President and he may exercise his powers either directly or through officers subordinate to him which includes a Minister also.

(c) It extends to matters with respect to which the Parliament has powers to make laws (Executive powers are co-extensive with the legislative powers).
However the Executive power does not extend to matters in the *concurrent list* with respect to which the State Legislature.*also* has power to make laws except as may be expressly provided by Constitution or law made by the Parliament.

(d) It extends to the exercise of such right, authority, and jurisdiction as are exercisable by the Government of India by virtue of any treaty or agreement (Article 73)

Powers of the Governor of the State:—

(a) They are similar to those of the President *except diplomatic, military and emergency powers of the President.*

(b) Executive powers vest in the Governor and he may exercise his powers either directly or through officers subordinate to him which includes a Minister also. Article 154
However this provision shall not be deemed to transfer to the Governor any functions conferred by any existing law on any other authority.
Likewise it shall not prevent the Parliament or the Legislature of the State from conferring by law functions on any authority subordinate to the Governor. (Article 154)

(c) The Executive powers of the State are co-extensive with the legislative powers of the State Legislature to make laws.
However in respect of matters in the concurrent list in which both the Parliament and the State Legislature have power to make laws- the Executive power of the State is subject to, and limited by the Executive power expressly conferred upon the Union or its authorities by the Constitution or by any law made by the Parliament. (Article 162)

8. All Executive actions of the Union are executed in the name of the President. They are authenticated in the manner specified in the rules made by the President. The validity of the authenticated order cannot be called in question that it is not an order made or authenticated by the President. He allocates the business of the Government of India amongst the Ministers. (Article 77)

All Executive actions of the State are executed in the name of the Governor. They are authenticated in the manner specified in the rules made by the Governor. The validity of the authenticated order cannot be called in question that it is not an order made or authenticated by the Governor. He allocates the business of the State Government amongst the Ministers *except such business with respect to which under the Constitution he has to act in his discretion.* (Article 166).

9. He appoints the Prime Minister. On the advice of the Prime Minister he appoints the other ministers of the Union, Judges of the Supreme Court and the High Court, the Governors of the State, the Attorney General, the Comptroller and Auditor General, the Chairman and the Members of the Public Service Commissions, Election Commissioners, Special officers of the Scheduled Castes and Scheduled Tribes, Backward Classes Commission. All of them hold office during the pleasure of the President.

He appoints the Chief Minister. On the advice of the Chief Minister he appoints the other ministers of the State.

C. Appointment of the Prime Minister

The Prime Minister shall be appointed by the President and the other ministers are appointed by the President on the advice of the Prime Minister [Article 74(1)]. In appointing the Prime Minister the President hardly exercises his discretion as we have adopted the English Cabinet system which works on conventions. Under the British convention the leader of the majority party of the Lower House is appointed as Prime Minister, that is, the person who is in a position to win the confidence of the majority in that House. When a single party gains an absolute majority in the Lok Sabha and has an accepted leader the President has no choice but to appoint such a person as the Prime Minister. This is the only condition because Council of Ministers with the Prime Minister at its Head shall be collectively responsible to the House of the People under article 75(3).

The President exercises some discretion where there is a multi-party system and a coalition Government is formed. Even here there are certain conventions:

(a) If the Government is defeated- President should invite the leader of the opposition to form a stable Government.

(b) If two or more parties have formed a coalition before the election its leader must be called upon to form the ministry.

(c) He should then invite the largest single party in the LS to form a Government.

(d) He must invite the leader of the coalition formed after the election.

The last two precedents have been followed in the States but not uniformly. Such a situation arose at the centre for the first time in 1979 when Congress Government headed by Indira Gandhi was defeated and Janata Party came to power.

D. Duties of the Prime Minister under Article 78 and of the Chief Minister under article 167

The Prime Minister shall communicate to the President (a) all decisions of the Council of Ministers relating to the administration of the affairs of the Union and proposals for legislation and furnish such information as the President may call for.

If the President so requires – to submit for consideration of the Council of Ministers any matter on which a decision has been taken by a minister but which has not been considered by the Council of Ministers. (*Likewise in the case of the State –it is the Chief Minister who communicates with the Governor.*)

E. Executive power of the President

As the Executive powers of the Governor and the President are analogous- the explanations offered for the Executive powers of the President are equally applicable to those of the Governor. Wherever there is a difference the same has been pointed out.

What is 'Executive power': The observations are applicable to the Executive power of the President under article 73 and of the Governor under Article 163.

In *Ram Jawaya Kapur* v. *State of Punjab*[1] the Supreme Court has held that it is not possible to exhaustively define 'Executive' power. It connotes the residue of the Government functions that remain after legislative and judicial functions are taken away. In *Ram Jawaya Kapur* the Punjab Government order acquired copyrights in selected text books by an Executive order because of which the private publishing houses were ousted from the text book business. It was challenged as the order was without any legislative sanction. It was held that under articles 73 and 163 the power is not confined merely to administration of laws already enacted but includes determination of Government policy, initiation of legislation, maintenance of law and order, promotion of social and economic welfare, direction of foreign policy *i.e.,* carrying on of supervision of the general administration of the State.

Extensive Executive powers are conferred on the President and the Governor. All Executive functions of the Union and the State are executed in the name of the President and the Governor respectively.

The President has power to appoint- the Prime Minister of India and other Ministers;[2] the Attorney-General of India[3]; the Comptroller and Auditor-General of India;[4] the Judges of the Supreme Court;[5] judges of the High Court of the State;[6] Governor of a State;[7] Inter-State Council;[8] Union Public Service Commission and a Joint Commission for a group of States;[9] Finance Commission;[10] Election Commissioners;[11] Special Officer for Scheduled Castes and Scheduled Tribes;[12] Commission on Languages;[13] President has the power to revoke the Ministers,[14] the Attorney-General,[15] and the Governor of a State.[16] The Governor has powers to appoint the Chief Minister under article 164; the Auditor-General who holds office during the pleasure of the Governor under article 165.

F. Election of the President

1. President is elected not directly but by an electoral college consisting of
   (a) The elected members of both the Houses of the Parliament; and
   (b) Elected members of the Legislative Assemblies of the State. State includes National Capital Territory of Delhi and Union Territory of Pondicherry. Nominated members of the LS, RS, and the Assembly

1. AIR 1955 SC 549: 1955 SCA 577: (1955) 2 SCR 225.
2. Article 74.
3. Article 76.
4. Article 148.
5. Article 124.
6. Article 217.
7. Article 155.
8. Article 263.
9. Article 316.
10. Article 280.
11. Article 324.
12. Article 338.
13. Article 344.
14. Article 75(2).
15. Article 76(4).
16. Article 156(1).

have no voting rights. Members of the Legislative Council have no voting rights.

2. The election is in accordance with the system of proportional representation by means of a single transferable vote.

For example, A,B,C, and D are the contesting candidates. Total number of valid votes are 15,000. A candidate must secure at least 7,501 votes in order to win. They have polled as under:

1st preference Votes	2nd preference Votes	**Total of 1st & 2nd pref. Votes**	3rd preference Votes	**Total 1st, 2nd, 3rd pref votes**	Result of election
A 5250	300	**5550**	1700	**7250**	Eliminated
B 4800	1050	**5850**	1900	**7750**	Winner
C 2700	900	**3600**	Eliminated		
D 2250	Eliminated				

Procedure: At the first preference vote count - no candidate has secured 7501. D has secured the least. He is eliminated first.

Second preference votes recorded as against D's first preference votes will be transferred to the respective candidates A,B,C, when the 2nd preference votes are counted – again nobody secures 7501. Hence C who has secured the least is eliminated.

The third preference votes recorded as against C's 2nd preference votes are transferred to A, and B. Here B emerges as the successful candidate as he has secured more than 7501 and A is eliminated.

3. It is by secret ballot.
4. Number of votes which each elected MP is entitled to cast is calculated by the following formula article 55(2)(a):

   Population means the population as ascertained in 1971 census.
5. Disputes regarding election: All disputes regarding the election of the President and the Vice-President shall be enquired into and decided by the Supreme Court whose decision shall be final (Article 71). If their election is declared void – acts done in the exercise of their powers shall not be invalidated. Parliament may by law regulate any matter relating to the election of the President or Vice-President. Their election cannot be challenged on the ground of existence of any vacancy for whatever reason in the electoral college.

$$\frac{\text{State population}}{\text{Total number of elected members}} \times \frac{1}{1000}$$

In *N.B. Khare* v. *Election Commissioner of India,*[1] the petitioner had prayed that the Presidential election be stayed because general election in certain parts of Punjab and Haryana had not taken place and therefore the electoral college was incomplete. The Supreme Court held that the election to the President could be challenged only after completion of the election and declaration of the successful candidate.

1. AIR 1957 SC 694: 1957 SCC 344: 1957 SCA 953.

After the elections he again challenged the validity of the election in *Dr. N.B. Khare* v. *Election Commissioner of India*[1] - the court held that under the Presidential and Vice Presidential Act, 1952 the election could be challenged only by the candidate or 20 (in case of President) or 10 (in case of Vice-President) electors. Dr. Khare was neither a candidate nor an elector and hence was not entitled to challenge the election.

In *Re Presidential Elections*[2] The Presidential election was challenged on the ground that the electoral college was incomplete as the Gujarat State Legislature was dissolved and that the Presidential elections must be postponed until Gujarat elections are held. It was held that the elections must be held before the expiry of the Presidential term under article 62(1), 54, 55. It is only when the successor has not entered in his office that the President whose term has expired can continue in his office.

G. Procedure for impeachment of the President (Article 61)

Following are the steps to be taken for impeachment of the President:

(1) ***For violation of the Constitution:*** He can be removed from his office for 'violation of the Constitution' by the process of impeachment.

(2) ***Proposal in LS or RS contained in a resolution*:** The impeachment charge can be initiated either in the LS or the RS. The charge must be in the form of a proposal contained in a resolution signed by not less than $1/4^{th}$ of the total number of members of House. It can be moved after giving at least 14 days' advance notice. Such a resolution must be passed by a majority of not less than $2/3^{rd}$ of the total membership of the House.

(3) ***Investigated by the other House:*** The charge is then investigated by the other House. If the other House passes the resolution by $2/3^{rd}$ majority after investigation it has the effect of removing the President from the office. The President has a right to appear and to be represented at such investigation.

H. Vice-President of India

(1) *Elected:* There shall be a Vice-President of India (Article 63) who is elected by the members of both Houses of the Parliament at a joint Session by secret ballot in accordance with the system of proportional representation by means of a single transferable vote.

(2) *Qualifications:* Qualifications are the same as that of the President except that he must be eligible for election to the RS.

(3) *Duration:* The term is for 5 years. He may resign before the expiry of the term.

(4) *Removal by resolution of RS:* He can be removed by a resolution of the RS passed by a majority of the House and agreed to by a majority of the LS such a resolution can be moved only after giving 14 days' notice of the intention to move the resolution (Article 67).

---

1. AIR 1958 SC 139: 1958 SCR 648: 1958 SCA 287.
2. AIR 1974 SC 1982.

5. *Functions*: He shall be the ex-officio Chairman of the Rajya Sabha. He presides over the meetings of the Rajya Sabha but has no right to vote as he is not a member of the Rajya Sabha. He acts as a President whenever there is a vacancy due to death, removal, resignation or otherwise until a new President is elected.
6. When the President is unable to discharge his functions due to illness, absence, or other cause he discharges the functions of the President until the date on which the President resumes his office.

I. Powers of the President

(1) Military powers

President is the Supreme Commander of the defence forces of the country. He has powers to declare war and peace. His powers are regulated by law. The Parliament is empowered to regulate or control the exercise of the military powers by the President. The military power of the President is thus subordinate to his Executive power which is exercisable by him on the advice of the Council of Ministers.

(2) Diplomatic powers

The President sends and receives Ambassadors, and other Diplomatic Representatives. All Treaties and International agreements are negotiated and concluded in the name of the President and subject to ratification by the Parliament.

(3) Legislative powers

He has powers to summon, prorogue the Parliament and dissolve the Lok Sabha. However not more than 6 months must lapse between the two sessions of the Parliament. [Article 85(1)]. He can call a joint sitting of both the Houses of the Parliament in case of a conflict between the two Houses of the Parliament in respect of an ordinary Bill. (Article 108). He addresses both the Houses in a joint session at the commencement of each House and outlines the policies of the Government. But his speech is prepared by the Prime Minister.

Every Bill passed by both the Houses of the Parliament is sent to President for his assent. He may give his assent to the Bill in which case it becomes a law. He may withhold his assent or in the case of the Bill other than Money Bill, may return it to the House for reconsideration on the lines suggested by him. If the Bill, is again passed by both the Houses with or without Amendment, he must give his assent to it, when sent for the second time.

Bills to be introduced with the President's recommendation:

1. A Bill for a recognition of new State or alteration of new boundaries can be introduced in either House of Parliament with his recommendations.
2. State Bills for imposing restrictions on freedom of trade and commerce require his recommendations – (Article 304).
3. Money Bills can be introduced only in the Lok Sabha with his recommendations.

President has to lay before the Parliament the Annual Financial Budget; report of the Auditor-General; recommendations of the Finance Commission; report of the Special Commission of Scheduled Caste and

Scheduled Tribe; Backward Classes Commission Report; Report of Special Officers of linguistic minorities.

(4) Ordinance making powers

Ordinance making powers of the President under Article 123 of the Governor under Article 213.

(Legislative power of the Union and State (Executive)

President's Ordinance making Power article 123	Governor's Ordinance making Power (article 213)
When *both the Houses* of the Parliament are not in session and the President is satisfied that circumstances exist making it necessary to take immediate action, he may promulgate an Ordinance as the circumstances appear to him to require.	When *Legislative Assembly* is not in session (or both the Legislative Assembly and the Legislative Council not in session) and the Governor is satisfied that circumstances exist making it necessary to take immediate action, he may promulgate an ordinance as the circumstances appear to him to require. The Governor shall not promulgate any such Ordinance without instructions from the President if, (a) A Bill containing the same provisions would require previous sanction of the President for the introduction into the legislature or the Governor would have deemed it necessary to reserve a Bill for the President's consideration or an Act containing the same provisions would be invalid under the Constitution unless it has received the assent of the President.
Such an ordinance has the same force and effect as an Act of the Parliament.	Such an ordinance has the same force and effect as an Act of the Legislature of the State.
Such an ordinance must be laid before both the Houses of Parliament and shall cease to operate at the expiry of 6 weeks from the reassembly of the Parliament or if before the expiry of 6 weeks, resolutions disapproving it are passed by both the Houses, it shall cease to operate upon the passing of the second of those resolutions. Where both the Houses reassemble on different dates the period of 6 weeks is to be calculated from later of those dates.	Such an ordinance must be laid before Legislative Assembly (and Legislative Council, if any) and shall cease to operate at the expiry of 6 weeks from the reassembly of the State Legislature or if before the expiry of 6 weeks, resolution disapproving it is passed by Legislative Assembly-(and the Legislative Council- if there is one) upon the passing of the resolution Where both the Houses, (if any), reassemble on different dates the period of 6 weeks is to be calculated from later of those dates.
Ordinance may be withdrawn at any time by the President.	Ordinance may be withdrawn at any time by the Governor.
If the Ordinance relates to a provision on which the Parliament cannot enact a law, it shall be void.	If the Ordinance relates to a provision on which the State Legislature cannot enact a law, it shall be void. However if the State Act is repugnant to the Act of the Parliament or repugnant to an existing law in the Concurrent list, an Ordinance promulgated under this article in pursuance of instructions from the President shall be deemed to be Act of the State Legislature which is reserved for consideration of the President and assented to by him.

An Ordinance under articles 123 and 213 stand on the same footing as held in *T. Venkata Reddy* v. *State of AP*, AIR 1985 SC 724: 1986 Lab IC 357: (1985) 3

SCC 198. An Ordinance can also be issued when only one House is in session because the law cannot be passed by one House. An Ordinance under article 123 has the same force and effect as an Act of the Parliament/Legislature. It cannot be treated as an administrative decision. The power is plenary within its field and there are no limitations except those which are there on legislative powers of the State. In exercising the power, the President/Governor acts on his own satisfaction. The court cannot enquire into reason or subjective satisfaction or into sufficiency of those reasons.[1] In reality the satisfaction is that of the cabinet on whose advice the President or Governor exercises his ordinance making power. The existence of the necessity for promulgating for decisions cannot be questioned in the court of law. The validity of the ordinance cannot be tested on the grounds on which judicial action is tested. Just as the motive for passing the legislation is not subject to the court scrutiny so also the motive, propriety, expediency and necessity for passing an Ordinance is not subject to the court scrutiny.

Judicial Decisions:

1. In *R.K. Garg* v. *Union of India,* AIR 1981 SC 2138: (1981) 11 Tax Caw Rev 277 (SC): (1981) 4 SCC 675 the Ordinance making power has been upheld. Special Bearer Bonds (Immunities and Exemptions) Ordinance, 1981 was held not *ultra vires* of article 123 of the Constitution. An ordinance making power is co-extensive with the power of Parliament to make laws and no limitation can be read into legislative power of the President. Article 123 or 213 cannot be said to be undemocratic.
2. In *A.K. Roy* v. *Union of India,* AIR 1982 SC 710: 1982 Cr LJ 340: (1982) 1 SCC 27 The National Security Ordinance was held not violative of article 14. Ordinance would be subject to the test of vagueness, arbitrariness and public interest and it must be passed only when Parliament/legislature are not in sessions. While considering the validity of the law the court has nothing to do with morality of the law.
3. *D.C. Wadhwa* v. *State of Bihar,* AIR 1987 SC 579: 1986 (4) Supreme 465: (1987) 1 SCC 378 is a glaring example for abuse or ordinance making power between 1967 and 1981, the Bihar Governor promulgated 256 Ordinances. They were kept alive 1-14 years by repromulgation. The court called it "a subversion of democratic powers and colourable exercise of powers. It amounted to fraud on the Constitution and hence unconstitutional. It was PIL filed by a Professor who contended that a people have a right governed by laws made by elected representatives and not by an executive.
4. *Satyapal Dang* v. *State of Punjab*[2] the Punjab Legislative Assembly was not in session. It was in a state of inaction because the Speaker had adjourned the House making it impossible to pass appropriation Bill before the end of financial year. As time was running out and the budget had to be passed. The Governor prorogued the Assembly on 11th March

1. *Emperor* v. *Banwari Lal Sharma,* AIR 1945 PC 48: 46 Cr LJ 589: 72 Ind App 57; *T. Venkata Reddy* v. *State of AP,* AIR 1985 SC 724: 1986 Lab IC 357: (1985) 3 SCC 198.
2. AIR 1969 SC 903: (1969) 1 SCR 478.

and promulgated an Ordinance on 13th March prescribing the procedure for passing the budget and the appropriation Bill for timely completion of financial business. The Ordinance provided that the House could be adjourned by the resolution of House. Assembly was re-summoned by the Governor to meet on March 18th. On March 18th the Speaker ruled that the House was illegally re-summoned and that his adjournment order of March 8th was still good. He then left the House. Thereafter Deputy speaker took over and certified the appropriation Bill and it was approved. The Speaker questioned the validity of an Ordinance. The Supreme Court held that the Speaker's ruling that the House could not be resummoned by the Governor when he had adjourned it, was based on a wrong assumption. It was held that the Speaker cannot pronounce about the validity of Government's Ordinance. It can only be challenged by Legislative Assembly by a resolution.

(5) *Pardon powers of the President and Governor*

The object of conferring pardon powers on the President and the Governor is to provide for a remedy.for there is always a possibility of error in human judgment even the 'most trained mind.' It is to provide a protection to life and personal liberty at all levels possible – *i.e.*, both at the Judicial and Executive level. The power is exercised on the aid and advice of the Council of Ministers.

Pardon powers of the President	Pardon powers of the Governor
President has the powers— To grant pardons, reprieves, respites or remissions of punishment; or To suspend, remit; or commute the sentence of any person convicted of any offence: (a) By Court martial; (b) Against any law relating to a matter to which the Executive power the Union extends; or (c) In all cases *where the sentence is one of death.*	Governor has the powers – to grant pardons, reprieves, respites or remissions of punishment; or To suspend, remit, or commute the sentence of any person convicted of any offence: (a) Against any law relating of a matter to which the Executive power of the Union extends. Thus as regards death sentences and military offences President is the only pardoning authority.

Pardon- Completely absolves the offender from all sentences and punishments and disqualifications and places him in a position as if he had never committed the offence.

Commutation is the substitution of one form of punishment for another of a lighter character, Example from rigourous imprisonment to simple imprisonment.

Remission is the reduction of the amount of sentence without changing its character, Example reduction of sentence from one year to six months.

Respite is the awarding of a lesser punishment on some special grounds for example pregnancy/existence of a small baby of a woman offender.

Reprieve means temporary suspension of death sentence.

Judicial decisions:

(1) *In K.M. Nanavati* v. *Union of India*[1] the Supreme Court held that the President and the Governor in India have the same powers of pardon as

1. AIR 1961 SC 112: (1961) 1 Cr LJ 173: (1961) 1 SCR 497.

is enjoyed by the King in Great Britain and the President in USA. Hence the pardoning power can be exercised before, during or after the trial.[1] It is submitted that the power is to pardon etc 'the sentence of any person convicted of any offence' under articles 72 and 161. This clearly means that the power can be exercised only after the sentence is passed for otherwise there would not be any question of 'person being convicted' if pardon were to be given at the trial stage. At the trial stage every person is presumed to be innocent until proved guilty. Hence it is opined that decision is wrong. The British Conventions can be relied upon only in case the text of the Constitution is not clear. When the text is clear – it is the literal interpretation which should prevail.

2. *Kuljeet Singh* v. *Governor of Delhi* the Supreme Court considered the scope of the President's power.[2] The petitioner contended that the power to pardon is coupled with a duty to act fairly and reasonably. As no guidelines were issued by the Government of India for the exercise of this Constitutional power the court stayed all the executions of all the convicts whose mercy petitions were pending. Later the court vacated the stay on Ranga and Billa's execution as even the most liberal use of the pardon power could not justify granting a pardon. It observed that President's power to commute the death sentence has to be examined on case to case basis; and that it is not a fit case for laying down of guidelines to guide the discretion of the President. By ruling that the exercise of the President's power will be examined on the facts of the case the court has retained the power of judicial review on President's pardon power.
3. In *Sher Singh* v. *State of Punjab*[3] the court held that the mercy petitions must be disposed of expeditiously and expressed languish at mercy petitions being pending even for 8 years.
4. *In Kehar Singh* v. *Union of India*[4] (Indira Gandhi murder case) Supreme Court held that the President is free to scrutinise the evidence on record and come to a different conclusion on the guilt and the sentence. He does not amend or modify or supercede the judicial record. The record remains intact. How the application is going to be considered is decided by the President. There is no right to be heard at this stage. The power is a very wide power. It is not possible for the court to spell out precise, clearly defined and specific guidelines for the exercise of this power. The President cannot be asked to give reasons for his order.[5]

---

1. *In Re Channugadu*, AIR 1954 Mad 911: ILR 1955 Mad 92: 1954 Cr LJ 1370.
2. AIR 1982 SC 774, Ranga and Billa had murdered two innocent children. Their death sentence was upheld at all levels and their Special Leave petition was dismissed by the Supreme Court. Their mercy petition was rejected by the President without assigning any reasons.
3. AIR 1983 SC 361: 1983 Cr LJ 693: 1983 (1) SCJ 288.
4. AIR 1989 SC 653: 1989 Cr LJ 941: (1989) 1 SCC 204.
5. In this case Kehar Singh's request for personal hearing was rejected by the President. The President had stated that 'he cannot go into the merits of the case finally decided by the Highest Court of the land'. So Kehar Singh's son filed a writ in the Delhi High Court. It is in this context that the Supreme Court held that the power to review the death sentence extends to reviewing the sentence and also the guilt. Such wide are the powers of the President and the Governor under the pardon powers.

5. *G. Krishna Gouda* v. *State of Andhra Pradesh*[1] was a case of murder for implementing a social ideology through terrorist technology. It was argued that because their crime was of a political nature it needed a different consideration. The Supreme Court rejected the contention. It held that all public powers however high the dignitary in whom the power is reposed – has to exercise it in good faith, and intelligent and informed care and honesty for public good. In the present case there was no indication of any *mala fides* or an abuse of power.
6. In *Epuran Sudhakar* v. *State of Andhra Pradesh*[2] Supreme Court has held that the Governor cannot exercise the pardon powers arbitrarily. A Congress worker was awarded death sentence by the trial Court for murdering a Telugu Desam worker. High Court of Andhra Pradesh confirmed the death sentence. The Governor granted pardon. The victim's son filed a writ application in the Supreme Court challenging the validity of the Governors' pardon. Supreme Court quashed the pardon and awarded the death sentence. It held that if the exercise of pardon power is based on caste, religion or political considerations the court can examine its Constitutional validity.

(6) Emergency powers

They are covered in detail in an independent chapter. (Articles 352-360 & 365)

J. Privileges of the President and of the Governor (Article 361)

1. The President/Governor is not answerable to any Court for the exercise and performance of the powers and duties of his office or for any act done by him in the exercise and performance of those powers and duties.
2. However any person has the right to initiate appropriate proceedings against the State Government or the Central Government.

   Note that the *President's* conduct can be reviewed by any Court, Tribunal or body appointed by either House of Parliament for investigation in an impeachment case under article 61 (this para not applicable to Governor)
3. No criminal proceedings whatsoever can be instituted or continued against the President in any court during his term of office.
4. No process for the arrest or imprisonment of the President/Governor can be issue from any court during his term of office.
5. No civil proceedings claiming relief against the President/Governor can be instituted during his term of office in any Court in respect of any act done or purporting to be done by him in his personal capacity whether before or after he entered upon his office as President/Governor until the expiry of two month's notice in writing delivered to the President stating the nature of the proceedings, the cause of action, the name description

---

1. (1976) 1 SCC 157.
2. (2006) 8 SCC 161.

and place of residence of the party by whom such proceedings are be instituted and the relief which he claims.

6. The President/Governor is not answerable to any Court for the exercise and performance of the powers and duties of his office or for any act done by him in the exercise and performance of those powers and duties. His conduct can be reviewed by any Court, Tribunal or body appointed by either House of Parliament for investigation.
7. No process for the arrest or imprisonment of the President/Governor can be issued from any court during his term of office.

K. Position of the President before and after the 42nd Amendment

Convention – President to act in accordance with advise: Article 53(1) says that the Executive power of the Union shall be vested in the President and shall be exercised by him either directly or through officers subordinate to him in accordance with the Constitution. Article 53 gives an impression that if the President minds he can become a dictator. But article 74 provided that there shall be a Council of Ministers to aid and advice the President with the Prime Minister at the head. A hotly debated question therefore was whether the President was bound to accept the advice of the Council of Ministers or was it just an advise which could or could not be followed. Under the British convention it was the practice that the King would act in accordance with the aid and advice given by the Council of Ministers. *This was the position before the 42nd Amendment.*

Council of Ministers is the smaller body of ministers who form the advisory Council for the President with the Prime Minister at its head. They frame the general policy of the Executive and also the more important legislative measures introduced by the Government in Parliament. The duty of the Council of Ministers is to aid and advice the President.

Under 42nd Amendment – President to act in accordance with advise: After the 42nd Amendment, article 74 was amended and it was provided that 'there shall be a Council of Ministers to aid and advice the President and the President shall act in accordance with such aid and advice.' This set at rest the controversy whether the President is bound to act in accordance with the aid and advice given by the Council of Ministers or whether he had the discretion to reject the advice as it provided that the President shall act in accordance with the aid and advice.

The 44th Amendment has further provided that the President may require the Council of Ministers to reconsider their advice either generally or otherwise. When after reconsideration advice is tendered to him the President must act in accordance with such advice.

Dr. Ambedkar said in the Constituent Assembly that 'President occupies the same position as the King under the English Constitution. He is the head of the State but not of the Executive. He represents the Nation but does not rule the Nation. He is the symbol of the Nation. His place in the administration is that of the ceremonial device on a seal by which the nation's decisions are made known. He will be generally bound by the advice of the Ministers. He can do nothing contrary to their advice nor can he do anything without their advice. '...the Crown must find advisors to bear responsibility for his action.'[1] So also under our Constitution Council of Ministers are the advisors who bear the responsibility for the President's action.

Supreme Court has consistently taken the view that the position of President and Governors under the Constitution is similar to the position of the Crown under the British System. The Council of Ministers – consisting of Legislative members is like a hyphen which joins the legislative part of the State with the Executive part.[2]

In *Judges Transfer* case[3] the Supreme Court has held that though the advice given by the Council of Ministers to the President cannot be inquired into by the courts but the materials on the basis of which such advice is given, are not secret, and can be scrutinised by the courts.

In *U.N. Rao* v. *Indira Gandhi*[4] Supreme Court held that even after the dissolution of the LS the Council of Ministers does not cease to hold office. Their presence is needed to aid and advice the President. Any exercise of power without such aid and advice will be unconstitutional in view of article 75(1). It was contended by the appellant that under article 75(3) the Council of Ministers is collectively responsible to the House of People. So how can the Council of Ministers be responsible to the House which has been dissolved? And hence Council of Ministers also cease to hold office when the House is dissolved. The Supreme Court rejected this argument. It held that the whole of article 75 must be harmoniously construed. And that article 75(3) is applicable only when the House of the People is not dissolved. Hence the Prime Minister and the Council of Ministers continue in office even when the House of People is dissolved.

L. Council of Ministers (Union: Articles 74-75, 78 Schedule 3; State: Articles 163, 164, Schedule 3, Forms V, VI)

Council of Ministers at the Centre	Council of Ministers at the State
There shall be a Council of Ministers with the *Prime Minister at the head* to aid and advise the President who *shall act* in accordance with such advice. President may require the Council of Ministers to reconsider such advice either generally or otherwise and the President shall act in accordance with such advice tendered after reconsideration. [Article 74(1)]	There shall be a Council of Ministers with the *Chief Minister at the head* to aid and advise the Governor in the exercise of his functions *except* insofar as he is by or under this Constitution, required to exercise his functions or any of them in *his discretion*. If a question arises whether the matter is one where the Governor is required to act in his discretion – the decision of the Governor is final and the validity of anything done by the Governor shall not be called in question on the ground that he ought or ought not to act in his discretion. [Article 163(1)(2)]. This means that the Governor is not required to act or even seek advice as his decision is final.

1. *Samsher Singh* v. *State of Punjab*, AIR 1974 SC 2192: (1975) 1 SCR 814: 1976 All Serv Rep 269.
2. *Ram Jawaya Kapur* v. *State of Punjab*, AIR 1955 SC 549: 1955 SCA 577: (1955) 2 SCR 225.
3. *S.P.Gupta* v. *President of India*, AIR 1982 SC 149: 1982 Raj LR 389: 1981 Supp SCC 87.
4. AIR 1971 SC 1002: (1971) 2 SCC 63: (1971) Supp SCR 46.

Whether any and what advice was tendered by Ministers to the President shall not be inquired into in any Court. (Article 74(2))	Whether any and what advice was tendered by Ministers to the Governor shall not be inquired into in any Court. [Article (163(3)]
Prime Minister is appointed by the President and the other members of the Council of Ministers are appointed by the President on the advice of the Prime Minister.	Chief Minister is appointed by the Governor and the other members of the Council of Ministers are appointed by the Governor on the advice of the Chief Minister and the Ministers shall hold office during the pleasure of the Governor. [Article 164(1)]
Total number of members including the Prime Minister shall not exceed 15% of the total members of the House of People. (91st Amendment 2003)	Total number of members including the Chief Minister shall not exceed 15% of the total members of the House of People.(91st Amendment 2003). Subject to a *minimum of 12 Ministers.* [Article 164(1A)]
Member of the LS or RS belonging to any political party who is disqualified for being a member of that House under Para 2 Tenth Schedule – is also disqualified from being appointed as a Minister from the date of his disqualification to the date of the expiry of his term of office as such member or if he contests any election for either the LS or RS before the expiry of such period – till the date on which he is declared elected which ever is earlier. [Article 75(1B)]	MLA (or an MLA or an MLC in States having both Houses) belonging to any political party who is disqualified for being a member of that House under Para 2 Tenth Schedule- is also disqualified from being appointed as a Minister from the date of his disqualification to the date of the expiry of his term of office as such member or if he contests any election to the Legislative Assembly (or Legislative Council) till the date on which he is declared elected which ever is earlier. [Article 164(1B)]
Ministers hold office during the pleasure of the President. Article 75(2)	Ministers hold office during the pleasure of the Governor. [Article 164(1)]
President administers the oath of office and of secrecy before Minister enters upon the office as set out in the Third Schedule.	Governor administers the oath of office and of secrecy before Minister enters upon the office as set out in the Third Schedule.
A Minister who for any period of 6 consecutive months is not a member of either House of Parliament shall at the expiry of that period cease to be a Minister. [Article 75(5)]	A Minister who for any period of 6 consecutive months is not a member of Legislature of the State shall at the expiry of that period cease to be a Minister. [Article 164(4)]
Council of Ministers shall be collectively responsible to the Parliament. [Article 75 (3)]	Council of Ministers shall be collectively responsible to the Legislative Assembly [Article 164(2)]
Under article (3) the President makes rules for the more convenient transaction of the business of Government of India. He also allocates the business amongst the ministers.	Under article 166(3) the Governor makes rules for the more convenient transaction of the business of the Government of the State. He also allocates to the ministers business not pertaining to matters where the Governor is required to act in his discretion.

Council of Ministers consists of 3 categories of Ministers:

1. *Ministers of Cabinet rank*: Council of Ministers is a wider body of which the Cabinet is a part. It consists of the top 15-20 ministers who stand designated as Cabinet Ministers. Only the Cabinet Ministers take part in the meetings presided over by the Prime Minister or the Chief Minister as the case may be. Other ministers attend when invited. A full meeting of the Council of Ministers is rarely held. It is the Cabinet which frames

the policy and not the Council of Ministers. However note that the Constitution nowhere speaks of 'Cabinet'. This is again a convention inherited from the British.

2. *Minister of State:* They are formally of the Cabinet rank and paid the same salary and they hold independent charge of their departments.
3. *Deputy Ministers*: They have no separate charge of a department. They assist Ministers with whom they are attached. They are paid lesser than the Cabinet rank Ministers.

It is the Government of the day, which decides which portfolio will be of the Cabinet rank and which shall be of the Minister of State rank. There is no hard and fast rule on the matter.

M. Principle of collective responsibility

Cabinet decisions are joint decisions of Council of Ministers: The principle of collective responsibility is the basic principle in a Parliamentary form of Government. In England this principle works on well established conventions. In India the Constitution has made specific provisions to give effect to this principle. In addition we are also guided by the English conventions. It means that the Council of Ministers – construed as a body, is responsible to the Lok Sabha for the general conduct of affairs of the Government. Council of Ministers works as a team. Whatever be the differences of opinion within the Cabinet, once a decision is taken – it is the decision of the Council of Ministers acting as a body. Actual decisions are discussed and debated in Cabinet meetings where all the Council of Ministers are not present. Yet the decision taken by the Cabinet are joint decisions binding the Council of Ministers. Lord Salisbury explains this principle "for all that passes in the Cabinet each member who does not resign is absolutely irretrievably responsible and has no right afterwards to say that he agreed in one sense to a compromise while in another he was persuaded by his colleagues."[1] The only alternative before a Minister who is not prepared to support and defend the decision of the Cabinet is to resign. He cannot remain inside and keep raising dissenting voices. It is a valuable concept which helps in maintaining unity and discipline in the Council of Ministers. Hence when the Ministry loses the confidence of the House or is defeated on any question of policy it must resign.

Minister's individual responsibility: Every minister is responsible for the acts of the officers of his department. He has to answer questions regarding the affairs of his department in the Parliament/State Legislature. If the minister has taken an action without the Cabinet's approval – the Cabinet may or may not support him. If it supports the action- the action becomes a joint action. If the Cabinet does not support the action- the Minister has to resign and not the Cabinet. Cabinet cannot retain the Minister and at the same time contend that the decision is not of the Cabinet but the individual decision of the Minister.[2]

---

1. Life of R.B. Salisbury Vol II pp. 219-20.
2. *Ram Jawaya Kapur* v. *State of Punjab*, AIR 1955 SC 549: (1955) 2 SCR 225.

N. Discretionary powers of the Governor

Comparing the provisions pertaining to the President and the Governor it is clear that the discretion which the Governor enjoys is not enjoyed by the President. Yet this does not mean that the Governor has the power to disregard the advice of his Ministers in any matter that he wishes to do so. It is only in the limited areas where the Constitution permits that he is empowered to act in his discretion. In the areas where he has the discretion he need not act upon the advice nor even seek his advice.

The Constitution does not define the discretionary powers. This has raised the question whether the Governor is merely the Constitutional head or whether he has any real powers. The language is a partial reproduction of section 50(1) of the Government of India Act, 1935 and it alarmed the Constituent Assembly Members. However because a Cabinet which is collectively responsible to the Legislature gives advice to the Governor in the discharge of his functions – occasions are almost non-existent where he can act contrary to their advice. The only case where the Government is expressly required to exercise his functions in his discretion are paras 9 and 18 of VI Schedule to the Constitution regarding the administration of tribal areas in Assam. Normally he will act in accordance with the advice tendered, but in times of crisis between the Governor and the Council of Ministers there is a possibility of Governor acting on his own discretion.

It is submitted that it is truly alarming that the Governor is given more discretionary powers than the President. Giving larger discretion to the Governor is an indication of more Central control over the Centre. It is argued thus: President appoints the Governor and he remains in office during the pleasure of the President. But the President always acts in accordance with the aid and advice of the Council of Ministers at the Centre. However, this is not true for the Governor. Governor can over-ride the advice of the Council of Ministers at the State level as his decision on the question of his discretion is final under article 164. The Centre can, if it so minds, prevail upon the Governor to act according to its instructions and even dismiss or dissolve the Legislature Assembly. A nominated Governor of a State— being made more powerful than Executive Head of the Nation (who is himself the appointer of the Governor — and also bound by the advice of the Council of Ministers) – is one more indicator towards a *'Federal country with strong unitary characteristics.'*

O. Governor's discretion

Following are the circumstances where the Governor will be called upon to act in his discretion:

(1) *Appointment of the Chief Minister* – Normally the leader of the majority party is appointed as the Chief Minister. But when it is doubtful as to who is the leader of the majority party, the Governor may have to exercise his discretion and appoint the Chief Minister. After the Third General Election such situations have arisen. But the Governors have not followed any uniform practice in the appointment of the Chief Minister. Following principles are generally recognised to guide the Governor's discretion:

(a) First in the normal circumstance he should invite the leader of the majority party.

(b) Secondly: He should invite the leader of the alliance or coalition front formed before the election and returned with majority.

(c) Thirdly: He should invite the leader of the single largest party.

(d) Fourthly: He should invite the leader of the front formed after elections.

As these guidelines were not followed Governor's discretion has been subject to lot of controversy.

2. *Dismissal of the Ministry*: Ministers hold office during the pleasure of the Governor under article 164. The term 'during the pleasure' has its own limitations.

(i) It does not mean 'at the sweet will'. In a Parliamentary form of Government – it means the – confidence of the majority in the Legislature.

(ii) Governor exercises his pleasure according to the advice of the Council of Ministers. Council of Ministers is collectively responsible to the Legislative Assembly of the State. This means that as long as the Ministry enjoys the confidence of the majority of the House – Governor cannot dismiss it. In India – the Governor may refuse to accept the advice of the Ministry which has lost the majority in the House. Whether the Ministry has lost the confidence in the House is to be decided on the floor of the House. According to well established conventions the Governor is not to rely on material extraneous to the Assembly.

In a coalition Government a peculiar Constitutional dilemma is created. *For example,* the Governor dismissed the Charan Singh Ministry in UP and recommended imposition of President's rule in the State as no party was in his opinion able to form a stable Government. The Governor proposed a new theory – that the Chief Minister of a coalition Government cannot be treated on par with the Chief Minister of a single party majority Government. In such cases – according to the Governor – the Chief Minister should resign first and then reconstitute the Government. Note that in a coalition even when one of the coalition party withdraws support- reducing the party to a minority- it can still prove its majority in the House with the support of the other political parties. In UP the Chief Minister had already summoned the Assembly to meet on October 6th 1970 and was ready to advance the date if the Governor so desired, but the Governor did not care to wait until the majority was decided on the floor of the House.

After this Constitutional crisis in UP the President appointed a Committee of Governors to study and formulate norms on the powers etc., of the Governors. Following were the recommendations:

1. If the Chief Minister shirks his responsibility of facing the Assembly within the shortest time to test the confidence of the Legislature – the Governor has the right to dismiss a ministry.

2. Whether the Chief Minister commands the confidence in the House must be tested by voting on the floor of the House. If the Chief Minister refuses to so test it is a *prima facie* proof that he no longer enjoys the confidence of the House.
3. If an alternative ministry can be formed which in the Governor's view commands a majority in the Assembly – he must dismiss the ministry in power and install an alternative ministry in office.
4. If it is not possible to form such a ministry then the last option is to report to the President under article 356 and recommend the dissolution of the ministry in office.
5. The Chief Minister of a coalition Ministry is in fragile position as compared to the Chief Minister of the Single Party majority. Hence he cannot advise the Governor as regards appointment or dismissal of the Ministries with the same emphasis as may be done by the Chief Minister of the Single Party majority. The Governor has the discretion to explore the possibility of alternative ministries being formed which would command the confidence of the House.
6. On the Governor's discretion the Committee observed that right from the commencement of the Constitution it is recognized that in the choice of the Chief Minister Governor's decision under article 164(1) is final and based entirely on his unfettered judgment.

   Karnataka provides the latest example regarding the tug of war between the Governor and the Chief Minister as regards discretionary powers of the Governor. Governor has been refusing to appoint Justice Bannurmath as the Lok Ayukta with an observation that the Government must search for 'more honest judges'. He returned back the recommendation with suggestions that someone other than J. Bannurmath be appointed. The Chief Minister has again recommended the same Judge. The Governor now says that he will on his own appoint a Judge as the Lok Ayukta.[1] Likewise in Karnataka the Governor is exercising his discretion and refusing to release some of the prisoners on the ground that they are harmful to the country.

(iii) *Dissolution of the Legislative Assembly*: Under article 174 the Governor summons, prorogues and dissolves the Legislative Assembly. Under normal circumstances the Legislature is dissolved only at the expiry of 5 years. When the Ministry has lost the majority and an alternative stable Ministry cannot be formed, he may dissolve the House. Is the Governor bound to accept the advice of the defeated Ministry to dissolve the House? There are two views – *one view* is that he is bound to accept the advice even of the defeated Chief Minister, the *second view* is that he may form an alternative Ministry. There are many examples where Governors have refused to accept the advice given by the defeated Chief Minister.

1. NIE dt.

(iv) *Report to the President to proclaim emergency under article 356:* The Governor's report to the President that the State is not being run in accordance with the Constitution can be made by the Governor in his own discretion.

P. Can a non-member become a Minister

A non-member can become a Minister: a Minister need not be a member of the Parliament. An outsider can be a minister, but he must become a member of the Parliament within 6 months. If he does not, he has to resign from the Parliament or the Legislature as the case may be. In *S.P. Anand* v. *H.D. Deve Gowda*[1] the petitioner had challenged the appointment of Mr. Deve Gowda as the Prime Minister of India as he was not a member of either House of the Parliament at the time of his appointment as the Prime Minister. Supreme Court held that on plain reading the Constitution permits a non-MLA or non MLC or a non-MP to become a Minister. The only condition under article 75(5) is that he must become a member within 6 months.

In *S.R. Chauhan* v. *State of Punjab*[2] it was held that a non-member who fails to get elected during the period of 6 consecutive months after he is appointed a Minister cannot be re-appointed as Minister. Tej Prakash – a non-MLA was appointed under article 164(4) as a Minister. He failed to get elected to the Legislature and so he resigned. Meanwhile another person was appointed as the Chief Minister. Tej Prakash was again appointed as a Minister. Supreme Court held his appointment unconstitutional. Article 164(4) is an exception to the normal rule that only members of the Legislature can be appointed as a Minister. The clear mandate of article 164(4) cannot be defeated by giving a gap of a few days and reappointing him as a Minister. The non-member's inclusion in the Cabinet is a one-time privilege.

In *H.S. Verma* v. *T.N. Singh* in the context of upholding the appointment of a non-member as a Chief Minister the Supreme Court observed that – Article 164(4) must be interpreted in the light of articles 164 and 163. Article 163(1) does not provide for any qualifications for the person to be selected by the Governor as the Chief Minister or Minister but clause (2) makes it essential that the Council of Ministers shall be collectively responsible to the Legislative Assembly. This is the only condition prescribed by the Constitution.

Q. Convicted person cannot be appointed as a Chief Minister

In a landmark judgment in *B.R. Kapoor* v. *State of Tamil Nadu*[3] Smt. Jaylalitha-was convicted and sentenced to imprisonment for more than 2 years under the Prevention of Corruption Act. Hence she was barred from contesting the elections. Her party had won the elections with a thumping majority and she was elected as the leader of the Party. The Governor appointed her as the Chief Minister. Supreme Court held the appointment unconstitutional. It held that a person convicted of criminal offence and sentenced to more than two years cannot be appointed as a Chief Minister. A non-member can be appointed only when

1. AIR 1997 SC 272: 1997 AIR SCW 18: (1996) 6 SCC 734.
2. AIR 2001 SC 2707: 2001 AIR SCW 3070: (2001) 7 SCC 126.
3. AIR 2001 SC 3435: 2001 AIR SCW 3720: (2001) 7 SCC 231.

he possesses the qualifications prescribed under article 173 and has not been disqualified under article 191 of the Constitution. However the Governor does have the privilege of appointing any person as the Chief Minister under article 164(4). Court rejected that argument that 'people's mandate is supreme.' It held that people's mandate is supreme within the framework of the Constitution.

R. Dissolution of Parliament

Article 85(b) provides that the President may from time-to-time dissolve the House of the People or prorogue the House. Article 174(2) gives a similar power to the Governor. Here too, he acts on the advice given by the Council of Ministers. So long as the Prime Minister and his Cabinet enjoys the confidence of the Lok Sabha, President is bound to dissolve the Parliament when so advised by the Prime Minister.

The overwhelming juristic opinion is that the advice of the Prime Minister or the Chief Minister is not binding on the President or the Governor in the following four cases:

(1) When he loses his majority.

(2) When he is unable to prove his majority.

(3) When a vote of no confidence is passed against the ministry.

(4) When he is not facing the Parliament or Assembly but the President or the Governor has proof that the ruling party does not have a majority.

In these cases the President or the Governor must try to find an alternative ministry if possible and avoid mid-term poll.

S. Dismissal of Minister

Under article 75(2) ministers hold office during the pleasure of the President. But President appoints the minister on the advice of the Prime Minister. It is for the Prime Minister to decide who shall be the minister in his team. It is only when he is given the unfettered discretion to select and to drop any Minister that the principle of collective responsibility works. "The Prime Minister is really the keystone of the arch of the Cabinet and until we create that office and endow that office with statutory authority to nominate and dismiss Ministers there can be no collective responsibility."[1] The same is true in case of the Governor's power to dismiss a State Minister under article 174(2).

T. Dismissal of the Cabinet

It is an established convention of Parliamentary type of Government that a Ministry that has lost confidence of the Lok Sabha must resign. If it insists on remaining in office the President can dismiss that Ministry.

If the Ministry enjoys the confidence of the Lok Sabha but has lost the confidence of the people can it remain in office is a Constitutional grey area. There are two views. According to Prof. Dicey the King can dismiss such a Ministry but according to Prof. Jennings the King has no such right until the Ministry enjoys the confidence of the House. In India there have been three such instances. In 1959 the Communist ministry in the State of Kerala was dismissed on the ground that it had lost the confidence of the people though

1. Dr. Ambedkar Constituent Assembly Debates Vol VII pg. 1159.

it enjoyed the confidence of the Legislature. In 1977 Congress Ministry in 9 States were dismissed on the ground that they had lost the confidence of the electorates. Again in 1980 Janata ministries in 9 States were dismissed on the ground that they had lost the confidence of the electorate. Prof. Shukla justifies dismissal of the Ministry when it has lost the confidence of the people while still enjoying the confidence of the House because people's will is supreme under our Constitution. But the real problem is how do you determine the true will of the people specially with regard to the set up under which our democracy is working- there is no issue based voting; votes are purchased or lured; elections are won on money and muscle power; there is wide spread illiteracy which leads to uninformed voters and poverty resulting in hapless voters worried about making two ends meet. We are guided by the decision in *B.R. Kapoor's* case where it was held that ultimately people are supreme only within the framework of the Constitution. This observation was made when Jaylalitha was appointed as the Chief Minister in spite of she being convicted of corruption charges and sentenced for more than 2 years due to which she was not eligible to contest election; yet her party won by a thumping majority and she was elected as the leader of the Party and appointed as the Chief Minister. The court did not agree that people's will is supreme and hence her appointment as Chief Minister is legal and proper.[1]

---

1. For an analysis of the case, see the article authored by this author titled: Reading Constitutional limitations into Article 164(4) – with special reference to *B.R. Kapoor* v. *State of Tamil Nadu*, AIR 2001 SC 3435: 2001 AIR SCW 3720: (2001) 7 SCC 231.

CHAPTER 21

UNION AND THE STATE LEGISLATURE

(Articles 79-122; 168-212)

SYNOPSIS

A. Introduction

Provisions pertaining to the Union Legislature and the State Legislature are almost parallel. Hence they have been dealt with in a single chapter and the differences pointed out for a more comprehensive understanding of the Constitutional provisions. Our system provides for a compulsory bicameralism at the Union level – that is – two Houses – the House of People (*i.e.*, the Lower House also known as the Lok Sabha) and the Council of States (*i.e.*, the Upper House also known as Rajya Sabha).

There is either bicameralism or unicameralism at the State Legislature level. Where there is bicameralism, there are two Houses – Legislative Assembly (also known as the Vidhan Sabha) and the Legislative Council (also known as the Vidhan Parishad). Every State compulsorily has a Legislative Assembly. But it is only in 5 States that there are Legislative Councils. That is, except 5 States all other States are unicameral.

B. Union Parliament—Provisions pertaining to Lok Sabha and Rajya Sabha

Three Organs: Parliament of India consists of three organs. The President, the Council of States (Rajya Sabha) and the House of People (Lok Sabha). President is not a member of either House of Parliament yet he is a constituent part of the Parliament because he performs important legislative functions like giving assent to the Bills, summoning and dissolving the House etc.

The two Houses of the Parliament are constituted on different principles and different functional view points. They are not of co-equal status. Following are some of the *differences between the Lok Sabha and the Rajya Sabha*:

1. Lok Sabha is a popular House directly elected by the people on the basis of adult franchise. Hence the Council of Ministers is collectively responsible to the Lok Sabha.

   Rajya Sabha is constituted mainly by indirect elections. Hence it is not a 'popular House'. So the Council of Ministers is not responsible to the Rajya Sabha.
2. As Lok Sabha is a democratic chamber it has a prime role in the affairs of the country as compared to that of the Rajya Sabha. Role of the Rajya Sabha is somewhat secondary though in certain areas the Rajya Sabha alone has powers.

C. Rajya Sabha [Articles 80, 83(1), 84, 89 to 92]

(1) Composition of the Rajya Sabha

Rajya Sabha has maximum membership of 250 out of which 12 members are nominated by the President. They are persons having special knowledge or practical experience in matters as literature, science, arts and social service [Article 80(1)(a) & (3)]. The remaining 238 shall be representatives of States and Union territories.

The seats in the House are allotted among the various States and the Union Territories based on their respective population. The allocation of seats is specified in Schedule IV.

The nominations to Rajya Sabha are made by the President on the advice of the Council of Ministers. The elected and the nominated members stand on an equal status. The only difference is that the nominated members do not form a part of the electoral college which elects the President.

Rajya Sabha is a continuing body. It is not dissolved as is the case of Lok Sabha. 1/3rd of its members retire every 2 years [Article 83(1)] and their seats are filled up by fresh elections and nominations.

(2) Chairman and the Deputy Chairman of the Rajya Sabha

The Vice President of India is the ex-officio Chairman of the Rajya Sabha. Rajya Sabha elects a member of the House to be a Deputy Chairman

(Article 89). When the office of the Chairman is vacant or he is discharging the functions of the President, his duties shall be performed by the Deputy Chairman. If the office of the Deputy Chairman is also vacant his duties are performed by such member of the Rajya Sabha as the President may appoint for that purpose. The Chairman presides over the House and in his absence the Deputy Chairman presides. If both are absent then such person as may be determined by the rule of procedure of the Council and if no such person is present, such other person as may be determined by the Rule of Procedure shall act as a Chairman.

The Deputy Chairman shall vacate his office if he ceases to be a member of the Council. He may resign his office by writing to the Chairman. He may be removed from his office by a resolution of the Council passed by a majority of all the then members present (Article 90). Such a resolution can be moved only by giving at least 14 day's notice. While a resolution for the removal of the Deputy Chairman or the Chairman is under consideration, the Deputy Chairman or the Chairman respectively shall not preside. The Chairman shall have the right to speak and take part but shall have no right to vote on such resolution or any other proceedings.

(3) Utility of Rajya Sabha

Though termed as the Upper House, the Rajya Sabha, in fact stands in an inferior position as compared to the Lok Sabha. For *e.g.*, a Money Bill can be introduced only in Lok Sabha. A vote of no confidence cannot be passed by the Rajya Sabha, even when a Joint Session is held in case of dead lock between both the Houses. The Lok Sabha stands on the higher footing due to its numerical strength. Due to the weak position of the Rajya Sabha, some Constitutional Jurists suggest for its abolition. The other opinion is that Rajya Sabha is desirable due to following reasons:

1. Senior Statesman and Politicians get an access into the administration of the country without undergoing ordeal of General elections necessary for entry into Lok Sabha.
2. Talent and expertise of such persons would be available to the country.
3. Lok Sabha is a popular House. It may be tempted to act hastily with an eye on mustering a public opinion. Rajya Sabha acts as a check and affords an opportunity for its reconsideration of hurried changes in Law by delaying its adoption for a limited period.
4. Rajya Sabha is a House where the States are represented keeping it with a federal principle.

D. House of People (Lok Sabha) (Articles 81-84, 93-96, 100, 112, 330-334)

(1) Composition of Lok Sabha

Lok Sabha is the popular House. Maximum number of membership is 550 out of whom not more than 530 are elected by the States and not more than 20 represent Union territories (Article 81). The President may nominate 2 members of Anglo-Indian Community if in his opinion they are not adequately represented in the Lok Sabha (Article 331). The representatives of States are directly elected by the people on the basis of Adult Suffrage. The Representatives of Union Territory are elected in the manner prescribed by the Parliament. Every citizen who is not less than 18 years of age and not disqualified on grounds of non-residence, unsoundness of mind, corrupt or illegal practice is entitled to be a voter. (Article 326).

Each State is allotted a number of seats in the Lok Sabha in such a manner that the ratio between the number of seats and its population is same for all the States. (Articles 81 (2) (a) & 81 (3)). This provision is not applicable to a State having a population of less than 6 millions.

[*State Legislature:* Composition in the Legislative Assembly is – maximum 500 and minimum 60 chosen by direct election].

(2) Territorial Constituencies

Each State is divided into territorial constituency in such a manner that the ratio between *population of each constituency* and number of seats allotted to it is the same throughout the State as far as practicable. This ensures uniformity between inter-States and intra-States[1]. After completion of each census, allocation of seats in Lok Sabha and division of State into territorial constituencies must be readjusted in the manner provided by the Parliament. Such readjustment does not affect the representation in the Lok Sabha until dissolution of the existing House. Upto the year 2026, for the purpose of seats allotment, 1971 census figures will be used to ascertain the population of the State. This means that the allocation of the seats through the State in the Lok Sabha has been chosen at the 1971 census. So no revision is to be made until the first census is taken after 2026. In short, whatever be the increase in the population allocation of seats is based on 1971 population.[2] This is introduced by 42ndAmendment as a proviso to article 81 & 82. Likewise, similar changes have been introduced by the same Amendment as regards composition of Legislative Assembly under article 170.

[State Legislature: Provision regarding territorial constituency of Legislative Assembly is dealt with under article 170(2)].

(3) Duration

Lok Sabha shall continue for 5 years from the commencement of its first session. Expiry of 5 years operates as a dissolution of the House. The President may dissolve it even earlier. When the proclamation of Emergency is in force, it can be extended by the Parliament for a period not exceeding one year at a time and in any case not exceeding 6 months after the proclamation has ceased to operate [Article 83(2)].

[*State Legislature:* Duration of Legislative Assembly is the same as that of the Lok Sabha Article 172(1).]

1. Inter-States (between one State and another) and intra-States (*i.e.,* between different constituencies in the same State).
2. Parliament has enacted Delimitation Commission Act, 2002. The Commission will demarcate each State into single member constituency equal in number to the seats allotted to the State in Lok Sabha. 1991 census figures are to be used. However there should be no readjustment of seats in the LS until 2026.

(4) Speaker and Deputy Speaker of the Lok Sabha (Articles 93-96)

The Lok Sabha elects two of its members as Speaker and Deputy Speaker respectively. When the office of the speaker is vacant, the Deputy speaker performs the duties of the Speaker's office. If the office of the Deputy speaker is also vacant, duties of the Speaker shall be performed by such member of the House, as the President may appoint [Article 95(1)]. Deputy Speaker also acts as the Speaker when the Speaker is absent from any sitting of the House. If he is also absent, such persons as may be determined by the Rules of the House and if no such person is present such other person as may be determined by the House may act as the Speaker [Article 95(2)].

The Speaker and the Deputy Speaker remain in the office as long as they are members of the House. The Speaker continues in the office even if the Lok Sabha is dissolved until newly elected Lok Sabha meets. They may resign their offices or they may be removed from their offices by the resolution of the Lok Sabha passed by the majority of all the members of the House [Article 94 (a) (b) & (c)].

Such a resolution cannot be moved unless 14 day's notice is given of the intention to move the resolution. When the resolution for removal of the Speaker is under consideration – the Speaker and when it is against the Deputy Speaker – the Deputy Speaker shall not preside over the sittings of the House, though he may be present.

The Speaker shall have right to speak in and take part in the proceedings of the House of People while any resolution for his removal is under consideration in the House and he is entitled to vote only in the first instance on such resolution for his removal or any other matter during such proceedings but not in case of equality of votes. The Speaker is the Chief Officer of the Lok Sabha. He presides over its sitting and controls its working. He upholds dignity and privilege of the House, once elected he must rise above party interest. The salary of the Speaker is charged on consolidated fund of India and is not subject to annual vote by the Parliament. He cannot be removed from his office by a resolution passed by the special majority.

(5) Functions and Powers of the Speaker

The position, power and duties of the Speaker of the Lok Sabha and Legislative Assembly are one and the same. The Speaker is an impartial and independent Presiding Officer. He presides over the meetings of the House and regulates the Proceedings of the House. He has no vote except in case of tie [Article 100(1)]. Disciplinary Powers vests with him. He maintains decorum in the House during debates. He Interprets the rules of the Assembly and decides all points of the order and questions of procedure. He can ask the Member to withdraw from the House for the violation of the rules of the House. He can suspend him for the whole session for disregarding the Authority and rulings of the Chair. He can adjourn or suspend the session in case of great disorder. He certifies whether a money bill is a bill or not. His rulings on the above point are final and cannot be challenged in the court of law. Thus he is custodian of the dignity of the House and an impartial arbitrator in its proceedings.

He enjoys the same honour and the same dignity as is enjoyed by the Speaker of the House of Commons in England. However it is unfortunate that we have instances where the conduct of the Speaker is not in tune with the high dignity attached to his Office. For *e.g.*, the Supreme Court disapproved the action of the Speaker in *A.K. Molhialgan* v. *Governor*, the Madras High Court held adjournment of speaker was not *bona fide* act of adjournment. There are instances of misuse of the power of the Speaker.

He is an officer of the House. He has to ensure orderly working of the House. He has no inherent power of his own under the Constitution. Hence he cannot arrogate to himself the function of the House. It is for the House to recognise the Ministry and not for the Speaker.

It is well accepted rule that Speaker does not give a ruling upon a Constitutional question nor decide a question of law. Such questions are meant for the court to decide. Speaker gives rulings only on the procedural matter. Speaker does not give rulings unless the matter is raised on the floor of the House.

[*State Legislature*: Provisions regarding Speaker and Deputy Speaker of the Legislative Assembly of the State is similar and is under articles 178, 179, 180(1)].

(6) Qualification for membership of Lok Sabha and Rajya Sabha

(a) He must be a citizen of India.

(b) He must not be less than 30 years of age in case of Rajya Sabha and not less than 25 years for Lok Sabha.

(c) He must possess such other qualifications as may be prescribed by the Parliament.

(d) He must take an oath before some person authorized in that behalf by election commission according in form set out in the third schedule. Article 84

(e) Under the Representations of People Act, 1951, his name should be registered as a voter in any Parliament Constituency.

No educational qualifications are prescribed for the Member of the Parliament.

[*State Legislature:* Qualifications for the State Legislature is contained under article 173].

(7) Disqualifications of members (Articles 101-104)

A person is disqualified for being chosen and for continuing as the Member of the Parliament if:

(a) He holds any office of profit under the Central or the State Government, other than the office declared by the Parliament by law not to disqualify its holder [Article 102(1)]. A Minister in the Central or State Government is not considered as holding office of profit.

(b) If he is of unsound mind and declared by the competent court.

(c) Undischarged insolvent.

(d) If he is not citizen of India or has voluntarily acquired citizenship of Foreign State or is under any acknowledgment of any allegiance or adherence to a Foreign State.

(e) If he is so disqualified under any law made by the Parliament.

[*State Legislature:* Provisions regarding disqualification of State Legislature members is under article 191]

(8) Disqualification under Representation of People's Act

(a) Corrupt practices in the Election.

(b) Conviction for an offence resulting in an imprisonment for 2 or more years

(c) Failure to lodge an account for election expenses.

(d) Having an interest or share in the contract for supply of goods or execution of any work or performance of the service to the Government.

(e) Being a director or a managing agent or holding an office of profit in a Corporation in which Government has 25% share.

(f) Dismissal from the Government service for corruption and disloyalty to the State.

(9) Disqualification on the ground of defection

The 52nd Amendment has added Schedule 10 to the Constitution which specifies the disqualifications on the ground of defection. It has amended articles 102 & 191 which provides that a member shall be disqualified for being a member of either House of Parliament or of State Legislatures if he incurs the disqualifications in the 10th Schedule:

(a) If he voluntarily gives up the membership of the political party on whose ticket he is elected to the House; or

(b) If he votes or abstains from voting in the House against any direction of the political party or any person or authority authorised by it in this behalf without the prior permission of such party and unless it has been condoned by the party within 15 days from the date of voting or abstention or

(c) If any nominated member joins any political party after the expiry of six months from the date on which he takes his seat in the House.

Exceptions: Above disqualifications will not apply:

(1) If a member goes out of the political party as a result of merger of his original political party with another political party provided 2/3rd of the members of the Legislature party have agreed to such merger.

(2) If a member after being elected as the Presiding Officer of the House – gives up the membership of the Party to which he belonged or does not join that Party or becomes a member of another Party.

The Constitution 91st Amendment Act, 2003 has added a new clause to articles 75 and 164 of the Constitution. Clause 1(B) provides that member of either House of Parliament belonging to any political party who is disqualified for being a member of that House on the ground of defection under 10th Schedule (Para 2) – shall also be disqualified to be appointed as a Minister under articles 75(1) and 164 until he is re-elected.[1] Consequently Para 3 of the 10th Schedule under which the exemption from disqualification was provided in case of split of 1/3rd members has been omitted.

Suppose in a State Legislature there are 30 members belonging to a particular party, say 20 or more members decide to join the ruling party. There is no defection by these 20 members and hence they can become Ministers. Under the earlier provision even if 10 members out of 30 had joined the ruling party it would not be considered defection and they could become Ministers.

If any question arises as to whether a member of a House has become subject to any of the disqualifications in the 10th Schedule the question shall be referred to the Chairman or Speaker of such House whose decision shall be final. The decision of the Presiding Officer shall not be called in question in any Court of law (Para 7). In a land mark judgment in *Kihota Hollohon* v. *Zachilhu*[2] Supreme Court has held Para 7 as unconstitutional as it takes away the judicial review powers which is the basic structure of the Constitution. In applying the Anti-defection Law the Speaker role is like that of a Tribunal and is therefore open to judicial review.

(10) Effect of disqualification [Article 101(3)]

A member's seat becomes vacant in the following 3 cases [Article 101(3), (4)]:

(i) by resigning his seat in writing under his hand addressed to the Speaker of the Lok Sabha or the Chairman of the Rajya Sabha.

(ii) if he remains absent from all meetings of the House for 60 days without the permission of the House.

(iii) if he becomes subject to disqualifications mentioned above.

(11) Penalty for voting by a non-qualified person (Article 104)

If a person sits or votes as a member of the Parliament before taking oath or knowing that he is not qualified or that he is disqualified or that he is prohibited from so doing by any law he becomes liable in respect of each day on which he so sits or votes to a penalty of 500 rupees to be recovered as a debt due to the Union.

Office of profit: The term 'office of profit' is not defined in the Constitution or in the Representation of People Act, 1951. The term 'office' implies that there is an existence of an office apart from the person who holds it. The 'office of profit' must be under the Central or any State Government. What is to be seen is whether the Government has the power of appointment; whether the Government has the right to dismiss him; whether Government pays the remuneration; whether the functions are performed for the Government;

1. Such a person cannot be appointed a Minister under Article 164(4).
2. (1992) 1 SCC 309: 1992 AIR SCW 3497: (1992) Supp 2 SCC 651.

whether Government exercises control over the performance of those functions are the questions which determine whether the office is an office of profit.

E. Conduct of Parliamentary business (Articles 85-88, 99-100, 104, 121-122, Sch. 3)

(1) Sessions, Prorogation, Dissolution

The President may from time-to-time summon the House or either House to meet at such time and place as he thinks fit; he can also prorogue either House or dissolve the House of the People but six months must not intervene between their first and last sittings.

Indira Gandhi v. *Raj Narain*, (1976) 2 SCR 347: AIR 1975 SC 2299: 1975 Supp SCC 1, the Supreme Court held that the Constitution 39th Amendment Act, was not illegal on the ground that a number of members of Parliament of the two Houses were detained under the preventive detention laws during the Internal Emergency.

Prorogation: It merely ends a session. It does not end the life of a House and hence a Bill does not lapse on prorogation of the session. The power to prorogue is vested in the President.

Adjournment: Terminates a sitting of the House. It is an act of the House and is exercised by the Presiding Officer of the House. It resumes the business when it meets again.

Dissolution : It ends the very life of the House and general election must be held to elect a new Lok Sabha. Rajya Sabha is a permanent body and is not subject to dissolution. Power to dissolve the Lok Sabha vests with the President who acts on the advice of the Prime Minister.

(2) President's address and special address (Articles 86, 87)

The President may address either House of Parliament or both Houses assembled together and for that purpose require the attendance of members. He may also send messages to Parliament whether with respect to a Bill then pending in Parliament or otherwise. The House to which any message is so sent shall with all convenient despatch consider any matter required by the message to be taken into consideration. (Article 86)

The President must at the commencement of the first session after each General Election to the Lok Sabha and at the commencement of first session of each year address both Houses assembled together and inform the Parliament of the causes of its summons. (Article 87)

(3) Oath by members

Every member of either House of Parliament before taking his seat must make and subscribe before the President an oath or affirmation in the prescribed form contained in Schedule III. (Article 99, Schedule 3)

(4) Voting in Houses and quorum (Articles 100, 104)

All questions of any sitting of either House or joint sitting of the Houses are to be determined by a majority of votes of the members present and voting. Some Constitutional questions require a special majority for example articles 61(2)(b), 61(4), 94(c), 108(4), 218, 249(1), & 368. The Chairman or the Speaker cannot vote in the first instance but has a casting vote in the case of an equality of votes. Under article 122(1) the validity of any proceedings in the Parliament cannot be called in question on the ground of any alleged irregularity of procedures.

> Quorum to constitute either House of Parliament is $1/10^{th}$ of the total number of members of the House. It is further provided that if at any time during a meeting of a House there is no quorum it is the duty of the Chairman or Speaker either to adjourn the House or suspend the meeting until there is a quorum. (Article 100(4)

F. Legislative Procedures (Articles 107, 111)

Article 107 provides for the introduction and passing of all Bills other than money and financial Bills.

(1) Introduction and originating of a Bill [Article 107(1)]: [Passing of ordinary Bills] [Article 107(2)]

A Bill may originate in either House of Parliament. A Bill is not deemed to have been passed by the Parliament unless it has been agreed to by both the Houses. Thus both the House have been given an equal status.

After the Bill is passed in one House and sent to the other the latter has four options:

(i) If the other House agrees to the Bill without Amendment it is deemed to have been passed by both the Houses and sent for President's assent.

(ii) The other House may reject the Bill altogether. The President may summon a joint sitting under article 108(1)(a).

(iii) It may pass the Bill with Amendments and return it to the other House. If the House which originated the Bill accepts the Amendments the Bill is sent to President for his assent. (Article 111)

(iv) If the originating House does not agree to the Amendments and no final agreement between the Houses is reached through negotiations the President may call a joint meeting of both the Houses. (Article 108(1)(b))

(v) It may take no action on the Bill *i.e.,* keep it lying with itself without returning it to the originating house. In such a case if 6 months have elapsed since the receipt of the Bill the President may summon a joint meeting. (Article 108(1)(c))

(vi) When there is a joint sitting the two Houses of the Parliament have equal powers as regards Bills other than money Bills.

(2) *Lapsing of the pending Bills* [Article 107(3)(4)(5)]

(i) A Bill pending in the Parliament does not lapse due to prorogation of the Houses.

(ii) A Bill pending in the Rajya Sabha does not lapse by dissolution of the Lok Sabha.

(iii) But a Bill which is pending in Lok Sabha or having been passed by the Lok Sabha is pending in Rajya Sabha does lapse on the dissolution of the Lok Sabha.

Effect of dissolution on the pending business

(3) *Joint Sitting of the Houses [Articles 108, 118(3)(4)]*

According to article 108 when a Bill passed by one House and sent to the other House:

(i) Is rejected by the House; or

(ii) The House disagrees to the amendments or

(iii) The other House does not pass the Bill and more than six months have passed the President may summon a joint session of both the Houses.

  (i) The President cannot summon a joint sitting if the Bill in question has lapsed due to dissolution of the Lok Sabha. If the dissolution takes place after the President has notified his intention to summon a joint sitting, such sitting is held notwithstanding the dissolution.

  (ii) The President may notify to the House by sending a message of his intention to summon them for a joint sitting for the purpose of deliberation and voting on the Bill in dispute. If the Houses were not in session the President may express his intention by public notification. When the President has notified his intention of summoning the Houses to meet in a joint session- neither Houses shall proceed further with the Bill. If at the joint sitting of the two Houses the Bill is passed by the majority of total number of members of both the Houses present and voting it shall be deemed to have been passed by both the Houses. [Article 108(4)]

  (iii) At a joint sitting of two Houses, no new amendments shall be proposed in the Bill except such as are necessary by the delay in the passage of the Bill. If at all any amendment is necessary the decision of the Presiding officers shall be final. [Article 108(4)(b)]

  (iv) At a joint sitting of the two Houses the Speaker of the Lok Sabha or in his absence such person as may be determined by the Rules of Procedure presides. [Article 118(4)]

  (v) This provision does not apply to money Bill. Lok Sabha has exclusive powers over money Bill.

(4) *Money Bills (Articles 109, 110, 117)*

Efficient handling of the Nation's finance is the backbone of the economic prosperity of any country. Hence Constitution provides special provisions in respect of Money Bills. Following are the provisions:

What is a Money Bill: Article 110(1) defines that Money Bill is a Bill which contains only provisions with respect to all or any of the following matters:

(a) Imposition, abolition, remission, alteration or regulation of any tax.

(b) The regulation of the borrowing of money or giving of any guarantee by the Government of India.

(c) The custody of Consolidated Fund or the Contingency Fund, the payment or withdrawal of money from such Fund.

(d) Appropriation of money from the Consolidated Fund of India.

(e) Declaring of any expenditure to be charged on the Consolidated Fund of India.

(f) Receipt of money on account of the Consolidated Fund of India or the Public Account of India or the custody or issue of such money or the audit of the affairs of the Union or of a State.

(g) Any matter incidental to any of the matters specified in sub clauses (a) to (f) above

But a Bill is not a Money Bill by reason only that it provides for

(a) The imposition of fines or other pecuniary penalties; or

(b) The payment of fees for licence or service rendered; or

(c) Imposition, abolition, remission, alteration or regulation of any tax by any local authority or body for local purposes. [Article 113(2)]

if any question arises whether a Bill is a Money Bill or not the decision of the Speaker of the Lok Sabha shall be final. So when the Bill is sent to the Rajya Sabha or presented to the President for assent a certificate of the Speaker shall be endorsed on it that it is a Money Bill. [Article 110(4)]

A Money Bill can only be introduced in the Lok Sabha and not in the Rajya Sabha. Article 109(1). A Money Bill can be introduced only with the recommendation of the President. However no recommendation of the President is necessary for the moving of an amendment making provision for the reduction or abolition of any tax. [Article 117(1)]

After the Money Bill is passed by the Lok Sabha it is sent to the Rajya Sabha for its recommendations. The Rajya Sabha must return the Bill to the Lok Sabha within 14 days from the receipt of the Bill with its recommendations. If the Lok Sabha accepts the recommendations made by the Rajya Sabha the Money Bill shall be deemed to be passed by both the Houses. If the Money Bill sent to Rajya Sabha for its recommendations is not returned to the Lok Sabha within 14 days the Bill is deemed to have been passed by both the Houses at the expiry of the said 14 days in the form in which it was passed by the Lok Sabha. Thus at most the Rajya Sabha can retain a Money Bill for a maximum period of 14 days. It is then sent to the President for his assent. President may either give or refuse his assent. Since the power to veto a Bill is exercised only on the advise of the Cabinet the President will be bound to give his assent.

(5) *Financial Bills*

Money Bills [article 110(1)], other Finance Bills, [(Article 117(1)] Bills involving expenditure [article 117(3)].

Financial Bills are of three kinds:

- Money Bills [article 110(1)].
- Other Financial Bills [article 117(1)].
- Bills involving expenditure [article 117(3)].

Distinction between Money Bills, Finance Bills and Bills involving expenditure

1. Money Bill- contains only matters in article 110(1).

   Financial Bill deals with matters in addition to matters in article 110(1). Thus Financial Bill is a Money Bill to which provisions of general legislation are also added apart from matters under article 110(1). Thus, all Money Bills are Financial Bills but all Financial Bills are not Money Bills.
2. Both the Money Bill and the Financial Bill can originate only in the Lok Sabha and with the recommendation of the President.
3. Finance Bills and other Bills involving expenditure can be amended or rejected by the Rajya Sabha like any ordinary Bill. Money Bills cannot be amended or rejected by the Rajya Sabha. In the event of a deadlock it can be resolved by a joint session of the Houses. Thus Rajya Sabha has some control over the Financial and other Bills involving expenditure unlike in the case of Money Bill.
4. As far as the procedure is concerned there is no difference between a Financial Bill and an Ordinary Bill except that the Financial Bill requires President's recommendation and it can be introduced only in Lok Sabha.
5. As far as President's assent is concerned, the President may either give or refuse his assent in case of Money Bill but in case of a Finance Bill – in addition he may refer it back to the House with a message for reconsideration.

(6) *Assent to Bills (Article 111)*

A Bill does not become a law unless and until the President assents to it. When a Bill is presented to the President after its passage in both the Houses of the Parliament, he is entitled to take any of the following three steps:

1. He may declare his assent to the Bill; or
2. He may declare that he withholds his assent to the Bill; or
3. He may in the case of Bills other than the Money Bills return the Bill for reconsideration of the Houses with or without a message suggesting amendments.

In case the President returns it back for reconsideration – and the Bill is again passed by both the Houses with or without amendment and again presented to the President he 'shall' give assent to it.

The Constitution does not prescribe any time limit within which to declare his assent or refuse assent or to return a Bill. The President thus has only a delaying veto under the Indian Constitution.

(7) *Annual Financial Statement i.e., Budget (Article 112)*

The President shall in respect of every financial year cause to be laid before both the Houses of Parliament an annual financial statement commonly known as the Budget. This expenditure is shown under two heads: sums charged on the Consolidated Fund of India and the sums required to meet other expenditure out of the Consolidated Fund of India.

Following expenditures are charged on the Consolidated Fund of India:

(1) Salary and allowances of the President and other expenditure relating to his office.

(2) Salary and allowances of the Chairman and Dy. Chairman of the Rajya Sabha and the Speaker and Dy. Speaker of the Lok Sabha.

(3) Debt charges for which Government of India is liable.

(4) Salaries allowances and pensions payable to judges of the Supreme Court, Comptroller and Auditor-General of India, judges of the High Court and Federal Court.

(5) Any sums required to satisfy any Judgment decree or award of any Court or Tribunal.

(6) Any other expenditure declared by this Constitution or by Parliament by law to be so charged.

(8) Discussion and voting on Budget (Article 113)

The expenditure which is charged on the Consolidated Fund of India shall not be submitted to the vote of Parliament. However the Houses are not prevented from discussing any of these items of expenditure. The estimates relating to this expenditure must be submitted to the Lok Sabha in the form of demands for grants. The Lok Sabha has powers to assent or refuse to assent to any demand or to assent to any demand subject to the reduction of the amount specified therein. No demand for grant is to be made except on the recommendation of the President.

(9) ***Appropriation Bills [Article 114(3)]***

No money can be taken out of the Consolidated Fund of India unless the Appropriation Act is passed. Therefore after the demands for grants under article 113 are passed by the Lok Sabha, a Bill known as Appropriation Bill is introduced in the Lok Sabha, the Bill specifies all the grants made by the Lok Sabha, the expenditure charged on the Consolidated Fund of India as shown in the previous statement before the Parliament. But no amendment shall be proposed to the Appropriation Bill which will have the effect of varying the amount or altering the destination of any grant so made or of varying the amount of any expenditure charged on the Consolidated Fund of India. Supplementary grants for unforeseen expenses can be made under article 115.

(10) ***Votes on Account, vote on credit and vote on exceptional grants (Article 116)***

Before the Appropriation Act is passed no money is to be withdrawn from the Consolidated Fund of India. But the Government may need money to spend before it is passed. Under article 116A the Lok Sabha can grant a limited sum from the consolidated Fund of India to the executive to spend until the Appropriation Bill is passed by Parliament. Lok Sabha can make a grant for meeting an unexpected demand upon the resources of India when on account of the magnitude or the indefinite character of the service, the demand cannot be stated with details ordinarily given in the annual financial statements.

Under clause 3 the Lok Sabha has the power to make exceptional grants which forms no part of the current service of the current financial year. However it is necessary that Parliament shall make a law for withdrawal of money from the Consolidated Fund of India for the purpose for which the Lok Sabha has sanctioned the grants either by Annual Appropriation Act or Supplementary grant, excess grant, votes on account, votes on credit or exceptional grant.

(11) *Parliament control over Financial matters*

The Parliament exercises control over financial matters through *Public Accounts Committee and the Estimate Committee.* Public Accounts Committee consists of 15 members of the Parliament including a Minister. It considers the appropriate accounts. It also considers the report of the Comptroller and Auditor General. The report is submitted to the House. The Committee examines such estimates (presented to Lok Sabha) to the Budget as may seem fit to the Committee, to suggest economy in the expenditure, improvement in the organisation and other steps for increasing efficiency to find out whether the money is well laid out and also to suggest the form in which the estimate should be presented to the Parliament.

(12) Parliamentary Committees

The Rules Committee has recommended setting up of 17 Committees each comprising 10 members from the Lok Sabha and 15 from the Rajya Sabha in order to examine in detail grants and other proposals regarding the functioning of various departments. 6 committees will be constituted by the Chairman of the Rajya Sabha and 11 Committees will be constituted by the Lok Sabha Speaker. Some Committees would be joint Committees.

Each Committee would be given a definite time limit to complete the discussion of each demand for grant (2/3 days) and then submit the reports to the Parliament within the stipulated time. These reports are placed before Parliament and the Houses discuss the demands in the light of these reports. There is no curtailment of the number of sittings of the Parliament.

This enables the Parliament to examine grants of the departments in detail and this will help proper scrutiny of the Budget and the performance.

G. General provisions (Article 120-121)

Language for transaction of business in Parliament shall be English or Hindi subject to the Constitutional provisions regarding official language. However the Speaker or the Chairman may permit any member to address the House in his mother tongue.

H. Comptroller and Auditor General of India (Articles 148-151)

He is appointed by the President of India. He takes oath before entering upon his office. His salary is charged to the Consolidated Fund of India and cannot be varied to his disadvantage. After he has ceased to hold office he shall not be eligible to hold any office under Central or State Government. He can be removed from his office on the similar grounds as the judge of the Supreme Court can be removed.

Duties and powers: CAG exercises such powers and performs such duties in relation to the accounts of the Union and the States as may be prescribed by law made by Parliament. He performs two duties. As an Accountant he controls all withdrawal of money disbursed by Central or State Governments. He shall keep the account of the Union and the States in the manner prescribed by the President (Article 150). The Report of the CAG relating to the accounts of the Union is submitted to the President/Governor who shall cause them to be laid before the Parliament/Legislature as the case may be.

I. Comparison and differences between the Union Parliament and the State Legislature

	Union Parliament	State Legislature
1.	**Constitution of Parliament:** President, Lok Sabha and Rajya Sabha. [Article 79]	Constitution of Legislature: Governor, Legislative Assembly (and Legislative Council in 7 States) [Article 168]
2.	Parliament is always bicameral. There is no question of abolition of any House.	Parliament can abolish or create a Legislative Council if the State Legislative Assembly passes a resolution to that effect by a majority of total membership of the Assembly and by a majority of not less than 2/3rd of members present and voting.[Article 169]
	Composition of Lok Sabha: (i) 550 (and *two* Anglo Indians if not adequately represented). (i) Each State allotted such number of seats that there is *inter-State equality* based on population of the State-(not applicable if the population does not exceed 6 million) (ii) Territorial constituency in each State are allotted such number of seats that *intra-State equality* is maintained based on population. [Article 81(2)(a)(b)]. (iii) Population means population at the last preceding census; as of now 2001 census until 2026 population census is taken and published. (iv) After census there is readjustment of *allocation seats in the States* and readjustment of division of territorial constituencies within the States. Article 81(2)(a)(b)	**Composition of Legislative Assembly:** (i) Maximum 500, minimum 60 (and one Anglo Indian if in Governor's opinion not adequately represented). Art. 170, 333 [such reservations to cease after 40 yrs. as per 45th Amendment to Constitution] Territorial constituency in each State are allotted such number of seats that *intra-State equality* is maintained based on population. [Article 170(2)] (iii) Population means population at the last preceding census; as of now 2001 census until 2026 population census is taken and published. (iv) After census there is readjustment of *total number of seats in each State* and readjustment of division of territorial constituencies within the States. [Article 170(2)]
3.	**Composition of the Rajya Sabha**: (i) 250(238 representatives of States and Union Territories + 12 nominated by President). (ii) The 238 RS members are elected by elected MLAs of the State. (iii) Members nominated by President must have special knowledge in literature, arts, social service. [Article 80]	**Composition of Legislative Council: (i)**shall not exceed 1/3rd of total number in Legislative Assembly subject to a minimum of 40. [Article 171] (ii) Out of the total number: 1/3rd elected by members of local authorities, municipalities and Dist. Boards 1/12th elected by persons residing in the State who are graduates in any university in India. 1/12th elected by teachers teaching in educational institutions not lower in standard than Secondary education. 1/3rd elected by MLAs of the State from amongst those who are not MLAs; The remainder are nominated by the Governor from persons having special knowledge in literature, etc. [Article 171]

4.	**Duration of the Lok Sabha:** 5years. (During emergency extended by one year at a time and not exceeding 6 months after emergency ceases). Duration of Rajya Sabha: not subject to dissolution but 1/3rd members retire on the expiry of every 2nd year. [Article 83]	**Duration:** Same as in the case of Parliament. **Duration of Legislative Council:** Same as in the case of Rajya Sabha. (Article 172)
5.	**Qualification:** Citizen of India and take oath under Schedule III; 25 years for Lok Sabha members 30 years for Rajya Sabha members Such other prescribed qualifications. (Article 84)	**Qualification:** Citizen of India and take oath under Schedule III 25 years for MLA 30 years for MLC Such other prescribed qualifications. (Article 173 for MLC)
6.	**Sessions:** *President* summons the sessions of *Parliament.* 6 months shall not intervene between two sittings. Article 85	**Sessions:** *Governor* summons the sessions each House of *legislature.* 6 months shall not intervene between two sittings. (Article 174)
7.	**Rajya Sabha Address and message:** *President* addresses both or either House of *Parliament. President* may send message regarding pending Bill or otherwise and the House must consider the matter messaged. (Article 86)	**Address and message:** *Governor* addresses both or either House of *Legislature.* *Governor* may send message regarding pending Bill or otherwise and the House must consider the matter messaged. (Article 175)
8.	**Special address:** *President* addresses a joint sitting at the commencement of first sitting after every general election to LS and the first session of every year. (Article 87)	**Special address:** *Governor* addresses the Legislative Assembly (and the Council- if any) at the commencement of first sitting after every general election to Legislative Assembly and the first session of every year. (Article 176)
9.	**Rights of ministers and *Attorney General*:** Right to speak and take part in proceedings of *either House of Parliament* and take part in proceedings of Parliamentary Committee of which he is a member, but has no right to vote. (Article 88)	**Rights of ministers and *Advocate-General*:** Right to speak and take part in proceedings of *Legislative Assembly (and Legislative Council- if any)* and take part in proceedings of Parliamentary Committee of which he is a member, but has no right to vote. Article 177
10.	**Officers of RS:** *(i) Chairman (i.e.,* the Vice President of India Executive-officio) & *Deputy-Chairman* - chosen from the RS members. (ii) **Officer of the LS:** Speaker and Deputy Speaker – both chosen from the members of the LS.	**Officers of the Assembly:** *(i) Speaker and Deputy* Speaker for Legislative Assembly –both chosen from the MLAs. **(ii) Officers of the Council:** *Chairman and Deputy Chairman* – both chosen from MLCs.
11.	**Vacation of seats:** No person shall be a member of both the Houses of the Parliament. Parliament must make a provision by law for the vacation of seat in one or the other House. (Article 101) No person shall be a member of both *the Parliament and the Legislature of a State.* His seat in the *Parliament* becomes vacant at the expiry of time mentioned in Prohibition of Simultaneous Rules, 1950 unless he has already resigned his seat in the Legislature of the State. [Article 101(2)]	**Vacation of seats:** No person shall be a member of both the Houses of the Legislature. Legislature must make a provision by law for the vacation of seat in one or the other House. (Article 190) No person shall be a member of the Legislatures of two or more States specified in Schedule I. Unless he resigns from one of the States before the expiry of time mentioned in Prohibition of Simultaneous Rules, 1950 *his seat in the Legislature of all the States become vacant.* [Article190(2)]

	If a member absents himself for 60 days without permission his seat falls vacant. [Article 101(4)]	If a member absents himself for 60 days without permission his seat falls vacant [Article 101(4)]
12.	**Disqualifications for membership:** Holding an office of profit; of unsound mind; undischarged insolvent; not a citizen of India; voluntarily acquired citizenship of foreign State; owes allegiance to foreign State; disqualified under Parliament made law. [Article 102]	**Disqualifications for membership:** Holding an office of profit; of unsound mind; undischarged insolvent; not a citizen of India; voluntarily acquired citizenship of foreign State; owes allegiance to foreign State disqualified under Parliament made law. [Article 191]
13.	**Legislative procedure in Parliament:** It is dealt with from article 107-117.	**Legislative procedure in the Legislature:** It is dealt with from article 196-207.

The provisions regarding legislative procedure in respect of the Centre and the State are broadly similar only with consequential changes. [For Example, in a Money Bill one must read 'Consolidated Fund of the State' instead of 'Consolidated Fund of India' ; borrowing by the 'State' instead of the 'Government of India'; and Bill presented for assent to the 'Governor' instead of the 'President'].

The other difference is that the Governor in certain circumstances reserves the Bill for the consideration of the President if in his opinion if it became a law it would so derogate from the powers of the High Court as to endanger the position which that court is under the Constitution designed to fill. (Article 200). When a Bill is reserved by the Governor for the President's consideration the President shall declare that he assents to the Bill or that he withholds his assent. When the Bill is not a Money Bill the President may direct the Governor to return the Bill to the House together with the message referred to in the first proviso to article 200 (to consider the Bill/specific provision/desirability of considering amendments recommended by him). The House must reconsider it within 6 months from the date of receipt of such message and if again it is passed by the House with or without amendments it shall be presented again to the President for his consideration. (Article 201).

CHAPTER 22

UNION AND STATE JUDICIARY

(Articles 124 To 147; 214-237)

SYNOPSIS

A. Introduction

The Constitution deals with the provisions pertaining to State and the Union Judiciary and the subordinate courts. Union Judiciary is dealt with under articles 124-147 and State Judiciary under articles 214-237.

India has a unified judicial system with the Supreme Court at the apex and State High Courts below it. Under each High Court there is a system of subordinate Courts. Supreme Court is the topmost in the judicial hierarchy. It is the supreme interpreter of the Constitution. It is the ultimate interpreter of the Constitution and the other laws of the land.

B. Similarities and differences between the Union and the State Judiciary

The following table highlights the similarities and the differences for a quick reference before taking up detailed consideration of the important provisions which have engaged the attention of the courts.

No.	Union Judiciary	State Judiciary
1.	There shall be a Supreme Court of India consisting of *Chief Justice of India (CJI)* and *30* other judges. Initially there were 7 Judges. Parliament can by law increase the number. Article 124(1)	There shall be a High Court for *each State* consisting a *Chief Justice* and such other judges as the President may from time-to-time deem it *necessary to appoint*. Articles 214, 216
2.	Supreme Court sits in Delhi or at such place as the CJI may appoint with the approval of the President. Article 130	There is a High Court in each State. Some States have in addition High Court Benches at some place other than the capital of the State.
3.	**Appointment:** Every Supreme Court judge *shall be* appointed by the President by warrant under his hand and seal after consultation with such of the *judges of the Supreme Court and of the High Courts in the States* as the President *may* deem it necessary. Article 124(2). For appointing a Judge other than the CJI- the CJI *shall always* be consulted.	**Appointment:** Every High Court judge is appointed by the President by warrant under his hand and seal after consultation with *CJI, the Governor of the State and* in the case of the appointment of a judge other than the Chief Justice – *the Chief Justice of the High Court* concerned. Article 217(1)
	Ad-hoc judges: If there is *no quorum of the Judges of Supreme Court* available to hold or continue any session of the court, *CJI may* with the previous consent of the President and consultation with the CJ of High Court concerned-request in writing a judge of the High Court to sit as an *ad-hoc* judge for such period as may be necessary. Such an *ad-hoc* judge must attend the sittings of the Supreme Court and has all the jurisdiction, powers and privileges and shall discharge the duties of the Judge of Supreme Court. Article 127	**Additional judges:** If due to *temporary increase in High Court business* or arrears of work, *President may* appoint duly qualified persons to be additional judges of the court – if it appears to the President that the number of judges needs to be increased for the time being. Article 224
4.	**Appointment of Acting CJI:** When office of CJI is vacant or he is unable to perform the duties of his office due to absence or any other reason - his duties are performed by one of the other *Supreme Court Judges* as the President may appoint. Article 126 (Note that there is no provision for acting Supreme Court judge but only acting CJI of the Supreme Court.)	**Appointment of Acting CJ:** Similar to article 126. (One of the other *High Court judges* is appointed as acting CJ by the President). Article 223 **Acting judges:** If a High Court judge other than the CJ is unable to perform the duties of his office due to his absence or any other reason- the President may appoint a duly qualified person to act as a judge of that Court until the permanent judge has resumed his duties. Article 224

5.	**Attendance of retired judges at Supreme Court sittings: CJI** may at any time with the President's previous consent request any person who was the Supreme Court judge or Federal Court judge or a High Court judge and is duly qualified for appointment as a judge of the Supreme Court – to sit and act as a judge of the Supreme Court. Such a retired judge is entitled to such allowances as the President may determine by an order. He has all the jurisdiction and powers and privileges as judge of that Court but is not deemed to be the judge of that Court. Such a person is so appointed only if he consents to it. Article 128	**Appointment of retired judges:** Provisions are similar to article 128. Here it is the *Chief Justice of the High Court* who requests any person who was the judge of that High Court or any other High Court. Article 224A inserted by 15th Amendment.
6.	There is no question at all of any transfer of Supreme Court judges as we have only one Supreme Court sitting at Delhi.	**Transfer of a High Court judge**: President in *consultation with CJI* may transfer a Judge from one High Court to another. He is entitled to receive in addition to his salary such compensatory allowance as may be determined by the Parliament and until as the President may fix by an order. Article 222
7.	Supreme Court shall sit in Delhi or in such other place or places as the CJI may with the approval of the President appoint. Article 130	Common High Court: Parliament may by law establish a common High Court for two or more States or for two or more States and Union territories. Article 231
8.	**Tenure:** Supreme Court judge holds office until he attains the age of 65 yrs. Article 124(2). *Ad hoc* judges are appointed for such period as may be necessary	**Tenure:** High Court judge holds office until he attains 62 years. (Article 217). An additional judge holds office for a period not exceeding 2 yrs and an acting judge until the permanent judge returns. But no acting or additional judge can hold office after attaining 62 years. Article 224(3)
9.	**Qualifications:** A person is not qualified for appointment as Supreme Court judge unless he is a citizen of India and (a) Has been for at least *5 years a judge of the High Court* or of two or more High Courts in succession; or (b) Has been for at least *10 years advocate of the High Court* or of two or more such courts in succession. For computing the 10 years the period during which he has held judicial office *not inferior to that of a district judge* after he became an advocate shall be included; or (c) Is in the opinion of the President a *distinguished jurist* [Article *124(3) and explanation II*].	**Qualifications:** A person is not qualified for appointment as High Court judge unless he is a citizen of India and (a) Has for at least *10 years held a judicial office* in the territory of India. After he has held any judicial office the period during which he has been an advocate of the High Court or was a member of the tribunal or any post under Union or a State requiring special knowledge of law is to be included for computing the 10 years; or (b) Has for at least *10 years been an advocate of a High Court* or of two or more such courts in succession. After he became an advocate the period during which he has held *judicial office* or the office of a *member of a tribunal* or any post under the Union or a State must be included for computing the 10 years. Article 217(2) and the proviso.
10.	Question of age of Supreme Court judge is determined by *such authority* and in such manner as *Parliament may by law provide*. Article 124(2A)	Question of age of the High Court judge is determined by the *President after consultation with the CJI* and the decision of the President shall be final. Article 217(3)

11.	**Resignation:** A Supreme Court judge may resign his office by writing under his hand addressed to the President. **Removal:** He shall not be removed from his office except by an order of the President passed after an address by each House of Parliament supported by a majority of the total membership of that House and by a majority of not less than 2/3rd of the members of that House present and voting has been presented to the President in the same session for such removal on grounds of *proved misbehaviour or incapacity.* Parliament may by law regulate the procedure for presentation of an address and for the investigation and proof of the misbehaviour or incapacity of a Judge. Article 124(4)(5)	**Resignation:** A High Court judge may resign his office by writing under his hand addressed to the President. **Removal:** He can be removed in the same manner as a Supreme Court judge under article 124(4) read with article 218. Parliament has enacted Judges (Inquiry) Act, 1968 and made rules in 1969 for removal of High Court and Supreme Court judges on grounds of proved misbehaviour and incapacity.
12.	**Oath:** The *President* or some person appointed in that behalf by him administers the oath or affirmation according to the form set out in Third Schedule.	**Oath:** The *Governor* or some person appointed in that behalf by him administers the oath or affirmation according to the form set out in Third Schedule.
13.	**Restriction on practice:** A person who has held office as a Supreme Court judge shall not plead or act *in any court or before any authority within the territory of India.* Article 124(7)	**Restriction on practice:** A person who has held office as a permanent judge of High Court shall not plead or act in any court or before any authority in India *except the Supreme Court and the other High Courts.* Article 220
14.	**Jurisdiction:** Supreme Court has original, appellate, writ, advisory jurisdiction, special leave to appeal. Articles 131, 133, 134, 143, 136	General jurisdiction *i.e.,* the same as was immediately before the commencement of the Constitution. Its jurisdiction and powers can be changed by the Parliament and by Legislature Article 225; powers of superintendence over subordinate Courts; writ jurisdiction. Articles 226, 227

(1) Salaries of the Supreme Court and the High Court Judges are such as may be determined by the Parliament by law and until then – as specified in the Second Schedule. Their allowances and rights in respect of leave of absence and pension are determined by the Parliament and until then as specified in the Second Schedule. They shall not be varied to their disadvantage after their appointment in order to preserve the independence of the Judiciary. (Articles 125 and 221.)

Both the Supreme Court and the High Court are *Courts of record* and have the powers to punish for contempt of itself. (Articles 129 and 215)

C. Subordinate Courts [Articles 233-234, 236(a)]

Appointment of District judges in any State are to be made by the Governor of the State in consultation with High Court.

District judges include City Civil Court, additional District Judge, joint District judge, assistant district judge, Chief Judge of a Small Cause Court, Chief Presidency Magistrate, Additional Chief Presidency Magistrate, Sessions Judge.

Appointments of persons other than District judges to the judicial service of a State are to be made by the Governor of the State after consultation with the State Public Service Commission and the High Court. (Article 234)

D. Appointment of the Supreme Court judges

Special role of the Supreme Court: Supreme Court is the guardian of the Constitution. With sharing of power in a Federal Constitution like ours there are bound to be differences between the States *inter se* and between the State and the Union. In addition the conflicting interests and rights of the vast majority of the populace *inter se* and between the citizen on one hand and the Government on the other also has to be addressed. This requires an independent and an impartial authority to arbitrate over the matter. The supremacy of the Constitution also is to be maintained. The Supreme Court has been assigned this crucial role under the Constitution. It has to balance individual liberty and social control; it is the guardian of the Fundamental rights. Granville Austin describes it as the 'guardian of the social revolution.'[1]

It has been seen from the Table above that it is the President who appoints the High Court and the Supreme Court judges. However the President acts on the advice of the Council of Ministers. In order to prevent politics from entering in the appointment of judges, the Executive is required to consult persons from the Judiciary in matters of appointment of judges.[2] In appointing CJI President is not bound to consult anyone, but in appointing other judges he is bound to consult the CJI.

(1) *The changing convention in appointment of Chief Justice of India*

(a) *Senior most SC Judge appointed:* Till 1973 the practice was to appoint the senior most judge of the Supreme Court as the CJI. The Executive followed it without any exception for 22 years up to 1973

(b) *Merit-cum-seniority basis suggested:* In 1956 the Law Commission criticised this practice and suggested that appointments be made on merit-cum seniority basis taking into account experience as a judge, administrative competence and merit. But the recommendation was not acted upon until 1973 when there were unfortunate circumstances and the recommendation was utilised as a justification for not following the convention.

(c) *Superceding of three judges:* On April 25 1973, within a few hours of the judgment in *Keshwanand Bharati case*- Mr. A.N. Ray was appointed CJI superceding three senior judges – Justices Shelat, Grover, and Hegde. Eight hours after the swearing in ceremony – the three of them resigned from the Supreme Court. Action of the Government created a controversy. The Government justified its action on following grounds:

   (i) That the President has absolute discretion to appoint anyone whom he finds suitable. But in this case a time tested convention of 22 years was ignored on political reasons as the Justices who had been superceded had given judgment against the Government in *Keshavanand case.*

   (ii) The Government contended that it had followed the recommendations of the Law Commission. This contention does not stand because the judges superseded had credible experience to their credit as judges and had administrative competence. The recommendations were not acted upon for 22 years and suddenly the Government woke up to the

1. The Indian Constitution – the Cornerstone of the Nation, p. 169.
2. CAD Vol. 8 p. 285.

recommendations after an unpalatable judgment was delivered by the three judges.

(iii) It was contended by the Government that it was entitled to take into consideration the social philosophy of the judges while making the appointment. This in other words means that the judges who subscribe to the social philosophy of the ruling party. This contention is in blatant opposition to the Constitution ethos, values and culture. No party or person is above Constitution. The judges must be expected to be true to the social philosophy of the Constitution and not any political party.

(iv) *Establishment of Judicial committee suggested:* In *Judges Transfer Case* Bhagwati J. has suggested for the appointment of judicial committee to make judicial appointments.

(d) *Appointment on seniority basis: Senior most Supreme Court Judge basis—revived:* After the internal emergency in 1975, in 1977 the Congress party was defeated and the Janata Party came to power. It had opposed the supersession of the judges. It revived the old practice of appointing CJI on the basis of seniority.

(e) *National Judicial Commission—Mooted:* National Judicial Commission for appointment of judges is being formulated by the Centre.

(2) *Appointment of judges – Judges Transfer case – Supremacy of the Executive*

Several questions have arisen before the Judiciary in respect of appointment of the Supreme Court judges like – can the President act in accordance with his own discretion or is he bound by the advice of the Council of Ministers? (it is now settled that he is bound by such advice); is the President bound to act in accordance with the consultation with the CJI? What is the meaning and content of consultation? These are the questions that have arisen in connection with Union and also State Judiciary and the observations made with respect to the questions are equally applicable for both. Following are the rulings in this respect:

(1) *Meaning of 'Consultation': In Sankalchand Sheth* v. *Union of India*[1] the word 'consultation came up for consideration in connection with article 222-transfer of the High Court judges. It was held that 'consultation' means full and effective consultation. For a full and effective consultation it is necessary that the three Constitutional functionaries *'must have for its consideration full and identical facts' on the basis of which they would be able to take a decision.* But consultation does not mean 'concurrence'. Hence the President has a right to differ from the judicial functionaries and take a contrary view.

(2) *S.P. Gupta v. President of India*[2] the Supreme Court agreed that the meaning of word 'consultation' in articles 124(2), 212 and 222 of the Constitution is one and the same *i.e.,* as explained in *Sankalchand.* It held that the ultimate power to appoint judges is vested in the Executive. This decision

1. AIR 1977 SC 2328: (1978) 1 SCR 423: (1977) 4 SCC 193.
2. AIR 1982 SC 149: 1982 Raj LR 389: 1981 Supp SCC 87.

has been criticized for it gives primacy to the opinion of the Executive in preference to that of the Judiciary and therefore the independence of the Judiciary is diluted.

3. In *S.C. Advocate on Record Assn.* v. *Union of India,* AIR 1994 SC 268: 1993 AIR SCW 4101: (1993) 4 SCC 441, popularly known as *Judges Transfer Case II* – a nine judge Bench of the Supreme Court overruled its judgment in *S.P. Gupta case* and held that:
   (a) in appointment of Supreme Court and High Court judges – the CJI must have the primacy and not the Executive.
   (b) The CJI should form his view after taking into account the views of two senior most judges of the Supreme Court. This reduces the individual discretion either of the Executive or the Judiciary so as to ensure that neither political bias nor personal favouritism nor animosity plays any part in the appointment of judges of the Supreme Court and High Court.
   (c) Constitutional functionaries must act collectively in judicial appointments.
   (d) CJI has the final say in transfer of CJs and High Court judges.
   (e) Transfers of CJs and High Court judges cannot be challenged in Courts.
   (f) Appointment of CJI must be by seniority.
   (g) No judge can be appointed by the Union Government without consulting the CJI.
   (h) Fixation of the strength in High Courts is justiciable.
   (i) Supreme Court decision in *S.P. Gupta* is overruled.

   This judgment was welcomed as it restored the freedom and independence of the Judiciary. It is submitted[1] that both the decisions were right in their own place. Going by the literal interpretation of Constitution which lays down that 'President shall appoint in consultation with ....' primacy was given to the opinion of the Executive. When that did not work as expected a revolutionary interpretation led to *S.C. Advocates on Record*. When this also did not work well the President referred the question of 'consultation process to the Supreme Court for its advisory opinion in *Re Presidential reference.*

4. *In Re Presidential Reference*[2] the nine judge Bench ruled unanimously that the recommendation made by the CJI on the appointment of Judges of Supreme Court and High Court without following the consultation process are not binding on the Government. The Government stand was upheld. The Supreme Court held that:
   (a) CJI must consult a *plurality of the judges for the purposes of articles 217(1) and 222(1).* Sole individual opinion of the CJI does not constitute

1. *For details of the criticism* – see *Veena Tonapi: Kilpar Research Series: A Seminal Approach to Constitutional Philosophy – a special study of the judgments of Justice V.R. Krishna Iyer and Justice P.N. Bhagwati, p.420-428.*
2. AIR 1999 SC 1: 1998 AIR SCW 3400: (1998) 7 SCC 739.

'consultation' within the meaning of the said articles.

(b) For appointment of Supreme Court judges under article 124(2) CJI must consult 'a collegium of four seniormost judges of the Supreme Court'. If two judges give adverse opinion the CJI must not send the recommendation to the Government. The Collegium must include the successor CJI. The opinion of the collegium must be in writing.

(c) In the appointment of High Court judges the collegiums should consist of the CJI and any two senior most Supreme Court judges.

(d) In regard to transfer of High Court judges in addition to the collegiums of 4 judges the CJI is required to consult Chief Justices of the two High Courts – one from which judge is being transferred and the other receiving him.

The decision has meticulously attempted to strike a perfect balance to ensure that there is no one-man play in the appointment and transfer of judges. Yet the system did not work well. Hence in a seminar in Delhi on Judicial Reforms it was opined that a National Judicial Commission be appointed. A Bill was introduced which lapsed when the Lok Sabha was dissolved.

E. Transfer of a judge from one High Court to the other under article 222

The President is empowered to transfer a judge from one High Court to another after consultation with the CJI. The transferee judge is entitled for compensatory allowance under article 222(2).

Can be transferred without consent: Opinion of CJI is only recommendatory: In *Union of India* v. *Sankalchand Himatlal Sheth*, AIR 1977 SC 2328: 1977 Lab IC 1857: (1977) 4 SCC 193, the Supreme Court held that a High Court judge could be transferred without his consent. The power to transfer can be exercised in public interest and not as a weapon to punish a judge who does not toe its line. President must consult the CJI and consultation must be full and effective as discussed above.

In *S.P. Gupta v. President of India*[1] getting advance consent of the *sitting additional judges* for being appointed as permanent judges outside their State was challenged and was held valid by the majority judges, but the minority opinion was that it affected the independence of the Judiciary as it had a coercive effect on the minds of the judges that if they did not give consent they would be transferred or not made permanent.

Regarding the transfer of judges, by a majority of 4:3, it was held that consent is not a necessary element of article 222. The only requirement was that President must have consultation with the CJI which must be effective. Power of transfer must be exercised in public interest. Transfers must not be by way of punishment. Held that transfer of the CJ of Patna High Court to Madras High Court was in public interest because certain persons were taking undue advantage of their close relationship with him. There was full and effective consultation before the transfer was recommended. The CJI had in fact recommended the transfer

1. AIR 1982 SC 149: 1982 Raj LR 389: 1981 Supp SCC 87.

in this case.

In *S.C. Advocates-on-record* v. *Union of India*[1] – *S.P. Gupta was overruled:* It was held that in the case of transfer of High Court judges the opinion of the CJI is determinative. But he has to consult two senior most judges of the Supreme Court. Consent of the transferred judge or the transferred CJ of the High Court is not required.

CJI to consult four senior most SC judges: In *Re Presidential Reference* nine judge Bench of Supreme Court held that in case of transfer of High Court judge CJI must consult four senior most judges of the Supreme Court and in addition also consult CJ of the two High Courts (one from which the Judge is transferred and the other receiving him).[2]

F. Cases on resignation and removal of judges of High Court and Supreme Court

(1) *In Union of India* v. *Gopal Chandra Mishra*[3] *it was held that* if the judge 'resigns *in presenti*' –resignation terminates his office immediately. But if he chooses to resign from a future date the act of resigning is not complete and he can withdraw it before that date.

(2) *K. Veeraswamy* v. *Union of India*[4] is a landmark case where the Supreme Court has held that the term 'misbehaviour' in article 124(5) includes criminal misconduct defined in Prevention of Corruption Act. The expression 'public servant' includes judges of the Supreme Court and High Court. The Supreme Court ordered the prosecution of Veeraswamy who was the CJ of Madras High Court for disproportionate assets.

(3) Impeachment of J. Ramaswamy is the first case of impeachment after the Constitution came into force. J. Ramaswany appointed as a judge of the Madras High Court – he was elevated to the Supreme Court judge. The Judges Inquiry Committee appointed by the Speaker found him guilty of 'wilful and gross misuse of office, purposeful and persistent negligence in the discharge of his duties, intentional and habitual extravagance at the cost of public exchequer and moral turpitude by using public funds for private purposes in diverse ways'. All this constituted 'misbehaviour' under article 124(4). Unfortunately impeachment motion was defeated not on merits but because the ruling party Congress MPs abstained from voting acting upon the Party whip. It is submitted that this was simply taking the Constitution itself for a ride by no less than the rulers of the country themselves. In its ultimate analysis no matter what safeguards are provided in any Constitution it is the people in power, true to their conscience and true to the issues involved, who should make them work.

(4) In *Sub-Committee of judicial Accountability* v. *Union of India*[5] Supreme Court held that dissolution of the Lok Sabha does not put an end to the motion for removal of Supreme Court judge. Inquiry Committee appointed by the

---

1. AIR 1994 SC 268: 1993 AIR SCW 4101: (1993) 4 SCC 441.
2. AIR 1991 SC 1: JT 1990 (4) SC 106: (1992) (Supp) 1 SCC 182.
3. AIR 1978 SC 694: (1978) 2 SCC 301: 1978 (2) SCJ 16.
4. (1991) 3 SCC 655: 1991 SCC (Cri) 734.
5. AIR 1992 SC 320: 1991 AIR SCW 3049: (1991) 4 SCC 699.

Speaker is an independent body outside the Parliament and a statutory body under the Judges (Inquiry) Act. Until it furnishes its report it maintains its separate identity.

(5) In *Sarojini Ramaswamy* v. *Union of India*[1] question was whether J. Ramaswamy was entitled to a copy of the Inquiry Report before it was submitted to the Speaker. Following important rulings were given:

(a) If the Inquiry Committee reaches the verdict of 'not guilty'- the matter ends and there is no question of a copy being given or the Parliament taking up the motion for his removal.

(b) If the committee finds him 'guilty'- then the Parliament has to fully consider the case on merits and then decide whether to remove him or not. The concerned judge also must be given an opportunity of commenting on the Inquiry Report and hence the Speaker must give him a copy of the Report.

(c) If the Parliament concurs with the findings of the Committee and finds him 'guilty' judicial review is permissible but only after the President passes an order removing him and not before. However the Committee is not a 'tribunal' because its finding is in the nature of recommendation which may or may not be accepted by the Parliament.

(6) *Forced resignation of judges – illegal: C. Ravi Chandran Iyer* v. *Justice A.M. Bhattacharjee*[2] is a landmark case where the Supreme Court has ruled that only the CJI can move against an erring High Court judge or CJ for his bad conduct which falls short of punishment by impeachment. For the first time the CJI was given the powers of in-house disciplining of an erring High Court judge in this case.

The Supreme Court held that the Constitution provides for removal of a Judge from his office by a process of impeachment under articles 217(1) and 124(4)(5). No other procedure or pressure tactics can be adopted.

In this case *J. Bhattacharjee* – CJ of Bombay had written books on Muslim law and Hindu law for which a London based publisher had given a royalty of 80000 and 700000 US dollars respectively. Bar Council of Maharashtra and Goa (BCMG), Bombay Bar Assn., Advocates Association of Western India passed a resolution seeking the resignation of the CJ Bhattacharjee as the royalty amount received by him was kept confidential and not properly explained and accounted; and that this would result in biased decisions. They also sought for a CBI inquiry and a direction to the Speaker to initiate impeachment action.

Now, the petitioner Ravi Chandran, a practicing advocate filed a public interest litigation under article 32 for restraining BCMG and others from coercing the CJ Bhattacharjee from resigning from his office.[3] The petitioner argued that such pressures would disturb the independence

1. AIR 1992 SC 2219: 1992 AIR SCW 2683: (1992) 4 SCC 506.
2. (1995) 5 SCC 457: 1995 AIR SCW 3768.
3. Meanwhile CJ Bhattacharjee did resign.

of the Judiciary. In addition the Constitution provides for voluntary resignation and compulsory removal and prescribes procedures for the same. Forcible resignation is unconstitutional, unknown to our legal system and deleterious (harmful) to the independence of the Judiciary. The Supreme Court upheld the contentions of the petitioner and held that such forced resignation does affect the independence of the Judiciary. It damages the efficacy and credibility of the Judiciary itself and shakes the confidence and competence of judges of integrity and ethical firmness. The Supreme Court held that no other authority like the CBI or the Reserve Bank of India had powers to investigate into the conduct of the judges. No mandate can be issued to the Speaker of the Lok Sabha or the Chairman of Rajya Sabha to initiate action for impeachment.

But then the question remains – how do you discipline an erring judge whose conduct does not warrant such a serious action as impeachment? The Supreme Court held that it is the CJI who could discipline the erring judge through an in-house-procedure. It held that independence of Judiciary extends to independence from any other pressure and prejudices and is not confined to only the Executive pressures and influences.

It highlighted the importance of 'judicial activism' with an observation that the judge cannot retain his passive role when he has to give effect to the Constitutional ideals under the complexity of modern litigation. Modern litigation requires him to not just declare the rights but to mould the relief and often command the Executive and other agencies to enforce and give effect to orders etc. In the process judge is required to take judicial notice of the social and economic ramifications consistent with the theory of law. This requires independence of the Judiciary and he must feel sure that such action of his will not lead to his downfall.

Disclosure of assets by the judges: The three Judge Delhi High Court gave a landmark ruling that CJI's office comes within the purview of the Right To Information Act and that the judges also will have to disclose their assets. "The judicial independence is not a privilege to a judge but a responsibility," (judgment Jan 10th 2010). It is for the first time that the Supreme Court filed an appeal in the High Court against the decision of the Delhi High Court. It is now settled that RTIA is applicable to the office of the CJI.

(7) In *Union of India* v. *Pratibha Bonnerjea*[1] the Supreme Court has held that judges and officials of the High Courts are not Government servants. There is no master-servant relationship. The whole concept of independence and separation of the Judiciary from the Executive would crumble if the master-servant relationship was conceded. The judge is the holder of a constitutional office. Hence on retirement he is entitled to pension under Part III of the First Schedule to the Constitution, Judges (Conditions of Service) Act, 1954.

1. AIR 1996 SC 693: 1995 AIR SCW 4713: (1995) 6 SCC 765.

G. Jurisdiction of the Supreme Court and the High Court

There is considerable difference as regards the jurisdiction of the Supreme Court and of the High Court. But as regards contempt jurisdiction and writ jurisdiction it is substantially the same.

H. Jurisdiction of Supreme Court and High Court as a Court of Record

Both article 129 and article 215 which make the Supreme Court and the High Court respectively, a Court of Record are similarly worded. They confer all the powers of a Court of Record *including* the power to punish for its contempt. A Court of Record is a Court whose records are admitted to be of evidentiary value and are not to be questioned when produced before the court. Power to punish for contempt must be sparingly used only when public interest demands.[1]

The Contempt of Courts Act, 1971 prescribes the powers and procedure for punishing contempt of court. It classifies contempt into civil and criminal contempt. Civil contempt is wilful disobedience of any decree, order direction writ or other process of the court. Criminal contempt means the publication – whether by words spoken or written by signs or by visible representation or otherwise of any matter or doing of any act which scandalises or tend to scandalise or lowers or tends to lower the authority of any court or prejudices or interferes or tends to interfere with the due course of any judicial proceeding or interferes or tends to interfere with or obstructs or tends to obstruct the administration of justice in any other manner.

A judge or a Magistrate or other person acting judicially shall be liable for contempt of his own court or of any other court in the same manner as any other individual is liable. But for his observations regarding a subordinate court in an appeal or revision pending before him –he shall not be liable.

Exemptions from contempt: Innocent publications and its distribution; fair and accurate report of judicial proceedings; fair criticism of judicial act; complaint made in good faith against presiding officers of subordinate courts; publication of fair and accurate report of a judicial proceeding before a court sitting *in camera*[2]

The term *'includes'* widens the jurisdiction of the court to punish also for acts which are inherently within the jurisdiction of the court or Record. Five police officers were sent to jail as they were found guilty of criminal contempt for harassing and handcuffing the Chief Judicial Magistrate of Nadiad in Gujarat.[3]

(1) In *Pallav Sheth* v. *Custodian*[4] Supreme Court has held that the powers of the Supreme Court and of the High Court under articles 129/215 cannot be abrogated or stultified. Contempt of Courts Act, 1971 provides for the quantum of punishment; defines acts amounting to

1. *Hira Lal Dixit* v. *State of Uttar Pradesh*, AIR 1954 SC 743: 1954 SCA 1263: 1954 SCJ 846.
2. In camera means proceedings conducted in the Chambers of the Judge due to its sensitive or personal nature as in the case of matrimonial proceedings like divorce etc where delicate and embarrassing matters would be addressed.
3. *Delhi Judicial Services Association* v. *State of Gujarat*, AIR 1991 SC 2176: 1991 Cr LJ 3086: (1991) 4 SCC 406.
4. AIR 2001 SC 2763: 2001 AIR SCW 3025: 2001 Cr LJ 4175.

and not amounting to contempt; it prescribes limitation for initiating an action in contempt. This does not amount to abrogation of articles 129/215.

(2) In *C.K. Dapthery* v. *O.P. Gupta*[1] Supreme Court did not agree that a scurrilous attack on the past judgment or on the judge for his conduct has no adverse effect on the administration of justice. In this case the pamphlet in question contained allegations of dishonesty of a Supreme Court judge while acting in his judicial capacity and held that it amounted to Contempt of Court.

(3) In *Mohd. Aslam* v. *Union of India*[2] Supreme Court held that the Chief Minister of UP, Kalyan Singh was guilty of contempt of court for violating the order of the court and the National Integration Council not to allow any permanent structure on the disputed land. Court said that though it is true that the State of U.P. was guilty of contempt it is equally true that the Minister or officer of Government is also liable in his official capacity or if there is a personal element contributing to contempt – then he is liable for contempt in his personal capacity also. Court awarded a token sentence of one day.

(4) Manipur Assembly Speaker Borobabu appeared before the Supreme Court and tendered an apology in contempt proceedings against him for terminating the services of the Legislative Secretary for acting in support of court order in implementing the Anti-Defection law judgment.[3]

(5) In *re Vinay Chandra Mishra*[4] Supreme Court has held that it has the power *suo motu* to take cognizance of contempt proceedings against the contemner. Power under article 129, 215 and 142[5] cannot be curtailed by Contempt of Court Act, 1971. The court did not accept the unconditional apology of senior advocate Vinay Chandra Mishra – President of Bar Council of India for misbehaving with Justice Kishore of Allahabad High Court and therefore suspended his licence to practice for 6 months for committing criminal contempt of court.[6]

(6) In *Supreme Court Bar Assn.* v. *Union of India,* 1998 AIR SCW 1706: AIR 1998 SC 1895: (1998) 4 SCC 409, Supreme Court overruled *Vinay Chandra Mishra* and held that power to punish for contempt under article 129 does not include power to determine whether an advocate is guilty of 'professional misconduct' in a summary manner. This power vests with the Bar Council under the Advocates Act, 1961. This judgment is criticized. It limits the Constitutional power by reference to statute law which is not correct. Such professional misconduct was putting

1. AIR 1971 SC 1132: 1971 Cr LJ 844: (1971) 1 SCC 626.
2. AIR 1995 SC 548: (1994) 6 SCC 442.
3. Dr. J.N.Pandey: Constitution of India (Central Law Agency: Delhi) 47th Ed. p. 506.
4. (1995) 2 SCC 584: AIR 1995 SC 2348: 1995 AIR SCW 3488.
5. Supreme Court has the power to pass any order or decree to do complete justice under article 142.
6. Apology was not accepted as there was no sincere regret for his act of disrespect and there was an admission of misdemnour.

the profession in bad light but there was no disciplining by the Bar Council. Ruling in *Vinay Chandra* had a salutary effect on irresponsible lawyers.

(7) In *DDA* v. *Skipper Construction Co. Ltd.*,[1] the construction company had collected 14 crores from the public for selling space in the buildings in spite of various directions from the courts like not to collect money, to stop construction until the bid amount are deposited with the Delhi Development Authority etc. Ultimately DDA re-entered and took possession of property along with the buildings. But by then they had already collected 14 crores from the public. The Supreme Court initiated *suo motu* contempt proceedings against the director of the company and his wife and sentenced them to imprisonment and imposed fine.

(8) Supreme Court has punished several erring bureaucrats in connection with corruption or for disobeying court's orders for enforcing Fundamental right of citizens.

(9) In *Indira Sawhney* v. *Union of India*[2] the Supreme Court had directed the States to appoint Commissions to identify the creamy layers so that they can be left out of the reservation scheme. Kerala State did not implement the direction for more than 3 years. Supreme Court held that it amounted to contempt of Court, but gave it one more chance to implement the same.

(10) A fine of *Rs. 5 lakhs was* imposed on the company for not removing the defects in its effluent treatment plant which was polluting the Gomati river.

I. Original Jurisdiction of the Supreme Court

Supreme Court exercises original jurisdiction in three kinds of disputes between:

(a) The Government of India and one or more States;

(b) Government of India and any State or States on one side and one or more other States on the other;

(c) Two or more States—

Insofar as the dispute involves any question – whether of law or fact – on which the existence or extent of any legal right depends. Article 131.

Original jurisdiction does not extend to the following three types of disputes:

(1) a dispute arising out of any treaty, agreement, covenant, engagement, sanad or other similar instrument which was executed before the commencement of this Constitution and continues in operation after such commencement or which provides that the said jurisdiction shall not extend to such a dispute.

If the dispute arises out of any provision of a treaty, agreement etc entered into or executed before the commencement of the Constitution by any

1. (1996) 4 SCC 622: 1996 AIR SCW 2401: AIR 1996 SC 2005.
2. AIR 1993 SC 477: 1992 AIR SCW 3682: JT 1992 (6) SC 273: 1993 Lab IC 129.

Ruler of an Indian State and to which the Government of the Dominion of India was a party. Article 363

(2) Under article 262 Parliament may provide for the adjudication of any dispute or complaint with respect to the use, distribution or control of the waters in any inter-State river or river valley. Parliament may provide that neither the Supreme Court nor any other court shall exercise jurisdiction in respect of any such dispute or complaint.

(3) In its original jurisdiction Supreme Court cannot entertain any suits brought by private individuals against the Government of India.

Original jurisdiction is strictly limited by the provisions of article 131. Hence it has to be between the parties mentioned above; it must involve a question relating to a legal right and not a political right over which Courts have no jurisdiction.

In *State of Rajasthan* v. *Union of India*[1] the Supreme Court held that the term 'State' includes within its scope 'the State Government'. After the defeat of Congress Government (after the internal emergency) in 1977 at the Centre and the victory of the Janata Party, there was Congress Government in several States. These States were advised to dissolve the State Assemblies and seek a fresh mandate. These State Governments filed suits against Central Government under article 131 to restrain the Central Government from dissolving their Legislative Assemblies under article 356. Central Government raised preliminary objections to the maintainability of the suit the court held that for attracting article 131.

(i) it is not necessary that the plaintiff must assert a legal right in itself.

(ii) It is enough that plaintiff questions the legal or Constitutional right asserted by the defendant Government.

(iii) In this case the question was whether the Central Government has the right to dissolve the Legislative Assemblies. In a Federation the States are interested in defining the powers of the Central Government on one hand and their own on the other. The State Governments had questioned the constitutional right of the Central Government to direct the State Governments to advise the Governors to dissolve the Assemblies. This was a legal issue and not a political issue.

In State of Karnataka v. *Union of India*[2] the Central Government appointed a Commission on Inquiry against the Chief Minister of Karnataka to investigate the charges of corruption, nepotism and misuse of power. Karnataka filed a suit under article 131 for a declaration that the appointment of the Commission under the Commission of Inquiry Act was illegal as it was a matter falling exclusively within the sphere of State Legislative and executive powers and if it did empower it was *ultra vires* the provision of the Constitution and the federal structure. The Supreme Court held that the suit was maintainable. The Union of India acting through Central Government was representing the whole of the people of individual States. When differences arise between

1. AIR 1977 SC 1361: (1977) 3 SCC 592: (1978) 1 SCR 1.
2. AIR 1978 SC 68: (1977) 4 SCC 608: (1978) 2 SCR 1.

the representatives of the State and of the whole of the country on questions of interpretation of the Constitution suit under article 131 does lie.

(3) In *State of Karnataka* v. *State of Andhra Pradesh*[1] a suit by Karnataka against Andhra Pradesh raising a dispute relating to non-implementation of the binding decision rendered by the Krishna Water Disputes Tribunal constituted under section 4 of the Inter-State Water Dispute Act, 1956 was held maintainable.

(4) In *State of Haryana* v. *State of Punjab*[2] under article 131 the Supreme Court issued a mandatory injunction[3] directing the State of Punjab to complete the Sutlej-Yamuna link canal within a year as per the agreement between Punjab and Haryana. Court also directed the Central Government to discharge its own constitutional obligation to ensure that the canal is completed as expeditiously as possible.

J. Appellate jurisdiction of Supreme Court

They are of four main categories:

(i) Constitutional matters. (Article 132(1))

(ii) Civil matters (Article 133)

(iii) Criminal matters. (Article 134 and 134A)

(iv) Special leave to appeal. (Article 136)

(i) Appeal in Constitutional matters

Article 132(1) lies to the Supreme Court only when the High Court issues a certificate for appeal under article 134A. Such a certificate can be issued if following 3 conditions are satisfied under article 132(1).

(a) *From HC:* The order appealed must be against a judgment, decree or *final* order of a *High Court* in civil, criminal or other proceedings.

(b) *Interpretation of the Constitution:* The case must involve a *substantial question of law* as to the *interpretation of the Constitution,* and

(c) *Certificate:* The High Court must certify that the case be heard by the Supreme Court.

When such a certificate is given, *any party* may appeal to Supreme Court on the ground that any such question has been wrongly decided.

'Other proceedings' includes all proceedings other than civil and criminal *e.g.,* - revenue, tax etc. Question is not a *substantial question of law* if it has been already decided by the Supreme Court. But if there is a difference of opinion amongst different High Courts and there is no direct ruling on the point by the Supreme Court- it would be a substantial question of law. As an exceptional case an appeal can lie from the decision of a single judge of the High Court.[4] Appeal cannot be on a ground other than the one on which certificate was granted.

---

1. AIR 2001 SC 1560: (2000) 9 SCC 572: (2000) 3 SCALE 505.
2. AIR 2002 SC 685: 2002 AIR SCW 303: (2002) 2 SCC 507.
3. Mandatory injunction is direction given by the court to do a particular act.
4. *Election Commission* v. *Venkat Rao,* AIR 1953 SC 210: 1953 SCJ 293: 1953 SCR 1144.

(ii) Appeal in civil cases (Article 133)[1]

An appeal shall lie to the Supreme Court from *any* judgment, decree or *final* order in a *civil* proceeding of a High Court *only if* the High Court certifies

(a) *Question of law-general importance:* That the case involves a substantial question of law of *general importance*

(b) *Needs to be decided:* And that in the opinion of the High Court it *needs* to be decided by the Supreme Court.

There must be a necessity for the decision of the Supreme Court on the question of law. 'civil proceedings' means proceedings in which a party asserts the existence of a civil right. A writ proceeding under article 226 is a civil proceeding.

No appeal lies from the judgment etc., of a single judge of the High Court unless the Parliament provides otherwise by a law to that effect. Article 133(2)

(iii) Appeal in criminal cases (Article 134)

(i) *Appeal in criminal cases without a certificate* 134(1)(a)(b)

An appeal lies to the Supreme Court from any judgment, final order or *sentence*[2] *without a certificate* from the High Court in two cases:

(a) *Reversed the acquittal:* If the High Court has – on an appeal – *reversed* the acquittal order and sentenced the accused to *death penalty* [or sentenced him to imprisonment for life or to imprisonment for a period of not less than 10 years].[3]

But if conviction has been reversed to acquittal- no appeal would lie to the Supreme Court.

(b) *Withdrawn to itself and convicted:* Has *withdrawn* for trial *before itself* any case from any court subordinate to its authority and has in such trial convicted the accused person and *sentenced him to death.* [or sentenced him to imprisonment for life or to imprisonment for a period of not less than 10 years][4]

(ii) *Appeal in criminal cases with a certificate. (Article 134(c))*

Supreme Court has laid down the following guiding principles on when grant the certificate:

- Certificate must be granted only in exceptional circumstances like where there is a grave and substantial injustice.

---

1. Substituted by 30th amendment in 1972. Before 1972 an appeal could lie to the Supreme Court only if the monetary value in dispute or the amount was not less than Rs. 20,000. Now an appeal lies only if the HC certifies that the case involves that substantial question of law of general importance.
2. Note – In criminal cases we don't use the expression 'decree' because decrees are passed only in civil cases. And 'sentences' are passed in criminal cases.
3. Under Article 134(2) the Parliament is empowered to extend the appellate jurisdiction of the Supreme Court in criminal matters. This extension is under section 2 of Supreme Court Enlargement of Criminal Appellate Jurisdiction Act, 1970.
4. Ibid.

- It should not be granted on a mere question of fact. Normally the Court does not review facts in appeal except in exceptional cases of grave illegality.
- Concurrent findings of the two courts are binding.

(iii) Certificate for appeal to Supreme Court (Article 134A)

It provides that every High Court passing or making a judgment, decree, final order of sentence under articles 132, 133(1), 134(1)

(a) *May* on its own motion if it deems fit to do so–

(b) *Must* if an oral application is made by or on behalf of the aggrieved party immediately after the judgment etc., determine the question of whether a certificate referred to articles 132, 133(1), 134(1) may be given in respect of that case.

(iv) Special leave to appeal by the Supreme Court [Article 136]

(1) Supreme Court may under its discretion grant special leave to appeal from any judgment, decree, determination, sentence, or order in any in any cause or matter passed or made by any court or tribunal in the territory of India.

(2) Nothing contained above shall apply to any judgment, determination, sentence or order passed or made by any court or tribunal constituted by or under any law relating to the Armed Forces.

Article 136 is of special importance. The jurisdiction and power of the Supreme Court under article 136 is a residuary one which is exercisable when the needs of justice so requires. The only two requirements are that the determination appealed from must be a judicial determination and the authority whose act is complained against must be a court or a tribunal. The Judiciary has made a great contribution in tracing the content of this widely worded article.

SLP can be against *any order and not only a final order* as under articles 132-135. Hence there can be an SLP against an interlocutory order also. SLP can be from the order of any Court or Tribunal and not just a High Court as in the case of articles 132-135.

The manner of exercising power under article 136: The Supreme Court has held that

(1) The power is to be sparingly exercised in exceptional cases[1]. Beyond that it is not possible to fetter the exercise of article 136 jurisdiction by any set formula or rule.[2]

(2) Supreme Court does not interfere with the concurrent findings of the trial court and of the High Court. Only in case of a patent error of law leading to grave and substantial injustice it may interfere.[3]

---

1. *Pritam Singh* v. *State,* AIR 1950 SC 169: 51 Cr LJ 1270: 1950 SCR 453.
2. *D.C. Mills* v. *Commissioner of Income Tax West Bengal,* AIR 1955 SC 55.
3. *Mst. Bega Begum* v. *Abdul Ahmed Khan,* AIR 1979 SC 272: (1979) 1 SCC 273: (1979) 2 SCR 1

(3) A new plea cannot be raised for the first time under article 136 jurisdiction[1]

(4) *P.S.R. Sadhanantham* v. *Arunachalam*, an SLP was preferred against acquittal for murder- not by the State but by the brother of the deceased victim of murder. The question was can the life of the accused who was acquitted be put in peril by a special leave filed by a private person? Krishna Iyer J. read power-cum-fair procedure into article 136 and allowed the petition. It was held that article 136 does not confer a right of appeal but a wide discretionary power to fight injustice. 'Justice is functionally outraged not only when an innocent is punished but also when a guilty criminal gets away with it stultifying the legal system.'[2]

(5) In *Union Carbide Corporation* v. *Union of India*[3] Supreme Court withdrew the criminal proceedings and the original suit filed against the Union Carbide and brought about a settlement between the parties. It held that under article 136 Supreme Court has an inherent power to withdraw or transfer the suit. Article 139A does not exhaust the power of withdrawal and transfer of cases to the Supreme Court under articles 136 and 142 of the Constitution.

(6) *Delhi Administration* v. *Madan Lal Nangia*[4] it was held that if SLP is summarily dismissed this cannot prevent other parties from filing a special leave petition against the same judgment.

The Law Commission has commented in its 14th Report that leave to appeal under article 136 is being granted very frequently- specially in criminal matters and that if this continues the decision of the High Court would have no finality and this does not add to the prestige of the High Court.

Tribunals: Under article 136 special leave petition can be filed against orders etc., of the Tribunals also. Supreme Court has laid down tests to determine whether a particular body is a Tribunal. It must be constituted by the State and be vested with functions of judicial power- *viz.*, to resolve disputes. It does not include Tribunals having only administrative or executive or legislative functions. Industrial Tribunals, Income tax Tribunals, etc., are Tribunals within the meaning of article 136.

In *Clerks of Calcutta Tramways* v. *Calcutta Tramways Co. Ltd.*[5] the Supreme Court has held that it can normally interfere with the decisions of the Tribunals when Tribunal has acted in excess of its jurisdiction or there is an apparent error

1. *Badri Kedar Paper Pvt. Ltd.* v. *U.P. Electricity Regulatory Commn.*, AIR 2009 SC 1783: 2009 AIR SCW 1366: (2009) 3 SCC 754.
2. AIR 1980 SC 856 (858): 1980 3 SCC 141: ILR 1980 HP 147 *also see Ramakant Rai* v. *Madan Rai*, AIR 2004 SC 77: 2004 Cr LJ 36: 2003 AIR SCW 5633.
3. (1991) 4 SCC 584: AIR 1992 SC 248: JT (1991) 6 SC 8.
4. AIR 2003 SC 4672: 2003 AIR SCW 5114: (2003) 10 SCC 321; *Hindustan Tin Works Pvt. Ltd.* v. *Employees of M/s. Hindustan Tin Works Pvt. Ltd.*, AIR 1979 SC 75: (1979) 2 SCC 80: (1979) 1 SCR 563.
5. AIR 1957 SC 78: 1956 SCR 772: 1956 SCC 518.

on the face of the decision; or the awards are made in violation of the principles of natural justice causing substantial injustice to the parties; or it has erroneously applied well-accepted principles of jurisprudence.

K. Advisory jurisdiction of Supreme Court (Article 143)

(1) If at any time it appears to the President that—

(a) A question of law or fact has arisen or is likely to arise, and

(b) The question is of such a nature and of such public importance that it is expedient to obtain the opinion of the Supreme Court upon it,

he may refer the question for the advisory opinion of the court and

the court *may* after such hearing as it thinks fit *report* to the President its opinion thereon.

(2) The President can also refer a dispute arising out of treaty, agreement, covenant, engagement, *sanad,* or other similar instrument which was executed before the commencement of the Constitution and has continued in operation after the commencement. The Supreme Court *shall* after such hearing as it thinks fit *report* to the President its opinion thereon. Note that such a dispute is barred from being referred to the Supreme Court under its original jurisdiction under the proviso to article 131.

The minimum of five judges hear such a matter. The report and the judgment is delivered in *open Court* with the concurrence of the majority of the judges. A judge who does not concur can give his dissenting judgment.

The power to consult the Supreme Court is known as the Advisory jurisdiction or consultative power of the President. The Constitution is silent as to whether the opinion given by the Supreme Court is binding on the President.

Article 143(1) says that the Supreme Court 'may give its report'. This means that the Supreme Court may refuse to give its report on the question referred. *For example* the five judge Supreme Court Bench unanimously refused to answer the controversial question –whether there was any temple or other Hindu religious structure at the site where the Masjid was demolished at Ayodhya. The reference by the President was described as 'superfluous and unnecessary.' Note that under article 143(2) in respect of a dispute regarding treaty etc., the Supreme Court must report its opinion.

The Government of India Act, 1935 empowered the Governor-General to consult the Federal Court.

Advisory opinion is not a judgment as there are no parties before it and therefore it does not provide root of title as in case of a judgment.

Prima facie an opinion under article 143 is not binding under article 141[1] (law declared by the Supreme Court is binding on all the subordinate courts in India). But Delhi Laws Act, case has been frequently followed and referred by the courts. But in *Re Special Courts Bill case* the Supreme Court has held that the views expressed by it in exercise of its advisory jurisdiction are binding on all

---

1. Re Kerala Education Bill.

courts in India. It held that the Parliament has the power to establish Special Courts for trial of emergency offences subject to certain safeguards.[1]

In *Cauvery Disputes Tribunal*[2] a Tribunal was appointed by the Central Government to decide Cauvery river water dispute between Tamil Nadu and Karnataka. Tribunal gave an interim order directing Karnataka Government to release a particular quantity of water to the State of TN. Karnataka Government was not happy with the order. It promulgated an Ordinance empowering the Government not to obey the interim order of the Tribunal. Tamil Nadu Government protested. President referred the matter to the Supreme Court under article 143. Court held the Ordinance unconstitutional as it nullifies the decision of the Tribunal appointed under Inter State Water Dispute Act, 1956 which in turn has been enacted under article 262 of the Constitution.

In Special Reference No. 2002 the question was whether the Election Commission was bound to hold Election of the Gujarat Assembly which was dissolved before the expiry of its five year term, within a period of 6 months as laid down in article 174(1). Supreme Court held that article 174(1) is not related to elections. Article 174(1) and article 324 operate on different levels.

In Re Berubari in 1960 Supreme Court opinion was sought to find out the manner in which territory of India could be transferred to Pakistan.[3]

In Re Customs Bill opinion was sought to consider the validity of Sea Customs Bill.[4]

In Special Court Reference case (Keshav Singh case) extent of privileges and the power of judicial review was referred.

Special reference No. 1998 was referred for removing certain doubts regarding consultation with the CJI regarding appointment of Supreme Court and High Court judges.

L. Power of the Supreme Court to withdraw and transfer cases (article 139(a)) and power of the High Court to transfer cases under article 228

If the Supreme Court is satisfied – on its own motion or on an application made by the Attorney-General of India, or by a party to any such case that cases involving the same or substantially the same questions of law are pending before two or more High Courts and that such questions are substantial questions of general importance the Supreme Court may withdraw the case or cases pending before the High Court and dispose of such cases itself. Likewise if it deems it expedient to do so for the ends of justice the Supreme Court may transfer any case appeal or other proceedings before any High Court to any other High Court.

The Supreme Court may withdraw the case, determine the question of law and then return the case to the High Court along with a copy of its judgment. The High Court must then proceed to dispose of the case in conformity with such judgment.

---

1. That only a sitting judge be appointed to the Special Court; appointment be made in 'concurrence' and not just in 'consultation'; and the accused be given a right to apply for transfer of case from one Special Court to another if he alleges bias.
2. AIR 1992 SC 522: (1991) 2 SCR Supp 497.
3. AIR 1960 SC 845: 1961 (1) SCA 22: (1960) 3 SCR 250.
4. AIR 1963 SC 1760: (1964) 3 SCR 787: 1964 (2) SCA 97.

This enables cases involving same questions of law to be determined by the same court thus avoiding delay and embarrassment if conflicting decisions are given by different courts.

In *A.R. Antuley* v. *R.S. Naik*[1] Supreme Court held that it has no power to withdraw a case from a special judge and transfer it to High Court. Article 139A contemplates transfers from a court in one State to a court in another State or withdrawal to itself. Inter-State transfers amongst Courts subordinate to a High Court is within the jurisdiction of the appropriate High Court.

In *Union of India* v. *Shiromani Gurdwara Prabandhak Committee*[2] the respondents claimed damages from the Union of India for damage to Gurdwara properties due to Operation Blue Star. The same was transferred from Punjab Court to the Delhi High Court due to its sensitive nature and the extraordinary situation in Punjab on an application made by the respondent Committee.

High Court's power to transfer cases: The High Court also has powers to transfer certain cases to itself under article 228. It has power to withdraw a case from a subordinate court if it is satisfied that a case pending in a subordinate court involves a substantial question of law as to the interpretation of the Constitution. It may then either dispose of the case itself or determine the question of law and return the case to the subordinate Court with a copy of its judgment. The subordinate court will then decide the case in conformity with the High Court's judgment.

Differences between Articles 139A and 228

Transfer of cases to Supreme Court (article 139A)	Transfer of case to High Court (article 228)
Supreme Court acts either *suo motu* or on application by Attorney General of India or party to case.	High Court acts *suo motu*.
Cases involve the *same question or substantially the same question of law of general importance.*	Case involves a *substantial question of law as to the interpretation of Constitution.*
Such cases must be pending before (i) the Supreme Court and one or more High Courts or (ii) two or more High Courts.	The case must be pending in a Court subordinate to itself.
Supreme Court may itself dispose of the case so withdrawn to itself or determine the question of law and return it to the High Court for being disposed of according to its judgment.	High Court may itself dispose of the case so withdrawn to itself or determine the question of (Constitutional) law and return it to the Court from which it was withdrawn for being disposed of according to its judgment.
For the ends of justice Supreme Court may transfer any case, appeal or proceeding pending in one High Court to another High Court.	High Court cannot transfer the case from one subordinate Court to another subordinate Court.

M. Miscellaneous jurisdiction

(1) Federal Court's jurisdiction

Federal Court's jurisdiction to be exercised by the Supreme Court under article 135.

Before the commencement of the Constitution there was a Federal Court created by the Government of India Act, 1935. It has been abolished by the Constitution. Supreme Court can exercise the jurisdiction of the Federal Court if article 133 and 134 are not applicable and it is a case in respect of which the Federal Court had jurisdiction.

1. AIR 1992 SC 1701: 1992 Cr LJ 2717: (1992) 1 SCC 225.
2. (1986) 3 SCC 600: AIR 1986 SC 1896: 1986 SCC (Cri) 348.

(2) Power of Review under article 137

Supreme Court has the power to review any judgment pronounced or order made by it. Article 137. This power is subject to law passed by the Parliament. Review will lie to the Supreme Court on discovery of new important matters of evidence; mistake or error on the face of the record; and any other sufficient reason.

A review of a judgment is an exceptional phenomenon only in case a glaring error is made out.

(3) Ancillary powers of the Supreme Court under article 140

Parliament may by law confer such supplemental powers on the Supreme Court as may appear to be necessary or desirable for enabling the court to exercise the jurisdiction conferred on it more effectively. Such powers must not be inconsistent with the provisions of the Constitution.

(4) Enforcement of orders and decrees of the Supreme Court under articles 142 & 144

Article 142 provides that the Supreme Court in exercise of its jurisdiction may pass such decree or order as is necessary for doing complete justice in the matter pending before it. The decree or order made by the court shall be enforceable throughout the territory of India in such manner as may be prescribed by or under any law made by the Parliament.

The power is an inherent power and can be used for doing complete justice. Inherent power cannot be used when alternative remedy is available or has been already availed. Under article 144 all civil and judicial authorities in the territory of India shall act in aid of the Supreme Court.

In *Spencer and Co. Ltd.* v. *Vishwadarshan Distributors*[1] Supreme Court has held that under articles 141, 142, 144 an order of the Supreme Court even if it is in the form of a request is binding on the High Court and if flouted contempt proceedings can be initiated against the erring judges. In this case instead of disposing of the appellant's case within three months as 'requested' by the Supreme Court – the Madras High Court after more than three months had passed an order that the appellant had to wait for his turn as there were a large number of cases.

Under article 145 the Supreme Court has power to make rules to regulate its own procedure. This is subject to law made by the Parliament.

(5) Law declared by the Supreme Court is binding on all the subordinate courts within the territory of India (Article 141)

Judgment of the Supreme Court is binding on all the courts in India. Following are the important points to be noted:

(a) Questions of fact cannot be cited as precedents. It is only the *ratio or the principle of a decision* which can be cited as a binding force.

(b) Supreme Court is not bound by its own decisions and may in proper case reverse its previous decisions. The question was considered in *Bengal Immunity Co.* v. *State of Bihar*[2] the court should not lightly dissent from its previous decision. Its power of review must be exercised with

1. 1994 AIR SCW 5188: (1995) 1 SCC 259.
2. AIR 1955 SC 661: 1955 SCJ 672: (1955) 2 SCR 603.

due care and caution and only for advancing the public well being in the light of surrounding circumstances of each case.

For example there are any number of cases where the Supreme Court overrules its own ruling. Were it to be bound by its own decision the error would have continued in perpetuity. For example *Shankari Prasad* and *Sajjan Singh* were overruled in *Golak Nath*. And *Golak Nath* was overruled in *Keshavanand case*. Thus the doctrine of precedent is followed in India to a limited extent.

The decision of the Supreme Court is binding on all pending proceedings also and not only the future cases.

N. Jurisdiction of the High Court

(1) Court of Record

Already discussed above.

(2) General jurisdiction

Constitution does not make a detailed provision to define jurisdiction of the High Court. It merely declares that their jurisdiction, their powers in the administration of justice, their rule making power are all the same as were enjoyed by them immediately before the commencement of the Constitution *i.e.*, as on 25th January, 1950. This is because these High Courts are in existence long before the Constitution came into force. The *status quo* in respect of the High Courts is subject to provisions of the Constitution and law made by the appropriate Legislatures.

(a) Thus the three High Courts of Bombay, Madras and Calcutta possessed admiralty jurisdiction and they continue to do so. Andhra Pradesh High Court being the successor of High Court of Madras also enjoys admiralty jurisdiction.

(b) In the following two aspects the *status quo* is not maintained:

   (a) Revenue matters were excluded from the original jurisdiction of the Bombay, Madras and Calcutta High Courts. They are now freed from this restriction.

   (b) All High Courts are now conferred with the writ jurisdiction under article 226. Before the Constitution came into force, only the High Courts of Bombay, Madras and Calcutta had the writ jurisdiction. All High Courts in India are now treated equally.

(3) Power of superintendence over all Courts by the High Court (Article 227)

Under article 227 every High Court has the power of superintendence over all *Courts and Tribunals* throughout the territories in relation to which it exercises jurisdiction. It may call for returns from the courts; make and issue general rules and prescribe forms in which book entries and accounts are to be kept. The power of superintendence includes both *administrative and judicial superintendence*. It can also settle tables of fees to be allowed to the officers of such court and to advocates and pleaders practising therein subject to any law in force and the previous approval of the Governor of the State concerned. The power is to be exercised sparingly to ensure that the subordinate court keep within the bounds of their authority.

Power to issue writs under article 226 is different from power of superintendence under article 227. Writs like *habeas corpus* etc., are directed against persons, authorities or the State; power of superintendence is over the subordinate courts and Tribunals to see that they act within the limits of their authority. High Court usually interferes when a court or a Tribunal has acted arbitrarily or refuses to act when it is legally bound to act; or exceeds jurisdiction or assumes erroneous jurisdiction or acts against natural justice.[1]

In *L. Chandra Kumar* v. *Union of India*[2] the Supreme Court has held that the power under article 227 is a basic structure of the Constitution.

Article 235 also invests the High Court with control over subordinate courts. Article 227 deals with the official acts with the persons occupying those posts. Article 235 gives the High Courts control over District Courts and the courts subordinate to the District Courts as regards posting, promotion, leave etc., without taking away the right of appeal which they have under their conditions of service.

(4) Transfer of cases to High Court under article 228

It has been dealt with along with the transfer of cases by Supreme Court above.

(5) Power of review of the High Court

Constitution has made no provision for review by the High Court as in the case of the Supreme Court. But the Supreme Court has held that High Court, being a Court of Record, has an inherent power to review its own judgment to prevent miscarriage of justice.[3]

(6) Power of the High Courts to issue certain writs under article 226

(1) Notwithstanding anything contained in article 32, every High Court is empowered throughout the territories to which it exercises jurisdiction to issue to any person or authority including the Government within those territories directions, orders or writs including writs in the nature of *habeas corpus, mandamus,* prohibition, *quo-warranto, certiorari* or any of them for the enforcement of the Fundamental rights or for any other purpose.

(2) This power may also be exercised by any High Court exercising jurisdiction in relation to the territories within which the cause of action[4] has arisen wholly or in part notwithstanding that the seat of such Government or authority or the residence of such person is not within those territories.

(3) Where an interim order is passed against a party without—

---

1. *Dahya Lala* v. *Rasul Mahomed Abdul Rahim,* AIR 1964 SC 1320: (1963) 3 SCR 1: 1963 (2) SCJ 450; *Union of India* v. *Adhoc Claims Commissioner,* AIR 1977 Cal 393: (1977) 1 Cal LJ 456: 81 Cal WN 649; *State of Maharashtra* v. *Milind,* AIR 2001 SC 393: 2000 AIR SCW 4303: (2001) 1 SCC 4.
2. AIR 1997 SC 1125: 1997 AIR SCW 1345: (1997) 3 SCC 261.
3. *M.M. Thomas* v. *State of Kerala,* AIR 2000 SC 540: 2000 AIR SCW 73: (2000) 1 SCC 666.
4. Cause of action means all those bundle of facts which the plaintiff must prove to be entitled to the relief claimed.

(a) Furnishing him the copies of the petition, and

(b) Without giving him an opportunity of being heard.

And if that party makes an application to the High Court for vacating such order, the High Court shall be bound to dispose of such an application *within two weeks*. If the High Court *fails to dispose* of the application within two weeks the interim order shall on the expiry of two months automatically *stand vacated*. [Inserted by Constitution (44th Amendment) Act, 1978].

(4) The power under article 226 shall not be in derogation of the power conferred on the Supreme Court under article 32(2).

Comments:

(a) *Discretionary jurisdiction:* It is a discretionary jurisdiction and subject to several self-imposed restrictions.

(b) *226 is wider than 32:* Jurisdiction of the Supreme Court under article 32 is for the enforcement of the Fundamental right whereas under article 226 it is for the enforcement of Fundamental right or any other purpose. It is thus wider than article 32.

(c) *Article 226 and 32- independent remedies:* Article 226 operates 'notwithstanding anything contained in article 32'. Hence both the jurisdictions are independent of each other. However the doctrine of *res judicata*[1] has been introduced by the courts in order to avoid multiple and overlapping writ petitions in both the Supreme Court and the High Court to get the same relief in the same fact situation.

(d) *Article 226 is a basic structure:* In *L. Chandra Kumar* v. *Union of India*[2] the Supreme Court has held that *under article 226 jurisdiction of the High Courts is a basic structure of the Constitution* and cannot be curtailed even by a Constitutional Amendment. Thus article 323A(2)(d) & article 324B(3)(d) which excluded the jurisdiction of the High Court under articles 226 and 227 were struck down. These provisions had excluded the jurisdiction of the High Courts over Service Tribunals established under Administrative Tribunals Act, 1988. Yet the Tribunals are competent to test the validity of the statutory provisions and rules. The result is that though they have lost the status they have not lost their jurisdiction. A person now cannot go to the Supreme Court directly from the decision of the Tribunal, without first going to the High Court.

(e) *Alternative efficacious remedy – policy rule:* High Court does not ordinarily issue a writ when an *alternative efficacious remedy* is

1. Under the doctrine, a matter that is heard and decided by a court of competent jurisdiction on merits cannot be reopened by the same parties or their representatives. This is in order to give finality to the decision of the courts.
2. AIR 1997 SC 1125: 1997 AIR SCW 1345: (1997) 3 SCC 261.

available. This is a self-imposed restriction by the Judiciary. Article 226 jurisdiction is not to be used to by pass the statutory remedies and statutory authorities who are competent to give relief. This rule is a *'rule of policy, convenience and discretion and not of law."*[1] *For example* for refusal of a driving permit – the aggrieved must first proceed under Motor Vehicles Act, as it contains a complete code for regulating issue of permits. Likewise the Industrial Disputes Act, the Income Tax Act, Delhi Municipal Corporation Act provide for statutory remedies which must be first exhausted before approaching the High Court under article 226. *For example,* the Registrar of Trade Marks gave a notice to the petitioner *suo motu* to show cause why the registration of his trade mark be not cancelled. Petitioner filed a writ questioning the notice on the ground that the Registrar had no power to issue any such notice. High Court dismissed the writ petition as the petitioner had not exhausted the remedy under the Trade and Merchandise Marks Act, 1958.[2] But the Supreme Court reversed the High Court ruling with an observation that the High Court should have examined whether the show cause was without any jurisdiction. It held that in spite of statutory remedies the High Court can examine when the authority is shown to have no jurisdiction or has usurped the jurisdiction without legal foundation.

If the alternative remedy is ill-suited, burdensome or the petitioner has lost it through no fault of his, or if Tribunal acts under an *ultra vires* law a writ under article 226 is not denied.

(f) *Locus standi: Who can apply:* Under the traditional rule only the aggrieved can file. But under the liberal interpretation of *locus standi* and the concept of public interest litigation (discussed in chapter) any public spirited person can file a writ under article 226 for the enforcement of constitutional and statutory rights of any other person or a class if that person or a class is unable to invoke the jurisdiction of the High Court due to poverty or any social and economic disability.

(g) Supreme Court has emphasised time and again that power of the High Court under article 226 is supervisory and not similar to appellate jurisdiction. It does not sit in appeal over the judgment of the subordinate Court. It is often said that judicial review is not directed against the decision as such but is confined to the decision making process.[3]

---

1. *State of U.P.* v. *Mohammad Nooh,* AIR 1958 SC 86: 1958 SCR 595: ILR (1957) 2 All 422.
2. *Whirlpool Corporation* v. *Registrar of Trade Marks,* (1998) 8 SCC 1: AIR 1999 SC 22: 1998 AIR SCW 3345; *Khaitan India* v. *Union of India,* AIR 2000 Cal 1.
3. Prof. M.P. Jain: Indian Constitutional Law.

(h) *Effect of laches:* No period of limitation is prescribed for a High Court to exercise its power under article 226. However the remedy must be availed of within a reasonable time. Court are hesitant to entertain stale claims which unsettle the settled matters. Hence writ petitions filed after inordinate delay are usually dismissed.[1] But this is not a rule of law but a rule of practice.

Limitation Act is not applicable to writs but it may provide a standard to measure the delay in invoking article 226. Maximum period fixed by the Limitation Act for filing suits can be taken as a reasonable time for filing writs. Yet it must be noted that depending on the facts petitions filed within the limitation period have been dismissed and those filed after the period of limitation have been entertained. Thus there is no rigid formula. It is a matter of discretion to be judiciously exercised. The petitioner must give a satisfactory explanation for the delay.

(i) *Questions of fact:* Theoretically the High Court can determine both questions of law and fact. But in practice it determines only questions of law as questions of fact are best determined in the lower Courts where oral and documentary evidences are adduced.

(j) *In a writ petition* necessary party must and proper parties may be impleaded. Who are the necessary party depends upon the nature of the writ. *For example* in a petition for *certiorari* the Tribunal whose order is sought to be quashed and the party in whose favour the order is issued are necessary parties.

(k) *Res judicata:* In order to ensure finality to the decision of the court. Thus a party is barred from filing one writ after another on the same cause of action. It has been held in *Daryo* v. *State of Uttar Pradesh*[2] disposal of a writ petition under article 226 by the High Court on merits bars a subsequent petition for a writ under article 32 based on the same facts and same cause of action. Supreme Court has held that the rule of *res judicata* is based on the principle of public policy.

(l) *Declaratory relief under writ jurisdiction:* Normally a mere declaratory relief is not granted under article 226. It is only in exceptional cases that it may so grant. *For example* unless a rule was declared unconstitutional the Tribunal could not give the relief under a University Service Rule. Hence the High Court declared the rule

---

1. *Durga Prasad* v. *Chief Controller of Imports and Exports*, AIR 1970 SC 769: (1969) 2 SCR 861: 1970 (2) SCA 1; *Roshan Lal* v. *International Airport Authority of India*, AIR 1981 SC 597: 1981 (I) LLJ 272: 1991 Lab IC 1; *Municipal Council, Ahmednagar* v. *Shah Hyder Beig*, AIR 2000 SC 671: 2000 AIR SCW 197: (2000) 2 SCC 48.
2. AIR 1961 SC 1457: (1962) 1 SCR 574.

as unconstitutional so that the petitioner could claim relief from the Tribunal.[1]

(m) Court have granted compensation to the victims of Government lawlessness under its writ jurisdiction.

(n) High Court may make interlocutory orders in order to preserve the *status quo* so that proceedings do not become infructuous or ineffective by any unilateral act of one side during the pendency of the case.

---

1. *M.C. Sharma, Lecturer* v. *Punjab University, Chandigarh,* AIR 1997 P&H 87: 1998 (1) ESC 11: 1996 (5) Serv LR 49.

CHAPTER 23

PARLIAMENTARY PRIVILEGES

(Articles 105-194)

SYNOPSIS

A. Introduction

Parliamentary privilege is a legal mechanism employed within the legislative bodies of countries whose Constitutions are based on the West Minster Model.

The classic definition of Parliamentary privilege is one defined by *Sir Erskine May's Treatise on the Law, Privileges, Proceedings and Usage of Parliament*[1]:

'Parliamentary privilege, is the sum of the peculiar rights enjoyed by each House collectively... and by Members of each House individually, without which they could not discharge their functions, and which exceed those possessed by other bodies or individuals. Thus, privileges, though part of the law of the land, is to a certain extent an exemption from the general law.

Object of Parliamentary privileges: These are the rights and privileges enjoyed by the members of the State Legislatures and the Parliament. They have to discharge functions of a very high order. Basically they perform duties and functions connected with making and unmaking of laws which could operate

1. May, 22nd Edn., p. 65.

for generations to come keeping in view the over all interest of the Nation and its people belonging to different faith, religions and communities as in India. They need to perform their duties and speak out their mind without fear or favour; without obstructions and hindrances and interferences from within the House or outside the House. Hence they are given a wider freedom of speech and more privileges than the ordinary citizens whom they represent in such Houses.

The privileges of the State Legislature under article 194 and of the Parliament under article 105 are identical hence most of the observations are common to both.

B. Privileges and immunities (Article 105)

Following are the kinds of privileges and immunities available to the members of the Parliament:

1. Freedom of speech which is placed at a higher level than that of the ordinary citizens. Immunity from any court proceedings initiated against them for anything said in the Parliament.
2. Immunity from any court proceedings for any vote given by them.
3. Immunity for publications.
4. Article 105.

(1) Freedom of speech

There shall be freedom of speech in the Parliament which shall be subject to the provisions of the Constitution and the rules and Standing Orders regulating the procedure of the Parliament.

Restrictions

Following are the restrictions on the freedom of speech:

(a) Regarding the conduct of judges

Article 121 (and article 211) of the Constitution restricts the freedom of speech. The conduct of a judge of the Supreme Court or of the High Court in discharge of his duties cannot be discussed in the Parliament except when a motion for his removal on the ground of proved misbehaviour is under consideration.

(b) Expenditure on consolidated fund

Likewise expenditure charged upon the consolidated fund of the State is not to be put to vote by the Legislative Assembly though discussions on the estimates are allowed.

(c) Unparliamentary language prohibited

Likewise under rules 349 to 356 of the Lok Sabha use of unparliamentary language is prohibited.

(2) Immunity from court proceedings

No member of the Parliament shall be liable:

(a) for any proceedings in any court in respect of anything *said by him* or

(b) any *vote given* by him in the Parliament or in the Committee of the Parliament.[1]

The protection is available only for words spoken within the House and not outside the House except when they are spoken outside the House in the discharge of his duties as a member of the Parliament.

In *P.V. Narasimha Rao* v. *State – CBI/SPF*[2] the Congress Party with Narasimha Rao as the Prime Minister was short of the requisite majority to form the Government. It was short by 14 members. The opposition moved a no-confidence motion against him. No confidence motion was defeated with 251 voting in favour of the motion and 265 against it. That is – the Narasimha Government survived. A complaint was filed before the CBI by the Jharkhand Mukti Morcha that MPs from different political parties were bribed so that they would vote against the no-confidence motion and that there was a criminal conspiracy between Narasimha Rao and others with this object. On the basis of these allegations prosecution was filed in the court under the Prevention of Corruption Act.

Two important questions arose in this case:

1. Whether a member of the Parliament is a public servant? It was held unanimously (collectively) that he is a public servant under section 2 of the Prevention of Corruption Act, and hence criminal proceedings can be initiated without the sanction of the competent authority *i.e.,* the authority competent to remove him from office. What is required is only the permission of the Chairman of the Rajya Sabha or the Speaker of the Lok Sabha.
2. Can a member of the Parliament claim immunity from protection under article 105(2) on the charge of bribery in a criminal court?

The appellants claimed immunity from criminal prosecution under article 105(2). The Supreme Court by a majority of 3:2 has held that immunities available to the members of the Parliament are not confined only to the judicial proceedings but the protection is available to all civil action and criminal proceedings for anything said or any vote given by them in the House of Parliament. It held that the MPs who had *taken* bribe and voted in the Parliament against the no-confidence motion moved against Narasimha Rao Government are entitled to protection of article 105(2) and are not answerable in a court of law for alleged conspiracy. But the MPs who had *given* bribe cannot claim immunity. Likewise MPs who have *accepted the bribe but not voted* cannot claim protection from judicial proceedings.

It is submitted that the minority ruling is more rationale and fits into the spirit of the Constitutional provision. They have held that criminal liability for accepting bribe arises independently and is totally different from that of making a speech or giving of vote in the Parliament. Immunity can lie for the latter but not for accepting bribe to cast a vote or to make a speech.

---

1. Article 105(2).
2. AIR 1998 SC 2120: 1998 Cr LJ 2930: 1998 AIR SCW 2001.

It is submitted that the majority ruling is against the whole ethos on which our Constitution is based. The object of giving Parliamentary privileges is to ensure that the representatives of the people act fearlessly and without favour and in the interest of the people; to protect them against illegal pulls and pressures and not to provide immunity for acting against the tenets of our Constitution. By no stretch of imagination can it be said that the framers of our Constitution intended to protect those MLA's and MP's who had accepted bribes for voting in a particular manner.

In Britain the freedom of speech in the Parliament became established with the famous case of *Sir John Eliot*[1]. He was convicted for making seditious speeches in the House of Commons. The House of Lords reversed this decision on the ground that the words spoken in the Parliament should be judged only within the Parliament and not outside. Finally the Bill of Rights, 1688 laid down that freedom of speech and debates and proceedings must not be questioned in any court or place outside the Parliament. Thus a member may say whatever he thinks is proper and he is immune from any action against him in the court of law.

(3) Authorized publication

No person shall be liable to any proceedings in any court in respect of the publication of any report, paper, votes or proceedings if the publication is done by or under the authority of either House of the Parliament[2]. [Article 105(2).]

(a) Parliamentary Proceedings Act, 1956

Parliamentary Proceedings (Protection of Publication) Act, 1956 was passed which provided that no person shall be liable to any civil or criminal proceeding in any court in respect of the publication of substantially true report of the proceedings of either House of Parliament unless it is proved that publication of such proceeding was expressly ordered to be expunged. This Act was repealed by the Congress Government in 1975 during internal emergency. Janta Government repealed the Amendment Act of 1976 and restored the freedom of publication of true reports of Parliamentary proceedings without prior permission of the Legislature.

(b) Article 361A

Article 361A was introduced by the Forty-forth Amendment Act, 1978 which provides that no person shall be liable for any civil or criminal proceeding for publication in a newspaper of substantially true reports of either Houses of the Parliament or the State Legislature. It shall be so liable only in two exceptional cases—

(i) if the publication is proved to be made with malice, or

(ii) they relate to secret sittings of the Parliament or the Legislature.

Article 361A provides the same immunity to reports that are broadcast through wireless telegraphy. Newspaper includes a news agency report containing

---

1. 3 State Trials 294.
2. Article 105(2).

material for publication in the newspaper. Article 361A puts the protection of publication of Parliamentary reports on a more stronger foundation.[1]

It is submitted that under article 361A to claim immunity from legal proceedings for publication of Parliamentary proceedings no authorization from the Parliament is needed; but under article 105(2) immunity can be claimed only if there is such an authorization. Both the provisions are contradictory to each other leading to confusion. In order to bring about clarity in the Constitutional provisions the phrase *'by or under the authority of either House of Parliament'* under article 105(2) be deleted and the contents of article 361A be incorporated in article 105(2) itself rather than scatter the provisions in different Articles.

(4) Powers etc., in other respects

In other respects, the powers, privileges and immunities:

(a) of each House of Parliament, and

(b) of the members of the Parliament, and

(c) the members of Committees of each House;

— shall be such as may be *defined by the Parliament by law.*

Until the Parliament so defines by a law it shall be those of that House and of its members and Committees immediately before the coming into force of section 15 of the Constitution (Forty-Fourth Amendment) Act, 1978. [Article 105(3)]

C. Other privileges

They are as mentioned below—

(1) Freedom from arrest

It is available against civil arrest. No such protection is available for a crime committed by the member. He can be preventively detained under the Preventive Detention Act *i.e.,* person is detained even before the crime is committed as a preventive step because there are reasons to believe that he is likely to commit some crime which will disturb law and order in the society. He can be punished for contempt of court.

When a member is so arrested or detained or sentenced to imprisonment- the Lok Sabha rules require that the judge or the Magistrate or the executive authority must intimate the same to the Speaker, and also intimate the reasons for arrest etc., and the place of detention or imprisonment, the fact of release

---

1. With the passing of article 361A ruling in *Suresh Chandra Banerjee* v. *Punit Goala,* AIR 1951 Cal 176: 55 Cal WN 745: 52 Cr LJ 1422, stands overruled. In this case an MLA had made a speech in the West Bengal Legislative Assembly which was published by the newspaper. The complainant filed a complaint against the newspaper in the Chief Presidency Magistrate Court for defamatory speech published by them and against the MLA. The court held that the MLA could not be prosecuted because the reports in the newspaper were not published by or under the authority of the State Assembly. It could not be held as in *Wason* v. *Walter,* LR 4 QB 73 (1868) -that advantage to the public through such publications is greater than the inconvenience occasionally caused through such reporting.

   Likewise the ruling in *Jatish Chandra* v. *Hari Sadhan,* AIR 1961 SC 613: (1961) 3 SCR 486: 1962 (1) SCJ 411, also stands over-ruled by the introduction of article 361A in the Constitution. It was held that a newspaper not being a publication authorized by the Legislature was not protected even if it published a faithful report of the debates in the House.

on bail (if any). The Speaker reads out the communication in the House. Failure to intimate amounts to a breach of privilege of the House.

In *K. Anandan Nambiar* v. *Chief Secretary-Government of Madras*[1] it was held that an MLA could be arrested under a valid detention order even when the sessions were going on.

(2) Right to exclude strangers from its proceedings

The Parliament has a right to exclude strangers from its proceedings and hold secret sessions. Today secret sessions are held on exceptional occasions.

(3) Right to prohibit publication of its reports and proceedings

(a) The British position

The House of Commons could prohibit such publications by passing resolutions even up to 1762 in order to protect the members from the wrath of arbitrary kings. Later the House even encouraged such publications for its obvious advantages but since the resolutions were still not withdrawn it was still technically a breach of privilege to publish the reports. But the House did not entertain complaints unless the secret proceedings were published. On July, 16, 1971 the House of Commons passed a resolution waiving its privilege.

(b) The Indian position

In India publication of reports or proceedings are governed by article 105(2) and article 361A dealt in detail above.

Breach of privilege with respect to publication: Following constitute breach of privilege in respect of publication of Parliamentary reports:

(i) In *Searchlight* case[2] - the Supreme Court has held that publication of inaccurate versions of speeches in the House or misreporting the proceedings amounts to a breach of privilege.

(ii) Misrepresentation of a Parliamentary Committee report of the Parliamentary proceedings; misrepresenting the speech of the member of the House.

(iii) Committee reports are not to be published before they are laid before the House.

(iv) No document presented to the Committee must be publicized before the Committee presents its report to the House.

In addition it should be noted that with the Parliamentary proceedings being relayed on the Television and other electronic media- the privileges have been consequently curtailed. *For example*- the Speaker may expunge some remarks but they would have been already relayed in live telecast of the proceedings. In addition under the Right to Information Act, the cabinet papers also can be asked for under certain circumstances.

1. AIR 1966 SC 657: 1966 Cr LJ 586: (1966) 2 SCR 406.
2. *M.S.M. Sharma* v. *Sri Krishna Sinha*, AIR 1959 SC 395: 1959 SCJ 925: (1959) Supp 1 SCR 806.

(4) Right to regulate internal proceedings

In India article 122 lays down that the validity of the proceedings in Parliament cannot be called in question in a court of law on the ground of any alleged irregularity of procedure. No officer or member of Parliament who has the powers under the Constitution to regulate procedure or the conduct of business or for maintaining order in Parliament shall be subject to the jurisdiction of any court in respect of the exercise of such powers.

(5) Right to punish members or outsider for contempt

The House has power to punish its member for contempt or breach of privilege. A member may be expelled, or suspended or expelled from the House or sentenced to jail. On expulsion his seat becomes vacant. In 1977 Lok Sabha created history by expelling the former Prime Minister Smt. Indira Gandhi from membership and sentencing her to jail for committing a contempt of Parliament while she was a PM. She had committed a breache of privilege by preventing the Parliament from knowing that her son's Maruti Limited was installing imported machinery in violation of the licence to manufacture an indigenous small car; she obstructed the officers deputed to collect the above information, committed contempt by refusing to take oath or affirmation before the privilege committee. But when Janata Government was defeated in the elections and Congress returned to power in 1980 Parliament passed a resolution withdrawing all the charges on the ground that all charges were politically motivated.

There cannot be an exhaustive list of contempt of court cases. They may take various forms like obstructing the House or its members in performing their functions; comments in the newspaper by individuals which lower the image of the Parliament or its members; misreporting of the proceedings, etc.

'In modern times the phrase-*'breach of privilege'* is more flexible and broader concept than the phrase *'contempt of court'*. Breach of privilege means not only breach of a recognized and accepted privilege of the House but also any action which though not breach of a specific privilege yet undermines the dignity or authority of the House'[1].

Usually the House drops the action against a person who infringes its privileges if he apologizes and accepts his mistake. House is not vindictive. The power is used to preserve and vindicate its dignity.

Matter of breach of privilege can be raised even after the dissolution of the House – *i.e.,* in its next House. This point got decided when the privilege motion was raised in the Sixth Lok Sabha for Smt. Indira Gandhi's conduct in the Fifth Lok Sabha. The Privileges Committee ruled that the dissolution of Lok Sabha does not imply discontinuity of the institution of Parliament, the Lok Sabha has the power to punish a breach of privilege and contempt of the earlier Lok Sabha. Thus the House decided to imprison Indira Gandhi till the prorogation of the House and expelled her from membership.

---

1. The case of *John Junor JI of Parl Inf.,* 75(1957) quoted by Jain, M.P. Indian Constitutional Law; 5th Ed, 2009 at p. 97.

D. Privileges etc, before the 44th Amendment

Before the 44th Amendment in other respects (*i.e.*, other than freedom of speech; right of publication) the privileges, powers and immunities of the House, its members and its committees were those of the House of Commons in England.

E. Committee of Privileges

Each House in the Parliament has a Committee of privileges to advise it in matters affecting its powers, privileges and immunities and those of its members. It consists of 15 members nominated by the Chairman. The Committee examines every question referred to it and determines whether there has been a breach of privilege having regard to the facts of the case. It performs an adjudicatory function *i.e.*, it has to be non-political and non-partisan and follow the principles of natural justice, hear all the sides and then make such recommendations as it deems fit. It may also state the procedure[1] to be followed by the House to give effect to its recommendation. The recommendation of the Committee is not binding on the House.

F. Privileges of the House of Commons

Following were the privileges of the House of Commons in UK:

The ancient and undoubted rights and privileges of the Commons claimed by the Speaker at the beginning of each new Parliament:

1. Freedom of speech;
2. Freedom from arrest;
3. Access of the Commons to the Crown (*via* the Speaker); and
4. That the most favourable construction should be placed upon the deliberations of the Commons.

Privileges not so claimed:

1. Right of the House to regulate its own composition;
2. Right of the House to regulate its own internal proceedings (to take exclusive cognizance of matters within the house);
3. Right to punish members and "strangers" for breach of privilege and contempt;
4. Right of impeachment; and
5. Right to control finance and to initiate financial legislation as against the Lords.

G. Privileges and Fundamental Rights

In case of conflict between the privileges and Fundamental Rights

The question is what is the relationship between the privileges of the House and the Fundamental Rights guaranteed under Part III of the Constitution. Generally speaking freedom of speech and expression under article 19(1)(a) is subject to reasonable restrictions under article 19(2) of the Constitution. Right

1. Rules 314, 315 of the Rules of Procedure of the Lok Sabha.

of speech under article 105 is an independent right. It is not subject to the restrictions of 19(2).

(a) Gunapati case

The confusion is – in case of a conflict between privileges under article 105 and the Fundamental Rights under articles 12 to 35 which one will prevail? For the first time the question arose in *Gunapati* case[1]. The Blitz paper published derogatory aspersions on the Speaker of the Uttar Pradesh Assembly in its news item. The Speaker referred the matter to the Privileges Committee. The Privileges Committee summoned the Editor to appear before it to clarify its position. He did not respond. Speaker issued warrant to arrest the Editor based on the resolution of the House. Editor was arrested in Bombay for contempt of UP Legislative Assembly.

Editor – D.H. Mistry was brought to Lucknow and lodged in the Hotel for a week without anything further being done. Writ of *habeas corpus* (produce the body of the person was issued in case of detention etc.,) was moved in the Supreme Court as his Fundamental Right under article 22(2) was violated. Under article 22(2) an arrested person must be brought before the nearest Magistrate within 24 hours of arrest. Supreme Court held that the editor's Fundamental Right under article 22(2) was violated and ordered his release. This pronouncement created an impression that Fundamental Rights control Parliamentary privilege. This means that the Parliamentary privilege must be so exercised as not to infringe or violate the Fundamental Rights under articles 12 to 35.

(b) Searchlight case

The Supreme Court held that privileges under article 105(3) or of Legislature under article 194(3) were not subject to article 19(1)(a). Hence prohibition of publication of its debates is valid even if prohibition contravenes the Fundamental Rights of speech and expression of publisher under article 19(1)(a). The court held that article 105(3) not subject to Constitutional provisions as expressly mentioned in article 105(1) (but article 105(1) is general in nature. It says there shall be Fundamental Right to speech in the House and therefore strictly interpreting 105(3) is an application of 105(1) and hence 105(3) also is subject to other Constitutional provisions).

It held that *Gunapati* case was not binding as it was not a 'considered opinion', all angles not thought of and discussed in the court. So it was held that article 105(3) and Fundamental Rights must be 'harmoniously construed'. Article 19(1)(a) is of a general nature and therefore when there is a conflict between article 105(3) which is of a special nature it must prevail over article 19(1)(a) which is general nature.

In *Search Light case* a Bihar MLA made a speech on the floor of the House. Certain portions were expunged (directed to be scrolled off or deleted). But Search light published the whole speech. Privileges Committee summoned the

1. *Gunupati Keshavram Reddy* v. *Nafisul Hasan*, AIR 1954 SC 636: 1954 Cr LJ 1704.

editor to answer the charges of breach of privileges. He filed a writ under article 32 before the Supreme Court that his Fundamental Right to freedom of speech and expression was violated. Supreme Court rejected the editor's contention.

Supreme Court held that his Fundamental Rights under article 21 also was not violated. Under article 21 no person can be deprived of his and personal liberty except according to the procedure established by law. Supreme Court held that under article 118 and article 208 the Parliament and the State Legislature can make rules regulating the procedures for enforcing its powers privileges and immunities. When this procedure laid down in the Rules is followed article 21 Fundamental Rights is complied.

Privileges Committee again began its proceedings against the editor of Searchlight. Editor again went to the Supreme Court and raised the same grounds in Search light II. Supreme Court refused to reconsider the matter. Court held that however if a person is deprived of his personal liberty on capricious or *mala fide* grounds by the Parliament he can file a writ of *Habeas corpus*. Whether any other Fundamental Right would apply to the Parliamentary privileges was not before the court.

(c) Keshav Singh case

In *Keshav Singh's* case[1] Supreme Court has held that when a person is adjudged guilty of contempt of the House and is detained after following rules of procedure laid down by the House, article 22(2) of the Constitution is not applicable and hence there is no need to produce the person before the nearest Magistrate.

Thus, there is no authoritative ruling or a Constitutional provision whether all the Fundamental Rights apply to Parliamentary privileges under article 105 [or 194(3)]. The position appears to be that it is wrong to suppose that no Fundamental Rights apply to the area of legislative privileges. Some Fundamental Rights like article 19(1)(a) do not apply. Perhaps article 19(1) to (g) would also not apply. But article 21 is applicable and the position with respect to article 22(1) and article 22(2) is not clear.[2]

If the Parliament codifies the privileges by a law under article 105(3), then the codified provisions must comply with right or else it would infringe article 13(2) under which a law which takes away or abridges the Fundamental Rights is void to that extent.

H. Privileges and the courts

The relationship between Parliamentary privileges and the courts show that there has been a tug of war between the law making bodies and the judiciary giving rise to several questions mainly because the privileges have not been codified like:

- Who decides whether a particular privilege claimed by the House exists or not; is the House a final judge of the way in which it is to be exercised? Can the courts go into the question of the validity of the contempt

1. *Keshav Singh* v. *Speaker, Legislative Assembly U.P.*, AIR 1965 All 349: (1965) 2 Cr LJ 170: ILR (1965) 2 All 281.
2. Jain, M.P.: Indian Constitutional Law, 5th Ed. 2009 at pp. 101-102.

proceedings initiated by the House? Is the working of the Committee on privileges questioned before the courts.

In 1689 the House of Commons called two judges of the King's Bench to its bar to explain their conduct and later these judges were ordered to be imprisoned. Their fault was that 7 years earlier they had ordered Jay to be released from the custody of the Sergeant at arms of the House.

In *Re Under Article 143* one *Keshav Singh* was not a member of the Uttar Pradesh Assembly. He was held guilty of contempt of the House and was sentenced to 7 days imprisonment. His advocate moved a *habeas corpus* petition alleging that his detention was illegal and *mala fide* because he was not given an opportunity to defend himself.[1] Allahabad High Court granted an interim bail[2] to Keshav Singh and he was released pending disposal on merit. The Assembly passed a resolution that Keshav Singh, his advocate and the two judges had committed contempt of the House and therefore be taken into custody and produced before them. Now the two judges and the advocate filed a writ under article 226 in the High Court alleging that the resolution amounted to contempt of court. The Full Bench stayed the implementation of the Resolution. Warrant against the judges was withdrawn but they were asked to appear before the House and explain their conduct. High Court once again stayed the modified resolution. At this stage the President of India referred the matter to the Supreme Court under article 143 for the Advisory opinion. Note that the alleged contempt was by a non-member; the contempt (if any) had taken place outside the House; Assembly had passed a general or an unspeaking warrant.

Two main questions considered by the Supreme Court were:

> Whether the Legislative Assembly is the sole and exclusive judge of its Privilege and whether it is competent to punish a person for its contempt taking place outside the Legislature? Whether the High Court which had entertained writ of *Habeas Corpus* challenging validity of the sentence passed by the Legislative Assembly under an unspeaking warrant had committed contempt of the Legislature?

By a majority of 6:1 the Supreme Court held that

(a) the two judges were not guilty of contempt of the House by issuing an interim bail order. High Court has the power to release a person from illegal detention. It is a Constitutional power under article 226. Courts can examine the validity of a general or an unspeaking warrant of the Assembly. In this respect the position is different in England. In England the courts cannot examine the validity of a general or an unspeaking warrant issued by the House of Commons. The House of Commons is the highest court in England. Hence general warrants issued by it is not subject to judicial scrutiny. In India the Legislature never discharges judicial function and they cannot be regarded as the courts of record. Hence the English practice is not applicable in India.

---

1. One of the basic principles of natural justice is that no person shall be condemned unheard. That is he must be heard before taking any decision.
2. It is granted if there is a *prima facie* case made out that the contentions of the applicant are in all probability true and correct.

(b) Legislative privileges under 194(3) [& Parliamentary privileges under article 105(3)] are subject to Constitutional provisions.[1] Article 211 prohibits discussions *in the State Legislature* on the conduct of the Supreme Court or High Court judges and article 121 prohibits discussions in the Parliament on the conduct of the Supreme Court and High Court judges.

(c) The House is the sole and exclusive judge in respect of its privileges if such privileges can be found in article 194(3). But whether such a privilege is found in article 194(3) or not is for the court to decide. This is because in our country Constitution is supreme. All the organs – Legislature, Executive and the Judiciary are subject to the Constitution. Interpretation of the Constitution is a judicial function assigned to the courts under our Constitution. Interpretation of the privileges of the Legislature and of the Parliament also is a judicial junction. Hence courts have jurisdiction. The court held that the privileges are subject to articles 21 and 22 of the Constitution without commenting on whether the privileges are subject to all the Fundamental Rights under Part III.

The ruling thus maintains the:

(i) Status and dignity, integrity of the judiciary

(ii) It prevents the Legislature from being omnipotent (all powerful) in the area of its privileges for it is well known that power corrupts and absolute power corrupts absolutely.

(iii) It prevents the Legislature from being answerable to no authority as regards its privileges.

(iv) It upholds the Constitutional role of judges as interpreters of Constitution.

(v) The courts have acknowledged the supremacy of the Legislature and of the Parliament in respect of privileges as shown above.

Note that these were the observations of the Supreme Court under its Advisory jurisdiction.[2]

After the Supreme Court gave its opinion the Allahabad High Court considered *Keshav Singh's* case on merits and dismissed his petition.

(i) It rejected that the facts found by the Assembly did not amount to contempt of the Assembly.

(ii) It refused to sit-in-appeal over the decision of the Uttatr Pradesh Assembly which committed *Keshav Singh* to contempt. It thus refused to go into the correctness, propriety and legality of the decision of the House.

(iii) It held that Legislative Assembly is the master of its own procedure and the sole judge of the question whether contempt has been committed.

---

1. Article 211 prohibits discussions *in the State Legislature* on the conduct of the Supreme Court or High Court judges and article 121 prohibits discussions *in the Parliament* on the conduct of the Supreme Court and High Court judges.
2. Supreme Court only gives its opinion on the questions raised by the President, but the case is not disposed of by the court. Such recommendations are binding on all the subordinate courts in India.

(iv) It held that there were no *mala fides* to be seen on the facts of the case.

(v) There was no violation of article 21 or the principles of natural justice.

I. Disciplinary powers over its members

The Parliament has power to enforce discipline to punish its members for their offending conduct in the House or to expel a member for his non-befitting conduct. *For example* Mudgal, a Lok Sabha member, used to accept monetary benefits for asking questions in the House, moving amendments etc. Prime Minister Nehru moved a resolution for his expulsion. Meanwhile he resigned.

In *Subramanian* case, the Madras High Court refused to issue writ of Prohibition prohibiting the speaker from even calling upon Subramanian to show cause why he should not be held to be guilty of committing breach of privilege. Such a writ would stifle the very existence of jurisdiction and render articles 105(3) or 194(3) nugatory.

In the *Eenadu Privilege* issue the Chief Editor of Telagu Newspaper Eenadu published a news item – Elder's Commotion – in his newspaper. He was found guilty of contempt of the House. He was ordered to appear before it for admonition. The Supreme Court had ordered the Secretary of the House not to arrest him. He now refused to appear 'unless arrested and taken'. The Legislative Council discussed the matter and opined that in respect of privileges the Council was supreme and the court had no place in the matter and so it should go ahead and arrest the Editor in spite of the Supreme Court order. At this stage the Chief Minister intervened to prevent a conflict between the Legislature and the Judiciary and requested the House to postpone the matter as he had requested the President of India to refer the matter to the Supreme Court for its advisory opinion.

In *Tej Kumar Jain*[1] some Lok Sabha members had allegedly made remarks against Shankaracharya on the floor of the House/hence suit for damages was filed before the Delhi High Court. It was dismissed. Appeal was filed in the Supreme Court against the High Court decision. Notice of lodgment of Appeal was sent to the concerned members. Speaker advised them to appear before the Supreme Court either in person or by an Advocate. At this stage question of privileges was debated in the Lok Sabha and now the members were advised not to appear before the Supreme Court and that if they so appeared before Supreme Court – they would be guilty of breach of privilege of the House. Court held that there is a difference between notice of lodgment and a summons. If summons is issued and the defendant does not appear the case is heard *ex-parte*. But it is only an intimation of the fact of lodgment of appeal – it is for the party to choose whether to appear or not.

After this clarification the matter was again discussed by the House and the Speaker ruled that whether the court issued a summons or a notice – it made no difference as ultimately privileges of the House were involved, it shows the House has been too possessive of its privileges even by opining against the reasonable and impartial judgment given by the judiciary.

---

1. *Tej Kiran Jain* v. *M. Sanjiva Reddy*, AIR 1970 SC 1573: 76 ITR 719.

Such cases would justify codification of the privileges. Hence J. Subba Rao strongly pleaded for codification of the law relating to privileges in Searchlight I case because: "this branch is in a nebulous state with the result that a citizen will have to make a research into the unwritten law of privileges of the House of Commons at the risk of being called before the bar of the Legislature". Codification has its own advantages and disadvantages. It will be practically impossible to contemplate all situations leading to contempt and a breach of privilege. Hence it will restrict the power of the House to deal with the privileges matters in the way it thinks best. It would lose the flexibility it enjoys today. But then it is equally true that the present demand for codification has arisen due to the unreasonable approach of the Legislatures wherein they claim to be put above the Constitution and superior to the courts which are also a Constitutional institution.

CHAPTER 24
PANCHAYATS AND MUNICIPALITIES

(Articles 243 to 243-O; 243P to 243-ZG)

SYNOPSIS

A. Introduction

Parts IX and IXA have been added by the Constitution 73rd and 74th Amendment Acts, 1992. The amendments intend to take administration to the grass root level. It provides for *Gram Sabhas and Panchayats.* It gives effect to the directive principle in article 40 which directs the State to take steps to organise village *Panchayats* and endow them with such powers and authority as may be necessary to enable them to function as units of self-Government.

The Constitution, elections, devolution of powers and authority relating to these institutions have been completely left within the purview of the States.

B. Panchayats

(1) Gram Sabha—foundation of Panchayat Raj

A *Panchayat* is defined to mean an institution of self-government constituted under article 243B of the Constitution. *Gram Sabha* is the foundation of the *Panchayat Raj* System. It performs powers and functions entrusted to it by the State Legislatures. A *'Gram Sabha'* is defined to mean a body consisting of persons registered in the electoral rolls relating to a village comprised in the area of a *Panchayat* at the village level.

(2) Three tier Panchayat system

Constitution provides a three tier *Panchayat* system at the village, intermediate and district level. District means a district in a State. 'Intermediate level' means a level between village and district level. 'Village' means a village specified by the Governor by public notification to be a village for the purposes of Part IX and includes a group of villages so specified. *Panchayats* at the intermediate level may not be constituted by the State whose population does not exceed 20 lakhs.

(3) Elections for Panchayat

All the seats in a *Panchayat* are to be filled by persons chosen by direct election from territorial constituencies in the *Panchayat* area. For this purpose the *Panchayat* area is to be divided into territorial constituencies in such a manner that the ratio between the population of each constituency and the number of seats allotted to it is the same throughout the *Panchayat* area.

(4) Representation of Lok Sabha etc.

The State Legislature may provide for representation of the following persons in *Panchayat*—

Chairpersons of the *Panchayat* at the Village, district and intermediate level; members of the Lok Sabha and the Legislative Assembly of the State representing constituencies which comprise wholly or partly a *Panchayat* area at the level other than the village level; the members of the Rajya Sabha and Legislative Council of the State where they are registered as electors.

(5) Reservation for Scheduled Castes and Scheduled Tribes women

Provisions are made for reservations of seats for the scheduled castes and scheduled Tribes and for women belonging to such castes and tribes.

(6) Duration

Every *Panchayat* is to last for 5 years from the date of its first meeting and no longer (unless dissolved earlier).

(7) Powers and authority

The State Legislature may endow the *Panchayats* with such powers and authority as may be necessary to enable them to function as institutions of self-Government. Such law may contain provisions for devolution of powers and responsibilities upon *Panchayats* subject to such conditions as may be specified therein with respect to:

(a) The preparation of plans for economic development and social justice;

(b) The implementation of schemes for social development and social justice as may be entrusted to them including those in relation to the matters listed in the 11th Schedule, like agriculture, land improvement, poverty alleviation programme etc.

(8) Power to impose tax

Article 243H provides that the Legislature of a state may by law—

(a) Authorise a *Panchayat* to levy, collect and appropriate taxes, duties, tolls and fees within specified limits.

(b) Assign to a *panchayat* such taxes, duties, tolls and fees and collected by the State Government.

(c) Provide for grants-in-aid to the *Panchayat* from the Consolidated Funds of the State.

(d) Provide for constitution of such funds for crediting all money received by or on behalf of the *Panchayats* and for withdrawal of money there-from.

(9) Control of electoral rolls in State Election Commission

Superintendence, direction and control of the electoral rolls for and the conduct of all elections to the *Panchayat* are vested in the State Election Commission. Article 243B.

(10) Election petition

Elections can be challenged only by an election petition presented to such *authority* and in such manner as may be provided by the State Legislature. Article 243-O.

(11) Finance Commission

Finance commission must be constituted by the Governor of the State to review the financial position of the *Panchayat* and make necessary recommendations to the Governor.

(12) Accounts and audit

The State Legislature may also make provisions with regard to keeping of accounts by the *Panchayats* and its audits.

(13) Reservations of seats in Panchayat

Seats shall be reserved for Scheduled Castes and Scheduled Tribes. The number of seats so reserved shall be in the same proportion to the total number of seats to be filled by direct election in that *Panchayat* as the population of the SCs and STs in that *Panchayat* area bears to the total population of that area and such seats may be allotted by rotation to different constituencies in a *Panchayat*.

Out of total number of seats reserved not less than 1/3rd seats shall be reserved for women belonging to the SCs and STs. Out of total number of seats to be filled by direct election in every *Panchayat* not less than 1/3rd (including the number of seats reserved for SCs and STs women) seats shall be reserved for women. Such seats may be allotted by rotation to different constituencies in a *Panchayat*.

The office of the Chairpersons in the *Panchayats* at the village or any other level shall be reserved for SCs/STs and women in such manner as the Legislature of the State may by law provide. But the number of offices of Chairpersons reserved for the SCs and STs in the *Panchayats* at each level in any State shall be as nearly as possible in the same proportion to the number of such offices in the *Panchayats* at each level in proportion of the total population of the SCs and STs in the State but not less than 1/3rd of the total number of the offices of Chairperson in the *Panchayat* at each level shall be reserved for women. The number of offices reserved under this clause shall be allotted by relation to different *Panchayats* at each level.

The reservation of seats and reservation of offices of chairpersons (other than reservation for women) shall cease to have effect on the expiration of the 50 yrs specified in article 334.

The State Legislature is empowered to make reservations of seats in any *Panchayat* or office of Chairpersons in the *Panchayat* State at any level in favour of backward classes of citizens.

C. Municipalities

Part IX A was added to the Constitution by 74th Amendment 1992 (Article 243 P to 243ZG). It has also added 12th Schedule relating to urban local bodies in the Constitution. It provides Constitutional basis to the urban self-governing institutions. It provides for regular elections. As in the case of *Panchayats* – it provides for three types of Municipal Corporations and reservation of seats in every Municipality for Scheduled Castes, Scheduled Tribes and women.

Municipal area means the territorial area of a municipality as is notified by the Governor. [Article 243P(d)]. Municipality means an institution of self government constituted under article 243Q.

Metropolitan area means an area having a population of 10 lakhs or more comprised in one or more districts and consisting of two or more Municipalities or *Panchayats* or other contiguous areas specified by the Governor by public notification to be a Metropolitan area for the purposes of this Part.

Following are the important provisions covered under these Articles:

1. The Constitution makes provision for—

   Nagar Panchayat – for a transitional area *i.e.,* an area in transition from a rural area to an urban area.

   Municipal Council – for a smaller urban area. And

   Municipal Corporation – for a larger urban area.

2. All seats in the Municipality are to be filled by persons chosen by direct election from the territorial constituencies in the Municipal area. For this purpose each Municipal area is to be divided into territorial constituencies known as *wards.*

3. The State Legislature may provide:

   (a) For the representation in a Municipality of persons having special knowledge or experience in Municipal administration, the members of the Parliament and of State Legislatures and Chairpersons of the various committees; and

   (b) For the manner of electing the Chairpersons of the Municipalities.

   In all cases of a municipality with a population of 3 lakhs or more ward committees are to be established. The State Legislature must provide for:

   (i) Composition and territorial area of a Ward Committee, and

   (ii) The manner in which seats of a Ward Committee are to be filled.

It also provides for reservation of seats for the Scheduled Castes and Scheduled Tribes and for women belonging to such Castes and Tribes.

4. Every Municipality is to continue for 5 years from the date of its meeting and no longer (unless dissolved sooner). The State may by law endow the Municipalities with such powers and authority as may be necessary to enable them to function as institutions of self-Government. In particular the State Legislature may by law:

(a) Authorise the Municipality to levy, collect and appropriate such taxes, duties, tolls, and fees within specified limits.

(b) Assign to a municipality such taxes, duties, tolls and fees as may be levied and collected by the State Government.

(c) Provide for Constitution of such funds for crediting all money received by or on behalf of the municipalities and for withdrawal of money therefrom.

5. The superintendence, direction and control of the preparation of electoral rolls for and the conduct of all elections to the Municipality are vested in the State Election Commission (Article 243ZA). No election to any Municipality can be challenged except in an election petition presented to such authority and in such manner as may be provided by the State Legislature. (Article 243ZG)

6. *Committee for District Planning:* Article 243-ZD provides for constitution of a District Planning Committee in every State. Its functions shall be to consolidate the plans prepared by the *Panchayats* and the Municipalities in the District and to prepare a draft Development Plan for the District as a whole. The Legislature may make provisions:

   (a) for the composition of the District Planning Committees.

   (b) the manner in which the seats in such committees shall be filled. Out of the total number of members of such Committees $1/4^{th}$ shall be elected by and from amongst the elected members of the *Panchayat* at the District level and the municipalities in the District in proportion to the ratio between the population of the rural areas and of the urban areas in the District.

   (c) The functions relating to District Planning which may be assigned to such Committees, and

   (d) The manner in which the Chairpersons of such Committees shall be chosen.

   Every District Planning Committee shall in preparing such draft Development Plan have regard to matters of common interest between the *Panchayats* and the Municipalities including spatial planning, sharing of water and other physical and natural resources, the integrated development of infrastructure and environmental conservation.

7. Likewise article 243ZE provide for the establishment of a Metropolitan Planning Committee for every Metropolitan area which will prepare a draft development plan for the whole of the Metropolitan area.

CHAPTER 25

RELATIONS BETWEEN THE UNION AND THE STATES

(Articles 245-293)

SYNOPSIS

A. Introduction

India has a Federal system. In a Federal system, there is a dual polity. *For example,* in India there is the Central Government having jurisdiction throughout the territory of India and State Governments having jurisdiction in their respective States. The citizens are thus subject to the laws and the administration of two Governments – the Centre and the States. Both the Governments are supreme in their own spheres. There are certain exclusive areas and also some over-lapping areas of jurisdiction. The Constitution lays down a division and sharing of the powers and functions between the Central and the State Government for smooth functioning of the country. One is not to invade upon the powers and functions of the other. If it does so, it would be a breach of the Constitution. It gives rise to a justiciable issue[1] to be determined by the courts.

In India we have a Federal Government with strong unitary features[2]. That is during emergencies and in certain respects even during normal times the Centre exercises control over the States.

Relation between the Union and the State is to be studied with reference to three different relationships – Legislative, Administrative and financial relationships.

B. Legislative relations[3]

The division of Legislative functions is two fold:

(i) Territorial jurisdiction *i.e.,* the *territory* in respect of which the Legislature can make laws. (Article 245)

(ii) Subject-matter jurisdiction *i.e.* with respect to subject matter of the Legislation *i.e.,* the *topics/subjects* on which laws can be made. (Article 246)

(1) Territorial jurisdiction

(a) Territorial applicability of laws

Parliament can make laws for the whole or any part of the territory of India and the Legislature can make laws for the whole or any part of the State. This power is subject to the provisions of the Constitution.

(b) Extra-territorial application of central law

Law made by the Parliament is *not deemed to be invalid*[4] merely because it has extra-territorial application.

(c) Extra-territorial application[5] of State law

A State law *is not valid* if it is made applicable to the person or property outside its territory.

---

1. An issue which can be raised in the courts of law.
2. Some call it a *quasi*-Federal structure because it is not strictly Federal.
3. Articles 245-255.
4. A 'deeming clause' involves a legal fiction. Here it means that 'a Central law which would normally be invalid if it is to operate outside its jurisdiction – is by a legal fiction (deemed) supposed to be not invalid.'
5. Article 245(2).

(d) Exception-territorial nexus

To this rule there is only one exception. If the State law having extra-territorial application has a sufficient nexus between the subject matter of the law and the State making the law it is valid.

In *Wallace* v. *Income tax Commissioner*[1] a company was registered in England. It was a partner in a Firm in India. Indian Income tax authorities levied an income tax on the entire income of the company including the income accruing in England. It was held that a major portion of the company's profits accrued from India and hence there was sufficient territorial nexus between the company and India for tax purpose.

In *State of Bombay* v. *R.M.D. Chamarbaugwala*[2] Bombay State levied a tax on lotteries and prize competition. The tax was extended to a newspaper printed and published in Bangalore but had wide circulation in Bombay. The respondent conducted prize competition through this paper. The court held that there existed a sufficient territorial nexus to enable the Bombay State to tax the newspaper.

(i) Test for sufficient nexus

Whether there is sufficient nexus or not is a question of fact in each case. There are no fixed rules to determine sufficiency. Following two aspects must be considered:

- *Real connection:* Connection must be real and not illusory.
- *Relevant connection:* Liability sought to be imposed must be relevant to that connection.

Under section 68d(3) of the Motor Vehicles Act, it is the State Government which gives approval to a scheme for inter-State routes for the State Transport Undertaking. Hence article 245(2) is not applicable.[3]

Contempt of Court Act is enacted by the Parliament. Under section 11 it provides that the High Court has the jurisdiction to try a contempt of itself or of any court subordinate to itself – whether the contempt is committed within its territorial jurisdiction or outside it.

(ii) Article 298 – Extra-territorial business

Likewise, under article 298 the State and the Union can carry on business outside its territory. In such a case executive power of the Union is subject to State legislation where the business is carried on – if the business is not one with respect to which the Parliament can make laws; and the executive power of the State is subject to Central legislation if the business is not one with respect to which the State can make laws.

In *State of Andhra Pradesh* v. *National Thermal Power Corporation*[4] the Supreme Court has held that generally speaking the Parliament alone can make laws having extra-territorial application. The State law can be extra-territorially

1. AIR 1948 PC 118: (1948) 2 Mad LJ 62: (1948) 16 ITR 240.
2. AIR 1957 SC 699: 1957 SCJ 607: 1957 SCA 867.
3. *Ch. Khazan Singh.* v. *State of Uttar Pradesh*, AIR 1974 SC 669: 1974 SCC 295: (1974) 2 SCR 562.
4. (2002) 5 SCC 203: AIR 2002 SC 1895: 2002 AIR SCW 1956.

applicable only when there is territorial nexus which is sufficient, real and not illusory.

(2) *Subject matter jurisdiction*

(a) Legislative power – Plenary

The powers of the Legislature to make laws is plenary[1]. The only limitation is with respect to the subject matters specified in Schedule VII and other Constitutional limitations. Laws can be made prospectively or retrospectively. That is, they can be made operative from the date on which they are passed and brought into force or even from a date before it was passed subject to Constitutional limitations. It can amend or alter or modify or repeal the law.

(b) Law cannot be made to declare a judgment void

In *State of Haryana* v. *Karnal Co-operative Farmer's Society*[2] the Supreme Court has held that Legislature has power to alter the legal basis of a law and thereby make the earlier judicial decision ineffective. *For example* in *Shah Bano*[3] case the Supreme Court had held that a Muslim husband must maintain his divorced wife if she is unable to maintain herself and if she has not re-married. The Parliament passed the Muslim Women's (Protection of Rights on Divorce) Act, 1986 restricting the period of maintenance by the husband only to the period of *iddat*.

C. Distribution of Legislative Powers

The essence of a Federal Constitution lies in the division of powers and functions between the Centre and the States. Those of national importance are allotted to the Centre and those of local importance are allotted to the States. Yet it is an *ad-hoc* formula varying from one Federal country to another. Subjects like defense, currency, foreign affairs are of national importance everywhere and hence given to the Centre. But beyond this, other subjects may be allotted to the Centre or the State depending on exigencies of the situation in the country, attitude of the people and the philosophy prevailing at the time the Constitution was framed and the experiences around it. *For example* American Centre enumerates the powers of the Central Government and the residuary powers rest with the State. In Canada there is a Central and Provincial List and residue rests with Centre.

In any country there would be two conflicting philosophies – one favouring Centralization with a strong Union and the other favouring decentralization based on religious, ethnic, cultural, linguistic differences across the country. The scheme which emerges is sought to be a balance between both the philosophies.

Schedule VII

It contains three lists—

List I- Union List the Parliament has an exclusive power to make laws in respect of subjects in the Union List. It consists of 97 subjects of national importance. Some of them are:

1. Full and complete power of the Government – without limits.
2. (1993) 2 SCC 363: AIR 1994 SC 1: 1993 AIR SCW 3432.
3. *Mohd. Ahmed Khan* v. *Shah Bano Begum*, AIR 1985 SC 945: 1985 Cr LJ 875: (1985) 2 SCC 556.

- Defence (entries 1-7) like defense of India, Naval, Military and Air Forces, arms, firearms, ammunition and explosives; industries declared by the Parliament to be necessary for defense purpose;
- Preventive detention (entry 9);
- Foreign affairs (entries 10-21);
- Transportation and communication (entries 22-31).
- Property of the Union (entry 32);
- Financial powers;
- Economic power;.
- Elections Parliamentary affairs etc.
- Judicial powers;
- Residuary powers .

Foreign jurisdiction is a jurisdiction which Indian Government can exercise within another country as per International treaty. Such agreements are governed by Foreign Jurisdiction Act, 1947.

Entering into treaties with Foreign countries: Parliament can enact a Legislation to implement a Treaty or even decisions and non-obligatory recommendations on International organizations and conferences even if the subject matter falls in the State List. Entering into treaty with a foreign country is an executive function of the Central Government. *For example* boundary dispute between India and Pakistan in the Runn of Kutch was decided by Arbitral Tribunal. Supreme Court held that settlement of boundary dispute was not cessation of Indian territory. Hence it could be implemented without a Constitutional amendment.

Inter-State trade and commerce; banking insurance and financial corporations but not including co-operative societies; stock exchange and future markets;

Patents etc.;

Industries declared by law to be expedient in public interest;

Judicial powers like constitution and powers of the Supreme Court and the High Court etc.

List II State List- It consists of 66 subjects. The State has an exclusive power to make laws in respect of subjects in the State List. They are of local importance.

Some of them are:

- Law and order, justice: Public order can be equated with public peace and safety[1]. Supreme Court has held 'law and order' to be broader than 'public order'[2]; police including railway and village police –subject to the provisions of entry 2A of List I; officers and servants of High Court; prisons etc.

1. *Romesh Thappar* v. *State of Madras,* AIR 1950 SC 124: (1950) 51 Cr LJ 1514: 1950 SCR 594.
2. *Ram Manohar Lohia* v. *State of Bihar,* AIR 1966 SC 740: 1966 Cr LJ 608: (1966) 1 SCR 709.

- Health, local Government relief of the disabled etc.
- Libraries, museums, historical monuments other than those declared by the Parliament to be of national importance.
- Communications – roads, bridges etc. not declared in List I
- Land and agriculture.
- Trade, commerce, industry – *i.e.,* inter-State trade and commerce.
- State property.
- Intoxicants.
- Entertainment.
- Elections to State Legislature subject to law made by Parliament.
- State Public services.
- Finance and taxation.

List III: Concurrent List: Both the Parliament and the States can make laws in respect of subjects mentioned in this List- subject to the rule against repugnancy contained in article 254. It comprises 52 items. These are matters where the States and the Centre can have a common interest. When the Centre makes a law regarding a matter in the concurrent list- to that extent the Legislative powers of the State gets curtailed because a State law repugnant (opposed) to the Parliament made law is invalid.

Some of them are:

- Basic procedural and substantive laws and administration of justice. It provides for a uniform framework with a provision for local variations. For example, joint family, succession etc., come under concurrent list. Hindu Succession Act is a Central Act. Karnataka, Maharashtra, Andhra Pradesh, Tamil Nadu amended section 6 to make the daughters also the coparcenors, subject to certain conditions. Later in 2005 the Parliament amended the law on the same lines and brought uniformity throughout India.
- Criminal law including matters included in the Indian Penal Code excluding those specified under List I and II. Public order under List II is different from terrorist activity under List III.
- Removal from one State to another State— of prisoners, accused persons and persons preventively detained in connection with security of the State, maintenance of public order or the maintenance of supplies and services essential to the community.
- Marriage, divorce, infants, minors, adoption, wills.
- Transfer of property other than agricultural lands; registration of deeds and documents.
- Contracts other than those relating to agricultural lands. Law banning prize chits falls under this list.[1]
- Actionable wrongs – *i.e.,* civil wrongs – Torts.

---

1. *Srinivasa Enterprises* v. *Union of India,* AIR 1981 SC 504: (1980) 4 SCC 507: (1981) 1 SCR 801.

- Administration of justice and constitution and organization of all courts except the Supreme Court and the High Courts. It includes the power to create new courts, reorganize the existing courts and alter the pecuniary or territorial jurisdiction of the courts.
- Certain public welfare activities like- nomadic tribes, lunacy, prevention of cruelty to animals, adulteration of foods, drugs and poisons, social security and social insurance.
- Forests.
- Certain aspects of labour Legislations – like trade unions, conditions of work etc.
- Education – this subject has been transferred from List II to List III subject to entries 63-66 of List I. Under entry 66 the Centre has the power to see that a required standard of higher education in India is maintained.
- Economic and social planning – In order to attain welfare for the people. Planning has to be inter-governmental co-operative effort. Hence it is placed in the concurrent list. Term Planning is vagues. The Planning Commission formulates 5 years plans and supervises their implementation by the various Governments.
- Population control and family planning.
- Price control.
- Electricity.
- Communications like ports, shipping.
- Legal, medical and other professions.
- Newspaper books and printing presses.
- Archaeological sites.

It is thus, to be seen that Central Government is vested with vast powers. Some entries in the Union list are so framed that they can be extended by the Centre itself.

Some entries in the State list are subject to entries in the Union or Concurrent list or subject to the law made by the Parliament.

Some entries in the Concurrent list are subject to laws made by the Parliament.

Residuary powers are with the Parliament.

At the same time nation building responsibility is with the States also. *For example,* public health, law and order, agriculture are with the States.

(1) Norms to interpret the entries in the List

The Supreme Court has held that the construction of the entries in the Lists is essentially an interpretation concerning the question of power exercisable by the Union or the State. It said that the subjects are such that for one aspect and one purpose it may fall within the powers of the State but for another purpose and another aspect the same subject may fall within the purview of the Parliament.

Most of the disputes regarding division of powers have been raised by private parties unlike in other Federations where inter-governmental controversies have arisen. The courts have mostly upheld the impugned legislation.

Courts have developed the following norms to interpret the entries in the List—

(a) Substantive power to enact is under article 246

Legislative powers are conferred not by the entries but by article 246. The entries only demarcate the area within which the State Legislature or the Parliament can operate.

(b) Each entry to be interpreted broadly

The entries in various lists must be given the widest possible meaning. A general word used must be extended to cover all ancillary or subsidiary matters which can be reasonably held to be included in it.[1] The courts begin with a presumption that the enactment is constitutional. A strong case has to be made out to hold it unconstitutional. *For example,* List II entry 30 says "Money lending and money-lenders: relief of agricultural indebtedness." Narrowly interpreted it would cover only agricultural debt relief. But it was broadly interpreted to include debt relief to non-agriculturists as well.[2] Thus, the express mention of agricultural indebtedness was held to be only by way of an illustrative example which would cover broader categories.

(c) Punitive measures for enforcing social legislation are part of the ancillary powers

The court held that sections 37 and 46 of the Bombay Sales Tax Act, 1959 which provided for the forfeiture to the Government tax which was illegally collected by dealers was a punitive measure to enforce the Act. The State Legislature was competent to enact it.

(d) The entries are not mutually exclusive

In other words they are not placed in water tight compartments. They are *enumeratio simplex* of broad categories.

(e) Harmonize the entries

Courts must try to harmonise and reconcile the entries. Only when this is not possible – the powers of the Union over-ride that of the State.[3]

(f) Overlapping entries – Harmonious interpretation

Article 246(1) confers exclusive power on the Parliament to legislate relating to matters in List I 'notwithstanding anything in clauses (2) and (3).'[4]

---

1. *Prem Chand Jain* v. *R.K. Chhabra,* AIR 1984 SC 981: 1984 Cr LJ 668: (1984) 2 SCR 883; *Elel Hotels and Investments Ltd.* v. *Union of India,* AIR 1990 SC 1664 (1669): (1989) 3 SCC 698: (1989) 74 STC 146.
2. *Fatehchand Himmatlal* v. *State of Maharashtra,* AIR 1977 SC 1825: 1978 (1) SCJ 1: 79 Bom LR 552.
3. *State of Bombay* v. *F.N. Balsara,* AIR 1951 SC 318 (322): 52 Cr LJ 1361: 1951 SCR 682.
4. Such a clause is known as a *non-obstante* clause. It means – in spite of whatever is contained in clause 2 or 3 – Parliament has powers to legislate on matters in List I.

- The Union List has predominance over the other two Lists;
- The Concurrent List predominates over the State list.
- In case of overlapping between an entry in the Union list and in the State List- the Union list entry prevails over the State List entry to the extent of overlapping.
- In case of overlapping between the entry in the Union list and the Concurrent list- the Union list entry prevails.
- In case of overlapping of Concurrent List and the State List – Concurrent list prevails thus giving both the Parliament and the State to legislate over the subject.

Yet these overlapping rules (*i.e.,* the *non-obstante* clause) must not be applied automatically as soon as some conflict appears. It must be applied only if the conflicting entries cannot be reconciled. This is the rule of harmonious interpretation of the various entries. This can be done by narrowly construing a broad entry or *vice-versa.*

(g) Residuary power of the Parliament – Restricted interpretation

When there is a competition between an entry in the State List and residuary powers of the Parliament under entry 96 List I- the State List must be broadly interpreted and must prevail over the residuary power. Residuary power must be resorted to only as a last measure.[1]

(h) Pith and Substance

Both the State and the Parliament are supreme in their own areas of legislation. Under this rule when the question is whether the Parliament or the State has encroached upon each other's Legislative power the court ascertains.

- The true object of the legislation, and
- Whether it falls within the competence of the Centre or the State as the case may be – if the true object of the Legislature relates to a matter with the competence of Legislature which enacted it – it is held as *intra-vires* though it may incidentally encroach on matters not within the competence of Legislature.
- True character of the legislation has to be ascertained having regard to the Act as a whole, its objects, scope and effect of the provisions. The sections in the Act must not be seen in piecemeal but in its entirety. *For example,* in *Praful Kumar Mukherjee*[2] Bengal Money Lenders Act, 1946 was held to be valid under the Provincial (State) List. Money lending fell in the State list but money lenders commonly take Pro-note as security for the loan. Promissory notes come under Central List. Privy Council held in pith and substance the Act dealt with money lenders

---

1. *International Tourist Corporation* v. *State of Haryana,* AIR 1981 SC 774: (1981) 2 SCC 318: (1981) 2 SCR 364. This case has neutralized the effect of *Union of India* v. *Harbhajan Singh Dhillon,* AIR 1972 SC 1061: (1972) 2 SCR 33: (1971) 2 SCC 779 where residuary powers of the Parliament were given a wide interpretation.
2. AIR 1947 PC 60: 74 Ind App 23: (1947) 2 Mad LJ 6.

and money lending. It was a State subject and hence valid though incidentally it touched Central List *i.e.,* Promissory note.

- Likewise in *State of Bombay* v. *F.N. Balsara*[1] Bombay Prohibition Act prohibited purchase, use possession, sale and transport of liquor. It comes under State List. Though it incidentally encroaches on the Centre's power of imports – it is valid under the doctrine of pith and substance.
- State prohibition law deals in pith and substance with intoxicating liquors and only incidentally with evidence and criminal procedure which comes under concurrent list. Hence it is valid.[2]
- Industrial Disputes Act, deals in pith and substance with industry and labour dispute under Concurrent List and not with local Government – which comes under State List though it also applies to employees of Municipalities.
- State law banning use of amplifiers after 10 p.m. is valid. Purpose is to protect 'health' which comes under State List though it incidentally touches Union List. [Entry 31 List I]
- Object of the Advocates Act, is to provide for a common Bar Council for the whole of India. In pith and substance it deals with qualification, enrolment and discipline of person entitled to practice as Advocate before Supreme Court or the High Court. Act falls under Union List and not State List.

(i) Colorable Legislation

This doctrine is based on the maxim that what the Legislature cannot do directly – it cannot be done indirectly also. The doctrine thus deals with the question of competency of the Legislature to make a law.

Following points are relevant for the purpose of this doctrine:

- Doctrine is in no way concerned with the motives of Legislation *i.e.,* with *bona fides* or *mala fides.* It is beyond court's jurisdiction to enquire into Legislative motive.[3]
- If the Legislature is competent to make law – *mala fide* motive will not take away the competency to make law.[4]
- If the Legislature is not competent to make the law – it will not confer the power to make law even with the best of the motives.
- If the Legislature is competent to do a thing directly then merely because it is attempting to do it indirectly will not make the law invalid.
- Constitutionality of a law depends on the question of Legislative power. Legislature may transgress its legislative power manifestly, patently or directly. The doctrine is not applicable to such transgression.

---

1. AIR 1951 SC 318 (322): 52 Cr LJ 1361: 1951 SCR 682.
2. *A.S. Krishna* v. *State of Madras,* AIR 1957 SC 297: 1957 Cr LJ 409: 1957 SCR 399.
3. *T. Venkata Reddy* v. *State of AP,* AIR 1985 SC 724 (733): 1986 Lab IC 357: (1985) 3 SCC 198.
4. *R.S. Joshi* v. *Ajit Mills Ltd.,* AIR 1977 SC 2279: (1978) 1 SCR 338: 1978 (1) SCJ 239.

- Legislature may transgress its powers indirectly through a disguise. This is known as colourable Legislation. That is – apparently –on the face of it, the Legislature purports to act within limits of its powers but in substance and in reality – it has transgressed its powers.[1] But the transgression is in disguise, hidden or a pretension. It is not explicit on the face of it. What is important is whether it has transgressed its powers under a pretension. Whether it has done so inadvertently or with *mala fide* or *bona fide* motive is immaterial for the purpose of this doctrine. It is a fraud on the Constitution.[2]

In *Naga People's Movement for Human Rights* v. *Union of India*[3] the Supreme Court rejected the argument that Armed Forces (Special Powers) Act, 1958 is a colorable legislation and held that if legislation falls within the competence of the Legislature, question of doing something indirectly which cannot be done directly does not arise.

For example State of Bihar v. *Kameshwar Singh*[4] is the only example of colourable legislation. Bihar Land Reforms Act, 1950 was held void on the ground that it apparently purported to lay down principles for determining compensation. In reality, it did not lay down any such principle and this indirectly sought to deprive the petitioner of any compensation.

The law provided for abolition of landlord system. It provided that arrears of rent due to the landlord before acquisition date would vest in the State and half of arrears would be given to landlords as compensation. Provision was held to be a colourable legislation for it meant taking half the arrears without giving any compensation. It amounted to confiscation of half the amount.

In *S.S. Bola* v. *B.D. Sardana*[5] it was held that if there is a colourable legislation-the law is void to that extent.

D. Repugnancy between the Central and the State Law (Article 254)

State law is void if it is repugnant to Central law. Following are the provisions of article 245—

1. If the State law:
   - is repugnant to a provision of law made by the Parliament which Parliament is competent to enact, or
   - to any provision of an existing law with respect to matters in Concurrent List

   — then the Parliament made law prevails over the State made law. It is immaterial whether Parliament has passed the law before or

1. *Jalan Trading Co.* v. *Mill Mazdoor Sabha*, AIR 1967 SC 691: 1967 (1) SCA 338: (1967) 1 SCR 15; *Jabalpur Bus Operators' Association* v. *Union of India*, AIR 1994 MP 62: 1994 (1) ACC 265: 1993 MPLJ 992.
2. *R.S. Joshi* case *supra* note 26. It is submitted that calling it a fraud will require proving the malintention on the part of the Legislature. Under the doctrine motives or intention should not be a part of any enquiry at all. What is to be addressed is the objective question whether the subject legislated falls within the relevant entry or not.
3. AIR 1998 SC 431: 1998 AIR SCW 8: (1998) 2 SCC 109.
4. AIR 1952 SC 252: 1952 SCR 889: 1952 SCJ 427.
5. AIR 1997 SC 3127.

after State made law or the existing law. Existing law means any law, Ordinance, order, bye-law, rule or regulation passed or made before the commencement of our Constitution by any Legislature, authority or person having power to make such law, Ordinance etc. State made law is not totally void. It is void only to the extent of repugnancy subject to clause (2) of article 245. [Article 254(1)]

2. If the provision in the State made law is repugnant to the provision of an earlier law made by the Parliament or the existing law with respect to that matter and the State law is reserved for consideration by the President and received his assent then such State made law prevails in that State. [Article 254(2]

However this provision does not prevent Parliament from enacting at any time any law with respect to the same matter including a law adding to or amending varying or repealing the State made law.

This makes Parliament's power to legislate on concurrent list supreme. Article 254(1) is applicable only when there is an inconsistency between a Central law and the State law relating to a subject in concurrent list.[1]

The test of repugnancy was summarized in *M. Karunanidhi* v. *Union of India*[2]. Following are the relevant principles:

1. There must be a clear case of inconsistency between State and Central Act such that they cannot stand together.
2. There can be no repeal by implication unless the inconsistency appears on the face of the two statutes.
3. If the two statutes occupy a particular field, but there is no possibility of both statutes operating in the same field- no repugnancy results.
4. Where there is no inconsistency but the statute occupying the same field create distinct and separate offences.

E. Administrative relations (Article 256-263)

For effective working of the Federal system the framers of the Constitution have made provisions for all possible eventualities resulting from the working of the federalism principle. The Union has control over the States even during normal times. In emergency the Government of India takes complete control over the State as if it is a unitary Government.

---

1. *Vijay Kumar Sharma* v. *State of Karnataka*, AIR 1990 SC 2072: JT 1990 (2) SC 448: 1991 AIR SCW 1697.

   Note that on a plain reading of Article 254(1) it appears that if there is a conflict between a Central law and a State law concerning an 'existing law'(pre-constitution law) in the Concurrent list, Central law will prevail. But if there is a conflict between a post – Constitution law 'which Parliament is competent to enact' – (which means either the Union List or the Concurrent List) – then the Central law will prevail over the State law, whether the matter comes under the Union List or the Concurrent List. But the judiciary has held that repugnancy arises only when there is a conflict between State and the Central law in the Concurrent List.

2. AIR 1979 SC 898: 1979 Cr LJ 773: (1979) 3 SCC 431.

(1) Control of the Union over the State

(a) Direction by the Union to the State Governments

(b) Delegation of Union functions to the States

(c) All-India services

(d) Grants-in-Aid

(a) Direction by the Union to the State Governments

This idea of Union issuing directions to the States is taken from the Government of India Act, 1935. Power to issue directions is given to the Union under article 256. Actual directions are given under article 237.

Article 256 provides that the Executive power of the State shall be so exercised as to ensure that the State complies with laws made by the Parliament. Executive power of the Union shall extend to giving such directions to the State as may be necessary for the purpose.

Under article 257 the States must so exercise their Executive power as not to impede the exercise of the Executive power of the Union in the State. The Union can give directions to the State as to the manner in which it should exercise its Executive power.

The powers of the Central Government extends to giving directions to the State in two specific matters:

- Construction and maintenance of means of communication which are declared to be of national or military importance.
- Measures to be taken for the protection of Railways within the States.
- The power of giving directions does not affect the power of the Parliament to declare highways and waterways to be National Highways or Waterways and to construct and maintain means of communication as part of its functions with respect to Naval, Military or Air Force works.

If in carrying out the directions of the Union Government the State incurs additional costs the Union Government shall pay to the State Government such sum as may be agreed. If they do not reach upon an agreement the matter is referred to the arbitrator to be appointed by the Chief Justice of India. [Article 257(4)]

If the State fails to comply with the directions or fails to give effect to any directions given by the Union Government then the President is empowered to declare an emergency to the effect that the State Government cannot be carried on in accordance with the provisions of the Constitution and assume all functions of the State. (Article 356)

(b) Delegation of Union's functions to the State

Under article 258 the Parliament may, *with the consent of the State* Government entrust either conditionally or unconditionally to that Government or its offices functions relating to any matter falling within the Executive powers of the Union. [Article 258(1).]

Parliament is also empowered to use State machinery for the enforcement of Union laws and for this purpose may confer powers or impose duties upon the State or its officers to see that the laws are made applicable to the State. Note that under this clause [Article 258(2)] the delegation of power is made without the consent of the State.

The State Government also can delegate its powers to the Union Government. Under article 258A the Governor of a State can, with the consent of the Government of India entrust to the Government or its officers functions relating to any matter to which the Executive power of that Government extends.

(c) All India Services

Article 312 provides for the creation of 'All India Services' common to the Union and the States. If the Rajya Sabha passes a resolution supported by not less than 2/3rd of the members present and voting that it is necessary or expedient in the Nation's interest to do so, Parliament may create an All India Service. This ensures greater inter-State co-ordination and implementation of the policies of the Central Government through its officers.

(d) Grants-in-Aid

They augment the financial requirements of the State which have to undertake a great many activities for social upliftment. Grants can be subject to conditions. It enables Centre to exercise control over the States and encourages Centre-State co-ordination and co-operation.

Public records, public acts, and judicial proceedings of the Union and the State are given full faith and credit under article 261. Final judgments and orders delivered and passed by civil courts in any part of the territory of India shall be capable of execution anywhere within that territory according to law.

(2) Disputes relating to waters

Article 262 authorises the Parliament to provide for the adjudication of any dispute or complaint with respect to the use, distribution or control of the waters of, or in, any inter-State river or river valley. Under clause (2) Parliament may provide that notwithstanding anything in the Constitution, neither the Supreme Court nor any other Court shall exercise jurisdiction in respect of any such dispute or complaint. The Parliament has passed River Board Act, 1956 for the regulation and development of inter State rivers and river valleys. It has also passed the Inter-State Water Disputes Act, 1956 which empowers the Central Government to set up a Tribunal for the adjudication of such disputes.

(3) Co-ordination between States Co-operative Federalism (Article 263)

In a Federal Constitution the Union and the States are independent and supreme in their own sphere. Yet for the effective functioning of the federal system co-ordination between the Union and the States is a pre-requirement. This co-ordination is known as co-operative federalism which is ensured through Inter-State Councils established under article 263.

(4) Inter-State Council

The Inter-State Council is appointed by the President if it appears to him that the public interest would be served by its establishment. It is charged with the following duties:

(a) Inquiring into and advising upon the disputes which may arise between States.

(b) Investigating and discussing subjects in which some or all the States of the Union and one or more of States have common interest.

(c) Making recommendation on any subject and for the better co-ordination of the policy and action with respect to that subject.

The Council has an advisory function.

Under the States Reorganisation Act, 1951, five Zones have been set-up – the Central, Northern Western, Eastern, Southern Zones. They promote co-operation and make efforts to solve problems of the member-States. It consists of the Union Home Minister as *ex-officio* Chairman of the Council, the Chief Minister and two other Ministers nominated by the Governor of the member State.

Sarkaria Commission has strongly recommended for the establishment of an inter-State Council to effect co-ordination between States.

President has constituted the Inter-State Council in 1990 consisting of the following members: Prime Minister, Chief Ministers of all States, Chief Ministers of Union Territories having a Legislative Assembly and administrators of Union Territories not having a Legislative Assembly, 6 ministers of Cabinet rank in the Union Council of Ministers to be nominated by the Prime Minister. The Ministers of State having independent charge in the Union Government may be invited when any item relating to their Ministry is to be discussed.

Prime Minister shall be the Chairman of the Inter-State Council and preside over the meetings.

F. Duties of the Council

The council shall be a recommendatory body and it shall perform the following duties:

a) Investigate and discuss subjects of common interest.

b) Make recommendations for the better co-ordination of policy and actions on such subjects.

c) Deliberate on such matters of general interest to the States referred by the Chairman to the Council.

The Council must meet atleast three times in every year; proceedings are held *in camera;* all the members including the Chairman shall form the questions for the meeting and all the questions shall be decided by consensus.

The Council shall have a secretariat consisting of such officers and staff as the Chairman thinks fit to appoint.

G. Financial relations between the Union and the State (Article 264-291)

"No system of Federation can be successful unless both Union and the States have at their disposal adequate financial resources to enable them to discharge their respective responsibilities under the Constitution."[1]

The Scheme of distribution of sources of revenue between the States and the Centre is based on the scheme laid down in the Government of India Act, 1935.

1. Basu, D.D.: Introduction of the Constitution of India p. 141.

(1) Finance Commission

The Constitution under article 280 provides for the appointment of Finance Commission within two years of the commencement of the Constitution and thereafter at the expiry of every 5th year or at such earlier time as the President considers it necessary. It consists of the Chairman and four other members appointed by the President. The Finance Commission has to (i) recommend to the President the requisite changes to be made in the distribution of taxes between the Union and the States. (ii) to define the principles on which the Union Government has to make grants-in-aid to the States. The Constitution thus introduces a unique element of flexibility while tackling the problems of public revenues. No other Federal Constitution makes such elaborate provisions as our Constitution regarding the Financial relation between the Union and the States. In fact by providing for the establishment of Finance Commission for allocating and readjusting receipt from certain sources the Constitution has made an original contribution in this complicated aspect of Federal relationship.[1]

(2) Taxation only by authority of law (Article 256)

No tax can be collected except by the authority of law. No tax can be imposed by an executive order. The law providing for imposition of tax must be a valid law *i.e.,* it should not be prohibited by the provisions of the Constitution. (*e.g.,* article 276-285). Tax law must not violate article 14.[2]

(a) Tax and fee – Distinguished

(1) The prohibition that no tax can be levied or collected without the authority of law is applicable only to taxes and not to fees. Tax is a common burden and the only return the tax payer gets is the participation in the common benefit of the State.

(2) Tax is compulsory exaction of money by public authority for public purposes. The payment is enforceable by law. Fee is a payment for services rendered, benefit provided or privilege conferred. The *quid pro quo i.e.,* the consideration need not be direct, it can be a mere casual relation with the service rendered. It can be a general benefit received.[3]

(b) Regulatory and compensatory licence fees

In *Secunderabad Hyderabad Hotel Owners' Association* v. *Hyderabad Municipal Corporation, Hyderabad*[4] the Supreme Court has held that a licence fee may be either regulatory or compensatory. When a fee is charged for specific services rendered in return, there is a consideration element but it need not be arithmetically equivalent to the service rendered. Licence fees are regulatory when they are charged for regulation of a particular activity without any service being rendered. In this case the licence fees for running a lodging and eating house was increased. It was challenged as there was no *quid pro quo* between the fee charged and the service rendered to them. It was held that the fee was

1. Pylee: Constitutional Government in India, p. 544.
2. *Commissioner, Hindu Religious Endowments, Madras* v. *Lakshmindra Thirtha Swamiar of Sri Shirur Mutt,* AIR 1954 SC 282: 1954 SCA 415: 1954 SCR 1005.
3. *Municipal Corpn. of the City of Baroda* v. *Babubhai Himatlal,* AIR 1989 SC 2091.
4. AIR 1999 SC 635: 1999 AIR SCW 286: (1999) 2 SCC 274.

a regulatory fee for which no *quid pro quo was* necessary though it should not be unreasonable.

(3) Double taxation

Article 265 does not prohibit double taxation.

(4) Distribution of Revenues between the Union and the State

Article 268 provides the scheme for distribution of the revenue between the Union and the States. States and the Union possess exclusive jurisdiction over the taxes enumerated in the State and the Union list respectively. The concurrent list includes no taxes. While the proceeds of the taxes in the State list are entirely retained by the States but the proceeds of some of the taxes in the Union list may be allowed – wholly or partially to the States.

Union taxes assigned to the States: Following are the Union taxes which are wholly or partially assigned to the States:

(a) Duties levied by the Union but collected and appropriated by the States

Under article 268 stamp duties and duties of Excise on medicinal and toilet preparations mentioned in the Union list shall be levied by the Central Government. These duties are collected by the States within which such duties are leviable. The proceeds of such duties are assigned to the States.

(b) Service tax levied by Union and collected and are appropriated by Union and State

as per the principles laid down by the Parliament by law. Article 268A (by 88th Amendment Act, 2003).

(c) Taxes levied and collected by the Union and assigned to the States

Article 269 (80th Amendment 2000): It provides that taxes on the sale or purchase of goods and taxes on the assignment of goods shall be levied and collected by the Government of India but shall be assigned and deemed to have been assigned to the States on or after 1-4-1996 in the manner prescribed by the Parliament by law. The expression 'taxes on the sale or purchase of goods' shall not include 'taxes on sale and purchase of newspapers' where it takes in the course of inter-state trade or commerce.

Net proceeds in any financial year of any such duty or tax do not form part of the Consolidated Fund of India, but are to be assigned to the States within which that duty or tax is leviable in that year and are to be distributed amongst those States in accordance with the principles of distribution as formulated by the Parliament by law. Parliament may by law formulate principles for determining when a sale or purchase of goods takes place in the course of inter-State trade or commerce.

(d) Taxes levied by the Union but distributed between Union and States

Article 270 as amended by 80th Amendment. It provides that all taxes and duties referred to in the Union list except:

(i) The duties referred to in articles 268, 269

(ii) Surcharge on taxes and duties referred to in article 271

(iii) Any cess levied for specific purposes by any law made by Parliament – are to be levied and collected by the Government of India and distributed between the Union and the States in the prescribed manner.

Such percentage as may be prescribed of the net proceeds in any financial year is not to form part of the Consolidated Fund of India but is to be assigned to the States within which the tax is leviable in that year and is to be distributed among those States in such manner or from such time as may be prescribed.

(e) Grant from the Union to the States

Article 275 empowers the Parliament to aid needy States by grants known as 'grants-in-aid' given to such States. It provides that such sums as Parliament or the President may by law provide are to be charged on the Consolidated Fund of India in each year as Grants-in-Aid of the revenues of such States as Parliament may determine to be in need of the assistance and different sums may be fixed for different States including Assam. But after a Finance Commission has been constituted no order can be made by the President except after considering the recommendations of the Finance Commission.

The Union or a State may make any grants for any public purpose notwithstanding that the purpose is not one with respect to which Parliament or the Legislature of the State - as the case may be – may make laws. (Article 282).

(5) Tax on Union Property

Property of the Union is exempted from all taxation by the State or any other authority within the State except as may be provided by the Parliament by law. (Article 285)

(6) Taxes on Electricity

No taxes on electricity consumed by the Union in the States or sold to the Government of India for consumption of the Union Government shall be taxed. It may be electricity produced by State agency or any other independent power producers.

This exemption includes power consumed in the constitution, maintenance or operation of any railway by the Government of India or a railway company operating that railway or sold to that Government or any such railway company for consumption in the construction, maintenance or operation of any railway.

(7) Taxes on water

Exemption of taxation by State in respect of water or electricity in certain cases (article 288) – it provides detailed provisions for not taxing electricity for projects regulating or developing any inter-State river or river valley.

(8) Property tax

Exemption of property and income of a State from Union taxation (article 289). Property and income of a State are exempted from Union taxation. (Clause 1)

Nothing in clause 1 above prevents the Union from imposing or authorizing the imposition of any tax to such extent if any as Parliament may by law provide in respect of a trade or business or any kind carried on by or on behalf of

Government of the State or any operation connected therewith or any property used or occupied for the purposes of such trade or business or income accruing or arising in connection therewith. (Clause 2)

Nothing in clause 2 above applies to any trade or business or any class of trade or business which Parliament may by law declare to be incidental to the ordinary functions of the Government.

(9) Borrowings by the Union and the States

Article 292 deals with the powers of the Union to borrow and article 293 deals with borrowing by States.

1. Executive power of the Union extends to borrowing upon the security of the consolidated fund of India and to the giving of guarantees within such limits as may be fixed.
2. Power of the State to borrow [Article 293(1)]: Executive power of the State extends to borrowing within India upon the security of the consolidated funds of the State within limits fixed by the Legislature and to the giving of guarantees within such limits as may be so fixed.
3. Power of the Union to make loans [Article 293(2)]: Government of India may make loan to any State or give guarantees in respect of loans raised by any State or any sums required for the purpose of making such loans is to be charged on the consolidated funds of India.
4. Power of State to raise loans [Article 293(3)]: a State cannot without the consent of India raise any loan if there is still outstanding any part of the loan which has been made to the State by the Government of India or by its predecessor Government or in respect of which a guarantee has been given by the Government of India.

CHAPTER 26

PROPERTY, CONTRACTS, RIGHTS, LIABILITIES, OBLIGATIONS AND SUITS

(Articles 294-300)

SYNOPSIS

A. Introduction

The State is the largest litigant with the new set up established after the independence.

State liability under the Constitutional provisions is to be studied under two main heads:

1. Liability under contracts and 2. Liability under Torts.

B. Liability under Contracts

Government liability under contract arises if the following conditions mentioned under article 299 are satisfied:

1. All contracts made in exercise of the Executive power of the Union or of a State must be made by the President or by the Governor of the State as the case may be.
2. All such contracts and all assurances of property must be executed on behalf of the President or the Governor by such persons and in such manner as he may direct or authorise. [Article 299(1)]

Failure to comply with these conditions nullifies the contract and renders it void and unenforceable. It cannot be ratified[1] and there is no question of estoppel.

(1) Liability of State same as of the individual

The contractual liability of the State under the Constitution is the same as that of the individual under ordinary law of contracts. The liability of the States is exactly the same as that of the East India Company before 1858.

1. Ratification: The act is already done and validated by complying with the conditions on a future date but effect is given from the past date on which the act of contracting was done.

(2) No personal liability of the President or the Governor

Neither the President nor the Governor is personally liable in respect of any contract or assurance made or executed in the exercise of that power nor is any person making or executing any such contract or assurance on behalf of any of them personally liable in respect thereof. (Article 299(2)

(3) Suits and proceedings

Under article 300 the Government of India or the State Government may sue or be sued by the name of Union of India or the State Government as the case may be - subject to the *provisions made by the* Act of the Parliament or the Legislature as the case may be. The Union and the States are juristic persons capable of entering into contracts and incurring liabilities and capable of suing and being sued. The Government of India can be sued in relation to their affairs in the like cases as the Dominion of India might have been sued if this Constitution had not been enacted. The position remains the same as it existed before the commencement of the Constitution so long as Parliament does not make a law providing otherwise.

C. Liability under Torts

Tort is a civil wrong. It entitles the person wronged to damages (compensation) from the wrongdoer. As the Parliament has not made any law regulating this aspect, the question whether a suit would lie against the Government has to be decided by seeing whether in a similar case a suit would lie against the Dominion of India before the Constitution came into force.

Before the Constitution came into force the East India Company and after the Constitution of India Act, 1858 the Secretary of State Council were liable for the tortous acts of their servants committed in the course of their employment.

(1) Sovereign and non-sovereign functions

The first leading case on the point is *P&O Steam Navigation Co.* v. *Secy. of State*[1] it was held that

(a) The Secretary of State was not liable for anything done in exercise of sovereign functions. Sovereign functions are functions which can be exercised only by a sovereign or a private individual to whom sovereign functions are delegated.

(b) But the Secretary of State would be liable for damages in respect of acts done which could also be done by private individuals without any sovereign power.

In this case the horses of the plaintiff were injured by the negligence of Government workmen engaged in non-sovereign functions. Hence the Government was liable to pay damages.[2]

After the Constitution came into force the first case on the point is *State of Rajasthan* v. *Vidyawati*[3] a driver of a jeep owned and maintained by the State of

1. (1861) 5 Bom HCR App 1: Bourke AOC 166.
2. Note the difference between 'damage'- which means injury; and 'damages' which means 'compensation'.
3. AIR 1962 SC 933: 1962 (2) SCA 362: (1962) Supp 2 SCR 989.

Rajasthan drove rashly and negligently while bringing it back from repairs and fatally injured a pedestrian. The State was held to be vicariously liable[1] because the negligent act was a non-sovereign function. It also observed that the objective of the Republican Government is to establish a socialistic State with its varied industrial and other activities employing a large army of servants. Hence there is no justification in principle or in public interest that the State should not be held liable vicariously for the tortous act of its servant.

In *Kasturilal Ralia Ram Jain* v. *State of U.P.*, (1965) 1 SCR 375: AIR 1965 SC 1039: ILR (1965) 2 All 175 police seized gold from Kasturilal on suspicion that it was stolen property. It was kept in Government *malkhana* but was misappropriated by a constable who fled to Pakistan. Kasturilal was acquitted of the charges. He filed a case for return of the gold and silver and in the alternative for damages. Supreme Court held that he was not entitled for damages as the act complained of was related to the sovereign function.

(2) Rejection of the doctrine of sovereign immunity

In *Nagendra Rao & Co.* v. *State of Andhra Pradesh*, 1994 AIR SCW 3753: AIR 1994 SC 2663: (1994) 6 SCC 205 the Court rejected the doctrine of sovereign immunity and held that distinction between sovereign and non-sovereign functions no longer exists. In this case huge stocks of fertiliser, food grains and even non-essential goods were seized by the Police Inspector, Vigilance Cell. It was placed in the custody of Asst Agricultural Officer under section 6A of the Essential Commodities Act. After the inquiry it was found that the appellant was guilty only of improper maintenance of accounts. Hence the Collector ordered the release of the seized grains. But the stock was all spoilt. It was held that State was vicariously liable for the negligence of its officers in discharge of public duty conferred on them under a statute. No legal system can place the State above law as it is unjust for a citizen to be deprived of his property illegally by the negligent act of the officers of the State and go without a remedy.[2]

In *Common Cause, a Regd. Society* v. *Union of India*[3] Supreme Court held that the doctrine of sovereign immunity laid down in *P&O Steam Navigation Company* is outmoded. With increase in the State activities it is difficult to draw a line between its sovereign and non-sovereign functions. The State must be liable for all tortous acts of its servants. The Law Commission drafted a Bill to define the scope of the State's tortous liability but no law has yet been enacted for the purpose.

The Courts have held many modern functions as 'non-sovereign'- for example Running of bus service by the State, Banking business run by the State, Activities of Public Works Department, Construction of reservoir to facilitate drinking water, Famine relief work.

In *State of Andhra Pradesh* v. *Challa Ramkrishna Reddy*[4] Supreme Court held that *Kasturilal case* has paled into insignificance. A prisoner had asked for protection

1. Under vicarious liability – one person is liable for the negligent act of another *e.g.*, master liable for the servant's act or the Principal liable for the negligent act of his agent.
2. 1994 AIR SCW 3753: AIR 1994 SC 2663: (1994) 6 SCC 205.
3. AIR 1999 SC 2979: 1999 AIR SCW 2899: (1999) 6 SCC 667.
4. AIR 2000 SC 2083: 2000 AIR SCW 1923: (2000) 5 SCC 712.

as he apprehended danger to his life. He was killed within the prison and even a police was a party to the conspiracy to murder. Court held that it was a case of violation of Fundamental right and hence the defence of sovereign immunity was not acceptable. Personal liberty must be given preference over sovereign immunity.

In Rudal Saha v. *State of Bihar*[1] he was kept in jail for 14 years after his acquittal. State of Bihar was directed to pay Rajya Sabha, 75,000 to the victim of tortous act done by the Government employees while discharging sovereign functions. Other examples are: Rs. 75,000 compensation awarded for illegal arrest and detention in police custody and deliberately preventing from attending Assembly session.[2]

D. Vesting of property in Government (Articles 294-297)

All property and assets which vested in His Majesty for the purpose of Government of the Dominion of India and all property and assets which were vested in His Majesty for the purpose of the Government of each Governor's Province, vest respectively in the Union and the corresponding State. All rights, liabilities and obligations of the Government of the Dominion of India and of the Government of each Governor's promise whether arising out of Contract or otherwise become the rights, liabilities and obligations respectively of the Government of India and the Government of each corresponding State subject to the adjustment made or to be made by reason of the creation of the Dominion of Pakistan. (Article 294)

Similarly all property and assets which were vested in the Indian State vest in the Union. (Article 295)

So also any property in India which, if this Constitution had not come into operation would have accrued to His Majesty or to the Ruler of the Indian State by escheat or lapse or as *bona vacantia* for want of a rightful owner— vests in such a State where the property is situated in that State and in any other case in the Union.

Escheat: It takes place when a man dies intestate (without leaving a Will) without heirs and leaves property.

Lapse: Certain funds lapse to the Government if the rightful owners do not claim them within certain period. *For example* – Court deposits.

Bona Vacantia: It means that there is no apparent rightful claimant to the property in which case the property accrues to the Government.

Likewise all lands, minerals, and other things of value underlying the ocean within the territorial waters of India or the Continental Shelf of India or the exclusive economic zone of India vest in the Union and are held for the purposes of Union.

---

1. AIR 1983 SC 1086: 1983 Cr LJ 1644: (1983) 4 SCC 141.
2. *Bhim Singh* v. *State of Jammu and Kashmir*, AIR 1986 SC 494: 1986 Cr LJ 192: (1985) 4 SCC 677.

CHAPTER 27

CONSTITUTIONAL RIGHT TO PROPERTY

Article 300A

SYNOPSIS

A. Introduction

Right to property has undergone quite a substantial change after the Constitution 44th Amendment in 1978. It has taken away the right to property from the category of Fundamental rights and has made it a right to be regulated by ordinary law. It has repealed article 19(1)(f) and article 31. It has inserted article 300A under the Heading 'right to property' in Part XII of the Constitution. It provides that 'no person shall be deprived of his property save by the authority of law.' The safeguards regarding acquisition of property of an educational institution run by a minority are now incorporated in article 30 by the addition of a new clause (1A).

Right to property can be studied under two headings—

(1) Position before the 44th Amendment, and

(2) Position after the 44th Amendment.

B. Position before the 44th Amendment

(i) Article 19(1)(f) guaranteed the Fundamental right to 'acquire, hold and dispose of property. However under article 19(5) the State could make reasonable restrictions on the exercise of the right to property in the interests of the general public or for the protection of the interests of the Scheduled Tribes.

(ii) Article 31 before its deletion laid down that:

(a) No person shall be deprived of his property save by the authority of law.

(b) No property shall be compulsorily acquired or requisitioned save for a *public purpose* and save by authority of a law which provides for compensation for the property so acquired or requisitioned, and either fixes the amount of compensation or specifies the principles on which and the manner in which the compensation is to be determined and given. No such law shall be called in question in any Court on the ground that the compensation provided by that law is not adequate. (Article 31(2))

(3) In the *Bank Nationalisation* case[1] the court laid down two important principles *viz.*, that the compensation under article 31 must be 'just' compensation. If no method of valuation is laid down or if such method is not reasonable the courts could interfere in the matter. The second principle laid down was that any acquisition of property must satisfy article 31(2) and also article 19(1)(f).

(4) The Parliament reacted by passing the 25th Amendment to the Constitution. The word 'compensation' was replaced by the word 'amount'. Such amount could be paid 'otherwise than by cash'. The Amendment further provided that article 19(1)(f) was not applicable to any law relating to the acquisition or requisition of property for a public purpose.

(5) After this Amendment article 31(2) stood as follows:

No property shall be compulsorily acquired or requisitioned save for a *public purpose and save by authority of a law* providing for such acquisition or requisition of property for an amount which may be fixed by such law or determined in accordance with such principles and given in such manner as may be specified in such law. *No such law can be called in question in any Court on the ground that the amount so fixed or determined is not adequate* or that the whole or part of such amount is to be given otherwise than in cash.

(6) This Amendment was challenged in *Keshavanand Bharati* case[2]. The full Bench upheld this Amendment. However the Court could determine whether the amount paid for property acquired by the Government is or is not adequate or whether it is arbitrary.

Where law does not provide for transfer of ownership or right to possession of any property to the State – it shall not be deemed to provide for compulsory acquisition even if it deprives a person of his property.

If the law relating to compulsory acquisition or requisition of property is passed by the State Legislature – it needs the assent of the President.

What is important is that property could be acquired compulsorily only for a *public purpose* and Courts could enquire whether there is in fact a public purpose in acquiring property. In *State of Bihar* v. *Kameshwar Singh*[3] Supreme Court held that definition of 'public purpose' is elastic and the concept changes with time and the needs of the society.

It was held in *State of West Bengal* v. *Subodh Gopal*[4] *that* there cannot be deprivation of property by an executive order.

1. *R.C. Cooper* v. *Union of India, AIR 1970 SC 564: (1970) 1 SCC 248: (1970) 3 SCR 530.*
2. AIR 1973 SC 1461: (1973) 4 SCC 225: 1973 Supp SCR 1.
3. AIR 1952 SC 252: 1952 SCR 889: 1952 SCJ 427.
4. AIR 1954 SC 92: 1954 SCA 65: 1954 SCR 587.

C. Position after the 44th Amendment

It brought about a drastic change in the right to property. A new chapter – Chapter IV was introduced in Part XII of the Constitution. It contains a new article 300A – 'no person shall be deprived of his property save by authority of law.

Its effect – in short is as follows:

(1) Right to property is no more a Fundamental right. It is now a Constitutional right.

(2) 300A is identical with the former article 31(1). Hence comments and judicial observations on article 31(1) hold good for article 300A subject to the fact that the right is no more a Fundamental right.

(3) In *Jijubhai Nanbhai Khachar* v. *State of Gujarat*[1] it has been held that right to property guaranteed by article 300A is not a basic feature of the Constitution and hence it can be amended by the Constitution.

(4) Meaning of 'property'- Supreme Court has said that the term 'property' must be given a liberal meaning. It should be extended to all those well recognised types of interest which have the *insignia* characteristics of property right. It includes both corporeal and incorporeal right. It includes money, contract, interest in property. *For example,* interest of an allottee, licensee, mortgagee or lessee of property. The *mahantship* of a Hindu temple and shareholders interest in a company are recognisable interest in property.

5. Right to receive pension is property.

D. Eminent Domain

In *Charanjeet Lal* v. *Union of India*[2]: Every Government has an inherent right to take and appropriate the private property belonging to individual citizens for public purpose. This power is known as *Eminent domain* .It is an offspring of political necessity. The right rests on the maxim *salus populi est superma lex. i.e.,* the welfare of the people or public is the paramount law and also on the maxim *necessita public major est quam i.e.,* public necessity is greater than private necessity. Thus property may be needed and hence Government may acquire it for Government office, libraries, slum clearance projects, public schools, colleges and Universities etc.

---

1. AIR 1995 SC 142: 1994 AIR SCW 4181: JT 1994 (4) SC 473.
2. AIR 1951 SC 41: 1951 SCJ 29: 1950 SCR 869.

CHAPTER 28

FREEDOM OF TRADE, COMMERCE AND INTERCOURSE

(Articles 301-307)

SYNOPSIS

A. Introduction

The Constitution has made provisions for preventing local barriers to economic activity in the country in order to ensure economic unity in the country. Economic unity is the backbone of political freedom. This has been done by providing for free movement of goods throughout the territory of India.

The framers of the Constitution seem to have kept in view three aspects while framing the provisions: (a) there must be free flow of trade – both intra and inter-State; (b) the regional interests must not be ignored; (c) Centre must have power of intervention in any case of crisis to deal with particular problems which may arise in any part of India.[1]

B. Provisions pertaining to trade, commerce, and intercourse

Articles 301-307 deal with domestic trade and commerce.

1. Subject to other provisions of Part XII, trade, commerce and intercourse throughout the territory of India shall be free. It includes the freedom of inter-State and intra-State trade covering all lawful activities. 'Trade' covers all forms of buying and selling. 'Commerce' covers all forms of transportation by land, sea and air. Term 'intercourse' means movement of goods from one place to another place. The sweep of 'trade, commerce and intercourse is very wide. It includes all activities in relation to buying and selling, or interchange or exchange of commodities and that movement from place to place is the very soul of such trading activities. Prize competitions which are in the nature of gambling activities are not covered by article 301. This article is based on the model of the Australian Constitution with the difference that in Australia- trade or commerce is 'absolutely free'- which means that the State can place no restrictions which created difficulties in that country.

---

1. *Automobile Transport Ltd.* v. *State of Rajasthan,* AIR 1962 SC 1406: 1962 (2) SCA 35: (1963) 1 SCR 491.

C. Exceptions to freedom of trade etc.

Articles 302-304 are exceptions to article 301. They provide circumstances under which restrictions can be imposed on the freedom of trade:

(1) *In public interest:* Parliament may impose such restrictions on the freedom of trade as may be required in *public interest.* (Article 302). But neither the Parliament nor the State Legislature has power to make any law giving any preference to one State over another or to make any discrimination between one State and another article 303.

It is relevant to note that after the signing of GATT we have thrown our economy open to the world at large. Let alone ban against discrimination between inter-States within the country or intra-State— under the concept of 'National Treatment – non-discrimination within a country' there can be no discrimination on goods produced within the country and the foreign goods.[1]

(2) *In public interest – previous sanction of the President:* State Legislature also can impose reasonable restriction in *public interest* on the freedom of trade, commerce or intercourse within or outside that State. (Article 304). However no Bill or Amendment can be introduced or moved in a State Legislature without the previous sanction of the President. (proviso to article 304)

(3) *No discrimination allowed:* The State Legislature may by law impose on goods *imported from other States or the Union Territories* tax to which *similar goods* manufactured or produced in that State are subject, in such a manner as not to discriminate between goods so imported and goods so manufactured or produced. (Article 304). The idea is that there must be no discrimination between goods manufactured in a State and imported from another State in the interest of the unity of the country.

Parliament may appoint an appropriate authority for carrying out the purposes of articles 301 to 304 and confer on the authority so appointed such powers and duties as it thinks necessary. (Article 307)

D. Article 19(1)(g) and Article 301

The relationship is somewhat uncertain.

(a) One view is that article 19(1)(g) deals with the rights of the citizens; whereas article 301 provides safeguards for carrying on the trade. But Supreme Court did not agree that article 301 provides freedom in the 'abstract' and in fact people have challenged laws on the ground of its effect on their right to carry on trade and commerce.[2]

---

1. Para 4 of the article III of GATT 1994 stipulates "the products of the territory of any contracting party imported into the territory of any other contracting party shall be accorded no less favourable treatment than that accorded to like products of national origin in respect of all laws, regulations, and requirements affecting their internal sale, offering for sale, purchase, transportation, distribution or use."
2. *District Collector of Hyderabad* v. *Ibrahim and Co.*, AIR 1970 SC 1275: 1970 (2) SCJ 609: (1970) 3 SCR 498.

(b) The second view is on the 'volume of trade' theory. That is, article 301 prohibits restriction on the volume of trade flowing through the country. This theory is rejected. It creates many difficulties including ascertaining the volume of trade before and after the challenged statute which is alleged to restrict trade.

(c) The third view is that article 301 can be invoked only when an individual is prevented from sending his goods across the State or from one point to another in the same State while article 19(1)(g) can be invoked when the complaint is with regard to right of the individual to carry on trade irrespective of the movement of the goods. Article 301 contemplates the right of 'trade in motion' *i.e.* It is invoked when one is prevented from sending his goods across the State etc.

(d) Article 19(1)(g) guarantees the freedom to practice any trade, profession or business etc., to the citizens. It is a Fundamental right. Article 301 confers a statutory right which can be claimed by non-citizens also. As it is not a Fundamental right it cannot be enforced by a writ under article 32 as in the case of article 19(1)(g).

(e) Article 301 says 'trade *throughout* the territory of India shall be free' whereas article 19(1)(g) gives the freedom to carry on any trade etc *'within'* the territory of India. Word 'throughout' and the word 'within' have different connotations. *'Throughout' means from one point to another. 'Within' means 'anywhere in India. Word 'throughout' implies geographical divisions within the territory of India.*[1]

'Free' under article 301: It does not mean freedom from laws and regulations. It means freedom from local barriers treating India as one whole unit. A purely *regulatory and compensatory law* is not violative of the freedom of trade and commerce. Such laws facilitate trade. Thus traffic regulations, licensing of vehicles, charging for the maintenance of roads, price control, marketing and health regulations prescribing minimum wages etc., are regulatory measures. Likewise a law which levies a tax or a toll for the use of a road or bridge is not a barrier on trade but helps in the free and smooth flow of trade. Such compensatory taxes are not violative of article 301.[2]

In *P.N. Kaushal* v. *Union of India* the Supreme Court has held that no one has a right to trade in intoxicating liquors. Lotteries have an element of chance and not skill and thus of a gambling nature. Sale of lottery tickets cannot be regarded as trade or commerce so as to claim it as a 'free trade' even if it has the authority of law. This means that restriction imposed on lotteries is not a breach of article 301.[3]

In *Fateh Chand* v. *State of Maharashtra* rural money lending was held not to be a trade as it was exploitative in nature. Under the Maharashtra Debt Relief Act, business of money lending was not prohibited but it

1. This analysis is given by Mr. M.P. Singh *see* Note 1 on p. 319 of this book.
2. *G.K. Krishnan* v. *State of Tamil Nadu*, AIR 1975 SC 583: (1975) 2 SCR 715: 1975 Tax LR 1361.
3. AIR 1978 SC 1457: (1978) 3 SCC 558: (1979) 1 SCR 122.

wiped out all debts due to the money lenders and they had to return back the securities. It was argued by the money lenders that 'trade' covers not only 'buying and selling of goods' but also trading facilities like advances, overdrafts, banking and insurance etc. It was held that anti-social unscrupulous money lending to economically weaker sections cannot be regarded as 'trade' within the meaning of article 301.[1]

In *Atiabari Tea Co.* v. *State of Assam,* AIR 1961 SC 232: ILR (1961) 13 Assam 257: (1961) 1 SCR 809 export of tea to Calcutta via Assam was taxed. It levied the tax directly and immediately on the movements of goods and therefore was void under article 301 because previous sanction of the President before enacting such a law was not obtained as required under article 304(b).[2] This decision laid down the 'direct and immediate effect' test to find out if article 301 is violated.

In *Automobile Transport Ltd* v. *State of Rajasthan,* AIR 1962 SC 1406: 1962 (2) SCA 35: (1963) 1 SCR 491 State Government imposed a tax on all motor vehicles used and kept within the State of Rajasthan. It was held valid as it was only a regulatory measure. The direct and immediate effect test laid down in *Atiabari* was affirmed by the court with a clarification that regulatory measures imposing compensatory tax do not come within the meaning of restrictions contemplated by article 301 and hence such measures need not comply with article 304(b).

---

1. AIR 1977 SC 1825: 1978 (1) SCJ 1: 79 Bom LR 552. For a critical analysis of this case see the article by Mr. M.P. Singh "Is money lending extra-commercium? Some thoughts on *Fateh Chand* v. *State of Maharashtra,* AIR 1977 SC 1825: (1977) 2 SCC 670: 1978 (1) SCJ 1.
2. AIR 1951 SC 232: ILR (1961) 13 Assam 257: (1961) 1 SCR 809.

CHAPTER 29

SERVICES UNDER THE UNION AND THE STATE

(Articles 308-323)

SYNOPSIS

A. Introduction

Government services play an important role. A country cannot progress without an efficient civil service and hence we have elaborate provisions concerning services under the Union and State Government in the Constitution. Its efficiency lies in protecting the services from political and individual influences. Services under the Union and the States are covered under articles 308-311, 335, 336. Public Service Commissions are covered under articles 315-323, 378. State does not include the State of Jammu and Kashmir for the purposes of this Part unless the context otherwise requires. (Article 308)

B. Recruitment and Regulation of Conditions of Services

The appropriate State Legislature may regulate the requirements and conditions of services of persons appointed to public services and posts in connection with the affairs of the Union and the State. The President of India in case of Union services and the Governor in case of State services may make necessary rules for such services and posts. (Article 309)

Every member of the defence service or civil service of the Union or an All India Services and every such member of the State holds office during the pleasure of the President or the Governor as the case may be. However if a person (not being a member of the defence service, or All India Service or of a Civil Service of the State or Union) is appointed under the Constitution to a post under a contract in order to secure his services in view of his special qualifications – the President or the Governor as the case may be – may provide him compensation if before the expiry of the agreed period, that post is abolished or he is for reasons not connected with any misconduct on his part required to vacate the post. (Article 310(2)

The mode of recruitment and the category from which the recruitment to a service should be made are all matters which are exclusively within the domain of the Executive. Courts do not sit in judgment over the wisdom of the Executive on these matters.[1]

C. Doctrine of Pleasure

The normal rule in England is that the civil servants hold their office during the pleasure of the Crown. This doctrine is incorporated in article 310 but with safeguards to protect the civil servants from political interference and to bring about transparency.

Restrictions on the Doctrine of Pleasure

Following are the *restrictions on the Doctrine of Pleasure*

1. The pleasure of the President/Governor are controlled by the provisions of article 311.
2. The tenure of the Supreme Court and High Court judges, Auditor-General, Chief Election Commissioner, Chairman and members of the Public Service Commission are not dependent on the pleasure of the President or the Governor. These posts are excluded from the operation of the doctrine of pleasure.
3. The doctrine of pleasure is subject to the Fundamental rights.[2]
4. Compulsory retirement simpliciter – *i.e.,* without any stigma attached is not punishment. It is a facet of the doctrine of pleasure.

   In *Union of India* v. *Tulsiram Patel*[3] the court observed that the doctrine of pleasure is embodied in the Constitution not because it is a special prerogative of the British Crown but because public policy requires it to be so. The following important propositions regarding the doctrine of pleasure were laid down by the court:

(a) The doctrine of pleasure need not be exercised by the President or the Governor personally.

(b) Satisfaction regarding dispensing with the inquiry need not be the personal satisfaction of the President or the Governor.

(c) If article 311(2) becomes applicable the opportunity of being heard is totally ruled out and it cannot be reintroduced by recourse to article 14.

(d) The power to dispense with the inquiry should not be exercised lightly or arbitrarily or out of ulterior motives.

(e) When disciplinary inquiry is dispensed with there is no obligation to communicate the reasons therefor to the Government servant but it would be better if reasons are communicated.

---

1. *State of Andhra Pradesh* v. *V. Sadanandam,* AIR 1989 SC 2060: 1989 Lab IC 2024: (1989) 2 APLJ (SC) 1.
2. *General Manager, Southern Railway* v. *Rangachari,* AIR 1962 SC 36: (1961) 2 SCJ 424: (1962) 2 SCR 586.
3. AIR 1985 SC 1416: 1985 Lab IC 1393: (1985) 3 SCC 398.

Articles 335, 336 must be read along with these provisions. Thus the claims of the members of the Scheduled Castes and the Tribes are to be taken into consideration consistently with the maintenance of efficiency of administration in the making of appointment to services and posts in connection with the affairs of the Union and the State.

D. Constitutional safeguards for the Civil Servants

Article 311 provides the following safeguards to civil servants against any arbitrary dismissal from their posts.

1. Dismissal only by rank of or above that of appointing authority

No person holding office under the Union or a State can be dismissed or removed by an authority subordinate to that by which he was appointed. He can be dismissed by an officer of the same rank.[1]

2. Removal only after an enquiry

He cannot be dismissed or removed or reduced in rank except after an enquiry in which he has been informed of the charges against him and given a reasonable opportunity of being heard in respect of those charges. Reasonable opportunity of being heard must be given only if:

(a) the employee is a member of the civil services of the Union or the State; or if he holds a civil post under the Union or the State; or is in All India Service, and

(b) He is sought to be dismissed, removed or reduced in rank. A person who is 'dismissed' is ineligible for re-employment; but a person who is 'removed' can be re-employed. However both result in penal consequences like forfeiture of the right to salary, allowances, or pension already acquired for past services due to their blameworthy conduct.

3. When opportunity of being heard need not be given

Such opportunity need not be given in three cases:

(a) if he is removed due to his conviction of a criminal charge; or

(b) it is not reasonably practicable to give him an opportunity of showing cause; or

(c) the President is satisfied that in the interest of the security of the State it is not expedient to give hearing to that person [Article 311(1)]. If any question arises whether it is reasonably practicable to give him an opportunity of being heard the decision of the authority empowered to dismiss, remove or reduce in rank is final. [Article 311(3)]

4. No entitlement to hearing on penalty

After the 42nd Constitutional Amendment in 1976, it is now provided that a penalty may be imposed on the person concerned on the basis of evidence adduced during the enquiry and no opportunity to make a representation on the penalty proposed to be imposed need be given. Before the 42nd Amendment

---

1. *Mahesh Prasad* v. *State of Uttar Pradesh*, AIR 1955 SC 70: (1955) 1 SCR 965: 1955 Cr LJ 249.

the civil servants were entitled to make a representation on the sentence sought to be imposed.[1]

5. What is resonable opportunity

Reasonable opportunity means that the authority must:

(a) Frame specific charges with full particulars.

(b) Intimate the charges to the civil servant.

(c) Give him an opportunity of being heard and then take the decision.

Refusal to provide a copy of the Inquiry Report to the delinquent (wrong-doer) amounts to denial of reasonable opportunity.

In *Khem Chand* v. *Union of India*[2] Supreme Court has held that reasonable opportunity includes an opportunity to deny guilt and establish innocence.

E. Termination of service when amounts to punishment

The protection of article 311 is available only when dismissal, removal or reduction in rank is by way of punishment. So the question is: when does termination amount to punishment. In *Purshottam Lal Dhingra* v. *Union of India*[3] Supreme Court laid down the following two tests to determine whether termination is by way of punishment:

(a) If the Government servant had a right to hold the post or the rank – then the termination etc., amounts to punishment and he is entitled to the protection of article 311.

(b) Whether he has been visited with evil consequences.

In this case – Purshottam Lal was appointed to officiate on a higher post. After two years he was reverted to his original post due to his inefficiency. Supreme Court held that he had no right to the post as he was only officiating on the post, he had no right over the post. He could still be promoted in future based on his work and conduct. Hence he could not claim the benefit of article 311.

(1) Reduction in rank

Reduction in rank means reduction from a higher to a lower rank or post. In *State of Punjab* v. *Kishan Das*[4] a police constable was charge sheeted for arrogance and indiscipline and charges proved after a departmental enquiry. His services were forfeited and hence salary brought down to Rs. 45 *i.e.*, the salary payable to a constable at the starting point of the service. Supreme Court held that it was not 'reduction in rank'. It only resulted in loss of salary for which the remedy lies under the service rules and not article 311(2).

From the post of Chief Secretary of a State (Assam) to the post of Secretary in the Central Government (a tenure post which was to expire in July, 1969) has been held to be a promotion to higher post. Hence when the appellant was

---

1. Hearing on sentence was the result of court decisions. It later had the Constitutional sanction by Constitution 5th Amendment in 1964. This is now taken away by 42nd Amendment.
2. AIR 1958 SC 300: 1958 (I) LLJ 167: 1958 SCR 1080.
3. AIR 1958 SC 36: 1958 SCJ 217: 1958 (I) LLJ 544.
4. AIR 1971 SC 766: 1971 (2) SCA 574: (1971) 3 SCR 389.

asked to chose between reversion to the original post in the parent State or go in for compulsory retirement – Supreme Court held that article 311 is attracted as it adversely affected his seniority and chances of promotion.[1]

In *State of Maharashtra* v. *Chandrabhan*[2] under the Bombay Civil Service Rule a suspended Government employee whose appeal was pending against his conviction was entitled to Re. 1/per month as subsistence allowance. The Supreme Court struck down the rule as unconstitutional because the amount is illusory and meaningless and it is just impossible for the civil servant to defend himself effectively with such meagre subsistence. Such meagre subsistence amounts to denying the reasonable opportunity to defend himself. It held that he is entitled to normal subsistence allowance until the appeal is disposed of.

(2) Suspension is not punishment

It is neither dismissal nor reduction in rank nor removal. Hence the person suspended during the disciplinary inquiry is not entitled to Constitutional guarantee of article 311.[3] Likewise when termination is due to abolition of the post held by the civil servant for *bona fide* reasons, article 311(2) need not be complied with. But he is entitled to arrears of pay and other benefits for service already rendered and for the period after suspension upto the date of abolition of the post.[4]

(3) Compulsory retirement simpliciter

Compulsory retirement simpliciter *i.e.,* without any stigma attached is not punishment. It is a facet of the doctrine of pleasure. The object of compulsory retirement is to weed out dead wood in order to maintain efficiency and initiative in the service. In public interest a premature retirement of a Government servant who has ceased to possess the standard of efficiency and competency and hence utility is made to compulsorily retire. Here the servant is not entitled to the protection of article 311(2).[5]

Termination due to reduction of the age of retirement from 58 to 55 years is not 'removal' within the meaning of article 311(2).[6]

F. Temporary Government servants

Article 311 applies both to temporary and permanent servants. But if a Government servant holding a temporary post is terminated after giving him reasonable notice he is not entitled to the safeguards of article 311(2) because he has no right to the post held by him.

---

1. *Debesh Chandra Das* v. *Union of India,* AIR 1970 SC 77: 1970 (1) SCJ 16: (1970) 1 SCR 220.
2. AIR 1983 SC 803: 1983 Lab IC 1128: (1983) 3 SCC 387.
3. *S. Sukhbans Singh* v. *State of Punjab,* AIR 1962 SC 1711: 1963 (I) LLJ 671: (1963) 1 SCR 416.
4. *Kesho Nath Khurana* v. *Union of India,* AIR 1982 SC 1177: 1981 Supp SCC 38: 1982 (1) SCJ 435.
5. *State of Gujarat* v. *Umedbhai M. Patel,* AIR 2001 SC 1109: 2001 AIR SCW 862: (2001) 3 SCC 314; *Shamlal* v. *State of Uttar Pradesh,* AIR 1971 SC 40. Guidelines for compulsory retirement have been laid down by the Supreme Court in *Baikunth Nath Das* v. *Chief Distt. Medical Officer,* AIR 1992 SC 1020: 1992 AIR SCW 793: (1992) 2 SCC 299.
6. *K. Nagaraj* v. *State of Andhra Pradesh,* AIR 1985 SC 551: 1985 Lab IC 746: (1985) 1 SCC 523.

In *State of Punjab* v. *Sukh Raj Bahadur*[1] Supreme Court summarised the law regarding temporary servants and laid down the following propositions:

(a) Services of a temporary or a probationer can be terminated under the rules of his employment and such termination without anything more will not attract the operation of article 311.

(b) Circumstances for termination have to be examined in each case. The motive behind it is immaterial.

(c) If the termination order results in evil consequences- or casts a stigma on his character or integrity – it is by way of punishment.

(d) A pre-termination enquiry only to ascertain whether the public servant should be retained does not attract article 311.

(e) If there is a full scale enquiry *i.e.,* enquiry officer appointed, charges framed, explanation called for and considered and then termination order issued- it attracts article 311.

Termination on the ground of negligence without complying with article 311 is unconstitutional.[2]

G. All India Services (Article 312)

If the Council of States has declared by a resolution supported by not less than two-thirds of the members present and voting that it is necessary or expedient in the national interest so to do, Parliament may by law provide for the creation of one or more all-India services common to the Union and the States and regulate the recruitment and conditions of service of persons appointed to any such service.

Services known at the commencement of this Constitution as the Indian Administrative Service and the Indian Police Service are to be deemed to be services created by the Parliament under this article 312.

H. Public Service Commission (Articles 315-323, 378)

Article 315(1) provides that there shall be a Public Service Commission for the Union and a Public Service Commission for each State. Two or more States can agree to a Joint Public Service Commission to serve the needs of those States after a resolution to that effect is passed by the House (or both the Houses of the State) and the Parliament may by law so provide for the appointment of the Joint Commission. (Article 315(2) Such law may contain provisions desirable or necessary for giving effect to the purposes of law.

The Chairman and other members of a Public Service Commission are appointed in the case of the Union Commission or Joint Commission by the State and in case of a State Commission by the Governor of the State. [Article 316(1)]

Term of office: A member of a Public Service Commission holds office for six years from the date on which he enters upon his office or until he attains in the case of the Union Commission the age of 65 years and in the case of a State Commission or a Joint Commission the age of 62 years. whichever is earlier.

1. AIR 1968 SC 1089: 1968 Cur LJ 687: 1970 (I) LLJ 373.
2. *Kanhailal* v. *Distt. Judge,* AIR 1983 SC 351: (1983) 3 SCC 32: 1983 All LJ 184.

Qualifications: One held of the members of every Public Service Commission should be persons who have held office for at least 10 years under the Government before being so appointed.

A member of the Public Service Commission may resign by writing under his hand addressed to President in case of Union Commission and to the Governor in case of State Commission.

How removed: The member of the Public Service Commission can be removed for misbehaviour by an order of the President after the Supreme Court has reported that he should be removed after conducting an enquiry.

Misbehaviour includes:

(a) Being concerned or interested in any contract or agreement made by or on behalf of the Government of India or the Government of State.

(b) Participating in the profits thereof or in any benefit or employment arising therefrom otherwise than as a member and in common with the other members of an incorporated company.

(c) The President may on his own motion remove such Chairman or member (i) if he is adjudged an insolvent, or (ii) engages in any paid employment during his term of office outside the duties of his office, or (iii) is in the opinion of the President unfit to continue in office due to infirmity of mind or body.

I. Prohibition as to holding of office by Executive-members of the Commission (Article 319)

On ceasing to hold office:

(a) The Chairman and members of the UPSC and the Chairman and members of SPSC *are ineligible for further employment under Union or State Government.*

(b) But the Chairman of the SPSC is eligible for appointment as the Chairman/ member of UPSC or Chairman of another State Commission.

(c) Or a member of the UPSC (other than the Chairman) is eligible for appointment as the Chairman of UPSC or Chairman of a State Commission.

(d) A member of the SPSC (other than the Chairman) is eligible for appointment as the Chairman or any other member of the UPSC or the Chairman of that or any other SPSC.

J. Functions of Public Service Commission (Article 320)

1. They conduct examinations for appointment to the services of the Union and the States respectively.
2. They assist other states in framing and operating schemes for front recruitment for any services for which candidates possessing special qualifications are required.
3. They advise on matters relating to–

   (a) Methods of recruitment to civil services and for civil posts;

(b) Principles to be followed in making such appointments and promotions and transfers from one service to another and on the suitability of the candidates etc.;

(c) Disciplinary matters affecting a Government servant including memorial or petitions relating to such matters;

(d) Costs incurred in defending legal proceedings in respect of acts done in the execution of his duty should be paid out of the Consolidated Fund of India or of the State;

(e) Claims for the award of pension in respect of injuries sustained by a Government servant and any questions as to the amount of any such award.

K. Report of Public Service Commission (Article 323)

UPSC/SPSC must present to the President or the Governor as the case may be, a report as to the work done by the Commission. President or the Governor must cause a copy thereof explaining as respects the cases where the advice of the Commission was not accepted, the reasons for such non-acceptance to be laid before each House of the Parliament or before the Legislature of the State.

CHAPTER 30

TRIBUNALS

(Articles 323A and 323B)

SYNOPSIS

Part XIVA was added by 42nd Amendment, 1976. It makes provisions for—

(A) Administrative Tribunals under Article 323A

(1) Article 323A authorises the Parliament to make laws to provide for the adjudication or trial by Administrative Tribunals of disputes and complaints with respect to recruitment and conditions of service of persons appointed to public services and posts in connection with the affairs of the Union or of any State or of any local or other authority in India or under the control of the Government of India or of any Government corporation. Such a law also makes provisions for—

(a) Provide for the establishment of Administrative Tribunal for the Union and for the States.

(b) Specify the jurisdiction, powers and authority which may be exercised by each of the said Tribunals.

(c) Provide for the procedure to be followed by the said Tribunals.

(d) Exclude the jurisdiction of all courts except the jurisdiction of the Supreme Court under article 136 with respect to the disputes and complaints referred to in clause (1) above. (This provision is held unconstitutional as it excludes effective judicial review without providing an efficient alternative dispute resolution mechanism.)

(e) Provide for the transfer to each such Administrative Tribunal of any cases pending before any court or other authority immediately before the establishment of such Tribunal as would have been within the jurisdiction of such Tribunal if the causes of action of such suits or proceedings are based had arisen after such establishment.

(f) Repeal or amend any order made by the President under clause 3 of article 371D[1].

(g) Contain such supplemental, incidental and consequential provisions as Parliament may deem necessary for the effective functioning of and for the speedy disposal of cases by and the enforcement of the orders of such Tribunals.

---

1. Special provisions regarding the State of Andhra Pradesh.

Article 323 takes effect notwithstanding anything contained in the Constitution itself or any other law in force.

(B) Tribunals for any other matters under Article 323B

(1) This article authorises the appropriate Legislatures to make laws to provide for the adjudication or trial by Tribunal of disputes, complaints or offences with respect to the nine matters with respect to which the Legislature has powers to make laws mentioned in clause 2.

(2) Clause 2 mentions the following:

(a) Levy, assessment, collection and enforcement of any tax;

(b) Foreign exchange, export, import across customs frontiers;

(c) Industrial and labour disputes;

(d) Land reforms by way of acquisition by the State of any estate as defined in article 31A or of any rights therein or the extinguishment or modification of any such rights or by way of ceiling on the agricultural land or in any other way;

(e) Ceiling on urban property;

(f) Election to either House of Parliament or the other House of Legislature of a State excluding matters referred to in articles 329[1] and 329A;[2]

(g) Production, procurement, supply and distribution of food stuffs and such other goods as the President by public notification declares to be essential goods for the purpose of article 323B and control of prices of such goods;

(h) Offences against law with respect to any of the matters specified above;

(i) Any matter incidental to any of the matters specified in sub clauses above.

(3) Such law made by the State Legislature may:

(a) Provide for a hierarchy of Tribunals;

(b) Specify the jurisdiction, powers and authority which may be exercised by each of the said Tribunals;

(c) Provide for the procedure to be followed by the said Tribunal;

(d) Exclude the jurisdiction of all Courts except the jurisdiction of the Supreme Court under article 136 with respect to all or any of the matters falling within the jurisdiction of the said Tribunals; (This provision is held unconstitutional as it excludes effective judicial review without providing an efficient alternative mechanism);

(e) Provide for the transfer to each such Administrative Tribunal of any cases pending before any court or other authority immediately before the establishment of such Tribunal as would have been within the jurisdiction of such Tribunal if the causes of action of such suits or proceedings are based had arisen after such establishment;

---

1. Bar to interference by courts in electoral matters.
2. Special provisions as to elections to Parliament in the case of Prime Minister – omitted by 44th Amendment 1978.

(f) Contain such supplemental, incidental and consequential provisions as the appropriate Tribunal may deem necessary for the effective functioning of and speedy disposal of cases by and the enforcement of the orders of such Tribunals.

Article 323B takes effect notwithstanding anything contained in the Constitution itself or any other law in force.

Article 323A	Article 323B
It is confined to matters relating to public service	It relates to all matters like taxation etc., mentioned therein.
There is no hierarchy of Courts	State may provide for hierarchy of courts.
It confer powers exclusively on the President.	The legislative power is divided between the Union and the State.

In exercise of the jurisdiction under article 323A the Parliament has passed the Administrative Tribunals Act, 1985 empowering the Central Government establish Administrative Tribunal.

The question was whether ousting of the judicial review by the High Court under articles 226 and 227 in service matters specified under section 28 of the Administrative Tribunal Act, was constitutional. The court has reiterated its decision in *Minerva mills*[1] that judicial review is a basic structure of the Constitution and it cannot be taken away. But the Parliament can provide for effective alternate institutional mechanisms for judicial review without violating the basic structure of the Constitution. What is important to be noted is that the alternative mechanism must be *as efficacious as the High Court.*

In *L. Chandra Kumar* v. *Union of India*[2] the Supreme Court struck down articles 323A(2d) &323B(3d) because while excluding the jurisdiction of the High Court it had not upgraded the competence of the Tribunal. The Supreme Court perused the Malimath Committee Report and the recommendations of the Law Commission of India and was convinced about the uninspiring character, composition and functioning of Administrative Tribunal. So it quashed the concerned Article.

Thus as the position stands today, the persons who are subject to the jurisdiction of the Tribunal have to approach the Tribunal first; if aggrieved by the Tribunal's ruling then approach the High Court and only next, as a last resort approach the Supreme Court under article 136.

---

1. AIR 1980 SC 1789: (1980) 2 SCC 591: (1981) 1 SCR 206.
2. AIR 1997 SC 1125: 1997 AIR SCW 1345: (1997) 3 SCC 261.

CHAPTER 31

ELECTIONS

(Articles 324-329A)

SYNOPSIS

A. Introduction

Constitutional provisions pertaining to elections are dealt with under articles 324-329 and 124(4).

Elections play an important role in the working of a democracy. India is known worldwide to conduct very smooth elections in spite of the varying degrees of problems due to poverty, illiteracy and politics played by the political aspirants. These provisions deal with the appointment of an Election Commission for superintendence, directions and control of elections. The importance and the role that can be played by the Chief Election Commission has become manifest specially from the period when Mr. T.N. Sheshan was the Chief Election Commissioner.

There is one general electoral roll for every territorial constituency. No person shall be ineligible for inclusion in any such roll on grounds only of religion, race, caste, sex or any of them. The elections to the Parliament and State Legislature are held on the basis of adult suffrage. Every person who is a citizen of India and not less than 18 years of age and is not otherwise disqualified under the Constitution or the Representation of Peoples Act, 1950 – on the grounds of non-residence, unsoundness of mind, crime or illegal practice has a right to be registered as a voter. (Articles 325 & 326)

B. Constitution of the Election Commission

Election Commission consists of the Chief Election Commissioner and such number of other Election Commissioners as may be fixed. All of them are appointed by the President. Their appointments are subject to the law made by the Parliament. [Article 324(2)]. Chief Election Commissioner is the Chairman of the Commission. [Article 324(3)]. The President may also appoint Regional Commissioners to assist the Election Commission in its functions in consultation with the Election Commission. [Article 324(4)]

Conditions of service and the tenure of the office of the Election Commissioners and the Regional Commissioners shall be such as the President may by rule determine. These rules are subject to the law made by the Parliament.

Independence of the Chief Election Commissioner is ensured by providing that he can be removed from his office only in the same manner and on the same grounds as a judge of the Supreme Court. *I.e.,* on grounds of proved misbehaviour. The conditions of service of the Chief Election Commissioner cannot be varied to his disadvantage after his appointment to the office. Other Election Commissioners and the Regional Commissioners can be removed on the recommendation of the Chief Election Commissioner. Their salaries are paid out of the Consolidated Fund of India.

Inter se position of the Chief Election Commissioner, Regional Commissioner and Election Commissioners

The Supreme Court has held in *S.S. Dhanoa* v. *Union of India*[1] that the protection available to the Chief Election Commissioner is not available to the Election Commissioners or the Regional Commissioners. Hence removal of two Election Commissioners was not a case of 'termination of service' but a case of abolition of the post. Hence it was legal and constitutional.[2]

The Parliament has enacted an Act to provide for two persons as Election Commissioners. It states that the decision of three members of the Election Commission shall as far as possible be unanimous. In case of a difference the matter should be decided by a majority. The allocation of business or work between the Chief Election Commissioner and the other Election Commissioners shall be done under the Act and Rules of Business. The Act has placed the Chief Election Commissioner and the other Election Commissioners on an equal footing thus over-ruling the decision in *Dhonoa.*[3]

In *T.N. Sheshan* v. *Union of India*[4] the five judge Constitution Bench unanimously upheld the validity of the Act which placed the Chief Election Commissioner and the other Election Commissioners on an equal footing as regards status, power and authority. He had argued that the Act was unconstitutional as it was inconsistent with the scheme of article 324 which did not give power to the Parliament to frame rules for transaction of business of Election Commission; the provision under the Act that the decision must be taken unanimously or by majority was unworkable; and that the whole exercise in passing the Act was because he was insisting on strict compliance with the Model Code of Conduct by all political parties. The Supreme Court unanimously rejected the contentions of the Chief Election Commissioner and held the Act as valid. It held that the scheme of article 324 provided for a multi-member Election Commission. Just because there is a difference between the mode of removal of office of the Chief Election Commissioner and the Election Commissioners- that does not place

1. AIR 1991 SC 1145.
2. AIR 1991 SC 1745: 1991 AIR SCW 1937: 1991 3 SCC 567.
3. The Act was a result of a serious conflict between CEC – Mr. T.N. Sheshan and the Government in 1993. He had claimed exclusive powers for the Election Commission to direct the Government to deploy Central Police Forces at the time of an election and also an exclusive jurisdiction to take disciplinary action against the staff on election duty. The Act was held valid in the case filed by Mr. Sheshan.
4. (1995) 4 SCC 611.

the Chief Election Commissioner on a higher footing. 'Nobody can be above the institution which he is supposed to serve. He is merely the creature of the institution....'.[1]

C. Functions of the Election Commission [Article 324(1)]

1. The superintendence, direction and control of the preparation of the electoral rolls for all elections to Parliament, State Legislatures and to the offices of the President and Vice-President are assigned to the Election Commission.
2. The conduct of all the elections.
3. Term 'election' is used in a wide sense so as to include the entire process of election consisting of several stages.
4. Article 324(1) is a plenary provision vesting the whole responsibility in the Election Commission for National and State elections for conducting free and fair elections. If the law makes no provision to meet a situation, article 324 enables the Commission to act to provide for free and fair election with expedition. It can order for a re-poll due to breakdown of law and order at the time of polling or counting of votes. Supreme Court has held in *Mohinder Singh* v. *CEC*[2] that the Commission should exercise its power of cancelling a poll according to the principles of natural justice. It can postpone the elections due to disturbed conditions in the State. Its power is subject to judicial review. The power must not be arbitrarily exercised[3]. Election Commission had limited the use of loudspeakers for election purposes between 8 a.m. to 7 p.m. it was set aside by the High Court as there was no nexus between the restriction imposed and the power under article 324. The Supreme Court held the order too restrictive and banned the use of the loudspeakers from 10 p.m. to 6 a.m., but did not decide whether the Commission has such a power.[4]
5. Central Government Rules under Representation of People's Act, 1951 empowers the Election Commission to specify symbols for candidates at the election and also to adjudicate upon disputes regarding recognition of political parties and rival claims to a particular symbol for election purposes. It has issued Election Symbols (Reservation and Allotment) Order, 1968. The courts have treated it as 'compendium of directions' to meet various kinds of situations relating to elections with particular reference to symbols. The Election Commission has the power to make such an order in its own right under article 324[5].
6. In *Common Cause – a Registered Society* v. *Union of India*[6] Supreme Court has held that article 324 empowers the Election Commission to issue

1. Justice Ahmadi.
2. AIR 1978 SC 851: (1978) 1 SCC 405: (1978) 2 SCR 272.
3. *Digvijay Mote* v. *Union of India*, (1993) 4 SCC 175: 1993 AIR SCW 2895.
4. *Election Commission of India* v. *All India Anna Dravida Munetra Kazahagam*, 1994 Supp (2) SCC 689.
5. *All Party Hill Leaders' Conference, Shillong* v. *Captain W.A. Sangma*, AIR 1977 SC 2155: (1978) 1 SCR 393; *Roop Lal Sathi* v. *Nachhattar Singh*, AIR 1982 SC 1559: (1982) 3 SCC 487.
6. (1996) 2 SCC 752: AIR 1996 SC 3081: 1996 AIR SCW 1537.

directions requiring the political parties to submit their election expenses for scrutiny to maintain the purity of elections and to bring transparency in the process of election.

7. In *Union of India* v. *Association for Democratic Reforms*[1] the Supreme Court directed the Commission to issue certain directions to candidates to file an affidavit detailing the information about themselves regarding aspects like the criminal cases against them; their assets and liabilities etc. It held that when law is silent, article 324 is a reservoir of power to act for the avowed purpose of ensuring free and fair elections. This power is to be exercised within the framework of the rule of law and not in derogation of it.
8. On 9-1-2012[2] the Election Commission passed an unprecedented order directing that all statues of Uttar Pradesh Chief Minister Mayawati and the elephants which is the symbol of BSP built in several parks in the State at Government cost – should be kept covered with immediate effect till the completion of the Election process. If kept open it would provide an opportunity to the BSP for publicity of its leader and the election symbol. The order is said to trigger a controversy. It is submitted that it is high time that a ban be imposed on constructing of any statues at all. They are leading to further division of the society. The Constitution under article 17 bans conferring of 'titles' like 'Sir, etc.'. Intention was to see that no person is made 'super-human' and to convey the concept that all men are equal. Statues of politicians or of any other person in whatever field idolises them and takes them to a status of not just 'Super-human' but of a 'super-power like God' which is unconstitutional. These statues are worshipped, garlanded and bathed with milk etc which is no less than the slave mind-set of the yester years. Anti-social elements desecrate them leading to social tensions. A way out would be to keep all existing statues in a museum and ban the 'statue culture'.
9. Once the election results are declared the Commission has no jurisdiction with respect to the election.[3]
10. The President and the Governor shall when requested by the Election Commission make available to the Election Commission such State or Central Government staff as may be necessary to discharge its functions. Thus the Election Commission generally has a few staff of its own. When required it can demand necessary staff from the Government. Services of State Bank of India employees cannot be requisitioned for Election purposes as State Bank of India is a statutory body.[4]

---

1. (2002) 5 SCC 294: AIR 2002 SC 2112: 2002 AIR SCW 2186.
2. NIE 'EC Orders covering of all Maya Statues, Elephants' 9-1-2012. It has cost the Nation one crore for the implementation of the Order.
3. *Chandan Kumar Sarkar* v. *Chief Election Commissioner, New Delhi*, AIR 1995 Gau 61: 1995 (1) Civ LJ 277: 1995 (1) Gau LR 87.
4. *Election Commission of India* v. *State Bank of India*, AIR 1995 SC 1078: 1995 AIR SCW 1095: JT 1995 (2) SC 61.

D. Advisory functions of the Election Commissioner [Articles 103 and 192(2)]

If a question arises as to whether a member of either House of the Parliament has become subject to disqualification for membership in the House as mentioned in article 102 – the President's decision is final. But the President must consult the Election Commission before giving the decision. (Article 103). Likewise in the case of disqualification of membership in the Legislature – the Governor must consult the Election Commission before taking a decision (Article 192). Here the Commission discharges a quasi-judicial function and hence has to follow the principles of natural justice. In *Election Commission of India* v. *Subramanian Swamy*,[1] the Chief Election Commissioner was directed to excuse himself from participating in deciding the question of disqualification against Smt Jaylalitha, Tamil Nadu MLA as there was a suspicion of bias against the Chief Election Commissioner and the Chairman of Election Commission Sri Sheshan as Dr. Swamy's wife was engaged as a counsel in a case filed by Sri Sheshan.[1]

At the commencement of the Constitution the Election Commission was empowered to appoint Election Tribunals for deciding doubts and disputes arising out of or in connection with elections to Parliament and to the State Legislatures. This provision was omitted by the 19th Amendment to the Constitution in 1966.

It is the prerogative of the Government to choose the timing of the general elections. The Election Commission's role is to take over the actual conduct and supervision of the elections.[2]

E. Power of the Parliament and State Legislatures with regard to election law (Articles 327 and 328)

Parliament is empowered to make provisions with respect to all matters relating to or in connection with Election to Parliament and State Legislature, the preparation of electoral rolls, delimitation of constituencies and all other connected matters. Parliament has enacted the Representation of People's Act, 1951 and 1952, Presidential and Vice-Presidential Elections Act, 1952; Delimitation Commission Act, 1952. Article 328 confers a similar power on the State Legislature. The State Legislature can make provisions regarding all the matters mentioned above insofar as provision is not made by the Parliament in that behalf.

It was held in *A.C. Jose* v. *Sivan Pillai*[3] the powers of the Commission supplement the law in the matter of superintendence, direction and control and not supplant (replace) the law powers of the Commission under article 324 and the powers of the Parliament and the Legislature to make laws given under schedule VII must be read harmoniously. In this case Government had

1. AIR 1996 SC 1810: 1996 AIR SCW 2100: (1996) 4 SCC 104.
2. PIL filed by Jammu and Kashmir Panther's Party challenging the Election Commission's order rejecting the request of the governor to hold Jammu Kashmir State Assembly elections before December 20, 1995.
3. AIR 1984 SC 921: (1984) 2 SCC 656: 1984 Ker LT 510.

refused permission to use voting machines whereas the Commission had issued directions for the use of voting machines. The order of the Commission was held unconstitutional. The Supreme Court ordered a re-poll where the machines were used.

F. Presidential reference under Article 143

The President referred the question regarding interpretation of article 174 and article 324 to the Supreme Court under its advisory jurisdiction under article 143. The Governor summons the House at such time and place as he thinks fit, but more than 6 months shall not lapse between two sittings. Hence if the Assembly is dissolved election must be held and the Assembly constituted to meet within that period. In *Presidential Reference 2002*[1] – after the Godhra incident in Gujarat where *Kar Sevaks* were burnt alive in the train while returning from Ayodhya there were communal riots. Assembly was dissolved and elections were recommended. The Election Commission took stalk of the situation and stated that the condition was not conducive for free and fair elections. It recommended imposition of President's rule under article 356.

The Supreme Court gave its opinion on three important legal questions

(1) Article 174(1) which mandates that more than 6 months shall not lapse between two Assembly sittings – is applicable only to a 'live Assembly' and not a 'dissolved Assembly'. Hence there is no inter-relation between article 174(1) and article 324. The outer limit of 6 months mentioned in article 174 is not applicable for the holding of elections. Under article 324 holding of elections is the exclusive domain of the Election Commission.

(2) Article 174 and 324 operate at different levels. Neither is subject to the other.

(3) Election Commission has full powers for holding and conducting the elections. But its power is subject to judicial review. It must complete the elections within an outside limit of six months unless there are over-riding reasons for going beyond six months. Ordinary law and order or public disorder should not be the occasion for postponing the elections and it is the duty of all concerned to assist and co-operate with the Election Commission in conducting elections.

There is no specific provision in the Constitution for appeals from the decisions of Election Tribunals. However judicial review of decisions of all Tribunals including an Election Tribunal is available under article 136 which is an extraordinary remedy or by a petition to the High Court under article 226 for an appropriate writ. These powers of the Supreme Court and the High Court cannot be fettered in any way by any legislation.

G. Election disputes

1. Bar to interference by Courts in electoral matters (Article 329):

Notwithstanding anything in the Constitution validity of law relating

---

1. AIR 2003 SC 87: 2002 AIR SCW 4492: (2002) 8 SCC 237.

to the delimitation of constituencies or .the allotment of seats to such constituencies of the allotment of seats to such constituencies shall not be called in question in any court.

2. Under article 329(b), Elections can only be called in question by an election petition presented to such authority and in such manner as may be laid down by law. It was held in *Ponnuswami* v. *Returning Officer*[1] that all disputes must be raised only after the election is over. This is in order to ensure that there is no dislocation of the time schedule for completion of the election. This is a self imposed discipline by the courts and not a matter of judicial powers. Election process begins with the notification of the election under Representation of People Act, 1951. In this case the candidate was not allowed to challenge the decision of the returning officer who had rejected the nomination papers due to certain reasons.
3. The position now is that there is a two tier system to decide election disputes. Election Tribunals are no longer appointed now. Election petitions are heard directly by the High Courts from which an appeal may be taken to the Supreme Court under articles 132, 133, 136.
4. In *K. Venkatachalam* v. *A. Swamickan*,[2] person who was not an elector in the electoral roll for an Assembly constituency for general election filed his nomination paper on affidavit by impersonating himself. No election petition was filed challenging his election. Supreme Court ruled that the High Court under article 226 could make a declaration that the appellant is not qualified to be a member of the Assembly. If he were to be allowed to continue to sit and vote in the Assembly his action would be a fraud on the Constitution.
5. Preparation of electoral rolls is prior to and not a part of election process. It can be challenged through a writ petition.[3] Preparation and revision of the electoral roll is a continuous process which goes on whether or not there is an election. The election roll which at the time when election is notified is the foundation for holding the election. There can never be a moment when some electoral roll is not in force.
6. Election of a candidate cannot be challenged on the ground that the electoral roll is defective.[4]
7. The High Court has no power to stay the elections on whatever grounds under article 226. The High Court has no power to rectify any error in the process of election at any stage prior to declaration of the result of election. Election Commission has the power to set right any such defect under article 324.[5]

---

1. AIR 1952 SC 64: 1952 SCR 218: 1952 Cr LJ 547.
2. AIR 1999 SC 1723: 1999 AIR SCW 1353: (1999) 4 SCC 526.
3. *Ponnuswami* v. *Returning Officer*, AIR 1952 SC 64: 1952 SCR 218: 1952 Cr LJ 547.
4. *Indrajit Barua* v. *Election Commission of India*, AIR 1986 SC 103: (1985) 4 SCC 722: 1986 (1) Supreme 289.
5. *Election Commission of India* v. *Shivaji*, AIR 1988 SC 61: (1988) 1 SCC 277: 1988 (1) SCJ 348.

8. *A.K.M. Hassan Uzzaman* v. *Union of India,* (1982) 2 SCC 218: 1982 UJ (SC) 371 is an unprecedented case. Calcutta High Court restrained the Election Commission from declaring a date for holding State Assembly elections in West Bengal. The Supreme Court agreed to hear the appeal and transferred the petition to itself for disposal on merits under article 136. It dismissed the petition. It held that in spite of article 329(b) the election laws can be challenged through writ petition but the High Court cannot pass any order, final or interim- which would postpone the election. In *Election Commission of India* v. *Ashok Kumar*[1] Supreme Court has held that without interrupting, obstructing or delaying the progress of the election proceedings, the court can remove the obstacles therein or smoothen the progress of the election proceedings or preserve a vital piece of evidence if the same would be lost by the time results are declared. It is opined that this is an important decision which marks a deviation from the earlier rulings where it was stated that article 329(b) bars the jurisdiction of the courts until the results are declared. It is an exception to article 329(b) carved out by the judiciary. In this case the Supreme Court quashed the High Court order which had stayed the manner of the counting of votes as directed by the Election Commission Order. The High Court had stayed it on the ground of *mala fides* of the Election Commission Order. Supreme Court found that *mala fide* was a bald statement which was made in the petition without any further elaboration of the *mala fides.* What is to be noted is that High Court order was struck down not because its jurisdiction was barred under article 329(b) but because the High Court had acted upon bald assertion of *mala fides. i.e.,* on merits the High Court was wrong.

---

1. AIR 2000 SC 2979: 2000 AIR SCW 3274: (2000) 8 SCC 216.

CHAPTER 32

SPECIAL PROVISIONS RELATING TO CERTAIN CLASSES

(Articles 330-342 & 366)

SYNOPSIS

A. Introduction

Our Constitution is based on the principle of equality. By equality it never meant treating all the like and the unlike alike. Hence we have special provisions for the persons who are dissimilarly placed. This is in tune with the directive principles under article 46 which provides that the States must take special care for promoting the educational and economic interests of the weaker sections of the people and in particular the Scheduled Castes and the Scheduled Tribes and to protect them from injustice. Any such provision made by the State cannot be challenged as discriminatory. *For example,* we have special provision which can be made in favour of the women and children under article 15(3); reservations in educational institutions and public services under article 15(4) in favour of socially and educationally backward class of citizens and in favour of backward class of citizens under 16(4).

The unique achievement of our Constitution is that it has abolished communal representation and separate electorates based on which the British ruled us on their concept of divide and rule. There is no separate electorate under our Constitution. All the voters vote under a general electoral roll (article 325) and there are no reservations of seats based on religion, community. To this rule there are some exceptions.

Articles 341, 342: Our Constitution does not define as to who are the persons belonging to Scheduled Castes and the Scheduled Tribes. Articles 341 & 342 empower the President to draw up a list of these castes and tribes. Under article 341 the President after consultation with the Governor of the particular State specify the castes, races, tribes or groups within castes, races or tribes for the purpose of their identification with respect to the State. Any inclusion or exclusion from the Presidential notification of any caste, race or tribe can be done by the Parliament by law. If any question arises whether a particular tribe is a tribe within the meaning of this article one has to look at the public notification by the President under article 341.[1]

B. Special provisions for Scheduled Castes and the Scheduled Tribes

Constitution provides the following special provisions in favour of Scheduled Castes and the Scheduled Tribes.

(1) Reservation of seats in Lok Sabha and Assembly

Articles 330 and 332 provides for Reservation of seats for Scheduled Castes and the Scheduled Tribes (except the Scheduled Tribes in the autonomous District of Assam) in the Lok Sabha and in the Assembly respectively. The number of seats reserved in any State or Union territory for such castes and tribes is made on the population basis. The expression population means the population ascertained in the preceding census of which the relevant figures have been published.

There is a proposal for providing 33% reservation in law making bodies in favour of women which was hotly debated and has become a contentious matter.[2]

(2) Reservations extended up to 2026

Under the 95th Amendment to the Constitution in 2009, reservations in Lok Sabha and State Assemblies is extended up to 70 years from the commencement of the Constitution *i.e.,* 2026. It is to be noted that though seats are reserved for them they are elected by all the voters in the constituency. There is no separate electorate for Scheduled Castes and the Scheduled Tribes. Article 325 expressly provides that there shall be one general electoral roll. This means that a member of the Scheduled Caste and the Scheduled Tribe may contest from a general seat.[3]

(3) Reservations – Not to hamper efficiency in administration

Claims of the Scheduled Castes and the Scheduled Tribes must be consistent with the maintenance of efficiency of administration in the making of appointment of services and posts in connection with the affairs of the Union or of a State under article 335. This article puts a limit on the extent of reservation. It must not go beyond a limit where it would affect the efficiency of administration. However facts have shown that reservations became an extremely contentious issue and there are any number of cases challenging the reservations as being made in excess by increasing the avenues of reservation like providing reservations in promotions; increasing the percentage of reservations; lowering the eligibility criteria for entry into jobs and educational institutions etc. Parliament came up with a Constitution 81st Amendment Act, 2000 which has added a new provision to article 335 which states that "nothing in article 335 shall prevent in making of any provision in favour of Scheduled Castes and the Scheduled Tribes

1. *Bhaiya Lal* v. *Harikishan Singh,* AIR 1965 SC 1557: 1965 (2) SCA 721: (1965) 2 SCR 877 and *B. Basavalingappa* v. *D. Munichinnappa,* AIR 1965 SC 1269: 1965 (2) SCJ 153: (1965) 1 SCR 316.
2. For a critical analysis of political reservations for women, see the article of this author titled 'Political Reservations for Women – Sheer Politics' – (Indian Bar Review) 1994 Vol. 25(4) p. 125.
3. *V.V. Giri* v. *D. Suri Dora,* AIR 1959 SC 1318: (1960) 1 SCR 426: 1960 SCJ 1149.

in relation to qualifying marks in any examination or lowering the standards of evaluation for reservations in matters of promotion to any class or classes of services or posts in connection with the affairs of a Union or of a State". This Amendment has been brought in to counter certain court rulings in 1996.

(4) National Commission for Scheduled Castes and Scheduled Tribes

In 2003 a separate National Commission has been established for the Scheduled Tribes and Scheduled Castes by 89th Amendment. Hitherto there was one Commission for the Scheduled Castes and the Scheduled Tribes. (Articles 338 & 338A)

(5) Representation of Anglo-Indians in law making bodies – Representation of the Anglo-Indian people in the Lok Sabha (Article 331)

Notwithstanding anything in article 81, the President may if he is of the opinion that the Anglo-Indian community is not adequately represented in the House of the People, nominate not more that 2 members of the community to the Lok Sabha.

(6) Representation of the Anglo-Indian people in the Legislature (Article 333)

Notwithstanding anything in article 170 the governor of a State may if he is of the opinion that the Anglo-Indian community is not adequately represented in the Legislative Assembly of the State, nominate not more than one member of the community to the Assembly.

An Anglo-Indian is a person whose father or any of whose other male progenitors in the male line is or was of European descent but who is domiciled in India and is or was born within such territory of parents habitually resident therein and not established there for temporary purposes only. [Article 366(2)]

CHAPTER 33

EMERGENCY PROVISIONS

Articles 352-360

SYNOPSIS

A. Introduction

Emergency provisions are provisions by virtue of which federal structure of our Constitution partakes the character of a unitary Constitution. This is an exceptional measure provided in order to overcome different types of emergency that the country may have to face. Thus in normal times it works like a Federal Constitution and during Emergencies it works like a unitary Constitution.

B. The Constitution provides for three kinds of Emergencies

(1) National Emergency – due to war, external emergency or armed rebellion (Article 352)

(2) State Emergency – due to failure of the Constitutional machinery in the State (Article 356)

(3) Financial Emergency – Article 360

C. National Emergency

(1) Security of India threatened by war, external aggression, armed rebellion

If the President is satisfied that a grave Emergency exists – due to which Security of India or any part thereof is threatened by war, external aggression or armed rebellion – he may make a Proclamation of Emergency in respect of the whole of India or any part of India as may be specified in the Proclamation. [Article 352(1)]. Such an Emergency can be made even before the actual occurrence of the event contemplated in Article 352 if the President is satisfied that there is an imminent danger of war, external aggression or armed rebellion.

(2) Proclamation varied/revoked

Such a Proclamation may be varied or revoked by a subsequent Proclamation.

(3) Decision to proclaim to be communicated to President

After the 44th Amendment in 1978 such a Proclamation cannot be issued or varied unless the decision of the Union Cabinet (*i.e.* the Council consisting of the Prime Minister and the other ministers of Cabinet rank appointed under Article 75) that such a Proclamation may be issued has been communicated to the President in writing.

In 1975 Smt. Indira Gandhi had adviced the President to proclaim Emergency without consulting her Cabinet. That was the darkest phase in the history of independent India. To avoid history being repeated in future- this Amendment was passed.

(4) When Proclamation ceases to operate

(a) It ceases to operate after one month, unless it has been approved by resolutions of both the Houses of Parliament before the expiry of that period.

(b) If Emergency is issued

(i) when Lok Sabha has been dissolved or

(ii) dissolution of Lok Sabha takes place during the period of one month referred to above and the Rajya Sabha has passed a resolution approving the Emergency but the Lok Sabha has not passed such a resolution before one month:

- the Proclamation ceases to operate at the expiry of 30 days from the date on which the Lok Sabha first sits after reconstitution. But if before 30 days the Lok Sabha also has passed a resolution approving the Proclamation – the Proclamation shall not cease to operate. [Article 352(4)]

(5) Emergency in force for six months

Emergency once approved by Parliament remains in force for a period of 6 months from the date of passing of the second resolution approving it under clause (4) unless revoked earlier.

For a further continuance of the Emergency beyond 6 months – approval by the Parliament is required every 6 months. [1st proviso to 352(5)]

If the Lok Sabha gets dissolved during the period of 6 months without approving the continuance of Emergency – but it is approved by the Rajya Sabha – Proclamation ceases to operate at the expiry of 30 days after the Lok Sabha sits after fresh elections unless before the expiry of 30 days it is approved by the Lok Sabha.

(6) Special majority needed to proclaim emergency

Resolution approving the Proclamation must be passed by special majority *i.e.* by a majority of the total members of each House and also by a majority of not less than 2/3rds of the members present and voting in each House. Before the 44th Amendment in 1978 such resolution could be passed by Parliament by a simple majority. [Article 352(6)]

(7) If the Lok Sabha disapproves – President to revoke emergency

Notwithstanding anything contained above the President shall revoke the Proclamation of Emergency or a Proclamation varying such Proclamation if the Lok Sabha passes a resolution disapproving it or disapproving its continuance. [Article 352(7)]. Note that the President must revoke acting upon the resolution of the Lok Sabha alone.

(8) Resolution for disapproving the continuance of Emergency

Where a notice in writing signed by not less than $1/10^{th}$ of the total number of members of Lok Sabha is given expressing their intention to move a resolution for disapproving the continuance of Emergency to

- The Speaker if the House is in Session or
- To the President if the House is not in session
- a special sitting of the Lok Sabha shall be held within 14 days from the date on which such a notice is received by the Speaker or the President for the purpose of considering the resolution (clause 8). In such a case a session must be convened for considering the resolution.

(9) Different Proclamations on different grounds

The power to proclaim Emergency includes the power to issue different Proclamation on different grounds- either war, external aggression or armed rebellion or imminent danger thereof, whether or not there is a Proclamation already issued by the President under Article 352(1) and such Proclamation is in operation.

(10) Grounds – War, external aggression, armed rebellion

Grounds on which Emergency can be proclaimed now are war, external aggression and armed rebellion. Before the 44th Amendment it was not 'armed rebellion' but 'internal disturbance'. Term 'internal disturbance' was vague, not as severe as the present 'armed rebellion' and gave wide discretion to the Executive to impose Emergency on flimsy grounds. In 1975 the then Prime Minister Smt. Indira Gandhi declared Emergency when there was nothing alarming on the law and order front or security front. It was a reaction to the call given by the opposition parties to launch a movement to compel her to resign as she was found guilty of corrupt electoral practices by the Allahabad High Court. And so the words 'internal disturbance' was substituted with a more grave situation 'armed rebellion'.

(11) Satisfaction of the President – Not personal but of the Cabinet

It is not the personal satisfaction of the President but the satisfaction of the Cabinet. This aspect is made explicit with the 44th Amendment which states that the President can proclaim an Emergency only on the *written advice* of the Cabinet.

In *Minerva Mills Ltd* v. *Union of India,*[1] Court has held that for the Proclamation of Emergency, satisfaction of the President that a grave emergency exists for proclaiming an Emergency is a condition precedent. If it is shown that there is no satisfaction of the President at all, the exercise of the power would be unconstitutional. Where the satisfaction is absurd or perverse or *mala fide* or based on wholly extraneous grounds it would be no satisfaction at all and could be challenged. But the courts cannot go into the question of correctness or adequacy of the facts and circumstances on which the satisfaction is based.

(12) Duration of Emergency

Before the 44th Amendment, Emergency could remain in force for two months initially and once approved by the Parliament it could remain in force indefinitely –*i.e.* as long as the Executive wanted it. After the Amendment it can remain in force for one month initially. If approved by the Parliament- then for 6 months unless revoked earlier. Before the Amendment resolution could be passed by a simple majority but now it has to be passed by a special majority. To continue beyond 6 months – it now requires Parliamentary approval every 6 months. Executive discretion has been curtailed by a considerable extent.

Take an example for a more clear understanding of when the emergency ceases to operate:

1. President proclaims emergency on ———————15th January
2. It ceases to operate after———————————15th February
3. If Lok Sabha approves it on ———————————25th January
   and the Rajya Sabha approves it on ————14th February (within one month of 15th January then

   It will cease to operate from ——————14th August (6 months from Rajya Sabha approval)
4. If Lok Sabha was dissolved already on————————10th January
   or Lok Sabha is dissolved within one month say————28th January
   but Rajya Sabha has approved it & fresh elections are held and LS reconstituted on ———10th April

   the emergency ceases on——————————————10th May

1. AIR 1980 SC 1789: (1980) 2 SCC 591: (1981) 1 SCR 206.

To continue beyond 10th May every 6 months it has to be approved by the Parliament – so the first approval for continuation—10th Nov.

D. Effects of Emergency

Following are the four important effects of Emergency:

(1) Extension of Union's Executive Power [Article 353(a)]

When Proclamation of Emergency is in operation the Executive power of the Union extends to the giving of directions to any State as to the manner in which its Executive power is to be exercised.

(2) Extension of Union's Legislative Power

The Union Parliament can make laws with respect to matters in the State list (*i.e.* those not in the Union list). The law-making power of the State is not suspended but it is subject to the over-riding power of the Union Parliament. [Article 353(b)].

(3) Alteration in Revenue Distribution

Centre can alter the distribution of revenue between the Union and the State as provided in Article 268-279. Every such order is to be laid before each House of the Parliament and will come to an end by the end of the financial year in which the Proclamation of Emergency ceases to operate.

(4) Extension of life of Lok Sabha

When Emergency is in operation the President may extend the normal life of the Lok Sabha by an year each time up to a period not exceeding beyond 6 months after Proclamation ceases to operate. Article 83(2)

(5) Suspension of Fundamental Freedoms under Article 19

While Emergency is in operation State can make law to take any Executive action taking away or abridging the rights guaranteed by Article 19 of the Constitution. Article 19 freedoms are automatically suspended. As soon as the Emergency ceases to operate Article 19 freedoms are revived and laws inconsistent with Article 19 cease to have effect to the extent of the inconsistency. However things done or omitted to be done before the law ceases to have effect shall remain valid. Note the two changes made under the 44th Amendment Article 19 freedoms can be suspended only when the Proclamation of Emergency is on the ground of war and external aggression and not when it is on the ground of armed rebellion. (b) only the Emergency laws are protected from being challenged as violative of Article 19. That is, the law must contain a recital that it is enacted in relation to the Proclamation of Emergency – only then it gets the protection.

(6) Right to Enforce the Part III Freedoms Suspended (Article 359)

It empowers the President to suspend the right to enforce freedom guaranteed under Part III (*except Article 20-21-* added by 44th Amendment). This can be done only by proclaiming an order to that effect. Suspension is not automatic as in the case of Article 358. As under Article 358 it is applicable only to the emergency laws and hence it must contain a declaration that the law is in relation to the Emergency.

E. Differences between Articles 358 and 359

Makhan Singh v. *State of Punjab*[1] Supreme Court pointed out the following differences between Article 358 and 359:

Article 358	Article 359
Article 19 freedoms are suspended automatically until the Proclamation under article 352 lasts.	It does not suspend any Fundamental rights but deprives the citizens of their right to move any Court for the enforcement of such of the Fundamental rights as are mentioned in the Presidential Order under article 359.
Suspension of article 19 applies to the whole country.	Order under article 359 may extend to the whole country or a part of it.
Suspension of article 19 continues for the entire period of Emergency.	Suspension of the right to move the court is either for the whole period of Emergency or for a shorter period is so specified by the Presidential order.
Things done or omitted to be done during Emergency cannot be challenged even after the Emergency is over.	As soon as the Emergency is over, action can be initiated to challenge the violation of the Fundamental rights whose enforcement was barred under article 359.

It was held in *Makhan Singh*[1] that However citizen can move the Court for a writ of habeas corpus if his detention is *mala fide* inspite of Presidential Order under 359. Detention can also be challenged for infringement of Fundamental rights whose enforcement is not barred under Article 359

In *Ram Manohar Lohia* v: *State of Bihar*,[2] it was held that where a person was detained in violation of the mandatory provisions of the Defence of India Act his right to move the Court was not suspended.

In *Mohd Yaqub* v. *State of J&K*[3] Presidential order under Article 359(1) is not 'law' under Article 13(2) and so its validity cannot be challenged with reference to Part III dealing with Fundamental rights.

The first Emergency under Article 352 was in operation from 1962-1968 during Chinese invasion. The second was proclaimed in 1971 when Pakistan attacked India and continued until March 1977. On 26th June 1975 Emergency was declared due to 'internal disturbance'. This was in addition to the Emergency declared in 1971.

This 1975 Emergency and the detentions made under MISA was challenged in *A.D.M. Jabalpur* v. *Shivkant Shukla*[4] *-habeas corpus* case. The High Courts held that in spite of Presidential Order suspending the enforcement of Fundamental rights conferred by Article 19, 21, 22 High Court could examine whether the detention order under MISA was in accordance with its provisions and whether it was *mala fide*. The Supreme Court held that in view of the Emergency and the Presidential order under Article 359 suspending the enforcement of the Fundamental rights under Article 14,21,22- no writ could lie- not even the habeas corpus writ to challenge the detention order on the grounds of *mala fides*. It held that Article 21 was the sole repository of right to personal liberty and hence there

1. AIR 1964 SC 381: (1964) 4 SCR 797: (1964) 1 Cr LJ 269.
2. AIR 1966 SC 740: 1966 Cr LJ 608: (1966) 1 SCR 709.
3. AIR 1968 SC 765: 1968 Cr LJ 972: (1968) 2 SCR 227.
4. AIR 1976 SC 1207: (1976) 2 SCC 521: 1976 Cr LJ 945.

was no question of relying on the common law or the statutory right to personal liberty under Article 226. The judgment was vehemently criticised. The western Newspapers wrote- 'the World's largest democracy has gone to sleep'. Lot of atrocities were committed by the Government during emergency. Thousands were detained without grounds being disclosed[1]; third degree torture was used in the jails of Independent India; leaders of the Opposition were put behind bars; judgments and Press Reports were censored; judges who gave decisions were transferred without their consent; amendments were made to the Constitution when opposition leaders were behind bars. The judgment in *Habeas Corpus* case facilitated the ruling party because the detenue could not go to the Court for a writ of Habeas Corpus even on the grounds of *mala-fides.*

After the 44th Amendment *Habeas Corpus* case is no longer a good case. However it is a good example for lessons to be learnt from past mistake.

F. Duty to Protect States Article 355

Following two obligations are imposed on the Union:

1. Duty to protect States from internal disturbance and external aggression.
2. Duty to see that every State is carried on in accordance with the provisions of the Constitution. It is this duty which empowers the Centre to take over the State Government under Article 356 if it is not being run in accordance with the Constitution.

For the first time Supreme Court interpreted the word 'aggression' in Article 355 in *Sarbananda Sonowal* v. *Union of India*[2]. It said 'aggression' is not confined to war. Aggression include 'war' and also other acts which cannot be said to be war. The non-stop influx of illegal migrants of Bangladeshis into Assam leading to a change in the population pattern of the State and the insurgency in the State undermining the national security is an act of aggression.

G. Financial Emergency (Article 360)

Financial stability of India threatened: If the President is satisfied that situation has arisen whereby the financial stability or credit of India or part of India is threatened he may be a Proclamation make a declaration to that effect.

After the 44th Amendment following are the provisions respecting financial Emergency. Such a Proclamation can be revoked or varied by a subsequent Proclamation. It has to be laid before each House of Parliament. It ceases to operate at the *expiry of two months,* unless it has been approved by resolutions of both Houses of Parliament before the expiry of that period.

If the Proclamation is passed when the Lok Sabha is dissolved; or if Lok Sabha is dissolved during the period of two months after the Proclamation and the Rajya Sabha approves the Proclamation by a resolution but no such resolution is passed by the Lok Sabha –Proclamation ceases to operate at the expiry of 30 days from the date on which the Lok Sabha first sits after its reconstitution unless

1. Disclosure of grounds of arrest was prohibited under the amended MISA – Maintenance of Internal Security Act.
2. AIR 2005 SC 2920: 2005 AIR SCW 3393: (2005) 5 SCC 665.

before the expiry of this period of 30 days resolution approving the Proclamation has also been passed by Lok Sabha.

Effects of financial Emergency: the Union Executive can give directions to any State to observe such canons of financial propriety as may be specified. It can direct for reduction of salaries and allowances of persons serving a State and the Union including High Court and Supreme Court judges. A provision requiring all Money Bills to be reserved for the consideration of the President after they are passed by the *Legislature of the State.*

H. Provisions in case of failure of Constitutional machinery in States (Articles 356, 357, 365)

If the President, on receipt of a Report from the Governor of a State or otherwise is satisfied that a situation has arisen in which the Government of the State cannot be carried on in accordance with the provisions of the Constitution, he may issue a Proclamation to that effect.

Following are the *effects of such a Proclamation*:

(1) President assumes powers of the Governor

The President may assume to himself all or any of the powers vested in or exercisable by the Governor of the State and Governor or any body or authority other than the legislature of the State [356(a)].

(2) Powers of the State Legislature exercised by Parliament

He may declare that the powers of the State Legislature shall be exercisable by or under the authority of the Parliament. Parliament can also authorise President to make laws for the States and also to delegate such power to other authority specified by him. [356(b)]

(3) Incidental provisions to give effect to Proclamation

President may make such incidental and consequential provisions as may appear to him to be necessary or desirable for giving effect to the object of Proclamation. He can also suspend the operation of any Constitutional provision- (in whole or in part) relating to any body or authority of the State [356(c)]

(4) President cannot assume powers of High Court

President cannot assume to himself any powers vested in the High Court or suspend the operation of any provisions of the Constitution relating to the High Court. [proviso to 356(c)]

Proclamation under Article 356 may be revoked or varied by the President by a subsequent Proclamation. [356(2)]

The Proclamation must be laid before each House of the Parliament.

(a) When it ceases to operate

(a) *After 2 months:* It ceases to operate after two months, but not if it has been approved by resolutions passed by both the Houses of the Parliament

(b) *If Lok Sabha dissolved- Proclamation ceases at expiry of 30 days of Lok Sabha sitting:* If the Proclamation is issued at a time when the Lok Sabha is dissolved or the dissolution takes place during the period of two months referred to above and if a resolution approving the Proclamation has been passed by the Rajya Sabha but no resolution has been passed by the Lok Sabha before the expiry of 2 months, the Proclamation ceases to operate at the expiry of 30 days from the date on which the Lok Sabha first sits after its reconstitution; but not so if before the expiry of the such 30 days a resolution approving the Proclamation has also been passed by the Lok Sabha which is reconstituted.

(c) *An approved proclamation ceases after 6 months:* A Proclamation so approved shall cease to operate on the expiry of a period of 6 months[1] from the date of issue of the Proclamation – unless revoked earlier. [356(4)]

(d) *Continuation of Proclamation:* But if both the Houses pass a resolution for the continuance of the Proclamation – it shall continue in force for a further period of 6 months from the date on which it would otherwise have ceased to operate- but no such Proclamation shall in any case remain in force for more than 3 years. (with respect to State of Punjab- it is 5 years) [proviso to 356(4)]

(e) *Conditions for continuation of Proclamation beyond one year:* Notwithstanding anything contained in Article 356(4) a resolution to continue a Proclamation beyond an year from the date of issue of such a Proclamation cannot be passed by either House of Parliament unless—

(i) Proclamation of Emergency is in operation in the whole of India or any part of the State at the time of passing of such a resolution &

(ii) The Election Commission certifies that the continuance of the Proclamation is necessary due to difficulties in holding general elections to the legislative Assembly of the State concerned. [356(5) proviso]. This proviso is not applicable to Emergency issued on 11th May in Punjab)

Satisfaction- is not the personal satisfaction of the President but that of his Cabinet. Satisfaction can be challenged on the grounds of *mala fides* and that it is based on extraneous grounds. It is held in *S.R. Bommai* v. *Union of India*[2] that the Court can examine whether the reasons disclosed for issuing Proclamation has a rational nexus with the satisfaction of the Governor (President) under Article 356.

Governor's report or otherwise: President acts on the Governor's report or otherwise. The President can act even without the Governor's report. This is justified under Article 355 under which it has to ensure that the States function in accordance with the Constitution.

---

1. When the Constitution was framed it was '6 months'; it was made into 'one year' by 42nd amendment during internal emergency in 1976; it was again replaced by '6 months' by 44th amendment in 1978 when the emergency ceased to operate and Indira Gandhi's Government was defeated at the elections and replaced by Janata Party Government.
2. AIR 1990 Kant 5: ILR 1989 Kant 2425.

Article 356 has been amended 4 times -by 44th, 48th, 64th, 67th Amendments. The last 3 deal with special provisions to deal with the Akali agitation in Punjab.

(b) Can a writ of mandamus be issued directing the President to impose President's rule

All the High Courts have held that no mandamus can be issued to direct the President to issue a Proclamation under Article 356.

(a) *K. Sukumaran* v. *Union of India*[1]: Kerala High Court refused to declare that State of Kerala was not being run in accordance with the Constitution. It was a matter for President's satisfaction and not court's direction.

(b) In *D. Satyanarayan* v. *N.T.Rama Rao*[2]: AP High Court refused to issue mandamus directing the Central Govt to decide whether conditions warranting President rule existed in AP and to initiate necessary action if so satisfied. It held that it would amount to encroaching upon the constitutional functions of the President.

(c) But in *Samyukta Nagrik Samiti* case[3] the Patna High Court held that the High Court also was competent to report to the President about the breakdown of Constitutional machinery in the State it is a stray case which is not consistent with the established constitutional principles of separation of powers and the text of 356. This was a public interest litigation pointing out the irregularities committed by the State Government in implementing Jawahar Rojgar Yojana which fact was confirmed by CAG also.

(c) Is the satisfaction of the President justiciable?

Question was raised for the first time in *K.K. Aboo* v. *Union of India*[4] Kerala High Court held that the courts cannot question the validity of the Proclamation. President is an integral part of the Parliament. The parliament would not approve the Proclamation if it was not impressed with the constitutionality, legality or the propriety of the Proclamation.

(a) In *Rao Birendra Singh* v. *Union of India*[5]: President's rule was imposed in Haryana and the Assembly was dissolved. Proclamation was challenged. High Court dismissed the petition as the legality, propriety or relevancy or material forming the basis for satisfaction was not subject to judicial review; President is not amenable to the jurisdiction of the court under Article 361(1); reconsideration of the proclamation is specifically vested with the Parliament.

(b) In *Gokulananda* v. *Tarpada*[6] the Calcutta High Court held that Article 356(1)(c) under which the President can make incidental and consequential provisions to give effect to the Proclamation also is not justiciable.

---

1. AIR 1987 Kant 212: (1987) 4 (1) IJ Rep 123.
2. AIR 1988 AP 69 (FB): (1987) 2 Andh LT 799.
3. The Hindu dt 12-8-1997.
4. AIR 1965 Ker 229: 1965 Ker LJ 502: ILR (1966) 1 Ker 101.
5. AIR 1968 P&H 441: ILR (1969) 1 P&H 176.
6. AIR 1973 Cal 233: 76 Cal WN 411.

(c) In *Re A. Sreeramulu*[1] the Andhra Pradesh High Court dismissed the writ petition challenging the President's rule in AP on the ground that satisfaction of the President under Article 356 is a political issue; Constitution does not enumerate the situations where President's rule can be imposed. Hence there is no satisfactory criteria available to the courts to judge the relevancy of the considerations based on which President formed his satisfaction.

(d) In *Hanumanth Rao* v. *State of Andhra Pradesh*,[2] the AP High Court held that the provisions of Article 356 are non-justiciable. The court has to show deference (respect) to the satisfaction of the President in proclaiming emergency and also the steps taken by him in tackling the situation. Courts cannot examine the appropriateness or adequacy of the grounds of President's satisfaction nor can he be attributed with bad faith. Courts must keep a 'judicial hands-off in connection with the Presidential exercise of emergency power.

(e) In *Bijayanand* v. *President of India*,[3] Orissa High Court refused to review the legality of the Proclamation which dissolved the Orissa Assembly. The wide source of information as contemplated by the expression 'or otherwise' under Article 356 gives ample indication that President's satisfaction is not justiciable as it is subjective in nature. Article 74(2) and 361(1) prevent the court from contesting the grounds of satisfaction. The emergency provisions under Articles 352, 356, 360 render the President's satisfaction non-justiciable.

In 1975 the Constitution (38th Amendment) Act, 1975 added clause (5) to Article 356 and laid down that 'notwithstanding anything in this Constitution the satisfaction of the President mentioned in clause (1) shall be final and conclusive and shall not be questioned in any Court on any ground.' The clause was added to preclude the courts from claiming jurisdiction to entertain the petitions questioning the validity of the Proclamations issued under Article 356(1). Clause 5 was deleted and replaced by a new clause (5) dealing with an altogether different subject matter. The clause was considered for the first time in *State of Rajasthan* v. *Union of India* discussed below.)

(f) *State of Rajasthan* v. *Union of India* Unprecedented use of Article 356: Nine assemblies were dissolved in 1977 and President's rule imposed. The circumstances were unprecedented. The Congress Government which had an overwhelming majority was routed out at the elections held after the internal emergency was over. Janata Party came to power at the Centre. The Home Minister wrote a letter to the Chief ministers of the Congress led State-Governments to advise their respective Governors to dissolve the Assemblies and go in for fresh elections because they had lost the

1. AIR 1974 AP 106.
2. (1975) 2 Andh WR 277.
3. AIR 1974 Ori 52: (1973) 2 Cut WR 1607: ILR (1973) Cut 1127.

confidence of the people as their Party (Congress) was rejected in the Lok Sabha elections. This led to an apprehension that Article 356 could be invoked.

It was under these circumstances that *State of Rajasthan* v. *Union of India,* AIR 1977 SC 1361: (1977) 3 SCC 592: (1978) 1 SCR 1 came up before the Supreme Court. It was contended that the grounds disclosed in the letter could not be a ground for invoking Article 356; that no dissolution of the Assembles can take place without ascertaining the wishes of both the Houses of the Parliament. Permanent injunction was prayed for- to restrain the Centre from giving effect to the Home Minister's directives. The petition was rejected by a unanimous judgment of 7 member Constitution Bench. It held that:

1. Satisfaction of the President cannot be questioned. Court cannot go into the correctness or adequacy of the facts and circumstances on which the satisfaction of the central Government is based. Satisfaction of the President can be based on material other than the Governor's report. The choice between re-election or dissolution of the State Assemblies is a matter of political expediency and strategy under a democratic system. Mere attempt to get more political power for a party is not Constitutionally prohibited or illegal.
2. But if the Satisfaction is *mala-fide* or based on wholly extraneous and irrelevant grounds, the Court has the jurisdiction to examine it for in such a case there would be no satisfaction at all.[1]

It may be noted that in 1980, the Congress again came to power and Janata party was defeated in 9 States. This time it was the Congress which used the same lines of argument and dismissed the non-Congress State Governments. This amounts to misuse of Article 356.

(g) *S.R. Bommai* v. *Union of India President can only suspend Assembly until Parliament approves:* In *S.R. Bommai* v. *Union of India* the Supreme Court did not agree with the reasoning in *Rajasthan.* It held that the President shall exercise the power of dissolution only after the Proclamation is approved by both the Houses of the Parliament. Until then the President can only suspend the legislative assembly. That is, President must not dissolve the assembly till at least both the Houses of the Parliament have approved the Proclamation. This is because dissolution of the House is an irreversible action and the only way out is a fresh election.

---

1. It is submitted that the judgment cannot be put to a practical implementation. How can the Court find out the *mala fides* without ascertaining the correctness of the facts – is a dilemma. It is urged that the judgment gives only paper powers and not actual powers to the Court to do justice. Secondly I have urged that the framers of the Constitution also have not done their home work well as regards article 356. For details see KILPAR Research Series "Seminal Approach to Constitutional Philosophy: Contributions of Justice Bhagwati and Justice Krishna Iyer: by the present author. (Chapter titled: President's Rule under Article 356: A Misfit? – pp. 446-456.

Court has laid down the following valuable guidelines[1] which should prevent the misuse of Article 356:

1. Presidential Proclamation dissolving a State Legislative Assembly is subject to judicial review.
2. If a State Government works against secularism President's rule can be imposed.
3. There can be no wholesale dismissal of opposition ruled State Governments when a new political party assumes power in the Centre.
4. If President's rule is imposed only on political considerations the Court can even restore the assembly.
5. Imposition of President's rule and dissolution of the assembly cannot be done together
6. State Assembly can be dissolved only after the Parliament approves Central Rule
7. Supreme Court or High Court can compel the Union Government to disclose material on whose basis President's rule is imposed on a State
8. President's power under Art.356 is a Constitutional power. Existence of material to form satisfaction is a condition precedent to imposing President's rule. It is not an absolute power.

In *Rameshwar Prasad* v. *Union of India*[2] Court held that the Governor had acted in undue haste in sending his report to the President based on the media reports that a political party was trying to gain majority by engineering defections. Court held that if defections was the problem- 10th Schedule[3] was the answer and not Article 356. But it did not revive the dissolved Assembly because the election process was at an advanced stage. Court left the matter to be decided by electorate which was the ultimate source of power.

---

1. Guidelines are valuable. There can be no two opinion on that. Yet some negative points must be noted. (1). Judgment was pronounced so late that in Karnataka, Nagaland and Meghalaya fresh elections has already taken place and the benefits of the case being decided in favour of the State Governments concerned could not be realized. (2). Test of secularism for dismissal of the State Governments is vague and untenable specially because 'secularism' has been greatly misunderstood and applied only as regards Hindu Fundamentalism while ignoring the Muslim fundamentalism.
2. (2006) 2 SCC 1: AIR 2006 SC 980: 2006 AIR SCW 494.
3. Provisions regarding disqualification on the ground of defections.

I. Differences between Articles 352 and 356

Proclamation of Emergency under articles 352	Failure of Constitutional machinery under article 356
It is 'Proclamation of *Emergency' under article 352*	It is 'Proclamation of *failure of Constitutional machinery* in a State' under article 356.
It can be proclaimed on grounds of war, external aggression, armed rebellion.	Can be proclaimed on ground that the State is not being run as per the Constitutional provisions.
Ceases to operate at the expiry of *one month* subject to other conditions.	Ceases to operate at the expiry of *two months* subject to other conditions.
Centre-State relations with *all the States in India* undergo a change.	Change is only as regards *the State where 356 is invoked.*
State authorities *do not cease to function.*	State Government *ceases to function* in certain aspects and the Centre takes over the affairs of the State.
Object is to make the *Union more powerful* to handle violent threat from inside or outside the country.	Object is to ensure that the State runs in *accordance with the Constitution.*
Right to move the Court for the enforcement of the Fundamental rights under article 359 *may be* suspended by Presidential Order. Article 19 freedoms are automatically suspended under article 358.	*Fundamental rights not affected.*
Has been used 3 times since independence. Misused in 1975-*i.e.*, 'internal Emergency' due to 'internal disturbance'.	Has been used more than 100 times. Instances of misuse from 1970 onward.

Since the commencement of the Constitution President's rule has been imposed under Article 356 more than 100 times. In most of the cases it has been imposed when a stable ministry could not be formed due to no clear majority of any one political party or due to coalitions and dissensions etc. On occasions, the Union has even refused to assume as in the case of Travancore-Cochin and the problem was solved without Union intervention. But of late, Article 356 has become so controversial that opinions are being expressed that it should be deleted from the Constitution. The first signs of misuse was in 1970 when the Governor – recommended President's rule when the House was scheduled to meet just one week ahead and was claiming to demonstrate its majority. **After the decision in Bommai's case, misuse of article 356 has come down. Between 2000 and 2012 only one case- Rameshwar's case has come up before the Supreme Court.**

CHAPTER 34

AMENDMENT PROVISIONS

Article 368

SYNOPSIS

A. Introduction

"Some men look at Constitution with sanctimonious (pious) reverence (worship) and deem them ... too sacred to be touched. They ascribe to the men of the preceding age a wisdom more than human, and suppose what they did to be beyond Amendment .... Laws and institutions must go hand in hand with the progress of the human mind.... As new discoveries are made new truths disclosed and manners and opinions must advance also and keep pace with the times. Each generation ... has the right to choose for itself the form of

Government it believes the most promotive of its own happiness...."[1] hence the need for Amendment provisions.

The ease or difficulty with which a Constitution may be amended is regarded as the yardstick for determining whether the Constitution is a rigid one or a flexible one. If no provision for Amendment were provided there would be a constant danger of revolution and if it was too easy there could be hasty changes. The Constitutional provisions make it possible to change the Constitution in an orderly fashion keeping in tune with the changing times and aspirations and needs.

B. Three classes of Amendments

Constitution provides for three classes of Amendments:

(1) By a bare majority

(Article 4 provides for amending the Schedules to suit the laws passed under articles 2 and 3)[2]; Article 169 (empowering the President to create or abolish Legislative Councils).

(2) By a special majority

Article 240 (empowering the President to make regulations for peace progress and good Government of certain Union territories): Article 368. Constitutional Amendments other than those mentioned above.

(3) By special majority and ratification by resolutions passed by not less than half of the States

They cover eleven categories of Amendments which seek to amend federal structure of the Constitution.

C. Power and Procedure to amend Constitution[3]

Article 368 prescribes a special procedure for the Amendment of the Constitution. Following are the steps through which it can be amended—

(1) Introduction of the Bill

It can be initiated *only* by the introduction of a Bill for the purpose either in the Lok Sabha or Rajya Sabha. Thus the process of amending is a legislative process and an Amendment is to be passed as a legislative measure.

(2) 2/3rd majority

When the Bill is passed in each House by a majority of the total membership of that House and by a majority of not less than 2/3rd of the members of that House present and voting it is presented to the President 'who shall give his assent to the Bill'[4]. Note that the President has no option but to give his assent unlike before the 24th Amendment.

---

1. Thomas Jefferson to S. Kercheval (1816) quoted by Krishna Iyer J.: The Indian Presidency, (1988), 53 (New Delhi, Deep and Deep Publications 1988).
2. Formation of new States by alteration etc., and addition of new States – require re-allocation of seats mentioned in Schedule 4.
3. Subs. by 24th Amendment Act, 1971 for 'Procedure for amendment of the Constitution'.
4. Subs. By 24th Amendment Act, 1971 for 'it shall be presented for his assent and upon such assent being given to the Bill'.

(3) Ratification by States

If the Amendment seeks to make a change in the following categories it needs a ratification by not less than half the number of States. *viz.,*

(a) Election of the President (Articles 54, 55);

(b) Extent of executive powers of the Union and the States (Article 73, 162);

(c) Articles dealing with Supreme Court, High Court and Union Territories (Article 124-147, 214-231, 241);

(d) Distribution of legislative powers between Centre and States (Article 245 to 255);

(e) VII Schedule lists;

(f) Representation of States in the Parliament;

(g) Article 368 itself.

Such ratification must be done before the President gives his assent.

D. Other provisions regarding Amendment

(1) *Article 13 not applicable to article 368:* Nothing in article 13 shall apply to any Constitutional Amendment made under article 368.[1] The State is barred from making any law taking away or abridging the Fundamental rights under article 13. This means that the Constitution can be amended to take away or abridge the Fundamental rights after the 1971 amendment.

(2) Under the 42nd Amendment 1976 two changes were introduced:

(i) No Amendment of the Constitution *including the provisions relating to Fundamental right* made or purporting to be made under article 368 could be called into question in any Court on any ground. (clause 4)

(ii) It also declared that there would be no limitation whatsoever in the power of the Parliament to amend by way of addition, variation or repeal any of the provisions of the Constitution. (clause 5)

In *Minerva Mills Ltd* v. *Union of India*[2] it was held that the provision barring judicial review was beyond the amending powers of the Parliament. Clause(i) which barred judicial review is unconstitutional. The Indian Constitution is founded on the bedrock of a judicious balance between the Legislature, Executive and the Judiciary. It is a power-cum-duty of the judges to pronounce on the validity of the laws. If this is taken away – Fundamental right would become a mere adornment and article 13 would become a dead letter.

As regards the second clause it gave vast and undefined unfettered discretion to the Parliament to amend the Constitution to the extent of distorting it beyond recognition. It held that a limited amending power is the basic feature of the Constitution.

E. Distinguishing features of Article 368

(1) No separate body for amending the Constitution

Amendment to the Constitution 'may be initiated *'only'* by introduction of the Bill' indicates that the ordinary Legislature of the Union *i.e.,* the Parliament

---

1. Note that a similar amendment is made in Article 13 by the 24th Amendment.
2. AIR 1980 SC 1789: (1980) 2 SCC 591: (1981) 1 SCR 206.

is vested with the constituent power to amend the Constitution. There is no separate body for amending the Constitution as in some Constitutions.

(2) Amendment to be moved only in the Parliament

Amendments can be moved only in the Parliament Houses – either the Lok Sabha or the Rajya Sabha and not in any State Legislature. There is no requirement of referendum or plebiscite or a reference to the Constitutional convention

(3) Every provision in the Constitution can be amended

F. Amendment of Fundamental right – From limited to unlimited powers

Whether the Fundamental right can be amended was a question that was raised before the Court several times – but on which no debate whatsoever had taken place in the Parliament. Following is the route taken by this important question.

(1) Shankari Prasad – Parliament can amend Fundamental rights

It came up for the first time in *Shankari Prasad* v. *Union of India*[1] when the First Amendment to the Constitution was challenged. It was held that the Parliament has the power to amend the Fundamental rights. Such power is contained in article 368; that 'Law' under article 13(2) does not include an Amendment of the Constitution made in exercise of the constituent power. Hence Fundamental right can be amended, abridged or abrogated by a Constitutional Amendment. It was a case where articles 31A & 31B were inserted which took away the Fundamental right conferred by articles 14 and 19.

(2) Sajjan Singh – Fundamental right can be amended

Then came *Sajjan Singh* v. *State of Rajasthan*[2] in which the 17th Amendment which had added several legislations to the 9th Schedule was challenged and was upheld by the Supreme Court relying on the *Shankari Prasad* case. The majority observed that if the framers of the Constitution had intended they would have laid down that the Fundamental rights cannot be amended. (Note that legislations inserted in the 9th Schedule cannot be challenged on the ground that they take away the Fundamental rights.)

(3) Golaknath – No power to abridge Fundamental right

In *Golaknath* v. *State of Punjab*[3] the 17th Constitution Amendment Act, which had inserted certain State Acts in 9th Schedule was challenged. The earlier rulings were reversed and it was held that the Parliament has no power to amend Part III of the Constitution so as to take away or abridge the Fundamental right. It based its judgment on the following reasons:

(a) Chief Justice rejected the argument that the power to amend the Constitution is a sovereign power – Superior to the ordinary legislative power and that therefore it had no limitations; and that the exercise of the power involves political questions and that therefore they were outside judicial review.

1. AIR 1951 SC 458.
2. AIR 1965 SC 845: (1965) 1 SCR 933.
3. AIR 1967 SC 1643.

(b) Power of the Parliament to amend the Constitution is contained in article 245 read with Entry 97 List I and not from articles 368. Article 368 merely lays down the procedure for Amendment of the Constitution. Constitutional amendment is a legislative process.

(c) 'Law' under article 13(2) includes every kind of law including an Amendment under article 368. Therefore if it takes away or abridges the Fundamental right it is void under article 13(2).

(d) The decision had only prospective operation and hence would affect only the cases coming up after *Golaknath*. Cases decided before *Golaknath* would continue to remain valid.

(4) Kesavanand Bharati – Basic structure cannot be amended

In *Keshavanand Bharati* v. *State of Kerala*[1] 24th Amendment Act, 1971 which was enacted to remove the difficulties created by *Golaknath* was challenged. It was decided by a 13 judge Bench. It laid down that though the Parliament has wide powers to amend the Constitution it does not have unlimited powers. It can amend so as not to destroy the basic structure of the Constitution. The 24th Amendment made the following changes:

(a) The marginal note to article 368 was modified from 'procedure to amend the Constitution' to '*Power of the Parliament to amend the Constitution and procedure therefor*'.

(b) A new clause (4) was added to article 13 to provide that article 13(2) shall not include an Amendment made under article 368. This means that a Constitutional Amendment can take *away or abridge the Fundamental rights*.

(c) Consequential Amendment was made to article 368 to state that article 13 shall not be applicable to article 368.

(d) The power of the Parliament to amend the Constitution was *extended* to add, vary or repeal the Constitution.

(e) It was made *mandatory* to give assent to the Constitutional Amendment Bill. It provided that the 'President *shall give his assent* to the Constitution Amendment' instead of 'it shall be presented to the President for his assent and *upon such assent being given to the Bill*.'

G. Theory of Basic Structure

The theory of basic structure of the Constitution was laid down for the first time in *Kesavanand Bharati case* popularly known as the *Fundamental rights case*.

Facts of Kesavanand Bharati

The writ was initially filed to challenge the validity of Kerala Land Reforms Act, 1969. During the pendency of the petition the Kerala Land Reforms Act was amended and placed in the 9th Schedule by the 29th Amendment, so that it could not be challenged on the ground that it violates Part III of the Constitution. 25th Amendment Act was passed in 1971, to remove the difficulty created by the *Bank*

---

1. AIR 1973 SC 1461: (1973) 4 SCC 225: 1973 Supp SCR 1.

Nationalisation case. It amended clause (2) of article 31 and laid down in effect that property could be acquired by the State on payment of an 'amount' instead of 'compensation' as provided earlier. It added clause (2A) to make it clear that the property-deprivation law cannot be challenged on the ground that it takes away the Fundamental right under article 19. It inserted article 31(C) providing that the law passed for giving effect to the directive principles specified in article 39(b) and (c) shall not be challenged on the ground that it is inconsistent with or takes away or abridges any of the Fundamental right under articles 14, 19, 31. The petitioner was allowed to challenge the 24th, 25th, 29th Amendments. It was held that the 24th and 25th Amendment were valid. That the 24th Amendment is only declaratory in nature and that even before the Amendment the Parliament had the power to amend all or any of the Fundamental rights.

Question involved in *Keshavanand Bharati was decided by 13 judges with 11 different Judgments.*

The question involved was what is the extent of amending power conferred by article 368?

The Union claimed was that an unlimited amending power; that short of repealing the Constitution any change could be effected.

Petitioner's contention was that the amending power was wide but not unlimited; that the Parliament cannot destroy the 'basic feature' of the Constitution.

Court ruling:

1. It overruled *Golak Nath* which had held that Parliament's power to amend the Constitution is limited.
2. That even before the 24th Amendment article 368 contained the power as well as the procedure for Amendment. 24th Amendment only made it explicit what was otherwise implied. 24th Amendment does not enlarge the amending powers of the Parliament. It is only declaratory in nature.
3. That under article 368 Parliament is not empowered to amend the basic structure of Constitution.
4. The first part of the 25th Amendment is valid (property – deprivation law passed to give effect to the directive principles cannot be challenged on the ground that it infringes Fundamental right under article 19). But the second part that 'no such law containing the declaration that it is for giving effect to such policy shall be called in question in any court on the ground that it does not give effect to such policy' – is invalid and unconstitutional as it takes away the judicial review powers of the Court.
5. In view of Preamble, the importance given to Fundamental right and the emphasis on economic, political, social justice, stricter provisions for amending articles 52, 53 & the other federal structures of the Constitution (need for ratification by the States) show an intention that the framers of the Constitution did not want to use the word 'Amendment' in the widest sense. Hence the Constitution can be amended in such a manner that any change or alteration in the Fundamental rights must be within the broad contours of the Preamble, Constitution and the objectives and the Directive Principles.

6. The court rejected the argument of the Union and the States that the concept of basic structure is vague and illusive and an unsatisfactory test.

The judges[1] enumerated the following as the basic structure, *viz.*, (a) supremacy of the Constitution; (b) republic and democratic form of the Government; (c)secular character of the Government (d) Separation of powers between the Legislature, Executive and the Judiciary; (e) Federal character of the Constitution. They made it clear that these were only illustrative and not exhaustive. They had to be determined as and when the cases come up before the courts. Hegde J. and Mukherjee J cited democratic character of our policy a unity of India as essential features of individual freedom and mandate to build a welfare State.

In *Indira Nehru Gandhi* v. *Raj Narain*[2] the Supreme Court applied the basic structure doctrine and struck down article 329A inserted by 39th Amendment, 1975 on the ground that it was beyond the amending powers of the Parliament. It established a body to be constituted by the Parliament – made law to handle election disputes pertaining to the Speaker and the Prime Minister. It also barred judicial review of the decisions of such body.

In *Minerva Mills Ltd* v. *Union of India*[3] the Supreme Court held that limited powers of the Parliament to amend the Constitution, rule of law, judicial review and democracy which implies free and fair elections, harmony between Fundamental right and Directive Principles, judicial review are the basic features.

H. 42nd Amendment and Article 368

Constitution Amendments under article 368 can be challenged on the ground that they destroy the basic structure of the Constitution.

In *Minerva Mills* v. *UOI– Article 368 (4) &(5) unconstitutional*: Article 368 (4) & (5) added by 42nd Amendment were held to be unconstitutional as it took away the judicial review powers of the Judiciary. Thus, it is the Constitution which is Supreme and not the Parliament because the Parliament is the creature of the Constitution. Parliament's power in connection with law-making is of two types—

(1) *Ordinary Legislative Power*: Under which laws are made and amended. It includes within its fold – making and amending all laws except the Constitutional law. This power also has to be exercised within the Constitutional framework. Thus if the law contravenes the provisions of the Constitution it is declared unconstitutional and therefore void.

(2) *The Constituent Power*: Under which the Constitution itself is amended. The constituent power of amending the Constitution is not unlimited. The Parliament elected for a fixed period of 5 years cannot be vested with the unlimited power to amend it.

In Waman Rao v. *Union of India*[4] *the decision in: Keshavanand* was given a prospective applicability and not retrospective. Thus, the Supreme·Court held

1. Shelat and Grover, JJ.
2. AIR 1975 SC 2299: 1976 2 SCR 347: 1975 Supp SCC 1.
3. AIR 1980 SC 1789: (1981) 1 SCR 206.
4. AIR 1981 SC 271.

that all Amendments to the Constitution including the Amendments to the Ninth Schedule, made before April 24th, 1973 *i.e.*, the date on which *Keshavanand* judgment was delivered were valid and the Amendments to be made after that date had to satisfy the 'basic structure doctrine.' In this case it was held that the protection of article 31B is available only to the Original Acts included in the Ninth Schedule but Orders and notifications made under the Acts included in the Ninth Schedule are not entitled to protection.[1]

Validation of certain Acts and Regulations – Article 31B – added by the Constitution First Amendment Act, 1951. It provides that none of the Acts and Regulations mentioned in the Ninth Schedule to the Constitution shall be deemed to be void on the ground that they are inconsistent with any of the Fundamental rights conferred by Part III of the Constitution. However the Legislature can amend and repeal these Acts. The validity of the amended and repealed Acts- if not saved under article 31A – (no law providing for acquisition of any estate shall be deemed to be void on the ground that it violates articles 14, 19 of the Constitution) can be examined by the Courts on merits.[2]

In *S.P. Sampat Kumar* v. *Union of India*[3] - Constitutional validity of the Administrative Tribunals Act, 1985 and article 323A was challenged. It had excluded the jurisdiction of the High Court under articles 226 and 227 regarding service matters. But it had not excluded the jurisdiction of the Supreme Court under articles 32 and 136. Necessary changes also were incorporated in the Administrative Tribunals Act. Hence it was held that – as there was an effective alternative institutional mechanism that was provided for dealing with the disputes- the power of judicial review – which is a basic structure of the Constitution was not taken away.

L. Chandra Kumar v. *Union of India*[4]: *Tribunals cannot replace the Supreme Court or the High Courts:* –The Supreme Court struck down article 323A(2d) and article 323B (3d) which provided for the exclusion of the jurisdiction of the High Court under articles 226 and 227 and of the Supreme Court under article 32 of the Constitution. These jurisdictions of the High Court and the Supreme Court are an integral feature of the Constitution and formed its basic structure. Other Tribunals and Courts can discharge a supplemental role of judicial review. There is nothing objectionable about it as long as the judicial review of the High Court and the Supreme Court is not taken away. They cannot totally replace the High Court and the Supreme Court.

M. Nagraj v. *Union of India*[5] – *77th and the 81st Amendments to the Constitution- valid:* The *77th and the 81st Amendments to the Constitution* were challenged. They added articles 16(4A) and 16(4B) to the Constitution. 77th Amendment provided for reservations in matters of '*promotion along with consequential seniority*' in favour of the SCs/STs. The amendment abrogated judicial decisions which held that promotions with consequential seniority unconstitutional. The 81st Amendment

1. *Prag Ice & Oil Mills* v. *Union of India*, AIR 1978 SC 1296.
2. *Sajjan Singh* v. *State of Rajasthan*, AIR 1955 SC 845.
3. AIR 1987 SC 386.
4. AIR 1997 SC 1125.
5. AIR 2007 SC 71.

laid down that the 50% ceiling on reservations laid down in so many judgments was not applicable while filling up the backlog unfilled vacancies for the SCs/STs. It was held that these amendments do not violate the basic structure doctrine. They are enabling provisions and apply only to the SCs/STs. The 50% ceiling limit rule, the creamy layer rule, post-based filling up of vacancies laid down in *Indira Sawhney* case is not obliterated. Article 16(4A) is applicable only to the SCs/STs; backwardness and inadequacy of representation are still the factors based on which reservations in promotions are to be given; articles 14, 15, 16 are not obliterated; relaxation in qualifying marks[1] are to be applied with regard to efficiency in administration provided in article 335.

It was held that the catch-up rule or the consequential seniority rules which were laid down by the Judiciary are not constitutional principles. They cannot be elevated to the status of an axiom like that of secularism or sovereignty. Hence they are within the amending powers of Parliament under article 368.

I.R. Coelho v. *State of Tamil Nadu*[2]*- provisions of the Acts added to 9th Schedule by Amendment-subject to judicial review:* Even if an Act is put in the Ninth Schedule by a Constitutional Amendment, its provisions can be challenged if they violate the basic structure of the Constitution. In this case, Gudalur Janmam Estate (Abolition and Conversion into Ryotwari) Act, was struck down by the High Court because it was not an agrarian reform. The Act was amended and inserted in the 9th Schedule by the 34th Constitution Amendment Act. In another matter in the same case, section 2(c) of the West Bengal Land Holding Revenue Act, 1976 was struck down by Calcutta High Court as being arbitrary and violative of article 14. SLP was filed against the judgment by West Bengal. It was dismissed. By 66th Constitution Amendment, West Bengal Land Holding Revenue Act, 1979 was inserted in the Ninth Schedule. The court held that in spite of the Acts being inserted in the 9th Schedule the court has the power of judicial review to see if it violates the basic structure of the Constitution.

Ninth Schedule initially inserted for protecting agrarian reforms has been misused and other Non-Agrarian Reformatory laws are inserted in the Schedule to insulate them from the fundamental rights. *For example* Tamil Nadu Government made 69% reservations and inserted it in the Ninth Schedule so that it should not be challenged as exceeding the 50% reservation limit laid down by the courts and as violating the Fundamental rights. It was struck down as unconstitutional.

I. Criticism of the *Kesavanand Bharati Case*

The *Keshavanand* case is the greatest Constitutional case and most frequently relied. However it has drawn much criticism. It is not only the Judgment which has drawn criticism but also the manner in which the judgment was delivered; the way in which the *Keshavanand* Bench was constituted; and the politics played by the direct and indirect players in the case. It represents a conflict between 'theory and ideology pertaining to judicial process and other allied matters on one hand and facts, realities and human behaviour on the other'. *For example,*

1. Proviso to Article 335 added by 82nd Amendment to Constitution.
2. (2007) 2 SCC 1.

the Constitutional ideal is that the Legislature and the Judiciary are the pillars of our democratic system and that they are expected to and designed by the Constitution to act in harmony with each other, but *Keshavanand Bharati* case and the prelude and the aftermath of the case is a classic example of 'a tug of war between them and hence a lesson on how not to deal with a case on hand'. It reveals the extent to which the Executive can go in order to establish its supremacy and 'rewarding or punishing' the judges for giving rulings not palatable to them. The *'The Keshavanand Bharati Case – The Untold Story of Struggle for Supremacy by the Supreme Court and Parliament'*[1] narrates how manipulations are worked out to ensure that a ruling favourable to the Parliament are given by the court. Following is the gist of what happened in and around *Keshavanand Bharati.*

(1) Kesavanand Bharati decided in surcharged atmosphere

Keshavanand Bharti case was decided in a surcharged atmosphere of tension between the Judiciary and the Parliament. It was a conflict of interpretations of the Constitution: Parliament claiming that it has the powers to amend the Fundamental rights and the Judiciary emphasising upon the Fundamental right to property and holding property abolition/restriction laws as unconstitutional.

(2) The case stands apart from others

The case stands apart for the way in which established norms and conventions were by passed by the judges and the counsels alike. Judges did not remain unbiased and the counsels argued with passion and antagonism rather than remain merely objective and detached. Hence Sri. H.M. Seervai arguing for the Kerala Government hoped that the 'likes of *Keshavanand* would never be seen in our Supreme Court'; C.J. Ray observed that the case was a *'nightmare'*; Granville Austin commented that manner of arriving at the decision *'reflected ill'* on the Bench and on the Judiciary as an Institution. The judges' deliberation process was bizarre. Their individual opinions were chaotically articulated. The relations of one or more judges with the Executive Branch were thought to have been improper.

(3) Judges with pre-determined views and pronouncements on the Bench

Judges who were parties to the earlier judgments to be tested in *Keshavanand* were also on the Bench deciding *Keshavanand.* As a matter of proprieties they ought not to have been on the Bench as they had already formed and expressed their opinions on the issues involved. *For example, Golak Nath* was questioned in *Keshavanand.* But, C.J. Subba Rao. Sikri, and Shelat who were parties to *Golak Nath* were also members of 13 member Bench in *Keshavanand.* This is in spite of three other non committed judges – Justices Vaidyalingam, Dua and Alagiriswamy who were not judges in *Golak Nath* being available for *Keshavanand Bench.*

Likewise judges who had voided Bank Nationalisation Act in *R.C. Cooper's case* on the ground of inadequacy of compensation for taking away right to property were justices in *Keshavanand.*

---

1. Authored by Sri T.R. Andhyarujina (Universal Law Publishing Co. Pvt. Ltd. New Delhi).

(4) Establishing Parliamentary supremacy – Became election manifesto

Overcoming Supreme Court judgments which hampered social and economic reforms of the Government and re-establishing Parliamentary supremacy became the Congress Party's election manifesto in 1971. Congress won with a thumping majority. Acting on the people's mandate, 24th Amendment was passed giving unlimited amending powers to Parliament by amending articles 368 and 13. In effect, it overruled majority decision in *Golak Nath*. By 25th Amendment, term 'compensation' was replaced by 'amount' under article 31(2); primacy was given to directive principles under article 39(b) &(c) over Fundamental rights under articles 14, 19, 31. 26th Amendment Act inserted Kerala Land Reforms Act, 1969 and Kerala Land Reforms Amendment Act, 1971 in Ninth Schedule to validate the provisions which were invalidated by Kerala High Court and Supreme Court as being violative of the Fundamental right to property. These amendments were a challenge to the court in *Keshavanand* to reconsider its earlier judgments. Thus *Keshavanand* laid down grounds for major political confrontations between the Judiciary and the Parliament.

(5) Appointment of judges based on their judicial attitudes

It is in this background that Supreme Court judges were appointed by Government keeping in mind judicial attitudes of the judges as indicated by their judgments.

After the election a Committee was appointed to advise the Prime Minister 'to introduce amendments so as to vest executive with full powers by over-ruling *Golak Nath case* and to appoint judges committed to a policy as highlighted in Parliamentary debates on this aspect.[1]

(6) Pre-determined views of the judges in Kesavanand case

Justices Shelat, Hegde, Grover were party to *Bank Nationalisation, Golak Nath, and Privy Purse cases.* They firmly held that Parliament's power to amend Fundamentals rights is limited. Justices Ray, Mathews, Beg, Dwivedi believed that Parliament's power to amend the Fundamental right particularly the right to property to further economic reforms is unlimited. These were pre-determined views of judges on *Keshavanand Bench.* Justice Jaganmohan Reddy commented that he got an impression throughout that 'minds were closed and views were pre-determined.'[2] Justices Khanna, Mukherjea, Jaganmohan Reddy and Chandrachud were non-committed. Views were so pre-determined that on one occasion, Justice Jaganmohan Reddy put a question to the Attorney General and it was answered by J. Hegde and J. Jagmohan Reddy had protested. On another occasion J. Hegde told Seervai (arguing for the Government) that there was no substance in his argument and J. Ray intervened to tell Seervai to 'go on as he wanted.'

Dwivedi J. spelt out his firm view point by observing that if Palkhivala (representing the petitioners) was prepared to say that Fundamental right to property can be amended he would procure from the Parliament that all other

1. Justice Jagmohan Reddy: 'The justice I served: Orient Longman" – quoted in *Ibid* p. 15.
2. *Ibid* at p. 21.

Fundamental rights can be left unamended.' Texts of the draft judgment came into the hands of the Government before their delivery on 24th April 1973. Justice Beg and J. Dwivedi were labelled as pro-Government.

(7) Threats and frictions and tensions

There were sharp exchanges between Attorney-General Mr. Niren De (who had appeared for Government in *Golak Nath, Bank Nationalisation and Madhav Rao Scindia)* and the court. Niren De was most arrogant and rude and said on an occasion that 'consequences would have to be borne if the decision went against the Government'.[1]

There was continuous friction between Palkhivala making arguments of political nature and Seervai and the Attorney General protesting at Palkhivala's approach.

There were tensions even between the Attorney-General and Seervai though both were defending the Parliament's power to amend Constitution.[2] Seervai claimed to argue before the Attorney-General though in law Attorney-General has the right of the first audience[3]. Strained relations were eased out at the instance of Mr. Fali Nariman and Sri Andhyarujina.[4]

(8) Hospitalisation of J. Beg and end of oral hearings

Abrupt end of oral hearings and breakdown of Court norms towards the end of *Kesavanand case* was most unfortunate and unprecedented. Justice Beg was hospitalised several times during the 66 days of *Kesavanand* hearing. J. Beg was clearly inclined in favour of Parliament's unfettered power to amend the Constitution. Possibilities of J. Beg being 'dropped' from the Bench were suggested by the Chief Justice as he was advised complete rest for 3 weeks upon the risk of his death and the judgment had to be pronounced before 25th April as the CJI was to retire on that day and then proceed abroad. Palkhivala insisted that he be allowed to make oral submissions as the Respondents had taken 34 days while he himself had argued for 31 days. The Attorney- General and Seervai threatened to withdraw from the case if J. Beg was not to be on the Bench. J. Hegde retorted that he thought that 'walkouts were confined only to the Parliament and not to the courts' and that 'if we can be threatened like this the next time they will threaten us if we do not write judgment they want.'[5]

The case was later posted for 'orders and hearing.' To the surprise of the Government side, even before the Chief Justice could state his decision, Palkhivala addressed the court making it clear that the petitioners too are anxious that J. Beg should participate in the judgment (note that J. Beg's firm mind set was against the petitioner argument and his absence could benefit the petitioners)

---

1. *Ibid* p. 25.
2. Seervai representing the Kerala Government and Niren De representing the Government of India.
3. Right to be heard first by the court.
4. Ultimately Seervai argued first. Niren De told the court that Seervai would begin the arguments as he himself was busy with an Afro-Asian Conference on the Law of Seas, this was considered by some as lowering the status of the post of the Attorney-General.
5. Untold Story of Struggle for Supremacy of SC & Parliament, p. 35.

and that the 'World's most momentous case in World's history and in the history of Democracy should not be clouded by pettiness, bitterness and he suggested that the case be treated as closed and the petitioners permitted to put in the main points of written reply and if any of the Lordships is unable to participate in the judgment the judgment be delivered by the rest of the learned judges.

(9) The judgment

The 13 judges on the *Keshavanand Bench* were C.J. S.M. Sikri, Justices J.M. Shelat, K.S. Hegde, A.N. Grover, A.N. Ray, P. Jaganmohan Reddy, D.G. Palekar, H.R. Khanna, K.K. Mathew, M.H. Beg, S.N. Dwivedi, A.K. Mukherjea and Y.V. Chandrachud, eleven judgments were delivered by 13 judges. The judgments reflected the selections and appointments of individual judges:

- 5 out of 6 sitting judges prior to the initiative of Government to appoint judges (*i.e.,* C.J. Sikri, Shelat, Hedge, Grover and Jagmohan Reddy) decided in favour of inherent limitations on amending powers.
- The 6th judge Justice A.N. Ray who was generally out of step with the rest in earlier judgments decided in favour of unlimited power of amendment.
- Of the 6 recent appointments on Government's initiative – 5 of them decided in favour of unlimited amending powers (Justices Palekar, Mathew, Beg, Dwivedi and Chandrachud).
- Only one decided in favour of limitation on amending power (J. Mukherjea who wrote a common judgment with Justice Hegde.)
- Justice Khanna decided midway – *i.e.,* that the limitation is only on amending the basic structure of the Constitution.

In the result Government's initiative to appoint judges expected to decide in its favour only partially succeeded.

The basic question was" is there a ratio that the basic structure of the Constitution cannot be amended?": The question is: "could it be said that there was a *ratio in Keshvanand case* that the Parliament has no power to amend the basic structure of the Constitution?"[1]

The way in which the argument took shape is interesting

- *Keshavanand Bharati Bench* was constituted to reconsider the correctness of *Golak Nath* which had held that while amending the Constitution, Parliament exercises its ordinary legislative powers under List I item 97, and that article 368 prescribes only the procedure. So the petitioners began by justifying the correctness of *Golak Nath.* But CJ Sikri (a party to the majority judgment in *Golak Nath*) took the petitioners by surprise by telling Palkhivalla that it may not be necessary to consider the correctness of *Golak Nath* in view of the Constitutional 24th amendment giving unlimited powers to the Parliament to amend the Constitution and hence the line of enquiry should be: Whether there were inherent and implied limitations on the amending powers in article 368. So the

1. Refer Chapter IV Ibid 'Untold story of Keshavanand Bharati'.

petitioners changed the course of their argument and challenged the amending powers of the Parliament on inherent and implied limitations on the Parliament to amend the Constitution. For all practical purposes, petitioners abandoned defending *Golak Nath. Golak Nath* was overruled by all except C.J. Sikri and J. Shelat.

- That article 368 does not enable the Parliament to alter the basic structure was the conclusion of only one judge – J. Khanna.
- References to expressions such as 'basic structure, basic feature, or basic elements or essential features or fundamental features etc.' used by 6 other judges were made in different contexts and from inherent and implied limitations on Parliament whereas J. Khanna held that limitation of basic structure arose only from the limited scope of the word 'Amendment as distinguished from the word 'abrogation'. He rejected the theory of inherent limitations on amending power. Hence there could be no view by the majority of 7 judges (signed by nine judges) that article 368 does not enable Parliament to alter the basic structure of the Constitution. Seervai also commented soon after the judgment was pronounced that there is an unbridgeable gap between concepts and lines of reasoning of J. Khanna and the 6 others.
- *View by the majority:* the 'untold story of *Keshavanand Bharati case* lies in the manner in which the view of the majority' was formulated. After all, the 11 judgments were orally pronounced in the court on 24th April, 1973. C.J. Sikri produced and read out in the court a paper titled 'the Views of the Majority' and passed it on to all the 13 judges for signature. It consisted of 6 propositions. Proposition No. 2 was lifted from J. Khanna's conclusion *viz.* that article 368 does not enable the Parliament to alter basic structure of Constitution. 4 judges (Justices Ray, Mathews, Dwivedi, Beg) refused to sign it. 9 others signed it. However all the 13 judges signed a unanimous Order *viz.*, that the Constitution Bench will determine the validity of the 26th Amendment Act in accordance with law.[1]
- There were no possibilities of any discussion between the Justices in order to form 'View of the Majority'. They were hastily drawn up by C.J. Sikri[2]. There was only one judicial conference of only the judges favouring limitations on Parliament's amending powers called prior to the delivery of judgment.

Never had the Supreme Court seen such a spectacle. These are the so-called 'Views of Majority' assumed to be the decision in *Keshavanand Bharati.*

---

1. These Orders are correctly reproduced only in Supreme Court Reporter and not in AIR or SCC. AIR reports 'views by majority' as 'summary' before headnotes and not at the end of judgment. P. 56.
2. Per J.Beg in Ibid p. 57.

(10) Views of the majority cannot be the 'ratio of Kesavanand'

'Views of the Majority' cannot be the *ratio* of *Kesavanand Bharati.*[1] Deriving the *ratio* could be done only after full hearing by a later Constitution Bench to which petitions were remanded for disposal according to unanimous Order of the court. No later Constitution Bench was convened to dispose of the petitions. Alternatively, the *ratio* could have been derived by any later Bench from the differing judgments as was done before.[2]

(11) 'Summary in Kesavanand' has no legal effect

Summary signed by 9 judges has no legal effect and is not the law under article 141. As there was a unanimous order there was no occasion for determining what the majority of the judges had decided. 13 judges had signed a unanimous order but 4 of them had refused to sign the summary showing that there was a difference of opinion.

Note that Seervai points out that *'summary in Kesavanand'* is defective as regards the 5th proposition dealing with the amended article 31C. (the first part giving primacy to the directive principles was held valid and the second part taking away the judicial review powers was held unconstitutional.) This is because 5 of the 7 judges held article 31 wholly void. One other Justice severed some parts of article 31 to hold it valid. It was only Justice Khanna who held that only the first part of article 31 is valid and the second part invalid as it destroyed the judicial review powers. Thus, Palkhivala summed up the 'majority dilemma' of *Kesavanand* – with his observation that 6 judges were in favour of the State; 6 in favour of the citizen; and one – Justice Khanna decided midway between the two conflicting viewpoints. "By a strange quirk of fate the judgment of Justice Khanna with whom none of the other judges agreed has become the 'law of the land'"[3]. By a strategic roping in of Khanna's views with 6 other Judges 'The View by the Majority' – a majority of 7 judges to 6 was *created and approved by 9 judges*.

(12) Approach of the later courts to the 'basic structure' concept

In *Indira Nehru Gandhi* v. *Raj Narain*[4], Justice Mathew observed that he would proceed on the assumption that law laid down by the majority in *Keshavanand* should govern the decision though he does not 'share that view.'[5]

Keshavanand Bharati case is popularly known as 'Fundamental rights case', because the 13 judge Bench was constituted to reconsider the correctness of *Golak Nath* which had held that Fundamental rights cannot be amended. The 'View by the Majority' stated that *Golak Nath* which held that Fundamental rights cannot be amended was over-ruled. It did *not state as a proposition that Fundamental right is a part of basic structure and hence could not be amended*. Palkhivala's argument

---

1. Keshavanand: Untold Story of Struggle for Supremacy of SC & Parliament, p. 58.
2. For *e.g., S.R. Bommai* case, AIR 1994 SC 1918 was analysed and its *ratio* determined in *Rameshwar Prasad* v. *Union of India,* (2006) 2 SCC 1: AIR 2006 SC 980: 2006 AIR SCW 494.
3. (1973) 4 SCC 57, quoted in Ibid p. 62.
4. AIR 1975 SC 2299: (1976) 2 SCR 347: 1975 Supp SCC 1.
5. 1975 Supp SCC 1 (119).

that Fundamental rights are one of the inherent and implied limitation or an essential feature of the Constitution – was accepted by C.J. Sikri led 6 judges. 7 other judges including J. Khanna rejected the theory of implied limitation on amending powers as 'essentially nebulous'. Even Palkhivala wrote that the majority (*i.e.*, 9 judges) did not save the 'essential features' including Fundamental rights from amending power which was the view of the 6 'citizen judges' led by C.J. Sikri.

In *Indira Nehru Gandhi* v. *Raj Narain*[1] J. Chandrachud observed that J. Khanna had held in *Keshavanand* that Fundamental rights are not the basic structure of the Constitution and therefore can be abrogated like any other provision. But J. Khanna in *Indira Gandhi* did not agree with this conclusion. But once the judge delivers the judgment he becomes *functus officio* and he cannot subsequently offer a clarification or an explanation to it because the judgment becomes the law of the land and falls into public domain.

There was an abortive attempt to review *Keshavanand case* by the successor Chief Justice A.N. Ray.

However the *Keshavanand* case is so deeply ingrained into our Constitution law that the concept is here to stay in spite of the knowledge of the process and the attitudes through which it came about.

---

1. AIR 1975 SC 2299: (1976) 2 SCR 347: 1975 Supp SCC 1.

CHAPTER 35

SPECIAL PROVISIONS REGARDING JAMMU AND KASHMIR

(Article 370)

Articles 369 to 393 deal with temporary and transitional provisions. Out of these article 370 deals with temporary provisions in respect of Jammu and Kashmir and grants special status to Jammu and Kashmir.

Basis for the special status[1]: Under article 370 of Constitution State of Jammu and Kashmir enjoy a special status. This is due to certain commitments made by the Government of India with the then Ruler of Jammu and Kashmir at the time of its accession to India. Along with India the State of Jammu and Kashmir also became independent in 1947. Maharaja Hari Singh initially did not want to be a part of India or Pakistan. He thought of independence. He offered to sign a stand-still agreement with both India and Pakistan aimed at continuing the existing relationship pending his final decision regarding the future of the State but for a variety of reasons, the stand-still agreement was not signed between India and Kashmir. When the people of the State saw that India had become independent, they demanded the establishment of a responsible Government. In the absence of British help, which he was hitherto getting to suppress the internal rebellion and external aggression, Maharaja found himself in a tight corner. In the absence of the formal agreement between the Maharaja and India, Pakistan interpreted it to mean that Kashmir would ultimately become a part of Pakistan. Pakistan was pressurising the Maharaja to join Pakistan. The people of the State were tired of uncertainty and there was a *'Poonch Revolt'* against the authority of Maharaja. Maharaja now realised that he could no longer hold the people to subjugation through his army and police.

On October 20th 1947, several thousand Tribesmen supported by Pakistan army attacked the Frontiers of the State, the raiders were fast approaching Srinagar. Maharaja was nervous and saw his dream of independence shattered. It was as a last resort that Maharaja approached the Dominion of India to accept accession. To save his life, he left Srinagar and went to Jammu. He appointed Sheikh Mohammed Abdullah- his Emergency Minister who advised him to accede to India and ask for immediate military help. Faced with such a serious crisis, Maharaja at last with great reluctance sent the Instrument of Accession duly signed by him. The Governor-General of India – Lord Mountbatton accepted the Instrument of Accession.

The execution of Instrument of Accession by the Ruler and its acceptance by the Governor-General of India finally settled the issue of accession of the State

1. J.N. Pandey: Constitution Law. p. 728-731.

of Jammu and Kashmir and it cannot be re-opened again. But the Government of India accepted this Instrument of Accession subject to the confirmation by the people of the State, the accession was confirmed by the people of the State through their Constituent Assembly on November 17th, 1957. Section 3 of the Constitution of Jammu and Kashmir says 'the State of Jammu and Kashmir is and shall be integral part of the Union of India.'

It is thus to be seen that at the commencement of our Constitution – Jammu and Kashmir was different and therefore article 370 was inserted in our Constitution.

Article 370: Under article 370, the President is empowered to issue orders and thus acts as a legislature in issuing orders under this article.

Although the State of Jammu and Kashmir is a part of the Indian Union, its status is different from the other States in the following respects:

(a) State of Jammu and Kashmir has its own Constitution and its administration is carried on in accordance with that Constitution.

(b) Provisions of Article 238 shall not apply to that State of Jammu and Kashmir.

(c) Power of the Parliament to make laws for Jammu and Kashmir is limited to.

  (i) Those matters in the Union List and the Concurrent List which in consultation with the Government of the State are declared by the President to correspond to matters specified in the Instrument of Accession.

  (ii) Such other matters in the Union and the Concurrent List only with the concurrence with the Government of the State – President may by order specify. This means that on such matters – laws can be made only with the consent of the State of Jammu and Kashmir.

(d) The provisions of article 1 and this article shall apply in relation to that State.

(e) Such of the other provisions of the Constitution shall apply to that State subject to 'such exceptions and modifications as the President may by order specify.' But no such order which relates to matters specified in the Instrument of Accession referred to in Para (i) of sub-clause (c) shall be issued without the consultation of the State Government and matters other than those specified in the Instrument of Accession shall be issued with the concurrence of the State Government.

It has been held by the Supreme Court that the President may by orders extend certain provisions of the Constitution to that State with such modifications and exceptions as he thinks fit.[1] President may subsequently make amendments to such orders.[2]

---

1. *Puranlal Lakhanpal* v. *President of India,* AIR 1961 SC 1519: 1962 (1) SCJ 670: (1962) 1 SCR 688.
2. *Sampat Prakash* v. *State of Jammu and Kashmir,* AIR 1970 SC 1118: (1969) 2 SCR 365: 1970 Lab IC 873.

Power to abolish the operation of article 370: Article 370(3) provides that notwithstanding anything in the foregoing provisions of article 370, President may by public notification declare that the article shall cease to be operative. But the President cannot issue such a notification without the recommendation of the Constituent Assembly of that State.

SUBJECT INDEX

N

P

S

•••